MW00333825

SENATOR JAMES EASTLAND

MAKING THE MODERN SOUTH

David Goldfield, *Series Editor*

SENATOR
JAMES EASTLAND

MISSISSIPPI'S JIM CROW DEMOCRAT

MAARTEN ZWIERS

LOUISIANA STATE UNIVERSITY PRESS
BATON ROUGE

Published by Louisiana State University Press
Copyright © 2015 by Louisiana State University Press
All rights reserved
Manufactured in the United States of America
First printing

DESIGNER: *Mandy McDonald Scallan*
TYPEFACE: *Whitman, Trend Sans*
PRINTER AND BINDER: *Maple Press, Inc.*

Library of Congress Cataloging-in-Publication Data

Zwiers, Maarten, 1979–
  Senator James Eastland : Mississippi's Jim Crow Democrat / Maarten Zwiers.
    pages cm
  Includes bibliographical references and index.
  ISBN 978-0-8071-6001-5 (cloth : alkaline paper) — ISBN 978-0-8071-6002-2
(PDF) — ISBN 978-0-8071-6003-9 (ePub) — ISBN 978-0-8071-6004-6
(MOBI) 1. Eastland, James O. (James Oliver), 1904–1986. 2. Eastland, James
O. (James Oliver), 1904–1986—Political and social views. 3. Legislators—
United States — Biography. 4. United States. Congress. Senate—Biography.
5. Democratic Party (U.S.) — Biography. 6. Legislators—Mississippi — Biogra-
phy. 7. Mississippi—Politics and government—20th century. 8. Mississippi—
Race relations—Political aspects—History—20th century. I. Title.
  E748.E135Z95 2015
  328.73'092—dc23
  [B]

                                                    2014045216

CONTENTS

ACKNOWLEDGMENTS

Many people and organizations helped me to complete this book. In particular, Doeko Bosscher at the University of Groningen and Adam Fairclough at
Leiden University offered thoughtful comments on the manuscript. Research
for this work began during my graduate studies at the University of Mississippi. Without the financial support of the Fulbright Commission, VSBFonds,
Prins Bernhard Cultuurfonds, and Hendrik Muller's Vaderlandsch Fonds, my
dream of living and studying in the Deep South would not have been possible.
The Netherland-America Foundation sponsored my exchange at the University of North Carolina at Chapel Hill and my master's degree at the University
of Mississippi, for which I am extremely thankful. I received grants from the
Netherlands American Studies Association, the Lyndon Baines Johnson Foundation, the Harry Truman Presidential Library, the Association of Centers for
the Study of Congress, the Roosevelt Study Center, and the Nicolaas Mulerius
Foundation. All were critical in the successful completion of my book. Discussing James Eastland and southern Democrats with my colleagues in the
Departments of History and American Studies at the University of Groningen
has been both illuminating and fun.

I have come to consider Oxford, Mississippi, my second home. I met great
people during my stay there—too many to name here, but they are all in my
heart. I am especially indebted to the faculty and staff of the Center for the
Study of Southern Culture. I traveled all across the United States for archival
research, and staying with friends not only made these trips financially possible, but also very enjoyable. However, most of the research for this book took
place in the Department of Archives and Special Collections at the University
of Mississippi, where I started out as a student worker. I want to thank Leigh
McWhite for hiring me in the first place and for her suggestions as I was working on the manuscript. My year in Zeeland as visiting fellow at the Roosevelt

Study Center was memorable. The folks at the Center made the Deep South of the Netherlands a pleasant place to live and work.

I met David Goldfield at the Southern Historical Association conference in Louisville in 2009, and I appreciate his early interest in my work on Eastland. Rand Dotson and Lee Sioles at LSU Press were very helpful in guiding the manuscript through the different stages of the publication process. Derik Shelor did a terrific job as copyeditor. Finally, I want to thank my family and friends for their continuing love and support.

SENATOR JAMES EASTLAND

INTRODUCTION

J AMES EASTLAND was having dinner at Duke Zeibert's steakhouse when
Joe Forer walked in. Located on the corner of Connecticut Avenue and
L Street, just a few blocks from the White House, Zeibert's restaurant
was an intricate part of Washington politics, a place filled with "laughter and
drinking and animated talking and table hopping and, underneath it all, the
endless Washington scramble for inside knowledge, position, and power."[1]
Senator Eastland of Mississippi, the influential chairman of the Senate Judiciary
Committee, was infamous for his rabid anticommunism and strong defense
of segregation. Forer was senior partner in Forer and Rein, the Communist
Party's leading law firm in the capital. He had defended people accused of
communist sympathies before Eastland's Internal Security Subcommittee on
several occasions. Forer represented a cause Eastland completely opposed, but
when the lawyer walked toward the senator's table, Eastland cordially shook his
hand and invited him to sit down. William Rusher, the publisher of *National
Review* and a former staff member of the Internal Security Subcommittee,
watched the encounter in disbelief. When he left the restaurant, "the arch-
segregationist 'Red-baiter' and the Communist Party's lawyer were chatting
cozily together." Rusher thought the meeting between Eastland and Forer at
Zeibert's steakhouse characterized "this complex Mississippian's personality."[2]

James Eastland's political power was based on his ability to compromise.
In historiography and public memory, Eastland is generally remembered as
a ranting southern extremist, "a mad dog let loose in the streets of justice,"
in the words of NAACP spokesman Clarence Mitchell.[3] But this image
tells only one side of the story. If we really want to fathom how effective
southern segregationists were in their politics, it is essential to understand
why a northern liberal like Senator Birch Bayh of Indiana called Eastland
"a straightforward . . . honorable gentleman" for whom he had "the greatest

respect."[4] Bobby Baker, Capitol Hill operator and longtime political advisor to Lyndon Johnson, found "Jim Eastland to possess one of the quicker, more brilliant minds in the Senate." Eastland understood the game of politics. "It's a tribute to his political genius that he's managed to satisfy the most reactionary element of his Mississippi constituency and, at the same time, remain a working power and influence among his Senate colleagues," Baker believed. "No dumb man could do that."[5] It is this Janus-faced quality of southern Democrats that delivered them the respect and power they needed to remain politically effective, both in their home states and in Congress.

Eastland's political nexus extended from his plantation office in Doddsville to Capitol Hill and the backrooms of Washington. His power manifested itself formally and informally, and he had access to the resources of the federal government to implement his worldview. The senator's network and influence were widespread, and he knew how to put both to effective use. Eastland's political instincts and the willingness of state institutions to accommodate him form an important explanation of why the civil rights movement had so much trouble generating a true transformation of southern (and American) race and class relations. "Senator Eastland understood power and its proper application better than anybody I've ever been around," his administrative assistant Bill Simpson recalled. "The senator understood what it was and how to use it properly and in the right degree. He never pounded a table, never screamed or hollered. He just got the job done."[6]

As a politician, James Eastland wore many masks. Before his supporters in Mississippi and the South, he called for a united, regional crusade against government intervention in race relations. Eastland depicted labor unions, civil rights organizations, and other liberal groups as part of a global communist conspiracy, which had also successfully coopted most of the justices on the Supreme Court. Against such a powerful enemy, compromise was not an option. The fate of the United States hung in the balance, and with every cession the power of the Red Menace grew stronger. Eastland's conservative ideology did not just focus on the defense of segregation, but included various other elements, such as a commitment to laissez-faire capitalism, strict immigration laws, and state sovereignty. He considered an undiluted Anglo-Saxon culture and local control to be the heart of Americanism, and it therefore made sense to him that the communists would attempt to destroy exactly these constitutive parts. James Eastland thought he was waging a war for the soul of America. And according to the planter-politician, that soul was located in the old Confederacy.

But Eastland's political performance often had a dual nature. While he publicly called for no compromise in the fight against desegregation and denounced the federal government for interfering in state matters, he also needed the federal government to secure his power. The distribution of federal patronage helped Eastland build his political machine in Mississippi, and he could reward his followers by wielding his clout as a U.S. senator. He used federal funds to investigate his enemies and he received agricultural subsidies from Washington to improve his plantation. Moreover, in the theater of national politics, compromise was often unavoidable, and Eastland did not shy away from it. But such negotiations normally took place behind the scenes, like in Zeibert's restaurant. This kind of flexibility was necessary to gain influence and reach political objectives, not only in Congress, but also in the national Democratic Party. "In public, he solemnly maintains that the Supreme Court has been 'indoctrinated and brainwashed by left-wing pressure groups' who have also managed to gain 'control of the government of the U.S.' In private, his lips quirk with suppressed laughter when the visitor challenges the authenticity of his statements," correspondent Fern Marja wrote after conducting an extensive interview with Eastland. "There is in his response the deep, amused cynicism of a politician trying to snatch up the torch he reluctantly helped his colleagues rip from the hands of Wisconsin's Sen. McCarthy."[7]

The interaction between southern Democrats and the national Democratic Party is the main subject of this book, and James Eastland is its main character. The study focuses on Mississippi because this state was the hotbed of massive resistance against racial integration, and Eastland was a frontman of the massive resistance movement. The ideals of white southerners—and of upper-class white southerners like Eastland in particular—began to clash with the agenda of the Democratic Party, especially in the postwar years. The political leadership of Mississippi nonetheless decided to keep the state in the Democratic ranks during the 1950s, and the national Democrats accommodated. Beneath the hardline façade of massive resistance, segregationists such as Eastland created a modus vivendi with the national Democratic Party, which was based on a mutual understanding of achieving and maintaining political power. Both sides practiced a give-and-take strategy. This strategy protected the status quo and enabled southern Democrats to entrench themselves in national and party politics in the period following World War II. Instead of examining the "no compromise" attitude of massive resisters, this work explores how concessions and reciprocity safeguarded segregation and kept the South in the Democratic Party after 1948. Eastland and other southern segregationists waged an independent presidential campaign that year, but their States' Rights Democratic ticket did not receive enough electoral votes to decide the outcome of the race. After the failure of this so-called Dixiecrat Revolt, James Eastland realized he needed affiliation with a national party to expand and sustain his power in the Senate.

The Dixiecrat Revolt also had repercussions on the policy of the national Democratic Party toward the South. Although the States' Rights Democrats did not succeed in their attempt to play a kingmaker role in the election, the southern rebellion impelled the leaders of the national Democratic Party to assume a more conciliatory approach to the region below the Mason-Dixon Line. In 1948, the party adopted a strong civil rights plank at its convention in Philadelphia. During the 1950s, the national Democrats abandoned this course and chose to appease southern whites instead, because their traditional adherence to the Democratic Party contributed significantly to electoral success, in particular to the achievement of Democratic majorities in Congress. This reliance on southern votes had a negative impact on the enactment of the progressive points in the Democratic program, however, especially in the field of civil rights. Because the electorate in the South kept sending the same conservative Democrats to Washington, these representatives exerted disproportionate influence on federal policy. Based on their growing seniority, southern Democrats such as Eastland obtained command of important committees. And once these southerners were in power as committee chairs, they were extremely difficult to dislodge. The leadership of the national Democratic Party believed it could ill afford to lose southern electoral support, although this support came at a heavy price. The 1950s constituted a crucial era in the establishment and perpetuation of southern influence on the course of the national Democratic Party during a period of increasing demands for civil rights.

The civil rights movement eventually won great victories with the passage of the Civil Rights Act in 1964 and the Voting Rights Act in 1965, but southern Democrats effectively blocked the structural change in race relations that the movement wanted to achieve. The Democratic Party continued to accommodate segregationists, but the southern branch of the Republican Party did not tap into the expanding group of southern black voters. Southern Republicans decided to capture the support of disgruntled whites instead. The established parties thus offered limited opportunities for true black advancement. Until the 1960s, the progressive message of the Democratic Party withered in the shadow of southern Democrats, while it sheltered the rebirth and development of the southern GOP. By the time Eastland retired, southern Republicans had fine-tuned their message to a white electorate that understood the racial implications of states' rights rhetoric.

When Eastland left politics in 1978, the Mississippi Republican Party had appropriated the senator's ideas and sanitized them into a colorblind program of local control and individual responsibility. In recent years, scholars have argued that the race issue has overshadowed economics and class to explain the rise of southern Republicans; Republican growth coincided with the rise of a middle class in the southern suburbs.[8] The Republican advance in Mississippi challenges this suburban model, however. Until this day, Mississippi remains a heavily rural state. By the 1970s, suburban growth was primarily limited to the capital of Jackson. The Republican economic program attracted these suburbanites, but their numbers were not large enough to win elections. In order to become competitive in the Magnolia State, Republicans needed to win over rural white Democrats who did not share the financial ideology of the GOP but were susceptible to racial appeals. Before passage of the Civil Rights Act of 1964 and the Voting Rights Act of 1965, white Mississippi Republicans "sounded virtually identical to their Democratic counterparts when it came to rights of black Mississippians."[9] These early Republicans shared the racial and economic agenda of James Eastland. During the 1950s, Eastland Democrats were active in Republican organizations such as the Citizens for Eisenhower movement. Although more progressive Republicans attempted to attract a biracial coalition of voters during the 1960s and 1970s, ultraconservatives eventually took control of the party. Senator Eastland's worldview thus found a new expression in the political program of the Mississippi Republican Party.

The Black Belt origins and influence on the organization of the southern Republican Party should not be neglected, and the positive effects of modernization and economic growth on a long tradition of racism should not be overestimated.[10] Although the differences between North and South have diminished significantly since the Second World War, fundamental regional distinctiveness persists. In the end, the core characteristics of the South remain largely the same, while the ideologies of political parties have changed. Both the Democratic Party and the Republican Party were relatively moderate organizations during the 1950s. The Democrats especially were a party aimed at consensus between its liberal wing and its conservative (southern) wing. By the 1960s, this consensus model started to fall apart; both national parties abandoned their middle-of-the-road politics and chose different ideological directions. The Republican Party became the home of fiscal and social conservatives, while the Democrats adopted a decisively progressive agenda. Conservative southerners therefore began to turn to the GOP, not simply because they started to make more money, but because the Republicans had begun to voice a message that was more in tune with southern traditionalism.[11]

A study of Mississippi Democrats and of James Eastland in particular reveals how southern segregationists remained effective in the national Democratic Party after its leadership had spoken out strongly in favor of civil rights in 1948, and how these segregationists subsequently stymied Republican growth in the South during the 1950s and 1960s. Mississippi formed the heartland of the States' Rights Revolt together with Alabama, and Eastland was the only U.S. senator who wholeheartedly campaigned for the Dixiecrat ticket. Moreover, as a Black Belt planter, he belonged to the white elite that led the exodus from the Democratic Party in the Deep South. The fact that such a neobourbon ideologue managed to climb the ranks of the party he had completely vilified as a Dixiecrat indicates Eastland's political flexibility, and it also signifies the uncertainty in Democratic ranks during the 1950s about which ideological course to follow. As the national Democrats pondered this question, Eastland worked his way up in the Senate. His position in Congress enabled him to ward off political challenges at the federal and state level, and to effectively protect the white southern way of life. The legacy of James Eastland persists until this day.

CHAPTER 1

A PRODUCT OF TWO CULTURES

J AMES EASTLAND LEARNED the game of politics in two distinct political cultures, the Mississippi Delta and the Hills in the eastern part of the state. Each summer, young James would travel by train from Forest in the Hill Country to the family plantation near Doddsville. The house in Forest and the Delta plantation were the two home bases of the Eastlands. James Oliver Eastland was born in Doddsville on November 28, 1904, but he grew up in Forest, where his father, Woods Eastland, ran a law firm. His ancestors had settled there in the early 1800s. James Eastland's paternal great-grandfather, Hiram, came from Tennessee and built his wealth as a merchant in Scott County. His maternal grandfather had served as an officer in Confederate general Nathan Bedford Forrest's cavalry. Woods Eastland divided his time between practicing law in Forest and managing the plantation in Doddsville.[1] In 1911, he was elected district attorney of the eighth judicial district in central Mississippi. During his campaign he endorsed Delta senator LeRoy Percy, which was politically hazardous in the Hill Country. The Delta and the Hills had opposite interests. Eastland nonetheless won the election with a twenty-seven hundred-vote majority, and with his rising influence his political network also started to grow.[2] For Delta planters with statewide political ambitions, getting support from the whites in the Hill Country was crucial.

The division between Delta and Hills defined politics in the Magnolia State up until World War II, and it continued to linger thereafter. "Mississippi politics may be regarded, if one keeps alert to the risks of oversimplification, as a battle between the delta planters and the rednecks," V. O. Key observed. The alluvial plain in the western part of the state, along the Mississippi River, is known as the Delta. This area was home to the planters, who built their wealth on black labor—first the slaves, and later the sharecroppers. The Hills run from the Tennessee border in the north all the way to the pine forests near the Gulf Coast. The Hill region almost reaches the river near the town of Vicksburg, where the Delta ends. The soil is not as rich as the land adjacent to the Mississippi. Poor white landowners predominantly lived in this part of the state, although some of them migrated to the Delta, thus diminishing the strict dichotomy between the Delta and the Hills. "Peckerwoods, planters say, have moved down into the delta, especially into the towns, and diluted its purity," Key wrote. "In the hills the growth of towns, the development of transport and communication, the extension of education have reduced rural isolation."[3] The planters from the cotton-growing counties tended to look down on the small farmers from other areas of Mississippi, while poor whites detested the plantation aristocracy and its haughty manners. In his book *Lanterns on the Levee*, William Alexander Percy, scion of a wealthy planter's family, vividly described a Hill Country crowd at a campaign rally of U.S. senator LeRoy Percy (his father), who ran against James Vardaman in 1911: "I looked over the ill-dressed, surly audience, unintelligent and slinking, and heard him appeal to them for fair treatment of the Negro and explain to them the tariff and the Panama tolls situation. I studied them as they milled about. They were the sort of people that lynch Negroes, that mistake hoodlumism for wit, and cunning for intelligence, that attend revivals and fight and fornicate in the bushes afterwards. They were undiluted Anglo-Saxons. They were the sovereign voter. It was so horrible it seemed unreal."[4]

The Delta had a more conservative voting record on economic issues. The Hills supported progressive economic measures. The two regions also had different ways of life. While the Hill Country was strongly in favor of statewide prohibition, the Delta joined the counties on the Gulf Coast and two of the larger urban centers in Mississippi (Jackson and Meridian) in their opposition to anti-liquor laws. A large majority of white Mississippians believed in the righteousness of segregation and Jim Crow legislation, but representatives from the Delta generally distanced themselves from the virulently racist rhetoric of demagogues like Theodore Bilbo and James Vardaman, who were both worshiped in the Hills. The plantation owners had good reason to offer some sort of protection to their black workers. After all, the cotton had to be picked and sold at profitable rates, which did not happen without cheap black labor.

Although economics (rather than humanitarianism) were foremost on the planters' minds, populists like Bilbo and Vardaman effectively used the more reserved attitude of the people from the Delta toward the race question as a sign that the plantation elite held blacks in higher esteem than working-class whites. The Percy family experienced the effectiveness of this demagogic approach firsthand. "The man responsible for tearing Father's reputation to tatters and saddening three lives was a pert little monster, glib and shameful, with that sort of cunning common to criminals which passes for intelligence," William Alexander Percy described Bilbo. "The people loved him. They loved him not because they were deceived in him, but because they understood him thoroughly; they said of him proudly, 'He's a slick little bastard.' He was one of them."[5] The Delta and the Hill Country represented different states of mind.

James Eastland "was destined to be the product of two cultures," a student of his early life stated.[6] In 1927, he won election to the Mississippi legislature as a representative of Scott County. The county was located in the Hills, and Forest was its capital. During his term in the State House, Eastland defended the interests of the small farmers and supported the activist agenda of Governor Theodore Bilbo, a champion of the poor whites. After Eastland retired from state politics, he moved to the Delta, and his economic views changed accordingly. By the time he received his appointment to the U.S. Senate, in the summer of 1941, Eastland voiced the worldview of the Delta planters. One factor remained central to Eastland's ideology, however: his belief in black inferiority and segregation. White supremacy formed the basis of his political career, a career he sustained through his double roots in the Hills and the Delta. James Eastland's political style incorporated the demagogic elements of the redneck populist, and the gentlemanly demeanor of the Delta plantation owner. The interplay between these two identities determined Eastland's years in the U.S. Senate.

In 1904, the year Jim Eastland was born, James Kimble Vardaman became governor of Mississippi. His victory inaugurated a new era in state politics. Vardaman urged lawmakers to aid poor sharecroppers, increase funding for public health programs, and outlaw child labor. Simultaneously, he favored extension of Jim Crow segregation and cut the subsidy of Holly Springs Normal Institute, a black teachers' college already suffering from a lack of financial resources. In contrast with Delta legislators, Vardaman did not assume a paternalistic attitude toward African Americans. He worked for the poor whites instead, who formed his most important electoral base.[7] Vardaman started a more activist phase in Mississippi government by calling attention to prison reform and the improvement of conditions in other state institutions. Theodore Gilmore "The Man" Bilbo expanded Vardaman's racist-progressive agenda when he became governor in 1916. The rise of Vardaman and Bilbo signaled the political empowerment of the white masses in Mississippi.[8]

The involvement of Woods and later James Eastland in Mississippi politics coincided with the rise of Vardaman and Bilbo. In 1912, Vardaman replaced LeRoy Percy as U.S. senator and Bilbo was inaugurated as lieutenant governor. Both campaigns had been bitter. Class warfare dominated the race between Delta planter Percy and redneck champion Vardaman, and Bilbo also resorted to scurrilous rhetoric to brand his enemies. In a speech at Blue Mountain, he called one of his opponents "a cross between a hyena and a mongrel, begotten in a nigger graveyard at midnight, suckled by a sow and educated by a fool." Bilbo received a pistol-whipping in retribution for his words.[9] Less is known about Woods Eastland's campaign for district attorney of the eighth judicial district, an area of five counties in central Mississippi. Eastland held the post for eight years, from 1912 until 1920. He also developed a successful law office in Forest that specialized in personal injury cases. Many large sawmills were located in Scott County and the surrounding area, which made the law firm extremely lucrative. Eastland used the money he made as litigator to expand his land holdings in the Delta. Through his work as a lawyer and the district attorney in the Hill Country and as a planter in the Delta, Woods Eastland formed an extensive network in both regions. By the end of his term, he had become an influential behind-the-scenes power broker in Mississippi politics.[10]

Woods used his influence to advance the political career of his son. James was the only child of Woods and Alma Austin Eastland, and he was very close to his father. "My father completely controlled me," he later said in an interview.[11] James attended the all-white Forest High School, where he joined the basketball and debating teams. One of his fellow students remembered Jim Eastland as a popular and very outspoken young man. His popularity increased when he got a car, a luxury none of his other classmates could afford. He graduated in 1922 and entered the University of Mississippi, the state's flagship school. The university was better known as Ole Miss, an institution catering to the planter class and steeped in the traditions of the Old South.[12] At Ole Miss, James Eastland was a member of the Hermaiean Society and the Debating Council, and he set up a campus political organization with a few friends, including his later campaign manager Joe Brown. After three years,

Eastland transferred to Vanderbilt University in Nashville, Tennessee, because he thought he would get a better legal training there. Eastland only stayed at Vanderbilt for one semester, however, and then moved to Tuscaloosa to attend the University of Alabama. He again became involved in campus politics, but never graduated. James passed the bar examination in 1927, dropped out of school, and returned home to Scott County. His father wanted his son to run for the state legislature. If the plan failed, James Eastland would return to Alabama and finish his education.[13]

At the University of Alabama, Eastland was already getting ready for the upcoming election. "Am trying to prepare for the representatives race next summer by taking an interest in speaking and debating over here," he wrote Delta lawyer Joe Howorth in February 1927.[14] W. D. Cook, a banker from Forest, was Eastland's most formidable opponent in the 1927 Democratic primary, but with the help of his father, James Eastland easily defeated Cook. The young state representative from Scott County (he was only twenty-four years old) traveled to Jackson and started his political career as a strong supporter of Theodore Bilbo, who had won a second term as governor. Bilbo's redneck liberalism was popular in the Hill county of Scott, and Eastland listened to the wishes of his constituents. Moreover, he had always held a higher opinion of The Man than Woods Eastland did, who belonged to the anti-Vardaman camp of John Sharp Williams. On a clear winter day in January, Bilbo delivered his inaugural address. Among other things, he promised better roads and hospitals, tax revisions, cheaper schoolbooks, and a child welfare program. The state press reported favorably on the governor's progressive plans, and some reporters even hoped that the era of factionalism had come to an end. Once the first legislative session started, however, those hopes quickly crumbled.[15]

James Eastland was one of the chief spokesmen for the governor's agenda. Together with Courtney Pace and Kelly J. Hammond, Eastland formed the "Little Three," the leadership of a bloc of country legislators that advocated progressive measures favoring poor and working-class whites. Their opponents were known as the "Big Four," who represented the interests of the Black Belt Bourbons. This faction included Speaker of the House Thomas Bailey and Delta planter Walter Sillers of Rosedale, the chairman of the Judiciary Committee. Although Bilbo's supporters formed the majority in the State Senate, the opposition controlled the House, which severely hampered the enactment of the governor's initiatives. Bilbo's first administration, from 1916 until 1920, had been very successful. But by 1928, a group of experienced conservative lawmakers were less easily swayed by Bilbo's powers of persuasion. Young representatives like Eastland and his comrades did not yet possess the political skills to thwart the power of the Bourbons. Scandals surrounding the construction of a state printing plant and the Highway Commission crippled the administration, and Bilbo's stubborn refusal to sign revenue acts that deviated from his own proposals added to the general malaise. When the Great Depression hit Mississippi hard in 1930, the governor eventually agreed on a compromise tax bill. During the final session of the legislature, the state government turned more active to deal with the ravages caused by the economic crisis. Numerous relief measures were passed to counter the effects of bankruptcies, foreclosures, and sharply declining cotton prices. By the end of Bilbo's administration, Mississippi was bankrupt and its economic life in shambles.[16] The governor's enemies hoped that the ignoble end of Bilbo's governorship also meant the end of his political career. The following obituary circulated in the 1931 elections: "Funeral Notice: The friends, acquaintances, and former political supporters of Theodough Graftmore Bilbo (alias Theodore G. Bilbo) are invited to attend his political funeral, which will be held at the governor's mansion on Tuesday, August 4 at 7 P.M. or as soon thereafter as the election returns can be counted. Final obsequies and internment at the Juniper Grove Baptist Church, adjoining the pecan orchard, near Poplarville. No flowers requested, no crying. Rest in Peace."[17]

Eastland decided not to run for reelection when his term ended in 1932. The solid resistance of older and more conservative legislators had become a source of frustration, and Bilbo supporters faced grim opposition in the 1931 campaign. Woods Eastland told his son it was better for him to focus on raising a family, his law firm in Forest, and farming. The same year James retired from state politics, he married Elizabeth "Libby" Coleman, a math teacher at Ruleville High School, close to the Eastland plantation. Two years later the couple left Forest for good and settled in Doddsville. James Eastland named two reasons for their move to the Delta. The first motive was economic. "I had always said that when cotton got back to ten cents per pound I was coming back because I could then make more money in Sunflower County," he stated. The second reason was his father's health. Woods Eastland was suffering from high blood pressure, and he wanted his son to manage the finances of the plantation. Woods remained in control of operations at the farm, however.

Jim opened a law office in Ruleville and retired from active politics. His first daughter, Nell, was born in 1933. Three more children—Anne, Sue, and Woods, named after his grandfather—followed. Although James Eastland no longer was in the political limelight, he mirrored his father's example as an operator behind the scenes. His term in the legislature had served him well. As state legislator, he had gotten to know people all over Mississippi whose influence was valuable. Eastland nonetheless rejected the idea of a career in politics. "I never intended to run for anything again," he said in 1931.[18]

In contrast with his lieutenant, Theodore Bilbo did not retire from politics. Undaunted by the failures of his second gubernatorial term, he ran an effective campaign for the U.S. Senate in 1934 and defeated incumbent Hubert Stephens. While Bilbo became an enthusiastic supporter of the New Deal, Mississippi's senior senator, Pat Harrison, began to take a different attitude toward the relief measures of the Roosevelt administration after the president's reelection in 1936. During the early years of the Great Depression, Harrison had been a strong advocate of FDR's initiatives. Conservative politicians from the South like Harrison supported the initial New Deal programs for a number of reasons. First of all, even southern traditionalists understood that at least some form of federal intervention was necessary to resuscitate the ailing economy of Dixie. Moreover, the elite were in firm control of most New Deal projects in the South. Oscar Goodbar Johnston, owner of the largest plantation below the Mason-Dixon line, was the comptroller for the agency set up by the Agricultural Adjustment Act (AAA), and he was in charge of its programs. According to W. M. Garrard of the Staple Cotton Cooperative Association, plantation owners had "profited more under the Triple A than [they had] ever profited in all the years before its establishment."[19] As chairman of the Senate Finance Committee, Pat Harrison had played a significant role in the passage of important New Deal legislation, such as the National Industrial Recovery Act and the Social Security Act. Harry Hopkins, director of the Federal Emergency Relief Administration, told a crowd in Mississippi that with the exception of Senate Majority Leader Joseph Robinson of Arkansas, "no man in Washington . . . has done more for the New Deal than Pat Harrison."[20]

After his landslide victory in 1936, FDR had already told David Lilienthal, head of the Tennessee Valley Authority (TVA), that the time had come to liberalize the South, in particular the leadership of the Democratic Party in the region. "One of the things I am proud of is that I made men like Joe

Robinson and Pat Harrison swallow me hook, line, and sinker," the president said. "But the young people in the South, and the women, they are thinking about economic problems and will be part of a liberal group in the South."[21] The elections of 1936 showed that the southern Democrats started to lose their grip on the national party. At the Democratic National Convention in Philadelphia that year, the two-thirds rule was abolished, which meant that a simple majority could appoint presidential nominees. The southern bloc in the party thus lost an important instrument to prevent the nomination of a candidate who was hostile to the white South's interests. At the same time, the Democratic Party became more receptive to the demands of black voters in the North. These developments were highly disturbing to southern Democrats. At the 1936 convention, delegates from the South were already haunted by what they perceived as bad omens for the future. South Carolina senator Ellison "Cotton Ed" Smith could hardly believe his eyes when he found out a black minister opened a session at the convention. "By God, he's as black as melted midnight!" he shouted. "Get out of my way! This mongrel meeting ain't no place for a white man!"[22]

The election results of the 1936 presidential campaign were another confirmation of the southern Democrats' waning power within the national party. The South again voted massively for Roosevelt, but so did other parts of the country. If Dixie had not supported the Democratic ticket that year, FDR still would have defeated his Republican opponent with a margin of more than 6 million votes. Democrats in the North and West started to realize elections could be won with the support of African Americans in the populous industrial states, and without the backing of the South. The results of the convention in Philadelphia and the emergence of the so-called FDR coalition of western and northern Democrats were some of the first signs of a revamped Democratic Party, whose leadership was trying the get rid of the ghosts from the old Confederacy. A northern liberal coalition supported by Roosevelt increased its influence on the course of the party, much to the alarm of southern conservatives and their allies.[23]

In the U.S. Senate, the first major clash between conservatives from the South and the administration came shortly after Roosevelt's second inauguration. In early 1937, the president announced his plans to reform the federal judiciary. FDR knew the success of his New Deal programs depended in large measure on judges who subscribed to his broad interpretation of the

Constitution. In February, he asked both houses of Congress to create fifty new federal judgeships, including six extra posts on the Supreme Court. Roosevelt received support from some southerners in the Senate (including Harrison and Bilbo), but other Democratic senators from the South were less loyal. Harry Byrd and Carter Glass of Virginia, Josiah Bailey and Robert Reynolds of North Carolina, Ellison Smith of South Carolina, Walter George of Georgia, and Tom Connally of Texas all opposed the president's reforms.[24]

During the following years, support of southern conservatives for the administration's plans continued to falter. Other progressive legislation also fell victim to the southern bloc. In 1938 for instance, senators from the South initiated a filibuster against an anti-lynching bill. "Is the faith of the South to be broken?" Pat Harrison asked during the debate. "Is its love for the Democratic party to be shattered?"[25] The White House remained silent, and the southerners killed the legislation.[26] During FDR's first years in the White House, traditionalists from the South had managed to find a precarious balance between federal intervention and their own political ideology, which was based on balanced budgets and states' rights. But when the New Deal turned more reformist, many southern politicians backed away from its progressive projects. Only the outbreak of World War II brought southern conservatives back in line, although their loyalty could not be taken for granted any longer.[27]

The split between FDR and Pat Harrison also had repercussions on state politics in Mississippi. In contrast with Harrison, Theodore Bilbo remained an unequivocal adherent of New Deal economic policies. Bilbo's economic liberalism reflected political and social divisions in the Magnolia State.[28] Harrison was not a reactionary fixated on protecting the status quo and opposing all forms of government intervention, however. He was more in line with southern business progressives, who desired to create a better climate for entrepreneurship and industrialization. The Balance Agriculture With Industry (BAWI) program of Hugh White, Mississippi's governor from 1936 until 1940, was a good example of such business progressivism. Harrison belonged to the group of southern lawmakers who played an important role in masterminding the economic emergency measures of the early New Deal. But when Roosevelt began to restructure the Democratic Party to serve the interests of the poor and oppressed, the resistance of these oligarchs in the Senate increased.[29]

The 1939 governor's race in Mississippi between Paul B. Johnson Sr. and Mike Conner pitted Pat Harrison against Theodore Bilbo. Roosevelt and Bilbo supported Johnson, while Harrison and Governor White backed Conner. Like Bilbo, Woods Eastland joined the campaign for Johnson, his old roommate at Harperville College in Scott County. Eastland had met his future wife at Harperville, and Johnson was his best man at the wedding. Two years before the race, Woods was already in the midst of surveying the political scene for a Johnson bid. "I have heard more people regret having voted for White in this section," Eastland wrote his friend in August 1937, referring to the Delta, "in fact, practically everyone here expects to vote for you for Governor next time."[30] In October of that year, Woods Eastland advised Johnson to get Bilbo "to quietly throw his organization your way but not make any speeches."[31]

Johnson and Bilbo were old political enemies; Johnson had defeated Bilbo for a U.S. House seat in 1918, and Bilbo had helped Hugh White in the 1935 governor's election against Johnson. By 1939, however, the two men needed each other. Bilbo wanted to break Harrison's power and prestige in the Senate and in Mississippi, and Johnson coveted the votes of the small farmers, who still adored The Man. Johnson aimed his race at the "average man," advocating measures such as free textbooks for children, better welfare for the aged, and educational improvements. In many ways, his campaign pledges resembled Bilbo's platforms of 1915 and 1927. Johnson spoke out strongly in favor of Roosevelt and the New Deal, while Conner's opposition to FDR's nomination in 1932 hurt him in the runoff primary. Because Harrison wavered in his support of the president, the endorsement of the senior senator did not help Conner much either.[32]

James Eastland stumped the Delta for Johnson. Voters in this part of the state generally did not identify with Johnson's concern for working-class whites. Besides winning ballots for Johnson, Eastland made many contacts on his campaign trips, which proved useful in later years. The planter's son also developed a distinct political style. "He seldom used flowery language; he used common language that people could understand; he came to the point with little repetition," Chester Eastland said. A long and deep friendship was the overriding reason why Delta elites such as the Eastlands supported populist candidate Paul Johnson. Johnson easily defeated Conner in the second primary. Woods Eastland now had an old and trusted comrade in the governor's mansion.[33] Johnson's victory proved to be crucial in launching James Eastland's Senate career.

On Saturday, June 28, 1941, James Eastland received a call from Paul Johnson. The governor asked him to come to Jackson in the afternoon and to bring his father. Pat Harrison had died the Sunday before. The senator's death sanctioned the governor to appoint a successor until special elections for Harrison's seat could be held. Johnson initially offered the post to Woods, but he declined and said that his son would take the job instead. His father's proposal surprised James, but he did not protest. In previous years, James had turned down political offers by Johnson because he preferred to continue his lucrative work as lawyer and planter. But he was not going to disobey his father. When Johnson introduced the new senator, the governor described him as "a man of great ability, culture, and refinement, splendidly educated and ideally suited for the job." James Eastland accepted the nomination and promised to support President Roosevelt's domestic and foreign policies.[34]

During his eighty-eight days in the U.S. Senate, James Eastland primarily focused on defending the interests of cotton planters. On July 24, 1941, he introduced S. 1775, a bill about the disposal of government-held cotton. The day before, the Department of Agriculture had issued a statement about its intent to sell cotton at less than parity. According to Eastland, this decision would wreak havoc on planters in the South and Southwest, in particular the small cotton growers and tenant farmers. "Cotton gins today are humming in Texas and within 3 weeks will be running in Mississippi and the Carolinas," he said. "It is extremely unfortunate that the Government, after spending millions of dollars in an attempt to put the cotton market at a parity with industrial products, should attempt by selling Government-held cotton deliberately to depress the cotton market right at the time when the cotton is in the hands of the producer, and thus deprive the cotton grower not only of a prosperous year but of the first opportunity to recoup his former losses."[35]

Woods Eastland was pleased with his son's performance, and so were the newspapers in Mississippi. "Your bill to peg the price of the C.C. [commodity credit] cotton was alright and your explanation of the bill was splendid," he told James. But besides these congratulations, the letter also contained a warning. "I trust to God you will lay off of demagoguery," Woods wrote, "as you would disgust and drive all of the intelligent people of the State away from you. There is nothing to it."[36] The Delta planter instructed his son he should not lower himself to the standards of Theodore Bilbo, champion of the white working class from the Hills and piney woods of Mississippi. Although James more or less heeded his father's advice during his short first term in the U.S. Senate, he often turned a blind eye to it in the years that followed.

One of Eastland's first major speeches also dealt with farming. On August

11, 1941, he took the Senate floor to attack the agricultural policies of the U.S. government, and in particular Leon Henderson, the administrator of the Office of Price Administration (OPA). "I have always known that there was grave discrimination against the South in the policies of the American Government," Eastland started his address. "However, until I came to Washington in an official capacity I never dreamed of the great discriminations and malicious injustices practiced and attempted to be practiced against the South and southern agriculture by certain high officials of this Government." Eastland's speech had three themes: the use of Brazilian cotton by Canadian manufacturers to make uniforms for the U.S. Army; the anti-southern stance of Henderson; and the attempts of the OPA to keep cottonseed prices down. All these issues had a common objective, Eastland believed. "What could be more unjust than to empower a man such as Henderson, a citizen of New Jersey, with no knowledge or experience, to put a ceiling on cotton prices and tell southern agriculture what it shall receive for its product," he asked. "This man has no knowledge of what a fair price is or should be. He would crucify the South. He would enslave the South. His every action speaks his intent to treat us unfairly."[37] Using rhetoric reminiscent of the period before the Civil War, Eastland denounced the administration, embodied in the northerner Henderson, for its discriminatory actions against the Southland.

Only a month later, he addressed another subject that also used to be a dominant topic in the antebellum South: the protective tariff. Together with Alabama senator John Bankhead, he proposed a law to make Dixie "highly prosperous . . . King Cotton would regain his American throne." The Bankhead-Eastland bill rebated the duties on imported goods if the profits made on these goods were used to purchase surplus farm products. According to Eastland, this "gateway through the tariff wall" did not hurt northern industries, because their products were still protected by the tariff. "There could not come into this country, under this bill, a great mass of foreign goods to close up the factories and destroy the standard of living of the industrial worker, as the protected industrialists howl when they clamor for swill and additional booty at the expense of the cotton-growing South and of the producers of grain in this country," the Mississippi senator explained.[38] For many years, Eastland argued, the U.S. government had treated the South unfairly. Now the time had come to right these wrongs.

By the end of his term, Eastland had established an outstanding reputation in Mississippi. When he received the governor's nomination to the U.S. Senate, many of Johnson's closest friends were taken by surprise, and even James Eastland himself could hardly believe he was going to represent his state on the national stage. But when Eastland returned to Mississippi, he had become a guardian of the cotton-growing South. After his anti-Henderson speech, the OPA decided not to put a ceiling on cottonseed prices, which resulted in a higher value for this product. Southern planters, including the Eastland family, made significant profits on their crop that year. Although the young senator had promised Governor Johnson he would not run in the special election for Harrison's seat, he geared himself for the regular primary in 1942. Eastland knew he could count on his father's network, but he also realized that the powerful political machine of Theodore Bilbo would be lined up against him. During his years in the state legislature, Eastland had supported the erstwhile governor in his progressive programs. But by 1942, the times had changed. Disillusioned with Roosevelt's reformist projects, many plantation owners now opposed the spirit of the New Deal. James Eastland, who had become a planter himself, understood the political wishes of his constituency in the Delta. But if he wanted to win his Senate seat back, Eastland also had to convince voters in other regions of the state to support him.[39]

Eastland's opponent in 1942 was Wall Doxey, a former U.S. representative who had won the special election to Harrison's seat. Doxey received the support of Bilbo, who was now strongly opposed to his former ally. During his short tenure in the Senate, Eastland had attacked the tariff, government intervention, and addressed the importance of a global free trade system. These issues were popular with Delta planters, but voters in other parts of the state were more critical of Jim Eastland's performance in Washington. The Eastland campaign thus faced a difficult challenge. It had to defeat the powerful political machine of Theodore Bilbo by siphoning off enough votes from the electorate outside the Delta. In the race against Doxey, Eastland presented himself as a friend of the people in the Hills and piney woods of Mississippi, and as a champion of the farmer and the South.[40]

In the summer of 1942, James Eastland delivered speeches all across the Magnolia State. He primarily talked about his successes in the U.S. Senate, education, old-age pensions, and World War II. Mississippi needed a new voice in Washington, Eastland believed. In an indirect attack on Senator Bilbo, he said: "I waited for the old politicians to take the lead and fight for our people, but they were too busily engaged in political intrigue and chicanery; so I determined to speak. It was my solemn duty to our people. I minced no words. I expressed the opinion of every patriotic citizen of the South."[41] Although his accomplishments in the Senate primarily benefitted large planters, Eastland wanted to show his legislative record was also profitable to small landowners. His fight against the dumping of government-owned cotton on the American market and his opposition to the import of large quantities of Brazilian cotton, his successful effort to remove the low ceiling price on cottonseed, the Bankhead-Eastland bill, and his attempts to increase cotton allotments indicated he represented the interests of all farmers in the South. "If elected, I shall continue to strive in every way possible to protect the interests of the farmers, and to secure for farmers parity prices which will guarantee them the American standard of living," he stated in the *Farm Bureau Co-Op News*.[42]

Eastland knew he had the support of the Delta, but some of his constituents from this region worried about his chances in other parts of the state, particularly the Hill Country. "I believe a Delta man can be elected, but it must be a Delta man who can shed the Pharisee attitude of the average Deltaite and see eye to eye with the little man from the hills," attorney Marcus Kaufman wrote.[43] He advised Eastland to study the career of James Vardaman, a politician who came from the Delta but who successfully appealed to the poor white vote. Eastland agreed with Kaufman, but he also believed many people overestimated the alleged prejudice of the Hill Country toward the Delta. "The people of the Delta come from every community in Mississippi," he answered Kaufman, "they have relatives, they have friends, they have acquaintances in every community in our state. They can go back in those communities and do any candidate a world of good." Eastland himself was a prime example of a Mississippian who was born and raised in the Hill Country, but who moved to the Delta at a later point in his life. This double identity was an important asset in the 1942 race and in the campaigns that followed. Depending on where he was in the state, Eastland could either position himself as a Delta planter or a Hill Country farmer.[44]

Woods Eastland's nexus of powerful friends was useful in his son's first Senate campaign, and he actively sought their support. "I don't think you should hesitate on casting your vote for Jim," Woods wrote Harry Murray, an attorney from Vicksburg. "I want you to get busy and we can easily make it a one primary affair. He can easily win on the first if my old friends will get behind him."[45] But not all of Woods Eastland's allies were certain about an easy victory for the planter's son. "I had the opportunity to go to the hill section of Carroll, Montgomery, and Attalla counties on three different Sundays," one of them wrote. "There seems to be an undercurrent whispered around that you were a 'great' and immensely rich Delta plantation owner, as they all seem to think this about Delta planters; they were using this against you in every way."[46] Woods tried to allay these fears. "Jim has some land in the 'rich Delta' but isn't a rich man by any means," he answered. "Of course, a Delta planter is like a snake, you have to wait until he is dead to measure his wealth, which is usually nothing like it is represented to be."[47]

Wall Doxey considered Eastland's attempts to portray himself as a Hill Country farmer preposterous. "We have the absurd picture of a rich, young Delta planter claiming to be 'the farmer's friend' because he introduced three little bills in the Senate while he was serving the 88-day term of that political-debt appointment," he complained. According to Doxey, Governor Johnson was "pulling every patronage string and applying every pressure upon state employees in his effort to ram his own little senator down the throats of Mississippi voters and expand his political machine to Washington."[48]

In the meantime, Doxey's mentor in the U.S. Senate, Theodore Bilbo, tried to convince Eastland to enlist in the military. Bilbo had also written the other members of the "Little Three," Kelly Hammond and Courtney Pace, to join the army. "Lose no time in laying your all upon the altar of your Country—lose no time in putting on your Country's uniform and let the world know that you are ready to fight and even die, if need be, for those things that are precious to every American citizen," Bilbo urged Eastland. "I want to see you succeed and be the great leader you are destined to be, because I know that obscurity will be the lot of everyone who fails his Country in this hour of need."[49]

James Eastland did not appreciate Theodore Bilbo's advice. "Of course, Senator, you did not expect me to swallow your bait without discovering the barbed hook it so poorly concealed," he responded. In the remainder of the letter, Eastland criticized Bilbo's record in the Senate, his mingling in local political affairs, and his earlier isolationist position on American military involvement in World War II. Eastland reminded Bilbo he had not joined the army when the United States was at war with Spain. "That war was fought before I was born, which was November 28, 1904, yet I killed just as many Spaniards as you killed; I freed just as many Cubans as you freed; I contributed just as much to the defense of my country as you contributed," Eastland wryly noted. He considered the letter an ill-fated attempt to divert attention from the "miserable records" of Wall Doxey and Bilbo himself, and he equated the senior senator with Hitler, Mussolini, and Tojo—the dictators Eastland was supposed to fight. "Senator, your advice does not spring from patriotism, neither does it spring from friendship," James Eastland stated. "It is prompted by your desire to have as your colleague a Senator whom you can dominate and control."[50]

Bilbo's interference in the Senate race did not bring victory for his protégé. Eastland easily defeated Wall Doxey in the primary. Doxey won twelve counties scattered across the northern and central parts of the state, while Eastland carried the other sixty. Although Theodore Bilbo backed Eastland's opponent, Doxey had trouble rallying the senator's constituency in the Hill Country around him. "When Bilbo was a candidate the delta-hill division appeared in more or less clear form," Key observed. "In other races there often appeared a confusing criss-crossing of lines between delta and hills. The advantage in such politics almost invariably goes to the delta. Even without formal political organization the lawyer-planter-merchant group can act in concert; about the only means for the expression of the hill viewpoint is through a personality such as Bilbo."[51]

In future campaigns, Eastland often employed the same strategy that had brought him victory in 1942. Besides the ideological fusion of Delta and Hills, he combined anticommunism, segregation, and the defense of free enterprise into a powerful message. In the years to come, the newly elected senator was on the forefront in the fight against communists, labor union leaders, and other "outside agitators" who tried to destroy the white southern way of life. The *Tupelo Daily News* believed Eastland was indeed the statesman who would restore Americanism in national politics. "During the serious and black period of reconstruction following the war—the South has a man who is steeped in the Spirit of the Old South—a man that Lee and Jackson and Jefferson Davis would have voted for had they been living," the newspaper reported. "The South should rejoice today in the fact that the most able young man since the days of Lamar, Stone and Harrison has been selected by all the people of Mississippi to again restore to the greatest 'All-American State'—Mississippi— the prestige once held by our Commonwealth." When James Eastland started his first full term in the U.S. Senate, Theodore Bilbo was not present to introduce his colleague from Mississippi. Kenneth McKellar of Tennessee did the honors instead.[52]

Shortly after Eastland moved to Washington, he met with President Franklin Roosevelt. "That's alright son, I got quite a kick out of those anti-New Deal cracks," FDR said, referring to Eastland's race against Doxey. "But now you're elected and we've got to play together. You can come see me whenever you want to."[53] Although the junior senator from Mississippi supported Roosevelt and his successor, Harry Truman, in foreign policy, he often clashed with the Democrats in the White House on domestic issues. James Eastland's first political target was organized labor, especially the Congress of Industrial Organizations (CIO), an integrated labor union that advocated anti-lynching legislation and abolition of the poll tax. Eastland believed the CIO had only two goals in mind: destruction of Americanism and mongrelization of the people of the United States. He argued that the nation should form a united front, not only on the battlefield but also at home. From Eastland's point of view, strikes did not just hurt the economy. They were unpatriotic acts of treason and they had to be crushed. During his first year in Congress, the senator introduced a total of three bills, all aimed at limiting the rights of laborers and giving managers the authority to break strikes.[54]

Eastland combined his work in Washington with the management of the family plantation. Before the mechanization of agriculture, an abundant supply of cheap labor was necessary to keep the cotton business profitable. World War II threatened this system based on black menial work. Thousands of southern African Americans left Dixie during the war in search of opportunities elsewhere in the United States. With the military industry running at full speed, they found plenty of jobs in defense plants across the country. In the meantime, black workers who stayed in the South assumed a better bargaining position because of the growing labor shortage in the region. James Eastland experienced these problems firsthand. "Even after three weeks of dry weather, there is lots of competition for labor and I think this reflects the big increase in cotton acreage," plantation manager Robert Ormond reported. "If the crop is good, the picking problem will be the difference between profit and loss for a big wage crop."[55] A couple of months before the end of the war, W. J. Godbold, another supervisor on the Eastland farm, wrote the senator about the distressing situation in the Mississippi Delta. "Will do everything in our power to bring order out of chaos that exists on your plantation," he noted. "Of course this is true of all the delta. You are entirely familiar with the backwardness of all farm work in this section as you were here only a few days ago. This situation is most serious." In the era before mechanized farming, a lack of cheap labor could have disastrous results for cotton planters.[56]

The economic base of the cotton-growing business produced a worldview that justified this system. In the planter's mind, blacks were content with their life in the South until civil rights groups and communist-inspired movements descended upon Dixie. In the U.S. Senate, Eastland battled all interference in southern race relations, whether it came from the federal government, communist front groups, labor unions, or civil rights organizations. The Fair Employment Practices Committee (FEPC) in particular was a thorn in the side of southern segregationists. Established in 1941 by President Roosevelt, the goal of the FEPC was to prevent discrimination on the basis of "race, color, creed, or national origin." Every employer or labor union engaged in federally funded defense projects had to adhere to the committee's rules. Civil rights leaders considered the establishment of the FEPC to be an important step toward racial justice.[57]

Eastland and other senators from the South saw the committee in a different light. During the debate over the extension of funding for the FEPC, which started in June 1945, they denounced the agency as yet another attempt by the U.S. government to create a monolithic super state, based on racial equality and Marxist doctrine. Southern segregationists hoped the new president, Harry Truman, would come to their aid. Truman was a Democrat from the border state of Missouri and had succeeded Roosevelt after his death on April 12, 1945. But Truman surprised Eastland and his colleagues from the South when he spoke out strongly in favor of civil rights, including the FEPC. Advocates of the committee saw prolongation of the agency as a concretization of the ideals the United States had been fighting for in the Second World War. The war still continued in the Pacific, and the FEPC also served as a clear signal to China and other allies in Southeast Asia that America took racial progress seriously. A final consideration was the prevention of race-related unrest through federal control. Lynchings and race riots had erupted after World War I, and civil rights activists expected that the FEPC could prevent a repetition of such outbursts of violence when soldiers began to return home. Southern senators received all these arguments with skepticism. They saw the FEPC as an emergency measure established during wartime, and definitely did not endorse continued federal meddling in southern labor relations.[58]

On June 29, James Eastland spoke in the Senate about the supposed communist nature of the FEPC and the undesirability of racial change in the South. Eastland completely opposed government interference in hiring practices. "It is all part of the Communist program to destroy America, to destroy the American system of economy, to destroy the American system of government, which we love, in order to sovietize our country," the senator stated. Eastland saw anti-discrimination measures such as the FEPC as a communist strategy to increase race and class-consciousness, and thus ignite social conflict. By making false promises to blacks, the communists wanted to stir them into revolution and topple the dominant system in the South. The establishment of a Marxist regime in the United States would then just be a matter of time. "The Negro race is an inferior race," Eastland said. The destruction of "safeguards which have been erected to maintain the purity and racial integrity of the white race" would not lead to racial equality, but to the ruin of American civilization. In order to substantiate his racist claims, Eastland accused black soldiers of dishonorable conduct. "The Negro soldier was an utter and dismal failure in combat," he claimed. They were cowards, deserters, and disobeyed orders. This information came from generals who remained anonymous during the debate. "Negro soldiers have disgraced the flag of this country," Eastland declared. Why would the U.S. government reward these troops through initiatives such as the FEPC? According to the Mississippi senator, the white soldier had won the war, and "there will be no FEPC, there will be no social equality, there will be no such un-American measures when the soldier returns." Despite his calls for white supremacy, Eastland did not consider himself an enemy of blacks. But when he told his listeners he was "not prejudiced against the Negro," the Senate galleries burst out in laughter.[59]

Eastland's speech on the FEPC and the black soldier received mixed reactions. The Southern Conference for Human Welfare (SCHW), an agency established in 1938 to further the goals of the New Deal in the southern states, researched press reactions in the South to Eastland's speech. James Dombrowski, editor of the SCHW newsletter *The Southern Patriot*, sought the opinion of white editors about the senator's statements. Newspapers across the region criticized Eastland's depiction of blacks in the military. "This speech of Senator Eastland's is one of the basest appeals to . . . prejudice and hatred we have ever read," the *Macon News* reported. "We hope that the entire South will repudiate it and that the senator's own state at the first opportunity will return him to the obscurity from which he came." The *Richmond Times-Dispatch* thought it was "humiliating to the South for two Mississippi demagogues [Eastland and Bilbo] to misrepresent the Southern people with their unfair diatribes." The *Courier-Journal* from Louisville, Kentucky, branded Eastland "as a dangerous enemy of national unity in his cowardly use of sweeping assertions designed only to discredit a loyal American minority."[60]

In mid-July 1945, SCHW president Clark Foreman sent Eastland a copy of the editorial response to his Senate speech. Foreman considered the senator's derogation of black soldiers "a gross misrepresentation" and "definitely detrimental to our war effort at home and on the fighting fronts." He believed the SCHW survey demonstrated that the southern press shared these sentiments. "We want you to know that most Southerners feel proud of the achievements of Negro soldiers," Foreman wrote. "We further believe that the reason that Senator Eastland could dare to make such statements is that only 15% of the people of voting age in Mississippi voted in the election in that state in 1944." Because such a small portion of the Mississippi electorate voted, Foreman refused to accept Eastland's standpoints as an expression of the majority's will in the Magnolia State.[61]

Other white southerners were more appreciative of Eastland's stand in the FEPC debate, however. Editor Frank Sharbrough of the *Deer Creek Pilot*, a newspaper from Rolling Fork in the Mississippi Delta, had little respect for the SCHW and for his colleagues who rejected the language of Bilbo and Eastland. Sharbrough's grandfather had fought for "the cause we are enjoying in Dixie," and he was disappointed that only a few southerners (including the two senators from his state) appeared to "have the back-bone" to fight for white supremacy. "If this FEPC Bill ever becomes a law, you may expect trouble and plenty of it here in Mississippi," Sharbrough warned, "and may God have mercy on our souls here in the Mississippi Delta, if such should be the case."[62] Eastland told Sharbrough the SCHW was a communist front organization, with close ties to the CIO. "Its objective is to break down the southern racial safeguards. FEPC if established on a permanent basis will destroy us." The senator believed the southern bloc in the Senate had enough votes to derail the bill, however.[63] In another letter to an editor from North Carolina, Eastland commented on the sources of misbehavior by black troops in the war, and why he used these sources. "The information that I gave the Senate in the filibuster on FEPC relative to the conduct of negro soldiers in Europe was accurate and was given to our entire Committee by very high Military Authorities." From

Eastland's point of view, this data confirmed blacks did not deserve preferential treatment through fair employment legislation.[64]

Walter Sillers condemned the FEPC on similar grounds. In the state legislature, Eastland and Sillers had been opponents. But when Eastland moved to the Delta and became a planter himself, his agenda began to resemble the worldview of his old political enemy, who owned a plantation in Rosedale. Sillers saw the FEPC as discriminatory to whites:

> The people of this country want fair treatment to all, discrimination in favor of none, and they want the god given privilege of conducting their business as a free enterprise without interference by some committee or bureaucrat for the purpose of discriminating against the white people of the country in favor of the negro, or discriminating against independent laborers (40,000,000) who do not belong to a union, in favor of those who do belong. We don't want discriminations against these minorities, and we do not want discriminations in favor of them. We want our own freedom as well as allowing them theirs.[65]

The letter Sillers wrote to Eastland demonstrates the centrality and interconnectedness of labor rights and racial equality to Delta planters. During a time of labor shortage, agricultural reform, and growing demands for anti-discrimination measures, wealthy white supremacists such as Sillers and Eastland became apprehensive about the maintenance of traditional race and class relations in the South. At the end of World War II, their opposition to government interference became more vocal and definitely more virulent. Sillers proposed to organize the southern states "into a strong minority group" to counter the growing influence of liberal groups on the national Democratic Party. He opposed any form of compromise. "We may get somewhere that way, but under the policies now adopted of giving in to the demand of the administration, the Northern democrats, negro organizations and labor groups, we are sure to be the step-child of the administration." Sillers did not differentiate between organized labor and civil rights activists. Both groups wanted to upset the status quo in the South and were therefore equally dangerous. In addition, he argued that white southerners were the real victims of discrimination by the federal government and the national political parties.[66] These two notions—the link between labor rights and civil rights, and the perceived oppression of the white South by outside forces—formed the core of the neobourbon worldview shared by Eastland and Sillers.

Although the filibuster by James Eastland and his southern colleagues in the Senate ensured the temporary status of the FEPC and cut down its budget, the agency was not dead yet. In January 1946, U.S. senator Dennis Chavez of New Mexico introduced a new FEPC bill, which would make the committee a permanent institution. The southerners again organized a filibuster. Eastland invoked the specter of Reconstruction and John Calhoun's nullification theory to oppose the committee. The FEPC, like the Freedman's Bureau of the post–Civil War period, had two clear goals, Eastland stated: to "mongrelize the races" and "export Harlem democracy" to the southern states. The future of American civilization was at stake, because "with mongrelization comes Marxism." Eastland thought "the cure for all the racial agitation" was to take "the doctrine of white supremacy to the American people," to show them "the value of race—that race is everything in American life." Advocates of the FEPC could not muster the necessary two-thirds majority to end the southern filibuster. After three weeks of continuous debate, Senate liberals gave up the fight, thus spelling the end of the FEPC. Without funding, the agency disappeared for good five months later.[67]

The FEPC controversy was an important moment in Eastland's political career, catapulting him to national prominence.[68] In the 1945 debate, the junior senator from Mississippi took the stage after Theodore Bilbo had been filibustering for two days. Eastland demonstrated he could easily match Bilbo's racist demagoguery with his speech on the conduct of black soldiers. He also presented a synthesis between anticommunism and the defense of segregation, a fusion that became an important element of southern conservative thought in the Cold War. During his early Senate years, Eastland had primarily focused on agriculture. But as the call for racial equality and workers' rights increased, he turned to the defense of business interests and white supremacy. After the FEPC debate, America recognized Eastland as a fierce anticommunist and devoted segregationist. Moreover, in his resistance to federal intervention in the southern race and economic structure, the senator no longer adhered to the noblesse oblige of the Delta planter aristocracy. Eastland thus combined the economic views of the plantation establishment with the racist language of the white working class that supported Bilbo.[69]

James Eastland's outspoken statements about black inferiority and his attacks on organized labor coincided with the growing influence of civil rights groups and unions on the Democratic Party. In the months before the 1944 presidential election, southern conservatives tried to reestablish control of the party and prevent a takeover by forces hostile to Jim Crow. The Supreme Court decision in *Smith v. Allwright* in April 1944 was a severe blow to segregationists. The Court ruled the use of the all-white primary by Texas Democrats unconstitutional, which also meant that Democratic parties in the other southern states had to give up this practice. In Mississippi, the installment of the all-white primary had been important in the political empowerment of poor whites, while it added an extra barrier to black participation in elections. *Smith v. Allwright* put this system under pressure. Across the South, hundreds of thousands of blacks began to register after the Supreme Court verdict.[70]

Against this background, southern Democrats started to organize for their party's convention in Chicago. In the summer of 1944, Franklin Roosevelt decided he was going to run for a fourth term. His health was deteriorating, however, which made the selection of a vice presidential candidate critical. Walter Sillers believed Mississippi was ready for a showdown with New Deal Democrats. "We will stand by the Democratic Party and the house of our fathers, and we shall not forsake real democracy and the house of our fathers for a lot of foreign ideologies and communistic policies," he wrote Eastland. "Furthermore we do not intend to have the New Deal or any other political party force upon us their equality with the Negroes." At their state convention, Mississippi Democrats had already adopted a number of defiant measures. If the national convention selected a presidential ticket that did not respect "the traditions of the South," the Democratic electors of Mississippi claimed the right to vote for "some other good Democrat" who opposed "to the end any attempt to force racial and social equality of the Negroes upon the whites of the South."[71]

James F. Byrnes and Henry A. Wallace initially were the main contenders for the vice presidency. They represented the two warring wings of the Democratic Party. Byrnes was a former senator from South Carolina, had served on the Supreme Court, and headed the Office of War Mobilization (OWM) in 1944. As OWM director, Byrnes earned the nickname "Assistant President" because of his influence on the national economy and military production. Southerners and conservatives endorsed the South Carolina politician, yet party leaders feared his candidacy might result in the loss of support from African Americans, organized labor, and Catholic voters, which were all important constituencies for the Democratic Party. The CIO and northern blacks favored Vice President Henry Wallace, whose liberalism made him anathema to the Democratic right wing. Roosevelt liked both men, but he also understood that he needed a compromise candidate to hold the party together. That candidate was Senator Harry S. Truman of Missouri, whose border state origins and pro-labor voting record made him acceptable to most southerners and northern liberals. In the months leading up to the convention, Roosevelt and a trusted cadre of White House advisers worked behind the scenes to play out Byrnes and Wallace supporters against each other and push Truman as FDR's running mate.[72]

On the eve of the convention, Byrnes decided to give up his bid for the vice presidency, but Wallace was still determined to win the nomination. For southern delegations, thwarting Wallace's nomination had top priority. When the convention started the process of selecting a vice presidential candidate, the Mississippi delegates voted for Senator John Bankhead of Alabama on the first ballot, despite James Eastland's pleas to back Truman. The Missourian had always maintained cordial relations with Mississippi. When he entered the Senate in 1935, Truman followed Pat Harrison's cues, and in later years he shared a desk with Eastland.[73] In Chicago, Eastland told his fellow delegates that "one of the outstanding traits of Senator Truman's character is his loyalty to friends; that he is friendly to the South and that Mississippi would make no mistake in supporting him for the nomination."[74]

The wake-up call for southern Democrats came when they learned about the results of the first ballot. Wallace led the race with 429.5 votes, against Truman with 319.5. Bankhead received only 98 votes, while Wallace was close to gaining a majority of 589 delegates. Just before the start of the second ballot, Chairman Robert Hannegan of the Democratic National Committee met with James Eastland. Hannegan, a close friend of Truman, told Eastland that Mississippi had a decisive influence on the vice presidential nomination. If Mississippi refused to switch its votes to Truman, Wallace had a real chance of victory on the second ballot. Eastland subsequently addressed his state's delegation in one of the caucus rooms outside the convention hall. He told the delegates about his conversation with Hannegan and urged them to support Truman. Walter Sillers and John Sharp Williams seconded Eastland's pleas. Although some Mississippians criticized Hannegan's attempts to control their delegation, Truman eventually received the votes of the Magnolia State on the second ballot. Other states also switched to Truman on the second roll call, and within a matter of minutes the Missouri senator received enough votes to secure the nomination. Thanks to the president's maneuverings, the support of powerful friends, and the assistance of Senator Eastland, Harry Truman became Roosevelt's running mate.[75]

Top-ranking Mississippi politicians endorsed the Roosevelt-Truman ticket, although not all Democrats in the state were satisfied with the outcome of the convention. The party platform did not mention a permanent FEPC, but southern delegates had failed to get a states' rights declaration in the platform.[76] On the last night of the convention, former governor Mike Conner of Mississippi organized a meeting in his hotel room to discuss a future strategy for the white South. Conner was displeased the Democrats had voted down a white supremacy plank and restoration of the two-thirds rule. "We were pretty well agreed that the Democratic Party as now constituted and the Republican party do not stand for the principles we advocate," Conner said about the conference. Not many southern delegates showed up at the gathering, however. Most of them had already left for home.[77]

Eastland promised to support Roosevelt and Truman. "The fight by certain southern delegations in my judgment is largely responsible for the defeat of Wallace and the very mild position of the party in the platform on the race question when compared to the Republican stand on this question," he declared.[78] The Mississippi senator told Tom McDonald of Utica a similar message. "I think all the Southern states should support the ticket," Eastland wrote McDonald. "I will do everything within my power to aid in the election of the President and Harry Truman."[79] Like previous years, the Democratic candidates won Mississippi in a landslide.

When FDR died in the spring of 1945, Truman became president, which initially pleased the southern political establishment. Walter Sillers believed the new chief executive understood southern mores. "He is friendly to the South, respects its traditions, and appreciates the support we gave him," Sillers wrote Eastland in April 1945. "Jim, that is my opinion of our president and I am glad I was given the opportunity to play a small part in the events which contributed to his elevation to the presidency."[80] James Eastland continued to defend the president, even in 1946. "Many people are apprehensive about the drift to the left in this country," he wrote Billy Snider of Clarksdale. "President

Truman is systematically seeking out and firing all Communists and crackpots in the Government Service. I think this program is wholesome and would be endorsed by the people of Mississippi if they knew the facts."[81]

But apparently James Eastland had underestimated Truman's liberal leanings. Although the president supported the fight against international and domestic communism, he did not equate the advancement of civil rights with a Soviet plot to overthrow the American government. Less than three months after the senator had written his letter to Snider, Truman created the President's Committee on Civil Rights, which had to study how the personal freedoms written down in the Constitution could be guaranteed to every American citizen. The committee's findings played a significant part in the growth of southern unrest and the rise of the States' Rights Democrats.

Scholars have described the 1944 convention as the start of the struggle over the progressive promises of the New Deal, and the influence of this liberalism on the future course of the Democratic Party. While the national Democrats tried to win the votes of northern blacks, they also continued to tolerate southern segregationists in their ranks. How could the party embrace a liberal agenda and simultaneously accommodate its segregationist southern wing?[82] For Eastland, Sillers, and other conservative southern Democrats, the answer was clear: any more concessions to labor unions, civil rights activists, and minority groups would have disastrous results, not just for the party of their fathers, but for the survival of American civilization. Their fight to preserve what they considered the basic tenets of Americanism—states' rights, segregation, and free enterprise—would eventually lead to an open revolt against the party the Solid South had always loyally supported. This desperate act of rebellion would be a clear indication that the national Democrats could no longer take the old Confederacy for granted. Like previous calls for united southern action to protect regional traditions, Mike Conner's attempt to form a front in defense of white supremacy and state sovereignty would fail as long as politicians such as Eastland managed to sell the compromise reached in Chicago as a victory for the white South. When the Democratic Party truly committed itself to racial equality in 1948, southern loyalty all of a sudden would prove to be not as self-evident as it always had been.

CHAPTER 2

JAMES EASTLAND'S RADICALISM

The Formation of the States' Rights Party

THE FIRST TWO MONTHS of 1948 were ominous for the supporters of Jim Crow. On January 7, President Harry Truman delivered his State of the Union address, in which he declared that the first obligation of the U.S. government was to secure basic human rights for all Americans. Truman directed his message at the South. He criticized its system of segregation and proclaimed that every form of discrimination was against the fundamental American belief in democracy and liberty. Less than four weeks later, the president addressed the same issue in a special message to Congress. Truman asked for the implementation of ten objectives, which were all aimed at guaranteeing constitutional freedoms to every U.S. citizen. The president's plan included the enactment of anti-poll tax and anti-lynching laws, protection of voting rights, and the prevention of discriminating practices in employment. Truman based his address on a report written by the Committee on Civil Rights, a council he had appointed in December 1946. The committee's findings, titled *To Secure These Rights*, pointed at the wide divergence that existed between the American ideals of equality and justice for all and the presence of blatant forms of racism in large parts of the country, a discrepancy the Russians were already eagerly using in their propaganda war against the United States. Truman understood that the problem of southern racism had to be confronted, but he also feared the consequences. "I sent the Congress a Civil Rights message," he wrote in his diary on February 2. "They no doubt will receive it as coldly as they did my State of the Union message. But it needs to be said."[1]

Southern segregationists were indeed shocked by the president's initiatives. From all over the South angry letters started to pour into the White House, condemning Truman for his stance on civil rights and the harmful effects it might have on Democratic unity.[2] The fact that leading elements in the party now seemed committed to desegregation was particularly troublesome for white southerners. A congressman from Louisiana regarded the civil rights message to be a declaration of war "by the chieftain of the National Democratic Party against the traditions and Caucasianism of the South," while others considered it far more dangerous than the threat coming from the Soviet Union or the atomic bomb.[3]

The anti-Truman rhetoric emanating from the South was rife with references to the regional past. The president had not only betrayed his race, but also the old Confederacy, his opponents claimed. Some could not imagine that a white man from the border state of Missouri—and moreover, the grandson of a slaveholder—was able to display such utter disregard for southern mores and traditions. These men and women believed that Truman's program would lead to the mixing of the races and the subsequent downfall of the South's social order.

Although whites across the entire South expressed their dismay about the announced civil rights plans, nowhere was the opposition to Truman's ideas more virulent than in Mississippi. Among the other southern states, Mississippi stood out as the ultimate breeding ground for white supremacist thinking. Poverty, racism, reactionary politics, and massive resistance to external intervention all placed the state in a class by itself, V. O. Key argued. The race question dominated the political culture of Mississippi. "On the surface at least, the beginning and the end of Mississippi politics is the Negro," Key wrote. "He has no hand in the voting, no part in factional maneuvers, no seats in the legislature; nevertheless he fixes the tone—so far as the outside world is concerned—of Mississippi politics."[4]

The state's political representatives only magnified this image of Mississippi as a place obsessed by the maintenance of the color line. In Congress, politicians such as James Vardaman, Theodore Bilbo, and John Rankin exhibited the raw side of racism in their attacks on civil rights measures. World War II definitely changed society in the South, but Mississippi remained a bulwark of pro-segregationist forces, even after the Allied victory over fascism and the modernizing impulses of the U.S. war economy.

The Delta provided much of the leadership for the anti-Truman forces in Mississippi. Planter-politicians such as James Eastland, Walter Sillers, and Governor Fielding Wright all hailed from this part of the state. These men did not hide their antipathy toward the president. Described by historian James Cobb as "the most southern place on earth," the Delta appeared to be the negative image of mainstream America. Its rural economy, the strong adherence to the laws of Jim Crow, and the near-feudal rule of the planter class set the area apart even from the rest of the South. Paradoxically, however, natives of the Delta like Eastland and Sillers considered their birthplace to be the heartland of America and described any attack upon its social structure as the outcome of a dark scheme aimed to destroy the ideals for which the United States had always stood. Moreover, the leadership of the Democratic Party, the party of the South, seemed to be part of this very conspiracy. The southern opponents of Truman's civil rights program therefore depicted themselves as defenders of Americanism and saviors of the legacy of Thomas Jefferson, who they regarded as the founding father of the Democratic Party.

During the early months of 1948, at different gatherings across the state, the political elite of Mississippi explicated its commitment to local self-government and the maintenance of segregation. As the States' Rights movement evolved, numerous debates erupted within the organization about its objectives and campaign strategy. The moderate faction desired to focus on constitutional issues and thus broaden the appeal to voters who were less concerned about the survival of Jim Crow. The extremist wing of the party knew no such inhibitions. The radicals firmly believed in the righteousness of segregation and they wanted to address the issue head-on.

James Eastland was a prominent spokesman of the radical cause. He assumed whites in the North and the South had similar ideas about white supremacy and he thought that a focus on the defense of segregation would actually attract more people to the States' Rights Democrats, or Dixiecrats. While Eastland advocated southern independence from the Democratic Party, other Democrats from the region attempted to find a compromise between their adherence to segregation and loyalty to the national party. Even in Mississippi, Loyalists attempted to resist the Dixiecrat Revolt. Although the States' Rights Democrats did not acquire enough electoral strength to influence the presidential election directly, their 1948 campaign would impact the course of the Democratic Party in the years to come.

On January 29, 1948, James Eastland addressed a joint assembly of the Mississippi state legislature. He used the speech to discuss the changing nature of the Democratic Party and to outline a strategy to retain southern influence on national politics. Eastland stated that since the end of Reconstruction, the former Confederacy had been the bedrock of the Democratic Party. But the political loyalty of the southern states to the national party had now been betrayed. During the 1930s, when the Democrats became more receptive to the demands of organized labor and minority groups, the worldview of the white South came under threat. "Our own party, the Democratic party, waves this banner of social equality and the destruction of segregation, the destruction of our social safe guards in the south," Eastland told his audience gathered in the capitol. "That cry was immediately taken up by the Republican Party, because the Republican Party cannot look to us for help, but there is a contest in the north for the favors of those groups."[5]

The state of affairs sketched by Eastland had significant consequences for the supporters of segregation. Within the established American party structure, they could no longer find protection for their interests. Although Eastland did not deny that the Jim Crow South had its back against the wall, he called upon his listeners not to despair and to take a defiant stand in the fight to uphold their way of life. Eastland did not want a program aimed at social equality to be part of the Democratic platform. But what would happen if the national party did come out strongly for civil rights? With the abolition of the two-thirds rule in 1936, the southern delegations no longer had the power to stop this kind of proposition at the national convention. Abandoned by the national Democrats and unwilling to join the Republicans, the party of Reconstruction and Abraham Lincoln, which way could the southern states turn to keep their social system intact?

According to Eastland, only region-wide unity could save the South. He argued that the time had come to make the national Democrats realize that their commitment to civil rights would result in the loss of the South for the party. With 127 electoral votes, the southern states were in fact "a sleeping giant" that could prevent the candidates of both major parties from gaining a majority in the regular presidential elections. In such a case, the U.S. House of Representatives had the constitutional authority to choose the next president. With each state delegation having one vote, a southerner in the White House became a real possibility. Eastland reasoned that northern Democrats in the House would prefer a southern Democrat to a GOP candidate, and that Republicans would rather support a southern member of the Democratic Party than a Democrat from the North.

Eastland foresaw victory for the South, but this victory could only be achieved through regional cooperation. Like their Confederate forefathers, white southerners again had to act in unison, Eastland declared. He invoked the spirit of John Calhoun at the end of his speech. "Mr. Calhoun predicted the Civil War and he outlined what it would take to save the south from degradation and from destruction, and that was to go back to the Constitution, act as a unit, and let our presidential electors protect our social structure. There is the great leader of the south, one of the creators of the Democratic Party—a man who loved the Democratic Party, but a man who lived [for] the south, her people, her customs and her culture more than he did any other consideration." Eastland concluded his speech with a rhetorical question: what advice would those southern rebels from an earlier age, "those who led the south—those men who wore the Grey—those men who gave their all for Dixie," offer that day, more than eighty years after the last shots of the Civil War had been fired? By linking time and space together, Eastland at least convinced his own bailiwick that the strategy he proposed was the right course to follow, but getting the other southern states in line for a secessionist movement turned out to be a far greater challenge.[6]

The difficulty of rallying the rest of the South for a bolt from the Democratic Party surfaced in the first week of February, at the Southern Governors' Conference in Wakulla Springs, Florida. Fielding Wright traveled to the Sunshine State, hoping that the other states would join Mississippi in its revolt against Truman. His call for secession did not arouse much enthusiasm among his colleagues, however. Although all governors denounced the president's civil rights program, the majority considered Wright's plan to leave the party and take independent action too drastic. They decided instead on a forty-day "cooling off" period and created a committee, headed by Governor Strom Thurmond of South Carolina, to find a middle ground between the civil rights proposals of the president and the maintenance of white supremacy in the South.[7]

Eastland had little patience with the restraint of the governors' conference. From Washington, he expressed the hope that the recommendations of the Thurmond committee did not result in "further appeasement and vacillation." He believed that swift and autonomous action was necessary to save southern institutions. The people of the South should realize that they alone were "the ultimate arbiters of their destiny and that they must, if necessity arises, act independently of the politicians to protect themselves."[8]

In another effort to present the southern cause as an honorable crusade, Eastland mounted the rostrum in the Senate to explain the South's predicament. He talked about the Democratic tradition in the region below the Mason-Dixon Line, betrayed loyalty, and the need to restore respect for the southern people. The speech demonstrates how southern Democrats embedded their battle for segregation and state sovereignty within a historical framework that stressed the bond between the national Democratic Party and the white South. It also illustrates Eastland's thoughts about the causes of the liberal turn of the national party. He was convinced that "un-American" ethnic groups in the northern metropolises had taken control of U.S. politics and that these groups were bent on destroying the South, the nation's heartland.

First of all, the Mississippi senator emphasized that white southerners did not want to leave the Democratic Party. Yet preservation of the South's social institutions transcended loyalty to the national Democrats. "Our people are steeped in democratic tradition," the senator said. "All they know politically is the Democratic Party." This was also Eastland's background. His forefathers had worn the uniform of the Confederacy and "did their part in throwing off the yoke of carpetbagger reconstruction and in setting up the present South with all that the name implies." In this context, it made sense to distrust the Republicans, because they had been responsible for the imposition of the Reconstruction regime on the southern states. According to Eastland, "the Republican Party attempted to destroy the white race in the South. It attempted to form Negro States there with Anglo Saxon people subservient to the blacks." During those days, the Democratic Party sided with the white people of the South. It helped restore the old order in the region. But there were also other factors involved in the destruction of Republican rule. Thanks to an "honest Supreme Court" and guided by "the superior intelligence and leadership of the Anglo-Saxon," white control was eventually established and the South again became part of the Union. Since then, southerners had given their lives for their country on battlefields across the globe. There should be no doubt about the patriotism of the southern people, Eastland stated.[9]

Patriotism and partisan loyalty had not resulted in political rewards, however. Senator Eastland contended that the Democrats had reached their powerful position in national politics because of southern support. He believed that this unwavering devotion was exactly the reason why the South was now victimized. Since the Democrats did not have to worry about receiving the southern vote, and since the Republicans did not stand a chance in the area, both major parties paid no attention to the region. "As a result of southern loyalty, we find the national Democratic leadership today attempting to barter the South's social institutions for the political favors of mongrel northern minority groups in politically doubtful states—groups which place their own special demands above the welfare of the Nation." Eastland thought that these groups in fact already controlled the national government, which explained why southern leaders received orders to lead their people to destruction. Under the guise of party loyalty and in exchange for patronage, "the pure blood of the South is mongrelized by the barter of our heritage by northern politicians in order to secure political favors in the slums of the great cities of the East and Middle West."[10]

Eastland described the combined drive for the vote of minority groups and the demand for racial equality as nothing more than political opportunism. The planter-politician said that he was in contact with African Americans on a daily basis and that segregation was beneficial for black and white. He saw northern discrimination as the main reason for poor living conditions in the South. The Civil War, high tariffs, absentee ownership, and the exploitation of the South's natural reserves by eastern capital had led to southern poverty. But according to Eastland, this situation was bound to change. Economic development and southern free enterprise would raise the standard of living for both white and black. "The South can now do it and will do it because the shackles of northern domination, the archaic system which has enslaved both white and black, is being thrown off. We now have the capital to develop our own resources."[11]

Based on this interpretation of economic growth, James Eastland charged that the agitation over racial equality had very little to do with the improvement of the quality of life for black Americans. "The issue is the destruction of segregation, the destruction of the sovereignty of the States, and the concentration of all power in the Federal Government," Eastland told the Senate. He described the Republicans and Democrats as "the errand boys, the flunkeys" of minority groups and believed that their goal was "the total destruction of segregation, with racial mongrelization as the inevitable result." For the defenders of Jim Crow, these developments were more foreboding than the legislation passed during the Reconstruction era. The fact that Democrats were the architects of the new civil rights initiatives made matters even worse. "We have here a Democratic Party attempting to reenact the same program which the Republicans attempted in the heat of reconstruction, which program was

responsible for making the South solidly Democratic." Eastland rebuked southern Democrats who deemed patronage and committee seats more important
than the heritage of their homeland, and he called for leaders who placed "the
welfare of the people above positions of power in any political organization." If
the South organized in an independent grassroots movement and use its power
in the Electoral College, the southern people would again obtain a respect-
ful place in national politics. Eastland hoped "politics and patronage do not
destroy our people, their culture and traditions. This is a question for southern
statesmanship. With firm leadership we can accomplish our salvation."[12]

In the address before the joint assembly of the Mississippi legislature and in
his Senate speech, Eastland articulated a radical strategy to counter the growing influence of liberal and minority groups on national party politics. The
white South needed to organize, and it had to do so decisively. There was no
room for compromise: southern politicians who treasured their congressional
standing more than the defense of the South's social structure were nothing
more than traitors in Eastland's eyes. If the white South did not unite, well-
organized blocs of immigrants and blacks—the "mongrel northern minority
groups" he spoke of—would assume control and concentrate all political power
in the central government. This would mean the end of state sovereignty and
segregation. A second Reconstruction would await the South. For years, its
loyalty to the Democratic Party had been taken for granted. For years, the region had been exploited by outside investors. Now, the moment had arrived to
rise up in an all-out campaign to protect white southern interests. Eastland,
inspired by tales of rebel chivalry, issued a clarion call for another secession.
The Anglo-Saxon identity of the old Confederacy and, in fact, the entire United
States was at stake. The time for committee compromises and "cooling off"
periods had passed.

Harry Truman left Eastland and his allies little choice. The president made
clear that he was not going to negotiate about his program and declined to
bargain with Thurmond's group. The lackluster attitude of most southern
governors toward Fielding Wright's proposals at the conference in Wakulla
Springs and Truman's disregard for Thurmond's committee did not dampen
the secessionist spirit of the states' rights partisans, however. On February 12,
they held a mass meeting in the city auditorium of Jackson, Mississippi, with
Wright as one of the speakers. Walter Sillers remained relentlessly positive
about the future of the states' rights movement. He believed gatherings like

the one in Jackson demonstrated that the beleaguered white South was becoming more unified in its opposition to the administration's civil rights program. "The more I think of the situation and the more I hear from the people of Mississippi and other states, the more optimistic I become over the ultimate results," Walter Sillers wrote Eastland. "The people of Mississippi are 100% behind this movement." Any group opposed to the states' rights cause would "be hopelessly in the minority, and if as a result thereof these measures are put over on the South, when the negroes begin to go to school with the white folks and eat in restaurants, sit by them in picture shows, on street cars and buses, I would hate to be one of that group of white men who didn't go along with this movement."[13]

Sillers's confidence was not completely warranted, however. Charles Hamilton, chairman of the Young Democrats of Mississippi, claimed that the "people of Mississippi are still loyal to the President and the Democratic Party" and called the states' rights meeting of February 12 a fraud. "The few hundred corporation lawyers who supported Byrd in 1944 and who met at Jackson last week represent only their employers," Hamilton stated. "Four years ago the same set of demagogues tried the same trick. We defeated them, 15 to 1. The common people of Mississippi were not heard from last week, but we will be heard from again in November, and as usual."[14]

Despite the pro-Truman sentiments expressed by Hamilton and a few others in the South, Thurmond and his colleagues continued their attempt to change the mind of the party leadership. They eventually set up a meeting with the chairman of the Democratic National Committee, Senator J. Howard McGrath of Rhode Island, who turned out to be just as intransigent about the civil rights issue as the president. The Thurmond committee, thwarted in its efforts to force the southern viewpoint on the Democratic Party, released a joint statement shortly after its discussion with McGrath. "The Southern states are aroused," it read, "and the Democratic Party will soon realize that the South is no longer 'in the bag.'"[15]

The resolution seemed to mirror the opinion of most white southerners. An editor of *U.S. News and World Report* found "the South ablaze with talk about Mr. Truman's civil-rights program. Whites are bitter and angry. Informed Negroes hope that the program will help to improve the lot of the Negro. But many are simply scared."[16] The South's political establishment made sure it was not identified with the administration's initiatives. Even more liberal politicians from the region, such as John Sparkman, Lister Hill, and Jim Folsom of Alabama—under pressure from their constituents—criticized the president's program.

Mississippi took the lead in engineering the revolt against the national Democrats. On March 20, all counties in the state organized party rallies to listen to a radio address delivered by the governor. Speaking from Natchez, Wright started his speech with the standard rejection of Truman's civil rights plans. He then called on his fellow Democrats to commit to the states' rights fight and elect delegates dedicated to the cause at the precinct elections of May 18. Wright also invited his listeners to attend the upcoming states' rights conference in Jackson, which was held eight days before the precinct elections. In general, Mississippi closed ranks behinds its governor and his call for radical action against the national party.[17]

Charles Hamilton's response to the previous states' rights meeting in Jackson's city auditorium had already demonstrated that not all Democrats in the state shared the zeal for secession. This time, Harold White Gautier of Pascagoula shattered the façade of unity Fielding Wright and his neobourbon allies tried to create. Gautier was a World War II veteran, chairman of the Jackson County Democratic Executive Committee, and one of the leaders in the fight against Wright's plans. Although he was a friend of the governor and even served as a colonel on his staff, Gautier did not think the southern revolt would lead to the desired results. In a letter to a number of prominent states' righters, including Senator Eastland, he expressed sympathy for the opposition to Truman's civil rights initiatives, but deplored the strategy Mississippi's political establishment employed to defeat it. Gautier declared that the states' rights movement falsely used the Jeffersonian Democratic designation to take over the local machinery of the state party without any form of popular approval. From his point of view, the ultimate objective of the movement was the destruction of the Democratic Party "in the South and turning over the remnants of it to the Republican Party of the North, which party, from our past experience and from present happenings in Congress, is as anxious as the National Party leaders to inflict upon the South the evils of the so-called 'civil rights' program." Gautier had lived in Mississippi long enough to "remember the necessity of our women folks having to deal with negroe postmasters and of those who sought federal employment being humiliated through having to approach negroe patronage dispensers." He wondered "if the plan to form a

New Party that will be dominated by Republican leaders in the North does not mean a quicker and more emphatic return to such evils."[18]

Harold Gautier turned the states' rights argument upside down. Instead of describing the rebels as true patriots and defenders of the southern Democratic tradition, he castigated them as traitors who handed over the South to the Republican Party, which would bring back all the horrors of Reconstruction. Gautier had no illusions about the chances of the national Democratic Party in Mississippi. He conceded that a large majority of the electorate supported the states' rights ticket. But this did not mean that the voice of the few Democrats who objected to the bolt should go unheard. "As a Democrat I insist that the five, ten or twenty per cent that would want to vote for the nominee of the National Democratic Party should not be deprived of that right," Gautier wrote, "and when anyone seeks to deprive them of that right, neither the wearing of buttons or the mask of Jeffersonian Democracy can make such wearers Democrats who believe in Democracy and its processes."[19]

He challenged the states' righters to reveal their true intentions: were they still Democrats committed to the ideals of Thomas Jefferson, or had they formed a new party that tried to claim the Democratic label through insidious methods? "I believe that you should make a positive announcement on this to all the people, so that if you intend to hold a New Party convention, ignoring the principles of Jefferson which you pretend to espouse, the real Democrats of Mississippi may be forewarned that preparation can be made by them to hold conventions and to prepare for a continuation of Democratic primaries in this state." Using the same rhetoric states' righters practiced to present their cause as a righteous crusade, Harold Gautier demanded that every qualified voter should have the opportunity to express his or her opinion at the ballot box, "so that the people may stand up and be counted in the fight to maintain Southern Traditions and our Southern Way of Life free from outside interference."[20]

The protest of Mississippi Loyalists against Wright's plan of action was fairly limited, particularly in comparison to other southern states. But the states' rights activists soon discovered that the progress of the cause in the Magnolia State formed no blueprint for their rebellion in the rest of the region. This problem revealed itself at the states' rights conference of May 10. Fielding Wright and Strom Thurmond were the main speakers at the meeting in Jackson. Both governors reminded the audience of the Reconstruction period. Thurmond blamed southern poverty and underdevelopment on economic discrimination practiced against the region. The convention had to show the nation a united front of anti-Truman forces in Dixie, but that goal was not completely accomplished. Not all delegates were authorized to speak as state officials, and the Georgia delegation left the meeting after its refusal to sign a resolution calling for secession from the national Democrats in case the party did not repeal the administration's civil rights program.[21]

At the convention in Jackson, the states' rights campaign already had to deal with some of the problems that would plague the insurgents during the coming months: a lack of solid support from prominent southern Democrats who were active on the national scene, the inability to take over Democratic Party machines in all southern states, and the failure to persuade voters in the former Confederacy to support a third-party effort instead of the party of their fathers. In spite of these bad omens, the leadership of the movement decided to plan ahead. In case the national Democratic Party adopted a strong civil rights plank, another states' rights convention would be organized in Birmingham, Alabama, for July 17. At this convention, the delegates would nominate their own candidates for president and vice president. If everything went according to plan, these nominees would then run as the official Democratic candidates of the state parties that had joined the states' rights cause.[22]

On the same day the states' righters convened in Jackson, James Eastland sent Fielding Wright a message in which he expressed his full support for the movement. The senator hoped that under the leadership of the Mississippi governor a strategy could be devised to preserve the southern way of life. According to Eastland, Congress and the U.S. Supreme Court were unified in their attempt to create a strong central government and destroy the autonomy of the states. "Those who oppose this program fight to preserve the racial integrity of all Americans," he wrote. "It is a fight to preserve for our children's children the Caucasian blood stream which is responsible for all civilization and culture." The senator was convinced that white Americans across the country would join forces to maintain racial purity. The states' rights movement had to unite them in the battle against a government "dominated by organized minorities, racial demagogues, refugees, cranks, and crack-pots." Only if America accepted the righteousness of the southern cause would the future of the nation be secure. "May God direct the deliberations of the Southerners who lay the plans and prepare to carry the message of liberty, freedom, justice, and equality to every section of the country to the end that the so-called Southern Revolt shall become the revolt of all America against the evil forces which now control us and which seek to enslave our children's children," James Eastland concluded his message. From his point of view, the states' rights insurgence was nothing less than a crusade to save the United States from the evil clutches of totalitarian rule.[23]

In many ways, James Eastland was the ultimate embodiment of the incipient states' rights campaign. He was a wealthy planter from the Mississippi Black Belt with strong segregationist views, a political philosophy based on state sovereignty and anticommunism, and a commitment to free market capitalism. Eastland represented the ideology of the movement and the core of its membership. Appreciative constituents sent their senator letters of support. This correspondence not only reflects the mindset of Eastland's followers, but also their economic background. "The best and final remedy for internationalism, socialism, and communism, is to return our government to the white Christians, who established our Constitution," George W. Armstrong of the Woodstock Plantation in Natchez wrote Eastland. "Please permit me to suggest you, and my friends W. Lee O'Daniel, John E. Rankin and other true courageous Southerners, get together and repudiate the Democratic Party, denounce the United Nations and socialism and communism." Armstrong also urged Eastland to proclaim his adherence to "constitutional government" and advocate the repeal of the first sections of the Fourteenth and Fifteenth Amendments, which protect the rights of U.S. citizenship and guarantee the right to vote regardless of racial identity.[24]

In response to another letter, James Eastland agreed with Armstrong's suggestion to organize a political movement in defense of the peculiar social institutions of the southern people. "There is only one course open for the South and that is to withhold its electoral votes from any candidate or political party which is bent upon the destruction of our institutions," he told one of his constituents. "The statement that some politicians make 'to fight it out in the Party' is a fraud. This is what the Northern bosses of the Democratic Party want us to say. We are a hopeless minority, and they will pay no attention to us as soon as they are sure that they will receive our electoral votes." The content of these letters summarize the basic philosophy and campaign strategy of the states' righters: attempt to unite all white southern Christians in a movement based on a firm commitment to capitalism and segregation, deny either the Republicans or the Democrats enough electoral votes to win the presidency, and thus force the election of president into the House of Representatives, where the South had more political power.[25]

While the states' rights partisans were setting up their own sectional political organization, Loyalist southern Democrats attempted to find a middle way between allegiance to the national party and distance from its position on racial equality. In contrast with James Eastland, they thought that secession was not in the interest of the South. Unwilling to join the states' rights cause, but unsure about Harry Truman's chances to win the upcoming election and averse to an open association with his civil rights initiatives, New Deal stalwarts such as Alabama senators John Sparkman and Lister Hill distanced themselves from their old friend. Together with Senator Claude Pepper, a staunch liberal from Florida, these southerners considered World War II hero Dwight D. Eisenhower a better candidate for the ticket than Truman.

Different factions within the Democratic Party were thinking along similar lines. By the early spring of 1948, with the president's popularity ratings at an all-time low, the "Draft Eisenhower" drive started to gain followers across the entire political spectrum. Besides Hill, Sparkman, and Pepper, the liberal lobbying organization Americans for Democratic Action (ADA), the leadership of important labor groups, and the sons of Franklin Delano Roosevelt joined the campaign. Big city bosses such as Jacob Arvey of Chicago and Frank Hague of Jersey City also jumped on the bandwagon. From the conservative side of the party, support for Eisenhower came from Harry Byrd and William Tuck of Virginia and Herman Talmadge of Georgia. Even reactionaries like Strom Thurmond and Mississippi senator John Stennis, who were both associated with the states' rights rebellion, thought that the general would be an acceptable Democratic candidate for the South. As such, the Eisenhower movement was an extremely unstable coalition of right and left wing Democrats. Indeed, the only issues that bound them together were their disaffection with Truman and the conviction that he would surely lose the race for the presidency.[26]

On June 22, Mississippi Democrats discussed strategy and ideology at their convention in Jackson. At the gathering, the official nomination of state and district delegates to the national convention took place. All of them had to pledge that they would withhold support from the national Democratic ticket in the upcoming presidential race if the party nominated Harry Truman, adopted a civil rights plank, or disregarded state sovereignty.[27] James Eastland delivered the keynote address, and he seized the opportunity to warn the public of foreign intruders taking over the country. He regarded the influx of a great number of foreigners, especially from Eastern Europe and Asia, to be a particularly threatening development for those who believed in state sovereignty and the righteousness of segregation. These immigrants had formed a united front with civil rights activists and labor unions to influence the programs of both major parties in the United States. "In the great cities of the industrial East there rises against us the babble of alien voices. In the slums of Harlem, in Brooklyn, in Chicago, Detroit and among mongrel racial groups, radicals . . . , these forces which are aligned with Black and Tan Conglomerates are getting set with all of their political power for the second conquest of the South."[28]

Eastland deemed the new waves of immigrants not competent enough to understand the American system of government. "As a rule the Eastern European, the Asiatic from the Middle East and the alien from nationalities and races which do not come from the parent stock which built America are unable to grasp Anglo-Saxon institutions, culture and governmental institutions." He declared that these people had no culture at all and that they were therefore incapable of comprehending the South's political order and its racial doctrine, which were "the same as that of all Anglo-Saxon and Aryan peoples." Eastland saw the southern system of segregation as the best answer to the race question. In fact, if state sovereignty and segregation fell, the "fairest civilization of the Western World will perish."[29]

With the National Democratic Convention less than a month away, states' rights leaders such as Eastland and Walter Sillers started preparing for a showdown in Philadelphia. In a letter to Horace Wilkinson, a virulent racist who was active in the Alabama branch of the states' rights movement, Sillers praised Eastland for his address at the convention of the Mississippi Democrats. According to Sillers, the senator was right in his appeal for unity among all "true Democrats" in order to protect the South's institutions and traditions. But the planter from Rosedale also understood that such an agreement was difficult to achieve. In Congress, many southern members feared that a break from the national party would result in the loss of favorable committee assignments and less influence on the administration. "Having these views I feel sure they are going to lean favorably toward conciliation or appeasement and a compromise so as to keep the Southern delegation from walking out of the Convention," Sillers wrote. "It is also my opinion that most of the Congressional delegations from other southern states will take a position similar to the above." But even without the support of the entire South, Sillers thought the states' righters should continue their campaign. When the national Democrats adopted a platform contrary to the segregationists' cause—and he believed this expectation to be "well founded"—they should leave the convention, regroup as soon as possible in Birmingham, "and there perfect an organization to carry on continuously in the future until we win this fight." Sillers doubted the liberal course of the Democratic Party could be changed. In his letter, he asked Wilkinson to reserve a room for him and his wife at the Tutwiler Hotel in downtown Birmingham for the night of July 16.[30]

In order to gain support for the southern cause, Eastland advocated the organization of an information bureau to "lay the case of the South before the people of the North." According to Eastland, such a campaign was important to inform northerners about the "drive to tear down our institutions." He believed it was crucial for the survival of Americanism to demonstrate "the length that opposition politics will go for votes and to show the control alien racial groups have on our country."[31] Eastland foresaw dire consequences for the entire nation if northerners ignored the warnings of their southern countrymen. To counter this threat, Eastland proposed a hardline campaign that did not evade the question of race or ethnicity. From his point of view, such a campaign was pure patriotism.

The factions within the states' rights alliance basically shared the same political philosophy and racial views, but their different ideas about framing the prime objective of the movement—racism or constitutionalism—obstructed the formation of a common base. Confusion was the logical result. Even Walter Sillers started to ponder the ideological direction of the states' rights campaign. Although he shared Eastland's views on segregation and the danger of outside interference (particularly by communists) in southern race relations, Sillers wondered about the political expediency of a vigorous racist message. "The Senator thinks we are making a great mistake in our efforts to place our fight on the issue alone of 'State's Rights,'" Sillers wrote John U. Barr, a renegade Democrat from New Orleans. Eastland expected that the "racial, social equality issue" actually had a broad appeal across the nation. Sillers undoubtedly hoped that Eastland's observations were astute, but perhaps he realized that raw racism could also lead to the loss of a substantial number of potential supporters outside the Deep South.[32]

In the days before the opening of the national convention, southern Democrats gathered in an attempt to come up with a plan that prevented explicit commitments to racial equality in the party platform. Simultaneously, they went in search of a candidate who would respect southern traditions, particularly in the field of race relations. Eisenhower had been acceptable to most southerners, but when he ruled out a run for the presidency in 1948 they had to find another nominee with the right credentials. Among the contenders were Thurmond, Wright, and Benjamin Laney, the governor of Arkansas. Both James Eastland and Walter Sillers traveled to Philadelphia as members of the Mississippi delegation. The delegates from Mississippi had received clear instructions: either a Truman nomination or the adoption of a strong civil rights plank was sufficient reason to bolt the meeting and head for Birmingham.[33]

On the eve of the convention, Texas oil tycoon H. L. Hunt wrote Senator Eastland to suggest General Douglas MacArthur for the Democratic candidacy. Eastland shared Hunt's admiration for the World War II hero and was particularly pleased that he was "poison to the so-called ADA within the Democratic Party . . . the fact that he did not have any of the ADA support is a compliment to his Americanism." Other members of the caucus were not too excited about MacArthur as Democratic candidate for the presidency, however. "I discussed his prospective candidacy with the Southern Caucus but the response was not enthusiastic," Eastland responded to Hunt. "This was due principally, I think, because a number of the more militant Southern leaders were determined that they were going to fight the battle through and they felt like General MacArthur would not go all the way and they should use the Convention to build up a Southern candidate."[34]

On the other side of the party's ideological spectrum, the liberals were also devising a strategy to make their agenda part of the Democratic program, with special attention to civil rights. The platform committee, chaired by U.S. senator Francis Meyers of Pennsylvania, consisted primarily of moderates who placed party unity above a crusade for equal rights. As such, the committee's position corresponded with the standpoint of the administration; although Truman had presented himself as an outspoken proponent of racial equality earlier, during the months preceding the convention he slowly distanced himself from his previous statements on the subject. By July, the White House voiced its preference for a modest civil rights plank reminiscent of the one introduced in 1944, which hopefully would placate both the South and the progressives.

This time the liberals were not willing to compromise, however. With Mayor Hubert Humphrey of Minneapolis as its spokesman, the ADA led the struggle to force the party into accepting a firm and specific pledge to end racial discrimination and secure equal rights for all Americans. Together with Andrew Biemiller, a congressman from Wisconsin who was active in the labor movement, Humphrey strived to convince the old guard to accept the suggestions of the ADA, which basically included all the legislation Truman had called for in his February message before Congress. After a heated debate, a majority on the committee rejected Humphrey's motions and approved the administration's plank. The liberals had to accept defeat in the first round, but they were not ready to give up their fight yet. They still entertained a hope that the next day, July 14, the convention would accept their minority report instead of the proposals endorsed by the platform committee.[35]

The liberal Democrats not only believed that the enactment of effective civil rights legislation was morally right, they also worried that a vaguely worded commitment to racial equality would drive the African American electorate away from the Democratic Party. The Wallace movement formed a suitable alternative for these voters, and so did Dewey's Republican Party. "The Republicans at their convention just a few weeks earlier had adopted a relatively forward-looking civil rights plank," Humphrey explained the liberal line of thought. "If we had been mild, the Republicans might have seized the issue by our default. . . . So I came down hard on the side of a strong civil rights plank, both as a matter of conscience and as an imperative of political pragmatism."[36]

But after the platform committee voted down his proposals, Humphrey started to have doubts about continuing the civil rights campaign. The committee meeting took place behind closed doors, but the proceedings of the convention were broadcast across the entire nation. He feared that an open floor fight about the issue would show America how divided the Democrats were and possibly tear the party asunder. Personal reasons also played a role. Humphrey was running for the U.S. Senate, and a strong stance against the wishes of the party hierarchy might wreck his political career. Still, he firmly believed in the righteousness of the fight for equal rights. After discussing the matter with various liberal groups, the Minnesota delegation, his father (a delegate for South Dakota), and his wife, Muriel, Humphrey made a decision in the early morning of July 14. Andrew Biemiller would introduce the minority plank, and Humphrey would deliver the speech that had to convince the delegates to accept their motion.[37]

The last day of the convention was the day of reckoning. The southern Democrats moved first by submitting their own minority resolution, which called for the insertion of a states' rights proviso in the party platform. The day before, George Vaughan, delegate from Missouri and member of the credentials committee, had filed a report that asked for the exclusion of the Mississippi delegates. Vaughan stated that the anti-civil rights decrees they adopted at their convention of June 22 were in complete disagreement with the progressive spirit of the Democratic Party. The Mississippians survived the vote on Vaughan's proposition, but his initiative proved to be a foreboding of the direction in which the convention was heading.

Walter Sillers had already seen the dark clouds gather over the states' rights cause before the actual start of the convention, but he wanted to make one last stand in Philadelphia. In submitting his minority report, he made a final appeal to the delegates, asking them to restore the primacy of state sovereignty, which he considered one of the founding principles of the Democratic Party.[38] Sillers's plea for the protection of local self-government stood in stark contrast with Hubert Humphrey's civil rights speech, which followed the motions introduced by the southern Democrats. Although Humphrey's address was only eight minutes long, his impassioned call "to get out of the shadow of states rights and walk forthrightly into the bright sunshine of human rights" aroused the delegates.[39]

When the votes on the resolutions rolled in, few denied that the southern voice had become the voice of a bygone era in the Democratic Party. The states' rights motion was defeated by 925 to 309 (only eleven votes from outside the South were cast in favor of the region's position), while the convention accepted the minority report introduced by Biemiller and Humphrey with 651.5 to 582.5. The support of the big city bosses had been crucial in the passage of the Humphrey-Biemiller plank. The Alabama delegation, dismayed by the voting results and ready to walk out of the hall, attempted to get the attention of Chairman Sam Rayburn to announce its departure, but Rayburn adjourned the conference before the Alabamians were able to issue a statement. The states' righters had to wait until the evening to make their dramatic exit.[40]

When the Democrats reconvened that night to nominate their candidates for the presidency and vice presidency, Rayburn first gave the floor to Handy

Ellis, the chairman of the Alabama delegation. Ellis told the audience that the adoption of the civil rights plank and the imminent nomination of Harry Truman forced the true defenders of state sovereignty to leave the hall. Using rhetoric that was strikingly similar to Jefferson Davis's adieu to the Senate, he declared that without "hatred and without anger, and without fear, but with disillusionment and disappointment, we are faced with the necessity of carrying out our pledges to the people of Alabama, and that we cannot with honor further participate in the proceedings of this Convention."[41] With a final goodbye, half of the Alabama delegation stood up, followed by the entire delegation of Mississippi. Waving the Confederate battle flag, the rebels walked out of the auditorium into the pouring rain. A young alternate delegate named George Corley Wallace, who represented Barbour County in the Alabama state legislature, was part of the group that decided to stay at the convention. Wallace followed the lead of Senator Lister Hill, who thought that independent action would only endanger southern traditions.[42]

Although Hill and his associates did not join the walkout, they made their objections to Truman and his civil rights program known when the balloting for the Democratic ticket began. Together with the other southern states that stayed in Philadelphia, the Loyalist faction of the Alabama delegation voted for Richard Russell as presidential candidate. Only the South supported Russell, however; Harry Truman eventually secured the nomination, 947.5 to 263. The delegates elected U.S. senator Alben Barkley of Kentucky as Truman's running mate. The tumult on the floor had considerably delayed the convention and Truman did not deliver his acceptance address until 2 a.m. the next morning.

The president initially had favored a more moderate stance on civil rights and loathed the divisive tactics of the Democratic left wing, but now that the party had been liberated from the albatross of hardline segregationism, Truman decided to take advantage of the walkout. In a stirring speech, he promised the delegates that he would call Congress back in session and force the Republican majority to enact the liberal legislation they had included in their party program.[43] "Now, my friends, if there is any reality behind that Republican platform, we ought to get some action out of the short session of the 80th Congress, and they could do this job in 15 days if they wanted to do it, and still have time to go out in the country," Truman exclaimed. "They are going to dodge their responsibility, and they are going to drag all of the red herrings they can across this campaign, but I am here to say to you that Senator Barkley and I are not going to let them get away with it."[44] After all the infighting that occurred during the previous months and on the convention floor, the president's address brought the Democratic Party (or what was left of it) back to life that night. Time would prove whether Truman's fighting spirit was strong enough to secure a Democratic victory in the general election.

As events in Philadelphia came to an end, the southern bolters prepared to regroup in the heart of Dixie. The opening of the states' rights conference was scheduled for Saturday, July 17, but delegates pulled into Birmingham the day before. James Eastland delivered a press conference on Friday night to outline the states' rights strategy. The senator was certain of a southern victory. In boisterous language he declared the time had come to carry the fight north, starting with the home states of Truman and Barkley. "We should invade Missouri and Kentucky, along with other border states, as well as several Northern [states]," Eastland said. "We are certain to carry the Solid South. This can easily be done, and the South will then be the real Democratic Party."[45] Truman would lose the presidential election, Eastland predicted, and if the states of the old Confederacy gave their traditional support to Democratic candidates running for Congress, southern Democrats would regain their old position of dominance within the party and subsequently dictate its course.

From Eastland's standpoint, the states' rights movement was the true protector of the Democratic tradition. He argued that the liberals who now controlled the national party had consistently denied this fact, but the upcoming campaign would prove them wrong and reveal the real political power of the South. Moreover, he firmly believed that the strong racist sentiments he championed were not confined to the southern states. The senator therefore constantly pushed for a nationwide crusade against the civil rights program of the administration. In 1948, Eastland already perceived a silent majority in the rest of the nation that shared the views of white southerners about other racial groups.

James Eastland and his colleague from Mississippi, John Stennis, were the only U.S. senators who openly supported the states' rights rebellion. By July, Eastland was certain he did not face any serious challengers for his Senate seat, so he could devote his energy to the southern campaign against the national Democrats.[46] Moreover, he had not much political capital to lose. In the summer of 1948, Senator Eastland was still a relatively young, unknown politician. During his early years in Congress, he had kept a low profile most of the time, which allowed participation in such maverick ventures as the states' rights movement. "Colorless, closemouthed and seldom consulted by his colleagues, Eastland was just another Southern Senator who supported low tariffs, opposed organized labor, and generally went along with the Administration on foreign policy," *Time* described the Mississippi planter. "His only noticeable personal interest was agriculture—especially cotton."[47]

However, with the rise of civil rights activism, Eastland's defense of southern segregation became one of his more prominent trademarks. The senator's passionate involvement in the FEPC debate of June 1945 caught the attention of the national media, earning him the reputation as one of the Senate's strongest protectors of white supremacy.[48] The states' rights movement formed an excellent opportunity to bolster this image at home and across the nation. Not yet hampered by the responsibilities of an important Senate committee chairmanship and without the urge to compromise, Eastland decided to put his hardline ideology into political practice.

This decision could count on the backing of the white Mississippi electorate in general and his constituents in the Delta in particular. From the start of the revolt against the national party, the Magnolia State was in the forefront of the crusade. The *Jackson Clarion-Ledger,* the state's largest newspaper, in fact headlined that the movement was "Born, Cradled and Raised by Sympathetic Mississippians."[49] In such a charged atmosphere it was political suicide to support the national Democrats. John Stennis, Mississippi's junior senator, was confronted with this reality when he initially hesitated to join the states' rights cause. Less outspoken in his racism than Eastland and just elected to the Senate, Stennis declared in January that he was "still a freshman" and could therefore not comment on Governor Wright's call for independent southern action.[50] But Stennis probably underestimated the animosity against Truman and the national Democrats that existed in his home state. After receiving a severe critique for his vacillating stance, the newly minted senator realized that enlisting in the states' rights movement was probably more beneficial for his career than remaining loyal to the national party.[51]

On the morning of July 17 a spirited crowd of states' righters gathered in Birmingham's Municipal Auditorium. At 11 a.m. the chairman of the Alabama Democratic Party, Gessner McCorvey, called the conference to order. Although the organizers attempted to present the states' rights cause as a nationwide affair by decorating the auditorium with national symbols instead of ornaments reminiscent of the Confederate past, the sectionalist nature of the meeting could not be denied. Only a small number of "delegates" from outside the southern states was present. Attendees carried their own Confederate battle flags to the convention, a group of Alabama students brought a framed portrait of Robert E. Lee, and the tunes of Old South classics such as "The Suwannee River" and "Dixie" filled the hall at regular intervals. In their oratory, the main speakers at the conference did not shun references to the Civil War and the Reconstruction era either. Diatribes against Harry Truman, his civil rights program, and the national Democrats were other dominant themes. "There is no more Democratic party in the United States except the Democratic Party represented here today," said Walter Sillers, who was elected permanent chairman of the states' rights convention.[52] In a preliminary speech, John Stennis castigated President Truman's civil rights initiatives and warned that the destruction of southern segregation would result in a national disaster. Not Truman, but Fielding Wright "was a fine symbol . . . of a true Democrat," Stennis declared.[53]

Behind closed doors, leading elements from Mississippi and Alabama gathered after the plenary morning meeting to discuss the political course of the states' rights movement. Those who were outside this inner circle did not really know what exactly was going on in Birmingham; there was uncertainty about terminology (was the assembly a real convention with official delegates or a conference of people who were just interested in the protection of state sovereignty?), about the nomination of candidates for the states' rights ticket, and about the actual reasons for the gathering.[54] The man who eventually became the frontman of the States' Rights Democratic Party, Governor Strom Thurmond of South Carolina, actually did not plan to attend the meeting in Alabama at all, and the upper echelons of the Dixiecrat movement at first did not regard him as presidential material anyway. Arkansas governor Ben Laney was still under consideration for the ticket, and the Alabama contingent attempted to convince Frank Dixon to assume the mantle of leadership.[55] Courtney Pace later claimed that on an informal basis James Eastland had also been asked for the candidacy. The senator had declined because the support of Mississippi for the Dixiecrat cause was not in doubt. Together with Governor Wright, he thought it would be better if a politician from another state received the nomination.[56]

When Laney announced he was not a candidate and Dixon also turned down the offer, Thurmond appeared as a viable substitute. He had been involved in the states' rights revolt since the governors' conference in Wakulla

Springs, he was a good public speaker, and he had amply demonstrated his dedication to the southern cause. When Dixon asked Thurmond whether he was interested, the South Carolinian did not immediately accept the proposal, however. He believed that the states' rights convention should have been organized with more deliberation and he also had doubts about a rebellion against the Democratic Party in the South, even with Truman at the helm. What would happen to his political career if a Republican won the White House because he had led the states' righters in their mutiny against the national Democrats? But Thurmond also realized that the leading position on the Dixiecrat ticket gave him the opportunity to stand up for his convictions and fight for them on the national stage. In the end, the governor accepted the appointment. Fielding Wright was put forward as his running mate.[57]

The spectators broke out in thunderous cheers when Horace Wilkinson, chairman of the resolutions committee, announced Thurmond and Wright as the nominees for the States' Rights Democrats. After Chairman Sillers managed to calm down the crowd by playing the national anthem, Senator Eastland climbed the stage to endorse the ticket. Together with Governor Wright, he had a prominent role in the outcome of the Birmingham convention, urging Thurmond to accept the appointment and promising the support of Mississippi for his nomination.[58] The delegates did not challenge the choice of candidates by the states' rights leadership. By voice vote, they officially nominated Thurmond and Wright. Although Thurmond belonged to the moderate states' rights faction that preferred to focus on constitutional arguments instead of racist appeals, he did not refrain from using blatant segregationist discourse in his acceptance speech. Not civil rights activists, but the "good southern people" were responsible for the progress of blacks in the South, Thurmond asserted. He defiantly proclaimed "there's not enough troops in the army to force the southern people to break down segregation and admit the Negro race into our theaters, into our swimming pools, into our homes, and into our churches." Thurmond's address demonstrated once more that beneath the thin veneer of constitutionalism, the race question was at the center of the states' rights crusade, even for those who were not on the radical fringe.[59]

Shortly after the Dixiecrat convention, Walter Sillers drafted an amendment to the Mississippi state constitution that required voters to be of "good moral character." Since white registrars had the authority to judge whether a citizen possessed the right qualifications to participate in elections, the moral character clause was another attempt by the Mississippi power structure to deny blacks their right to vote. James Eastland fully supported Sillers's motion. He called adoption of the amendment "urgent" and promised to stump the state and prompt Mississippians to endorse the measure. Like Sillers, the senator foresaw that Congress would enact some sort of civil rights law soon and he expected that federal legislators were going to address the poll tax first. To avoid the stigma of sectionalism, Eastland stated that Connecticut had a similar moral character code in its constitution. He argued that the Sillers amendment should therefore not be seen as legislation typical of southern racism. Members of the state legislature criticized the proposition for other reasons, however. World War II veteran Boyce Holleman, a representative from Stone County in southeast Mississippi, believed the amendment "would leave entirely too much authority in the hands of election officials in passing on the moral character of those seeking to vote . . . they could object to a man's moral character simply because he may not belong to the same church as they."[60]

Views similar to Holleman's found little resonance at the state Democratic convention, which reconvened on August 3. Journalist Bill Minor described opposition to the Dixiecrat Revolt as "a voice in the wilderness," and he wondered where the Truman supporters had gone. "Where were the reported opponents who planned to place a set of 'loyalist' electors on the ballot in opposition to the states' righters? No one knew," wrote Minor. "Many Mississippi political observers began to doubt that the much-talked-about move to give the voters of the state an opportunity to vote for the Democratic nominees in November would ever materialize in the surge of states' rights sentiment." To make the Dixiecrat revolution complete, the delegates also adopted a resolution calling on all persons holding or seeking political office to come out for the states' rights cause. A few students protested the proceedings at the convention, but this did not lead to any tangible results. "Certainly no one of political stature in the state or anyone planning a political career will join any movement to oppose the states' righters at this point," Bill Minor concluded.[61]

Confident about a positive outcome in the elections, Mississippi states' righters set course for Houston, Texas, where the official nomination of the presidential ticket took place. The "States' Rights Special" train—with Fielding Wright and James Eastland on board—traveled through New Orleans and reached Houston early in the morning of August 11. Without a trace of irony in his voice, Eastland predicted that the presidential contest was a race between the Thurmond-Wright ticket and the Republicans. "The least we can get from the states' rights movement is to become the minority party and thus control minority committee appointments and elect the minority leaders of the House and Senate." He then warned that "if the South doesn't take a stand now, this whole civil rights program . . . will be enacted. . . . We can put a stop to it by taking our stand this fall."[62]

The Dixiecrats convened in Texas for a clear reason. Winning the twenty-three electoral votes of the Lone Star State would greatly enhance the chance to force the presidential election into the House of Representatives. James Eastland was convinced that Texas had to be won for the states' rights cause. "I hope Texas comes through and supports Thurmond and Wright. It is the only chance the South has," he mentioned in a letter a few days before the Houston conference.[63] But support for the states' rights cause was not wholehearted in Texas, to say the least. The threat to segregation was undoubtedly an issue in the state, especially in the eastern part of Texas, where a significant African American population resided. Nonetheless, the response to the administration's civil rights initiatives was rather restrained, particularly in comparison to the Deep South. Governor Beauford Jester expressed his resentment against federally enforced integration at various occasions and also preferred Eisenhower to Truman, but he eventually decided that a bolt from the national party was not a wise course to follow. For many Texans—including Jester—securing state control over tidelands oil was a more important matter and they believed that the most effective way to achieve this objective was through national party channels.[64]

Not surprisingly, the States' Rights Democrats were critical of the stand Jester and his allies took. At a press conference after the Houston convention, Thurmond expressed his dismay with the about-face of the Texas governor. "It is difficult for me to see how some people can fight the Truman proposals so bitterly, and then turn around and support him."[65] Prominent Texas politicians were noticeably absent from the Dixiecrat convention. Besides Mayor Oscar Holcombe of Houston, not a single member of the state's political establishment made an appearance at the meeting. For now, the Dixiecrat hopes were placed on the conference of the Texas Democratic Party, which convened in Forth Worth on September 14. If the renegade Democrats managed to engineer a takeover of the party there, an opportunity might still exist for a states' rights victory in the Lone Star State.

A day after the Dixiecrat conference in Texas, H. L. Bramlett of Houston congratulated his friend James Eastland on his performance at the convention. Bramlett thought Eastland's "speech at Houston was good—it 'key-noted' the whole meeting." The Texan hoped the convention had ignited the battle against "the political gangsters" who wanted to impose a second Reconstruction on the South. Southern politicians such as James Eastland formed the vanguard in this fight to clear "the shades of Thaddeus Stevens and his crowd [which] now stalk the paths that our children must walk." Like the Civil War, the contest between southern Democrats and national Democrats revolved around the heritage of the South. Bramlett warned if "the arrogant and communistic East can do so, they will repeat the ruthless despotism of the 1870s and even cram down our throat the cruelties of the era. The industrial north, with its red 'new look' is on the march."[66]

Eastland was in complete agreement with Bramlett's views. From his office in Ruleville, he wrote a response explaining how the southern bolt prevented the enactment of civil rights legislation during the special session of Congress in late July and the beginning of August. "The Republicans helped us because they wanted to encourage the fight within the Democratic Party. The New Deal Democrats quietly helped us because they wanted to make up." The senator believed that if the states' righters had not left the national convention, both parties probably would have enacted the civil rights program. It was therefore of the utmost importance that the South stand together in defense of state sovereignty and segregation. Like Thurmond, Eastland had little respect for southern politicos like Beauford Jester, who were harsh in their criticism of Truman but stayed with the national Democrats in the end. "I cannot understand your Governor," Eastland told Bramlett. "If the South is crushed, it will be because of politicians who are afraid to defend their people."[67] The senator himself clearly did not belong to this group. To demonstrate his strong antipathy toward Harry Truman, he even removed the autographed picture of the president from his office in Washington.[68]

Reconstruction and the assumed threat emanating from northern cities were again dominant themes in a Dixiecrat campaign speech by James Eastland, delivered on the night of September 10 in Bellevue Park in Memphis, Tennessee. Standing on a platform decorated with Confederate battle flags, Eastland said how proud he was to speak on behalf of Strom Thurmond, "worthy successor to Wade Hampton, to that great leader of the South 100 years ago, John C. Calhoun," and Fielding Wright, "a man who measures up to Jefferson Davis." After giving a short constitutional history of the United States—with heavy emphasis on the Tenth Amendment—he delved into the background and origins of the rising call for civil liberties. "In the great cities, the metropolitan areas, there are many people from the countries of Southeast Europe. They have organized along racial and religious lines." The senator also accused the Methodist Church (which he attended himself) of uniting with African American activists who fought for "racial amalgamation" and social equality. "Behind it all is the Communist Party, because they desire strife" he claimed. Such internal strife could eventually destroy the United States, opening the way for communist world domination.[69]

Eastland told the crowd how the Democratic leadership mocked southern senators by adopting a strong civil rights plank. Presuming that the South supported the party no matter what, the national Democrats now tried to broaden their appeal in urban areas, which Eastland described as nothing more than a "bold, brazen attempt to gain support from Red Mongrels in the slums of Eastern cities!" In the field of civil rights, he saw little difference between Truman, Dewey, and Wallace. The only way for the South to retain its self-respect and its time-honored customs was a vote for Thurmond. "We are face to face with another reconstruction. It is more devastating than the Force Bills of the 1870s. It is more devastating than the reconstruction following the Civil War, born in the hatred of war."[70]

According to Eastland, a federal anti-poll tax bill meant the elimination of state control over elections and the establishment of a "racial, alien-dominated Congress." A law against lynching set the country "on the high road to have every precious right swept away into the strong arms of national government." And a permanent FEPC might very well lead to an edict putting "negroes as foremen over white women in Memphis." Using public education in New York as an example, Eastland warned of the dangers integration entailed. Some schools in the state had a black-white ratio of 50–50, and in those institutions "policemen have to patrol the corridors. Criminal assaults of little white girls is frequent."[71]

In the upcoming presidential campaign southern voters had the power to decide whether their region would follow the example set by New York. Eastland predicted that the race was between Thurmond and Dewey and claimed that the states' rights movement could prevent another "disgraceful fracas" like the national convention in Philadelphia. At the end of his speech, the senator described a vote for Truman as "a vote against the Jeffersonian Democrats, a vote against such leaders as Robert E. Lee, Nathan Bedford Forrest, Jefferson Davis and Stonewall Jackson." As the audience applauded loudly, James Eastland concluded his speech with a call upon the citizens of Memphis and the South to "march to the tune of Dixie under the banner of Thurmond and Wright."[72]

In the senator's home state, a small but determined band of Loyalist Democrats was still struggling to get Truman and Barkley on the ballot. Under the direction of Philip Mullen, associate editor of the *Oxford Eagle* and a member of the state legislature, nine Mississippi Democrats were recruited to serve as electors for the national party. Although the Loyalist point of view on civil rights did not differ from the Dixiecrat position in Mississippi, the Truman supporters feared that important accomplishments achieved during the New Deal would disappear if the national Democrats did not win the presidential election. Mullen and his Loyalists believed "that TVA, REA, Soil Conservation Service, the price support program for cotton, will be protected only in a Democratic administration . . . further progress, economically, educationally and for the general welfare of the people in the South can be obtained only under a Democratic administration." Emboldened by the endorsement of the National Democratic Executive Committee, the group commenced the formation of a Loyalist party machinery, with the establishment of a state executive committee and the election of a national committeeman and committeewoman.[73]

The Loyalists constituted one of five different slates that were on the ballot in Mississippi. Despite the support of the national Democratic Party and the creation of a rump organization in the state, Governor Fielding Wright declared that the Loyalists had "no semblance of legality." But Wright could not prevent the qualification of the pro-Truman electors. Besides the States' Rights Democrats and the national Democrats, the Republicans also had two different lists of electors. In contrast with the Democrats, both Republican slates were committed to the Dewey-Warren ticket, but the race question also divided the Mississippi GOP. The so-called Black and Tan Republicans under African American attorney Perry Howard formed the faction that had the official endorsement of the national party. However, the Lily-White independent Republicans of George Sheldon had attracted more votes in the past. The Progressives were the only party in Mississippi with black electors, something that had not occurred in the state since the end of Reconstruction.[74]

In the meantime, the battle for the electoral votes of Texas continued. The States' Rights Democrats were determined to campaign actively in the state. A large contingent of prominent Dixiecrats planned to assemble in Houston on October 18 for a fund-raising barbecue. Tickets for the gathering were sold for "one day's income to save the South." Houston oilman and local campaign manager Robert W. Milner Jr. announced that the day after, speakers would start traveling across the state "until every town in Texas is covered."[75] The *Jackson Clarion-Ledger* reported that Senator James Eastland was heading "a delegation of political orators" from Mississippi in the ballot blitz dubbed by the newspaper as "Operation Texas." The Mississippians met with a group of Alabama states' righters at the Jackson airport on the day of the rally, and flew to Houston together.[76]

Although seven thousand tickets were sold for the barbecue, only twenty-five hundred Dixiecrat supporters showed up on the night of October 18 to listen to Governor Ben Laney (the keynote speaker) and other leaders of the revolt. Oil baron H. R. Cullen introduced Laney. Cullen condemned both major parties for their stance on segregation but praised Jack Porter, the Republican candidate for the U.S. Senate, who tried to beat his Democratic opponent Lyndon Baines Johnson on a states' rights platform. Charles K. Smith Jr. and W. H. Reed, two labor leaders from Houston, were also present at the gathering and spoke in favor of the states' rights platform. Reed stated that under the FEPC, "my right of employment, my working conditions, my right to seniority and promotion, and my right to continue work" were taken away. He asserted that the working class shared the Dixiecrats' concern about local control and state sovereignty.[77]

The big guns of the Dixiecrats—men such as Thurmond, Wright, and Eastland—barnstormed Texas for two weeks after the rally in Houston, but they clearly faced an uphill battle. By the end of October, an *Atlanta Journal* poll showed that only Louisiana, Alabama, South Carolina, and Mississippi followed the states' rights banner and that Texas backed Truman. In the end, even a devoted rebel like James Eastland had to admit that the Lone Star State was not going to vote for Thurmond. Back on his Delta plantation after the Texas tour, the senator conceded that the state was safely in the column for Harry Truman.[78] Eastland was right; the four Deep South states named in the *Atlanta Journal* poll backed the Dixiecrats, but the rest of the old Confederacy (including Texas) remained loyal to the national Democrats or went to the Republican camp.

A lack of organization, money, and grassroots support confined backing for the Thurmond-Wright ticket to the Black Belt, where a small group of powerful planters ruled over a majority of blacks. The white elite in this part of the region was able to identify the most with the party's reactionary segregationist message. Moreover, the Dixiecrats were the official Democratic candidates in these Black Belt states. In other southern states, where the states' rights movement ran as a third party, loyalty to the Democrats prevented a Dixiecrat victory. Fearing loss of seniority, prominent southern politicians such as Senators Richard Russell of Georgia and Olin Johnston of South Carolina remained loyal to the Democrats, thus denying the Dixiecrats the official status of the Democratic Party of the South. Indeed, James Eastland was one of the few national Democratic representatives that supported Strom Thurmond.

In spite of the Dixiecrat defeat, some Mississippians who voted for Thurmond were content about the outcome of the election. "We Coahoma countians are [definitely] pleased with the results of the election . . . , we feel that the northern democrats now can never say again that the south is in the bag," a planter from Clarksdale wrote Eastland, "your election comes from the people of Mississippi who [love] the south as we found it given to us by our forefathers that cleaned the carpet baggers from [its] borders."[79] James Eastland concurred. He did not doubt that Mississippi voters made the right decision in voting for the States' Rights Party. The state's support for the Dixiecrat movement had been a clear signal that white southerners did not remain loyal to the Democratic Party at all costs. "I would rather fight this thing to its conclusion. If the other Southern states had followed us, we would have won a tremendous victory. In fact, if it were to be done over again I would follow the identical course that I followed and I have no apologies to make." Eastland not only stressed the importance of southern unity, but also proclaimed a defiant stance that became one of his political trademarks.[80]

Harry Truman won the 1948 election without the support of the Deep South and the industrial East, although his victory was narrow. The president was in a confident mood after his presidential campaign and prided himself on the defeat of sectionalism within the national party.[81] Thurmond supporters across the southern states also realized this. They wondered about what course to follow to keep white supremacy alive. "Our little president is back in the saddle more firmly seated than ever before," Charles Clark of the Ashton Land Company in Clarksdale wrote Eastland. He asked the senator if some working agreement could be reached with the Republicans to stop the Democratic Party's program of economic liberalism. Clark worried about the Democrats' alignment with organized labor, but he feared the party's stance on civil rights even more. "I much prefer to deal with this and all like matters by chicanery; by trading, by compromise, by filibuster." Clark deemed the defeat of the Dixiecrat movement a sign of the impracticability of a political party based on the assumption of strong regional unity, but he hoped that some sort of conservative national organization could be formed to safeguard Americanism and the institutions of the South. "If this election has really sounded the death knell of the Republican Party, cannot we and its remains band together to form a new Nationalist Party of America," he asked. "Now that we have been repudiated by the Democrats, surely we must have enough gumption to align ourselves in some way with their principal opponents."[82] That plan never materialized, however. James Eastland and many other southern segregationists remained in the national Democratic Party, although their continued membership in an increasingly liberal political organization became a troublesome affair in the years to come.

Scholars have argued that the Dixiecrat Revolt marked the beginning of the end of the solid Democratic South, but it was also significant in other ways. Ideologically, the revolt revealed the southern segregationist worldview in one of its purest forms. Conspiratorial ideas were central to this doctrine. States' righters like James Eastland believed that a foreign force was attempting to destroy American culture through infiltration of the major political parties and the federal government. According to the theory, this force was considered to be well-organized. Behind the different minority groups and liberal organizations clamoring for the attention of the Democrats and Republicans, the communists were at work trying to overthrow the American system of checks and balances and create a police state without any form of freedom for its citizens. Although the liberals claimed they were fighting for racial equality, the communist masterminds were not really interested in the plight of African Americans and just used the issue of segregation to foment internal strife. This strife would hasten the downfall of the United States and would break the last barrier for the global Marxist revolution.

From an historic point of view, white southerners could relate to the fear of outside intrusion and federal control. States' righters used the stories of the Civil War and Reconstruction regularly to remind voters of the horrors that the loss of home rule entailed. Simultaneously, through a process of inversion, states' rights Democrats described Confederates as ideal Americans and heirs to the legacy of the founding fathers. The Dixiecrats placed their movement within this tradition of southern lore and depicted themselves as the true guardians of Americanism and constitutional government. Only state sovereignty could prevent the centralization of all power in one totalitarian regime. States' rights therefore constituted the essence of American political culture to them.

The Dixiecrats couched their crusade in rhetoric about betrayed loyalty and challenged southern honor that had to be redeemed. Moreover, they frequently mentioned instances of presumed northern prejudice against the South, which was primarily economic in nature. The states' righters wanted southern voters to believe that all these issues—lost power in the national party and in national politics, broken honor, and discriminating practices by northerners—could be resolved through unanimous regional support for the Dixiecrat movement. But this main prerequisite for states' rights success, the backing of the Solid South, eventually proved impossible to achieve. Southern adherence to the Democratic Party and a relatively pragmatic attitude by most Democratic politicians from the South toward the civil rights plank defeated the quest of the hardliners who formed the core of the Dixiecrat Party.

For James Eastland, the states' rights episode constituted an important learning moment. At the beginning of 1948, he displayed a strong conviction that the white South—and indeed, white America—welcomed an independent political effort by southern segregationists. The sound defeat of the Dixiecrats in the presidential election demonstrated that Eastland had severely overestimated the willingness of southern whites to vote for the states' rights ticket, however. The election confirmed that secession from the national party was not a viable option to protect southern interests. From then on, Dixiecrat politicians such as Eastland had to engineer strategies to remain politically effective within the national party structure without losing their credibility as defenders of the Jim Crow South.

CHAPTER 3

TAKING CONTROL

The Beginning of Eastland's Rise to Power

"I AM NOT A PARTY HACK. I will vote my convictions on all measures," James Eastland declared in the spring of 1949. The Dixiecrat was back in the ranks of the national party, but he did not intend to follow the party line. He proudly proclaimed that he was probably number one on Truman's unpopularity list and that he planned to oppose most of the president's programs.[1] Eastland's statement revealed the predicament Truman and the national Democrats faced. At first sight, 1948 looked to be a triumphant year for the Democratic Party. Harry Truman had won the presidential election against great odds and the Republicans suffered defeats in the House and Senate. With the establishment of Democratic majorities in both houses of Congress, it seemed Truman was finally in the position to implement the liberal promises of his campaign. But things were more complicated than they appeared. In general, many southern Democrats were critical of the president and some of them had opposed Truman outright during the 1948 race. Senator Eastland belonged to the latter group. He displayed little remorse for his defection to the states' rights camp.

For the leadership of the national Democratic Party, the issue of party loyalty was vexing. Liberal Democrats and organizations such as the ADA and NAACP tried to convince President Truman and DNC chairman Howard McGrath to discipline renegade Democrats. Both men agreed with this line of thought, but they also feared the deleterious effects such disciplinary actions might have on party unity and the successful enactment of the administration's political agenda. Based on their seniority, conservative southerners still occupied important posts in Congress, a fact Truman and McGrath could not easily ignore. Moreover, although Harry Truman had managed to defeat his Republican opponent without the support of the Solid South, it remained to be seen whether future Democratic presidential candidates would be so fortunate.

Six days after Truman's victory, McGrath made a first, cautious statement on the position of states' rights rebels within the national party structure. He declared "the great bulk" of Thurmond supporters actually had "understandable motives" which did not negatively affect their standing in the national party, but he also made it clear that the more extreme states' righters could not count on such leniency. McGrath emphasized that his comments only applied to party matters and not to the organization of Congress, where the members themselves decided on committee assignments and related issues.[2]

As a former senator, the president recognized the independent status of the legislative branch to manage its own affairs, although he met with House Speaker Sam Rayburn shortly after the elections to discuss the viability of refusing Dixiecrats committee positions and seniority.[3] Different civil rights advocates urged Harry Truman to issue some sort of reprimand against the states' righters in Congress. The National Negro Council and the National Conference on Civil Rights telegraphed the White House to lobby against the seating of Senators Russell Long of Louisiana, John Sparkman of Alabama, Burnet Maybank of South Carolina, and Eastland, because their states had "officially, publicly, and illegally" denied voting rights to 2 million blacks.[4]

Truman and McGrath attempted to engineer a strategy that took the wishes of liberals and civil rights organizations into account and simultaneously prevented the loss of support from southern Democrats. The party leadership decided to follow a middle road through the system of patronage, a presidential prerogative on which members of Congress usually have substantial influence. By ignoring States' Rights Democrats in the distribution of patronage appointments and rewarding Loyalists in the South with federal largesse, the DNC and the administration hoped to bring southern rebels back in line without encroaching too much on congressional privileges. Truman and his advisers anticipated that this course would also bolster more liberal southern Democrats at the expense of the conservative clique that dominated politics below the Mason-Dixon.[5] McGrath emphasized that he "did not intend to forget those in the South who stood loyally by the party," referring to the Loyalist groups in South Carolina and Mississippi that opposed the Dixiecrats.[6]

Despite Eastland's strong words about the beneficial effects of the States'

Rights Revolt on the attitude of the national Democratic Party toward the South, the Dixiecrat rebellion had created mixed results for those who had supported Thurmond. The dispensation of patronage slipped through their hands and the Republican Party considered the Dixiecrat victory in the Deep South to be a sign that the traditional southern loyalty to the Democrats was no longer as self-evident as it used to be. The grand idea behind the states' rights crusade was the unification of the former Confederacy in defense of its customs and traditions, but after the dust of the campaign had settled, the Solid South appeared to be more fragmented than ever. In order to regain control of the political scene, States' Rights Democrats needed to check the Loyalist movements and the Republicans at the local level, while a balance had to be found between listening to the voice of a white constituency disgruntled with the national Democrats on the one hand, and remaining politically effective within the national party on the other. The election taught Eastland and his friends that independent political action toward the liberal leanings of the Democratic Party worked well on the home front in the Deep South, but that it also resulted in the loss of political favors that formed cornerstones for their base of power at the state level. How could they balance these conflicting interests?

Although both senators from Mississippi participated in the states' rights movement, the Truman administration decided to discipline only Eastland. In contrast with John Stennis, who attended the convention in Birmingham but did not get involved in the Dixiecrat campaign, Eastland displayed little qualms about his open support for the Thurmond-Wright ticket. During the final weeks of 1948, Eastland appeared as one of the main targets in Truman's patronage policy. By then, the White House had also decided to refrain from interfering with the organization of congressional committees and seniority status. The president suspected that such a course most likely would lead to another intraparty struggle that might push conservative southern Democrats further into a coalition with northern Republicans, thus creating a formidable bloc against his legislative plans. Moreover, the patronage issue alone had already caused enough problems in the Senate, where the administration normally first confers with each senator on federal appointments in his or her respective state.[7]

Eastland did not have to be concerned about his standing in Congress, but the patronage affair did pose a challenge to the senator's power base in Mississippi. The Loyalists, led by Philip Mullen and Clarence Hood, who had been elected national committeeman of the Truman Democrats in the fall of

1948, were eager to take charge of the dispersal of federal patronage in the state, and the Democratic leadership seemed willing to accommodate. In January 1949, Howard McGrath notified the heads of all federal departments that patronage appointments in Mississippi first needed to be approved by the Mississippi Loyalists.[8]

Shortly after McGrath gave his orders on patronage, Eastland started his assault on the Truman Democrats in Mississippi. Philip Mullen, editor of the *Oxford Eagle*, was the first Loyalist that came under the scrutiny of the senator's office. Administrative assistant Courtney Pace requested Cullen Curlee, one of Eastland's most trusted deputies in Mississippi, to start research on Mullen, in particular on the editor's anti-Eastland writings in the local newspaper. Rumors were that the president planned to nominate Mullen as collector of internal revenue in Jackson. Eastland wanted to obstruct this appointment. Curlee first provided Pace with Mullen's critical editorials on Eastland written during 1947 and 1948. On February 9, the results of more research followed, covering the period 1942–1943, when James Eastland ran against Wall Doxey for the U.S. Senate. During that campaign Philip Mullen managed public relations for Doxey in Lafayette County.[9]

For other members of Congress representing Dixiecrat states, the policy of the Truman administration involving patronage had already lost much of its initial rancor by the beginning of 1949. After Alabama tax collector Mortimer Jordan resigned because he did not want to comply with fair employment practices, Secretary of the Treasury John Snyder consulted with Senators Hill and Sparkman before naming a successor. Although Hill and Sparkman had not joined the Dixiecrat movement, they had not actively campaigned for Truman either and their state went to the Thurmond-Wright ticket. Snyder's decision to first discuss federal appointments with the senators from Alabama revealed the position of the White House in patronage affairs; as long as southern politicians had not been overtly hostile toward Truman during the campaign, they could count on acknowledgment from the president, even when their state went to the states' rights camp.[10] John Stennis actually received the backing from McGrath when he requested that Harry Truman replace Loyalist Democrat Chester L. Sumners, the U.S. district attorney for northern Mississippi, with his friend James P. Coleman, who had supported the national ticket in the 1948 election.[11]

Although the president opposed Coleman's nomination, the Truman Democrats in Mississippi considered these developments highly disturbing.

With the exception of census takers, the Loyalists had not received any federal jobs yet, and the fact that McGrath approved of Stennis's proposal to nominate one of his confidants for a powerful position in state politics made matters even worse. Moreover, the political establishment in Mississippi seemed impervious to Truman's threatening remarks about the denial of patronage. "I haven't asked for anything. I don't expect to get anything," James Eastland stated.[12]

Stennis also announced his voting would not be influenced by pork barrel, while Governor Wright accused the president of "attempting to play gang politics" in his efforts to control Congress. Wright declared he himself did not have the "slightest interest" in directing federal appointments at the state level, but he did believe the congressmen and senators from Mississippi should be involved in discussions on patronage. "After all," he said, "they do represent the democrats of this state."[13]

But who really represented the Mississippi Democrats? The states' righters that occupied seats of power in Congress, or Truman supporters such as Philip Mullen and Clarence Hood, who tried to set up a Loyalist rump party in the heartland of states' rights? In May, Hood and Mullen traveled to Washington to meet with the president and discuss how they were going to be rewarded for their work. After conducting preliminary talks with Harry Truman and representatives of the DNC, Clarence Hood announced on May 24 that his group desired a substantial number of prominent federal jobs in Mississippi, including the post of internal revenue collector. Although Hood declined to say exactly what Truman had told him, he came out of the meeting "very optimistic." Speaking from the lobby of the White House executive offices, he declared the Loyalist Democrats would file their own list of candidates for the 1950 congressional election because he did not "consider any of the incumbents as good Democrats." Pointing at the great unpopularity of the administration's civil rights program in their home state, Eastland and the other members of Congress from Mississippi immediately dismissed the viability of Hood's plans to replace them with Truman supporters.[14]

Clarence Hood explained that his goal was not absolute control over money and jobs coming from the administration. "Various state editors are loudly proclaiming that I and the Central committee are trying to establish political dictatorship in the state through the use of Federal patronage. I have repeatedly stated that I have no political ambition personally or otherwise and am not in the least bit interested in obtaining any political prestige." Hood stated that his primary objective was the restoration of the Democratic Party in Mississippi, a party based on the philosophy of the New Deal. He depicted the Dixiecrats as closet Republicans, who employed racist demagoguery to further their reactionary agenda. The Loyalists, Hood argued, wanted to "prevent the complete destruction of the Democratic Party in Mississippi, because we believe sincerely and conscientiously that the preservation of the Democratic Party with its liberal ideals is essential to the economic well-being of Mississippi and the South."[15]

According to Hood, the process of alienation from the Democratic Party was not a recent phenomenon. In 1928, "Republicans in the state masquerading as Democrats" had already tried to swing the Democratic vote to the GOP. This situation had only grown worse in the years that followed. Since the deaths of Governor Thomas Bailey and Senators Pat Harrison and Theodore Bilbo (politicians Clarence Hood described as "liberal leaders"), a group of "selfish" reactionaries took complete charge of the party machinery in Mississippi. Afraid to call themselves Republicans, these pseudo-Democrats actually seemed "to be pledged to work with the Republican party hand in glove to oppose all of the Administration program, good or bad." Hood called upon those Democrats "who are pledged to the principles of Republican conservatism" to come out in the open, instead of trying to mislead the electorate with appeals to base sentiments. With his statement, the Loyalist leader clearly defined the southern Democratic tradition as a tradition founded on the principles of New Deal economic liberalism. The states' righters claimed they were the true Democrats, but from Hood's viewpoint their white supremacist rhetoric was just a cover to hide their leanings toward the fiscal conservatism of the Party of Lincoln.[16]

People close to James Eastland abhorred the liberal economic policies the president and his supporters in Mississippi were advocating, and they applauded Eastland's disapproval of Fair Deal legislation, including Truman's national health care initiative and the farm plan engineered by Secretary of Agriculture Charles Brannan, which was aimed at supporting small farmers and limiting government subsidies to large, commercial landholders. The specter of Marxism was often invoked to criticize this kind of government activism based on a progressive agenda. In the words of Cullen Curlee, the Brannan Plan, "should it become law, would only be another step in socialism or communism. I see very little difference in Truman's socialistic program or Stalin's communistic program."[17]

In Mississippi, the Regular Democrats, who represented the traditional Democratic Party that had supported Thurmond, were determined to retain control over party politics in the state. Chairman Knox Huff of the State Democratic Executive Committee (SDEC) announced on June 23 that he had authorized the reactivation of the States' Rights Campaign Committee, this time to "submarine" a planned conference of the Loyalists in Jackson on July 15. States' rights partisans such as Fielding Wright and Wallace Wright were again prime movers in the organization of resistance against the president and his allies in the Magnolia State, and Walter Sillers also joined in condemning the Loyalist faction. Sillers warned that any Democrat who participated in the meeting of July 15 was in fact endorsing "the national committee's program for FEPC; non-segregation of the races; anti-poll tax, anti-lynch and other of the civil rights proposals."

The goal of the campaign committee was the coordination of a vigorous grassroots drive to demonstrate the presumed illegality of the Loyalists' claim that they represented the Democrats in Mississippi. The Regulars wanted to prevent a big turnout at the upcoming conference of the pro-Truman group at all costs, because they assumed that heavy attendance at this meeting might be interpreted by the national leadership as a sign that Mississippians actually favored a regime change. The strategy of the states' righters was therefore clear: portray the Loyalists as power hungry and dishonorable opportunists who "were sniping our congressional representatives from the rear" and who would give up white supremacy for a few federal dollars.[18]

A week later, the executive committee again met and adopted several resolutions of policy condemning the maneuvers of the Loyalist Democrats. In the words of the Regulars, their opponents were nothing more than "patronage seeking pretenders and usurpers" who betrayed their own representatives in Washington by following Democratic leaders seeking "defeat of all Southern congressmen who are fighting to preserve a free America." Members of the committee argued that since the Loyalists agreed with the program of the national party, they were actually in support of desegregation, "kindred Socialist measures . . . and all the other South-destroying and freedom-loving legislation proposed by said national leadership." If Truman Democrats in Mississippi denied their approval of these initiatives, they implicitly acknowledged federal patronage was all they were after. Pointing at state laws that allowed political parties to hold conventions once every four years, the states' righters accused the Loyalists of bolting the official state Democratic Party because they organized their own conference only a year after the previous meeting in Jackson. The Dixiecrats had engaged in similar secessionist activities the year before, but that did not seem to matter now. After all, following states' rights logic, Thurmond and his followers represented the true Democratic tradition and the Mississippi electorate had overwhelmingly endorsed their cause in the presidential election. The Regulars stated that real Mississippi Democrats were convinced their crusade was just and that they had "a vital role to play in defense of liberty" against the money-grubbing Trumanites. The executive committee stressed that it absolutely did not intend to lead the state into the Republican Party and that Loyalist assertions about this matter were false.[19]

The Truman Democrats, mindful that they might violate state laws, decided to call their gathering a forum. There, the first steps toward the reorganization of the Mississippi Democratic Party would be discussed. A few days before the Loyalist forum, the *Clarion-Ledger* reported that Mississippi congressman John Bell Williams had uncovered links between Truman supporters and communist front organizations. Williams contended that a representative of these subversive groups was in Mississippi to assist the faction led by Clarence Hood with the coordination of their upcoming meeting. The paper revealed that these connections with leftist movements were disclosed to the office of James Eastland.[20] Governor Wright also contributed to the blacklisting of the Trumanites. In a radio speech, he urged Mississippians not to be deceived by Hood and his henchmen, whose only alleged objective was personal enrichment through federal patronage. Wright also praised Senator Eastland for his "valiant fight and stand" in the U.S. Senate.[21]

The Loyalists were undeterred by the propaganda campaign of the Mississippi political establishment and its media outlets. On July 15, between four hundred and five hundred Truman Democrats met in Jackson to decide on a future course for the state party. They announced their adherence to the 1948 platform adopted in Philadelphia—except the civil rights plank— and advised the states' righters to seek forgiveness, rejoin the national party, and give up their attempts to "fool the real Democrats by appeals to fear and prejudice."[22] State Senator Marvin Henley of Philadelphia, Mississippi, was one of the few Democratic politicians who attended the forum. Like Hood, Henley also feared that the economic accomplishments of the New Deal would be reversed if the Dixiecrats in Congress were not checked. "I hate to think of our representatives in the national congress cutting our throats and sending us back into depression," he told the audience.[23]

Many branches of the state Democratic Party backed the stand of the Regulars, however. In Alcorn County, where Cullen Curlee played a leading role in Democratic politics, the county committee confirmed the legitimacy of the Huff group. Curlee expected other sections of the state party to follow this lead.[24] The motion by the Attala County Executive Committee was particularly scathing. Its drafters called the Loyalist forum an assembly of "political scalawags" bent on destroying the South because of their support for "the oppressive, distasteful and repugnant Civil Rights Program of the little man who now occupies the White House."[25]

In August 1949, J. Howard McGrath gave up his Senate seat and resigned as chairman of the DNC to become attorney general. William M. Boyle of Missouri, the DNC assistant director and a longtime friend of Harry Truman, replaced him. Like McGrath, Boyle wanted to restore party unity and favored a moderate approach toward the southern rebels. As an intermediary between the president and the Dixiecrats, the objective of the Democratic National Committee was the pacification of the two camps. This strategy of appeasement had its limits, however. "Mississippi is being handled gingerly," columnist Doris Fleeson reported. "Even the sweet-tempered McGrath gave up on the bitter Dixiecrat senior Senator, Mr. Eastland; it is hoped by kind treatment to reclaim Senator Stennis, an ex-judge in control of his temper."[26]

Howard McGrath took a conciliatory stance to get Stennis back on board, but he was less compromising in the management of the DNC. One of his last feats as chairman was his refusal to invite national committee members from Mississippi and Louisiana who were supporters of the Dixiecrats. On August 23, John B. Snider and Mrs. Hermes Gautier, who represented the Regular Democratic faction in Mississippi, appeared before the credentials committee of the DNC to protest McGrath's decision. Snider argued that he represented the Democrats of Mississippi, who had overwhelmingly endorsed Thurmond in the 1948 election. As spokesman for this party, he therefore could not have backed Truman even if he had wanted to. Snider's argument did not convince the members of the credentials committee to recognize the Regular bloc as the Democratic Party of the Magnolia State. They advised the DNC to grant seats to the Loyalists instead. Clarence Hood and Mrs. John Clark thus became the Mississippi delegates on the national committee.[27]

The same day Hood and Clark were admitted to the DNC, Truman proclaimed the Democratic Party had truly become a national organization. At a dinner honoring William Boyle as the new chairman, the president told the audience that the Democratic victory in 1948 signified the end of sectionalism. "The Democratic Party is a national party, and not a sectional party any more. The tail no longer wags the dog," Harry Truman said. "We won the election last November without New York, without the industrial East, and without the solid South."[28] Truman added that these sections were of course welcome in the new, restructured national party.

James Eastland considered the dismissal of states' righters from the DNC and the president's call for unity another indication that the national Democrats were only trying to attract new voters in the North. "Frankly, I do not think the Administration desired to seat the committeemen from Mississippi, Louisiana and Alabama as they would prefer making political capital with the Eastern minority groups," he wrote a friend from Mississippi shortly after the banquet.[29] Although Curlee considered the pro-Truman forum in Jackson "a complete failure," the leadership of the national party now recognized the Loyalists as the real Democrats of Mississippi.[30]

Around the same time, rumors started to circulate about possible tax evasion by Clarence Hood.[31] The charges against Hood came in the midst of congressional investigations of graft in the Truman administration. Eastland had already been in the process of gathering data on the tax evasion matter.[32] In September 1949, he released a statement that the pro-Truman movement in Mississippi was paid by outside organizations and received help from liberals such as Senator Hubert Humphrey of Minnesota. According to Eastland, the work of the Hood forces was an "attempt by the Congress of Industrial Organizations, the National Association for the Advancement of Colored People, Americans for Democratic Action and racial equality organizations and Communist organizations to take over and dominate Mississippi."[33]

The senator declared carpetbaggers and scalawags were working together to destroy civilization in Mississippi in exchange for federal patronage. Eastland warned "all the groups in this country who practice social equality, who advocate the things we do not believe, and who are attempting to destroy private enterprise and the American system are lined up behind those promoting Mr. Hood and his group." He also promised to publish "other angles" to the controversy around the Mississippi Loyalists in the near future.[34]

Clarence Hood branded Eastland's charge as a "malicious falsity" and emphasized that the Loyalists financed their own program and that it (according to Hood) gained new supporters in the state each day. "But poor Jim and his cronies have been trying to sell his Delta cotton to Fascist Spain so long he is likely to fly off on a tangent any time—especially where real Mississippi problems exist," Hood retorted, "as far as I am concerned his [Eastland's] long line of service to the common man of Mississippi speaks for itself."[35] Having secured the official recognition of the national party, Hood thought he was in the position to publicly scorn Mississippi's senior senator. But he recklessly underestimated Eastland's resources to upset the Loyalist effort and restore Regular control of state politics.

In the meantime, Eastland worked his way up in the Judiciary Committee. The chairman of the committee was Democrat Pat McCarran, an iron-willed rancher from Nevada who shared James Eastland's antipathy for communism and Harry Truman. After two unsuccessful bids in 1918 and 1926, McCarran won election to the U.S. Senate in 1932 on a platform of state sovereignty and opposition to the Hoover administration. The freshman senator immediately obtained nominations to two of the most important committees in the Senate: Appropriations and Judiciary. McCarran understood that his membership on these committees enabled him to secure a solid base of power in his home state. Judiciary handles the bulk of Senate legislation and decides on federal judicial appointments, while Appropriations directs the flow of money coming from the national government. McCarran used control of federal employment and federal dollars to build up a strong political machine in Nevada that ensured his reelection to Congress. The system of patronage created a mutually reinforcing bond between the senator and the electorate in his state; each victorious Senate campaign meant an increase in seniority for McCarran, which automatically meant more influence on the legislative process and on the distribution of government jobs and funds. As McCarran's authority in Congress grew, so did his ability to reward his followers. The senator was zealous in his efforts to create an extensive network of loyal supporters; according to Nevada governor Richard Kirman, "Pat [wanted] every job in the state."[36] In later years, James Eastland closely followed McCarran's use of patronage for his own political advantage.

Pat McCarran's worldview was very close to Eastland's political philosophy. Both men hailed from rural states and they despised the liberal establishment in the big cities. An almost constant fear of outside intrusion fueled the politics of the two senators. This encroachment came in different forms, but foreigners, communists, and the federal government constituted the most important dangers that needed to be checked, especially when these three enemies of the American way of life seemed to combine forces.[37] McCarran and Eastland adhered to a states' rights interpretation of the Constitution, which expressed itself in strong opposition to the liberal policies of the New and Fair Deals.

From the start of his Senate career, McCarran fought the expansion of power of the federal government, in particular the growing impact of the executive branch on lawmaking. On March 13, 1933, defying Senate traditions, the freshman senator rose from his seat to announce his objection to one of the first pieces of New Deal legislation proposed by Franklin Roosevelt. During his campaign, McCarran had pledged to support FDR, although this promise did not automatically translate in granting congressional powers to the president, even in times of grave economic depression. Senator Pat Harrison of Mississippi was able to thwart McCarran's attempt to reject Roosevelt's initial series of economic emergency laws by asking the Senate to table his motion, but this defeat did not stop McCarran from repeatedly voting against the president and the party line in the years to come.[38] Defending their version of Americanism was the highest priority for both Pat McCarran and James Eastland. For Eastland, segregation constituted an inherent part of the American way of life.

McGrath's resignation from the Senate opened up new avenues for Eastland to protect the system of Jim Crow more effectively. On April 28, 1949, before he resigned, McGrath had introduced an omnibus civil rights bill that contained anti-lynching and anti-poll tax provisions and prohibited discrimination in employment. The next day, Hubert Humphrey submitted an additional bill that authorized the creation of a federal civil rights commission. These two bills, S. 1725 and S. 1734, were referred to the Judiciary Subcommittee on Civil Rights, chaired by McGrath. The subcommittee had two other members: Republican Alexander Wiley of Wisconsin and James Eastland.

When Truman appointed McGrath as attorney general on August 24, 1949, McCarran made sure one of his conservative allies replaced the senator of Rhode Island. To the dismay of civil rights activists, he declared Eastland was the new chairman of the subcommittee. "Walter White, the negro leader, said he told President Truman in Washington there is 'widespread resentment' because Sen. Eastland . . . heads a Senate judiciary subcommittee on civil rights," the *Memphis Press-Scimitar* reported. "He said Mr. Truman reminded him there is nothing he can do about congressional appointments." The *Natchez Democrat* was more enthusiastic about Eastland's nomination. "The appointment of Senator Eastland of Mississippi as chairman of a Judiciary Subcommittee handling 'civil rights' legislation will undoubtedly come as a shock to Fair and New Dealers," the newspaper noted. "Whatever reasons were behind Senator McCarran's appointment of Eastland, the plain fact is that it is a recognition that the persons most likely to be affected by 'civil rights' legislation are entitled to a strong voice in that legislation."[39]

The promotion of Eastland to the chair of the Civil Rights Subcommittee meant the end of S. 1725 and S. 1734, and the anti-poll tax measure died in a Rules Subcommittee chaired by John Stennis. On October 3, Majority Leader Scott Lucas signaled the failure of prompt Senate action on civil rights issues when he announced that, according to him, it seemed "doubtful that a prolonged discussion of any civil rights bill at this session would be helpful."[40]

McCarran appointed Eastland right before he embarked on a journey to Europe, where he intended to investigate the status of refugees. World War II had displaced millions of people, and although the war had ended more than four years earlier, almost five hundred thousand people were still living in refugee camps. In 1946, Harry Truman had asked Congress to draft legislation aimed at admitting displaced persons into the United States. It took two years before the president could sign a new immigration bill into law, which he did reluctantly. Truman anticipated a liberal statute that would allow a substantial number of refugees to enter the United States, but the powerful conservative bloc on Capitol Hill was not very eager to open the borders for these victims of war. The consequence was a limited bill that only let a small quota of displaced persons into the country. Matters of immigration fell under the jurisdiction of the Judiciary Committee, where Pat McCarran had senior status. The senator from Nevada actually preferred to keep the American mainland closed to all refugees, wanting to relocate them to the territory of Alaska instead. When the Democrats regained control of Congress in the 1948 elections, Truman hoped the members of his party on Capitol Hill would design a less restrictive law. But with McCarran as chairman of the Judiciary Committee, hope was all the president could cling to.[41]

At the start of the new Congress, New York representative Emanuel

Celler and Senator J. Howard McGrath submitted proposals for a revised displaced persons law. Their idea was to significantly liberalize the 1948 act, but the subcommittee appointed by McCarran to study this legislation was outright hostile to any progressive amendments. Republican William Jenner of Indiana and James Eastland were on the committee, and these senators already considered the previous law too radical. Immigration reform had been buried in committee for almost four months when Pat McCarran made his announcement to the Senate that he needed to go to Europe to make a personal assessment of the refugee situation there. The trip was another delaying tactic to keep the bill from reaching the floor. McCarran trusted that senatorial courtesy would prevent a Senate debate while the chair was away.[42]

Yet a few weeks after McCarran's departure for Europe, Harley Kilgore of West Virginia, the acting chairman, called the Judiciary Committee to order. Kilgore was a liberal Democrat and a reliable supporter of the Truman administration. He was not going to wait on McCarran to debate displaced persons legislation. On October 15 the bill was sent to the floor without recommendation. James Eastland joined the chorus of conservative senators in criticizing discussion of the bill while the chair was not present. "I submit that the treatment of the chairman of the Senate Judiciary Committee was outrageous," Eastland stated. "He was under a leave of absence from the Senate, and was studying conditions zealously and sincerely, in an earnest endeavor to work out a bill which would be to the best interests of our country."[43]

The senators advocating restrictive displaced persons legislation were able to hold their ground in the debate. The Senate was ready to adjourn and McCarran's supporters successfully employed the weapon of filibuster to recommit the bill to the Judiciary Committee. By a vote of 36 to 30, the chamber adopted a motion introduced by Republican Harry Cain of Washington and James Eastland to send the bill back to the committee until the beginning of the next session. The conservative coalition once again prevailed; nineteen Republicans banded together with seventeen Democrats to vote for the motion. The majority of Democrats who backed the recommendation submitted by Eastland and Cain came from former Confederate states.[44]

On January 24, 1950, the Judiciary Committee finally submitted a displaced persons bill for discussion on the Senate floor, although hearings continued through March. The legislation reported out by the committee was Emanuel Celler's House bill, but Pat McCarran amended Celler's proposal to such an extent that the congressman from New York described the final result as a fraud. McCarran maintained some of the basic premises of the Celler bill, but the provisions added to the Senate version reveal a distinct preference for particular groups of refugees. The measure introduced by McCarran broadened the definition of displaced persons from victims of the Nazi regime to all people forced to leave their homes because they were persecuted or feared persecution during the period between September 1, 1939, and January 1, 1949. Moreover, the Senate bill retained the clause from the 1948 Displaced Persons Act which stipulated that 40 percent of the refugees were to come from annexed territories in Europe and that 30 percent of the displaced persons allowed into the United States were to be laborers involved in agriculture. These features harbored an inclination toward *Volksdeutsche* farm workers who had fled Eastern Europe after the postwar communist takeover. This addition came at the expense of other displaced persons, including Jewish people.[45]

Senator Eastland in particular expressed a keen interest in the fate of *Volksdeutsche* refugees. During the debate on displaced persons in October 1949 he had made the claim that no single "group of people in the entire history of the world ever suffered more than they did."[46] On March 3, 1950, when the bill was under discussion in the Senate, Eastland compared the Germans to the white people of Mississippi, who he described as being "of as pure Anglo-Saxon blood as can be found in the United States." According to Eastland, one "of the greatest crimes in all history was the uprooting [of Germans] from their homes, where their people had lived for centuries, of men, women, and children, whose only offense was that through their veins flowed Germanic blood and that a thousand years ago their ancestors had been of German stock."[47] Such rhetoric aroused criticism from liberals like Democratic senator Herbert Lehman of New York, who declared that the McCarran forces on the Judiciary Committee were trying "to change the entire nature of the [displaced persons] program from one of relief for displaced persons to one of relief of German expellees."[48]

The debate on the displaced persons bill turned into a dogged fight between liberal and conservative senators. McCarran and his allies resorted to sharp rhetoric and parliamentary maneuvers to thwart any form of reformist legislation. In one of his speeches on the refugee situation, James Eastland targeted the Displaced Persons Commission (DPC), a body appointed by President Truman to administer the 1948 Displaced Persons Act. The commission had three members, all progressives, who were more concerned with aiding immigrants coming to the States than with examining their communist leanings, which was a top priority for both McCarran and Eastland.[49] The Mississippi senator regarded "the administration of the present displaced-persons law . . . shocking," and charged the DPC officials with "moral treason" because they had set up a system through which "Communist saboteurs and agents and officers of the Russian secret police have been filtered into the United States."[50]

Prospects for enactment of McCarran's bill were unfavorable, but the chairman and his allies did everything in their power to influence the final outcome. For thirteen hours he attempted to slow down the vote by offering 130 amendments, first to his own version of the bill and then to Kilgore's substitute legislation. McCarran argued that increasing the number of immigrants would result in rising unemployment, housing shortages, and general economic crisis. He introduced measures that discriminated against Jewish victims of the war and that reduced the total number of refugees permitted into the United States. He also attempted to make the 8 million Germans living in communist-occupied territories eligible for displaced persons status, thus overloading the quotas for displaced persons allowed to enter the country. The Senate rejected all motions offered by McCarran and replaced his bill with the version drafted by Kilgore, which passed by a vote of 58 to 15. The senators voting against the bill were either Republican or southern Democrat. In the end, Pat McCarran cast his vote in support of the Kilgore substitute so that he could sit on the conference committee tasked with resolving the differences between the Senate and House versions of the displaced persons bill. The Nevada senator intended to stack the committee with strong conservatives such as James Eastland, but Majority Leader Lucas successfully thwarted that plan. In early June 1950, after McCarran had again tried to stall work on the refugee bill in various ways, President Truman finally signed a new displaced persons act into law. The defeat of the McCarran forces in the struggle over revised displaced persons legislation was not absolute, however. Eastland's allegation about communist infiltration in the Displaced Persons Commission was only part of a systematic attempt by conservatives to brand the officials involved in the execution of the 1948 act as subversives, or at least as Marxist sympathizers. The result was that the administrators who had appeared before the Judiciary Committee became less willing to admit refugees to the United States and that screening procedures intensified significantly. McCarran, Eastland, and their allies lost the battle in the Senate, but indirectly their influence was felt in the final implementation of displaced persons legislation.[51]

In the debates and hearings on the displaced persons bill, James Eastland did not waver from the views he articulated during the 1948 campaign. He had little appreciation for legislation that did not prioritize the immigration of *Volksdeutsche* farmers, who he considered close to the white people of his home state. "Do Senators know that under this bill a person who took up arms against Russia when the Russian Armies invaded his country, and who fought to protect his country, is ineligible to come into the United States as a displaced person under the Celler bill which we are asked to pass," Eastland asked his colleagues. He then declared "this bill is founded in discrimination. It stinks of discrimination against loyal, patriotic groups who should be permitted to come here, and who would be an asset to our country."[52] Parts of the *Volksdeutsche* population had collaborated with the Nazis, and this stigma blemished the entire community after the war. For Eastland, this discrimination was unwarranted. Because the senator based his interpretation of the refugee question on the premise that the enemy of your enemy is your friend, Germanic fugitives from communist oppression did not form a threat to the American way of life, especially in comparison with refugees from Eastern and Central Europe that had different ethnic backgrounds. An obvious link existed between the speeches Eastland delivered for the Dixiecrat cause and his rhetoric in the displaced persons debate. Under a liberal displaced persons bill, the groups of foreigners that pushed the Democratic Party away from Americanism and toward Marxism only increased. Senator Eastland did not oppose immigration, as long as the newcomers possessed the right ethnicity and had clearly displayed their anticommunist credentials.

During the spring of 1950, the cold warriors in the U.S. Senate engaged in a vigorous drive to enact a stricter antisubversion program. On February 9, Senator Joseph McCarthy delivered his now famous speech in Wheeling, West Virginia, where he charged that communists had successfully infiltrated the Truman administration and that he possessed the evidence to prove it. McCarthy's allegations came a few weeks after the Alger Hiss trial and Harry Truman's announcement that he had authorized the development of a hydrogen bomb. With Cold War tensions on the rise, right-wing politicians such as Eastland, McCarran, and Republican senator Karl Mundt of South Dakota moved to put these fears into legislative action. The sense of emergency only intensified when the Korean War broke out at the end of June. Truman himself actually gave the cue for McCarran and his allies to introduce their far-reaching series of measures to weed out communism in the United States. On August 8, the president asked Congress to slightly alter existing antisubversive legislation, thus enabling an easier prosecution of espionage and sabotage. Although Truman desired tougher laws to deal with infiltration, he also warned that his request should not be interpreted as a clarion call to start a witch hunt for Reds. Truman wanted to show that he took the dangers of communism seriously, but at the same time he intended to assure Americans that they did not need to develop irrational fears of internal subversion.[53]

McCarran, however, was less sanguine about domestic security. The Nevada senator had met defeat in the displaced persons debate, but the internal security issue offered an ultimate chance for retaliation. Two days after the message from the president, McCarran introduced an omnibus bill that combined most of the anti-subversion proposals pending in the Senate. The McCarran Act offered a comprehensive response to almost every form of un-American activity as defined by the right-wing bloc in Congress. Among other provisions, the law established a subversive activities control board to register members of communist and front organizations, denied passports and government jobs to Marxist sympathizers, tightened espionage legislation, and made the deportation of subversive foreigners easier.

Despite liberal opposition, the bill passed Congress on September 20, but Truman refused to sign it. He considered the McCarran Act a totalitarian piece of legislation that disregarded basic civil liberties, and he sent it back to Capitol Hill with the request they study the bill more carefully. The president anticipated that enactment of McCarran's plan would turn the United States into a police state with the authority to harass not only aliens, but also U.S. citizens. The House and Senate were not impressed by Truman's ominous predictions, however. Congress overrode his veto, and the Internal Security Act of 1950 became law on September 23.[54]

Two months later, on November 30, James Eastland introduced Senate Resolution 366, which created the Senate Internal Security Subcommittee (SISS). The main task of the subcommittee was to examine the administration of the Internal Security Act, but it also had the power to investigate "the extent, nature, and effects of subversive activities in the United States, its Territories and possessions." After introducing the resolution, Eastland emphasized it was necessary to conduct "a continuous study and investigation of the operation of our laws relating to espionage, sabotage, and the protection of the internal security of the United States, and the ever-recurring problems of the Communist menace in the United States."[55] McCarran became the chairman of SISS and filled the panel with the most reactionary members of the Judiciary Committee. Eastland was one of them.[56]

As chair of the Civil Rights Subcommittee and as a member of the Internal Security Subcommittee and the Agricultural Committee, Eastland maneuvered into a position where he could safeguard the interests of his most important constituencies, the business and farming elite. While his authority on the national scene slowly expanded, Eastland also wanted to establish control over partisan politics at the regional and state level. He faced the complicated task of finding the right strategy to combat his opponents inside and outside the southern Democratic Party.

A year earlier, Eastland had described the States' Rights effort as the most effective way to protect Americanism and the traditions of the South. As the only U.S. senator that gave his wholehearted support to the Dixiecrat movement, Eastland placed principle above pragmatism in the 1948 election. Thurmond, well aware of this fact, thanked his friend from Mississippi for the "splendid cooperation and support in our States' Rights movement. You gave freely of your time and talents and I wish you to know that I am deeply grateful for the magnificent contribution you made to this great cause." Although he did not win the presidency, Thurmond had no doubt the Dixiecrat attempt demonstrated "that the South can and will be independent when a matter of principle is involved, and that we will no longer be the doormat of any Party."[57]

Eastland concurred with Thurmond, claiming that the movement "made great progress and can be a tremendous benefit to the South." He called the South Carolina governor "a fine candidate [and] the best man in the race" and proposed discussing the future of the States' Rights Party sometime in the spring of 1949.[58] After the Dixiecrat defeat in the presidential election, however, the few prominent politicians in the movement withdrew their active support, including Strom Thurmond. Instead of trying to sustain an independent political organization to defend state sovereignty and southern customs, Thurmond aspired to a career in national politics. Thurmond's retreat from the states' rights group seemed to confirm the belief that he had merely used the movement as a stepping-stone to the 1950 Senate election.

As the former leader of the Dixiecrat Revolt, no one could possibly doubt his commitment to segregation and state sovereignty. Moreover, the campaign had provided him with useful media attention.[59]

One of the most daunting challenges the Dixiecrats faced was the effectiveness of Democrats from the South within the national party. This reality constituted the great irony of the Dixiecrat movement: the states' righters argued that southern members of Congress connected with the national Democratic Party were nothing more than traitors to their homeland and that their partisan affiliation led to the destruction of the white South. Despite the claims made by the Dixiecrats, however, the southern Democratic bloc on Capitol Hill proved to be well equipped to uphold the time-honored customs of their region through established political channels, making the States' Rights Party practically expendable in the defense of the very cause for which it was fighting.

Senator Eastland, one of the prime movers behind the Dixiecrat campaign, was an excellent example of the southern Democrats' influence on national politics. Although Eastland had been part of the States' Rights Party challenge, he returned to the Senate as a Democrat, and this status delivered him the chairmanship of the Civil Rights Subcommittee. An opinion piece titled "Southern Senators Control Ace in the Hole" called attention to the strategic position southern Democrats occupied in the Senate. With fifty-two Democrats and forty-six Republicans in the upper chamber, the eight senators from the Dixiecrat states held the swing vote. "Therefore, it behooves the Truman Democratic leaders to be generous and kindly toward the States' Righters. Their votes in the Senate will control the balance of power which may become vital upon many issues."[60]

Lister Hill was one of the senators from a States' Rights stronghold who used his position in Congress and the Democratic Party to confront the Dixiecrat movement in Alabama. Although he did not bolt the national Democrats in 1948, Hill could hardly be considered a foe to Jim Crow. In a statewide radio address delivered a few weeks before the 1950 election of the State Democratic Executive Committee, the senator declared that he in fact was a true states' rights Democrat, and that the Dixiecrats were Republicans in disguise. Hill used Eastland's chairmanship of the Civil Rights Subcommittee as validation that the South would only have political significance if it remained in the Democratic Party. "Senator Jim Eastland is chairman of this subcommittee because of his membership in the Democratic Party," Hill told his listeners.[61]

These kinds of statements infuriated the states' righters. They called Hill a "professional politician and federal patronage-dispenser," a Truman crony who took pleasure in deriding "rank and file Alabama Democrats." The Dixiecrats criticized Hill's suggestion that Eastland's affiliation with the Democratic Party delivered him the chair of the subcommittee. Eastland might be a Democrat, they stated, but he was a Mississippi Democrat who campaigned for the states' rights crusade two years earlier. Reviled by the party establishment, Eastland was not "trying to sack up Mississippi Democrats and deliver them to the Trumancrat machine, the nauseous trick that Hill would pull in Alabama."[62] For the Dixiecrats, Senator Eastland was the living proof that loyalty to the national party was not a prerequisite for congressional power.

Although Dixiecrat leaders disavowed the notion that their organization was secretly cooperating with the GOP, the Republicans considered the results of the presidential campaign an indication that the South's loyalty to the Democratic Party was no longer certain. The Dixiecrat Revolt did not exactly achieve the goals its architects were aiming for, but it did crack open the Solid South. The Republican Party nonetheless still had a long way to go before it would be able to profit from the work started by the states' righters. First of all, the Republicans needed to shed their unfavorable stature in the region. Since the beginning of the Civil War, most southerners considered the GOP the party of the North, of big money, and the dominant force behind Reconstruction and the Great Depression, both traumatic experiences in the mind of the white South. Besides this negative image, southern Republicans also had a major leadership problem. In the words of James Sundquist, the southern branch of the party was nothing more than a "hopeless, discredited band of stragglers, disreputably led, without tradition of victory or prospect of it."[63] If the Republicans wanted to make inroads into the former Confederacy, they had to improve public relations and local party management first.

The Republicans in Mississippi faced similar problems. In 1924, Perry Howard assumed leadership of the state party. Howard was an African American attorney from Holmes County who had moved to Washington, D.C., in 1921 to become special assistant to the attorney general in the Harding administration. After he relocated to the nation's capital, Howard never lived or voted in Mississippi again. The bloc under Howard's control was known as the Black and Tan Republicans, who had the official recognition of the Republican National Committee.

The Black and Tans were not the only group in the state that claimed the Republican badge, however. A rival faction named the Lily-Whites also vied for recognition from the national party leadership. George Sheldon, a former governor of Nebraska who had moved to Mississippi in 1909, formed the Lily-White Republicans in 1927. The two camps had been fighting each other ever since. The situation in Mississippi illustrated the challenges the Republican Party faced in the South. A lack of viable candidates and efficient leadership, combined with intraparty strife, a dismal reputation, and the absence of a strong electoral base, limited the role of the Republicans in Mississippi to patronage brokers during Republican administrations.[64] What the Grand Old Party in the South needed was a political message that resonated with the majority of the electorate in the region and leaders who were able to rally these voters and achieve unity among feuding Republicans.

A Chicago-based group called the National Republican Roundup Committee (NRRC) was particularly active in trying to lure southerners away from the Democratic Party. The head of the organization's executive committee was Fred Virkus, who traveled to Mississippi in September 1950 to do two statewide radio speeches. Virkus also went to Clarksdale in the Mississippi Delta to meet up with a number of (what he termed) "old line Democrats." The people present at the meeting decided to set up another conference between southern Democrats and Republicans later in the year to draft a states' rights plank for the 1952 GOP platform. Virkus expected significant progress for Republicans in the South if the party adopted the plank, because conservative Democratic voters "feel that they have nowhere else to turn to help prevent State Socialism and the destruction of our Free Enterprise System of Economy."[65]

He also anticipated that a meeting of southern Democrats and Republicans was going to reduce the stigma of voting Republican in the South and simultaneously encourage the professionalization of GOP branches in the region. According to Virkus, responsible southern business leaders (who were all Democrats) were behind the effort to revive the Republican Party in the South. Their effort demonstrated that they placed the welfare of their country above party politics, Virkus believed. The NRRC had little to lose and much to gain if it managed to remove sectionalist feelings, induce southern Republicans to show their true colors, and enlist independent voters in the South into Republican ranks. A pro–states' rights stance of the national Republican Party would attract "those Democrats who admit they want to defeat Truman and his New Deal," Virkus stated. The realization of his plan—the start of a two-party system in the South—might be the rebirth of American conservatism, the dawn of a new "epoch in American political history."[66]

In mid-November, Virkus invited a select group of businessmen and political leaders, including states' rights Democrat John U. Barr of New Orleans, to attend a meeting at the Robert E. Lee Hotel in Jackson on December 1 and 2. The invitations made clear that the Roundup Committee was not going to take a grassroots approach to reconstruct the southern Republican Party. The NRRC wanted to round up a particular group of Mississippians: the economic elite of the state. Although he did not speak for the Republican National Committee, Virkus believed the South could have a significant influence on the future course of the national party. The plan for the conference was to bring "representatives of the States' Rights group and other Jeffersonian Democrats together with a group of prominent Republicans" and design a strategy to defeat "the New Deal Party" in the 1952 elections. Virkus emphasized the meeting was off the record and that no Republican officeholders or officials of the RNC would be present.[67] Perhaps that would come at a later stage; for now, it was important to see if common ground existed between Republicans and southern Democrats.

Virkus was convinced the two groups needed each other. In a letter written shortly after the 1950 elections, he composed a list of ten "cold, hard facts" to prompt southerners disaffected with the national Democratic Party into action. The Republican Party could not win the upcoming presidential election without the support of the South, Virkus thought, and the voice of the states' righters would most likely not be heard at the Democratic National Convention. "Consequently, there *must* be a coalition of like-minded Americans, *a political rebirth,* with new faces and new ideals, in order to get rid of the Truman-Socialist administration in Washington—to save our Constitutional Republic," he continued. Without the formation of such an alliance, Virkus expected that "the same discredited and unacceptable hand-picked delegates" would be seated at the convention to "misrepresent the South." This thinly veiled reference to Perry Howard and the Black and Tans, combined with the appeals to states' righters such as John U. Barr, demonstrate that the race question was at least a latent part of the NRRC agenda.[68]

But southern Democrats were not very enthusiastic to join the Republicans. Barr was not present at the meeting in the Robert E. Lee Hotel, which was chaired by Delta planter Tom Gibson. "I am, indeed, interested in any movement that has for its purpose the preservation of our Constitutional form of Government," he wrote Virkus, "but also recognize that proper procedure must be used, if results are going to be obtained."[69] Apparently, a fusion between Dixiecrats and Republicans was not yet one of these proper procedures. Cullen Curlee reported on the conference to James Eastland, noting that he "would not care to have any part in it."[70] For Eastland and other conservative Mississippi Democrats, there seemed to be little reason indeed to get involved with organizations such as the NRRC.

In 1948, James Eastland considered the States' Rights Party to be the best vehicle to defend the southern way of life, but after Strom Thurmond abandoned the movement, the Mississippi senator did very little to prevent its collapse. Although white southern Republicans started to become more organized after the failed Dixiecrat Revolt, their power was not strong enough at the beginning of the 1950s to offer a viable alternative to traditionalist national Democrats like Eastland.[71] In Mississippi, Republicans faced difficulties similar to those of the Dixiecrats in other Deep South states; they were unable to establish a foothold and attract voters. With politicians like Eastland in Congress, conservative Mississippians saw little need to switch their allegiance to the GOP. Yet a change was underway, and the states' rights challenge largely precipitated this change.

In a study of Alabama politics during World War II, historian Glen Feldman argued that the planter and business elites in the state successfully combined their conservative economic views with the defense of white supremacy to suppress working-class challenges to their authority. Feldman called this integration of economic and racial conservatism the "Great Melding," which resulted in an alliance that cut across class lines to uphold the system of segregation. The main result of the Great Melding was the destruction of Alabama's liberal tradition and the gradual exodus of white Alabamians from the Democratic Party, first to the Dixiecrats and later to the Republican Party.[72] The NRRC advocated a similar ideology of laissez-faire economics, fused with implicit appeals to white supremacist sentiments. For Mississippi Democrats such as James Eastland, it became imperative to keep their ideological brethren in the southern Republican Party at bay and simultaneously suppress the Loyalist challenge to their control of the state party machinery.

In February 1951, Eastland had finally gathered enough information to declare on the Senate floor that the pro-Truman group in his state was involved in all sorts of corrupt practices. Eastland's charge came shortly after an investigative subcommittee chaired by Senator William Fulbright released its report on favoritism in the Reconstruction Finance Corporation (RFC), a federal government agency established during the Great Depression to provide loans to banks, railroads, and other businesses.[73] Eastland's allegations and the report of the Fulbright committee fit in a long string of investigations of corruption in the Truman administration. For Eastland, the discovery of widespread corruption in the Loyalist Democratic Party in Mississippi helped him in two ways: it offered an opportunity to eliminate his opponents at the state level and he could use it to discredit the Truman administration.

Eastland called the attention of his colleagues in the U.S. Senate to the alleged barter and sale of government jobs in Mississippi. Both Eastland and John Stennis had received numerous reports that members of the Loyalist Mississippi Democratic Committee were asking for money in exchange for positions in federal organizations such as the Office of Price Stabilization (OPS) and the Post Office. Eastland had also heard rumors that the group tried to sell government deals to war contractors. People charged with income tax fraud received suspended sentences after contacting the Loyalist group and were now in charge of patronage disbursement. The two senators obtained this information from an investigator in the state, who also secured two affidavits that served to substantiate Eastland's claims.[74]

Eastland could not emphasize enough that the Democratic National Committee was responsible for setting up the ring "which calls itself the Mississippi Democratic Committee." This group, he stated, was "the official representation" of the DNC in Mississippi, "its agent . . . its instrumentality." Eastland recalled that he had made suggestions to the White House about people in Mississippi who were friendly to the president and capable of dealing with patronage matters. If Truman had accepted these recommendations, "there would be no scandal attached to the Democratic administration," he remarked. Eastland and Stennis now called for a special Senate committee "to investigate the sordid aspects of the entire set-up in Mississippi."[75]

Two days after Eastland made his allegations of fraud against the Mississippi Loyalists, Frank Mize and Clarence Hood sent telegrams to the president and to DNC Chairman William Boyle claiming that Eastland's charges were without foundation and that his only intention was to disturb the upcoming Jefferson-Jackson Day Dinner organized by the Trumanites. "We consider this just another chapter in the vicious efforts of 'Dixiecrats' and Republicans to smear the administration and to attack President Truman through his friends," Mize and Hood wrote. They described Eastland's attack as a desperate effort to disrupt the progress of the Loyalist cause and prevent the Truman Democrats from influencing the upcoming governor's election in the state.[76] The White House decided not to acknowledge the telegram.[77]

The denunciations by the Loyalist leadership in Mississippi were to no avail. On February 26, William Boyle relieved Clarence Hood of his duties as acting national committeeman and the next day John Stennis introduced a resolution authorizing an investigation of federal government activities in Mississippi. Boyle wrote Eastland and Stennis that he welcomed their initiative to examine the activities of the Mississippi Democratic Committee and he promised to cooperate fully in the investigation.[78] Senator Clyde Hoey of North Carolina chaired the subcommittee that traveled to Jackson in early April 1951 to hold hearings on the dealings of the Mississippi Loyalists. Senators Karl Mundt of North Dakota and John McClellan of Arkansas were the other members of the committee who joined Hoey. Stennis delivered the opening statement.[79]

During three days, the committee examined the leaders of the Mississippi Loyalists and citizens from the state who testified about their interactions with the Trumanites. Based on the hearings, it appeared that the Loyalist leadership in Mississippi was after two things: political and personal gain through federal contracts and patronage. The hearings of the Hoey Committee demonstrated that the patronage strategy of the DNC and the administration did not always result in stronger Loyalist chapters, at least not in Mississippi. Appreciation for Eastland in fact rose after the investigations. "There is no doubt that your popularity has reached an all time high," Curlee reported to the senator. "Your constituents are very grateful and many have asked me to express to you their complete satisfaction in the final conclusion of the investigation."[80]

A number of factors led to the failure of the Mississippi Loyalists. In a state where 87 percent of the electorate cast its vote for Strom Thurmond in 1948, the political climate for the formation of a pro-Truman party was not optimal, to say the least. Almost twenty thousand Mississippians nonetheless voted for the president, which gave the Loyalists a small base to work from. The way they proceeded to set up their organization confirmed their amateur status and doubtful intentions, however. Through lumberman Clarence Hood, the leaders of the Mississippi Loyalists came in touch with people in the administration who were often engaged in dubious businesses. Hood exploited his position as national committeeman to make deals not only for his political associates, but also for himself.[81] Loyalist chairman Frank Mize insisted his group merely wanted to use patronage to build up a pro-Truman movement in the state. "Our plan was to use patronage in a legitimate way to further the interests of the Democratic Party in Mississippi," he testified.[82]

Senator Hoey did not agree with Mize's interpretation. When he submitted his report in the Senate on June 20, 1951, he strongly denounced the Trumanites and praised Eastland and Stennis for notifying Congress about the conditions in Mississippi. "It developed that control of the Mississippi Democratic Committee was usurped by a small group of willful men who corruptly extorted political contributions from a substantial number of persons seeking recommendations for appointment to postal jobs." Hoey also accused the Loyalists of trying to sell jobs in the OPS that were nonexistent and reproached them for how they manipulated their political position for personal profit in the form of defense contracts and RFC loans. For Hoey, it was "gratifying to report that the nefarious activities of this clique have been brought to an end." Federal patronage was restored to the congressional delegation, and the Department of Justice initiated a grand jury investigation of the situation in Mississippi.[83] A month later, the entire leadership of the Loyalist Mississippi Democratic Committee was indicted on charges of conspiracy in connection with the sale of federal jobs, although in February 1952 a federal judge dismissed the conspiracy indictments of ten Trumanites, including Clarence Hood.[84]

The downfall of the Loyalist movement in Mississippi can largely be blamed on the ineptitude of its headmen. But other factors also contributed to the failure of this group. The DNC was ambivalent in its support of the Mississippi Loyalists. The national committee expressed its devotion to forming organizations in the South that opposed the Dixiecrats, but simultaneously it attempted to appease those same Dixiecrats. During the hearings of the Hoey Committee, several witnesses stated that the DNC did not want to upset the states' rights Democrats in Congress. "The national committee told us all the time that they had the olive branch out to Eastland, Stennis and all the Congressman and we were to trade with them, just as soon as they quit," said Curtis Rogers, secretary-treasurer of the Mississippi Loyalists. "In other words, they wanted to turn the patronage back there if they could get them to quit fighting the administration, I assume."[85]

The outcome of the hearings was a severe setback for the Truman Democrats in Mississippi. Besides the lack of commitment on behalf of the DNC, the Trumanites simply did not command the same resources that established politicians such as Eastland had to wage successful political campaigns. During the hearings, Hood had charged that James Eastland employed an investigator who was on the federal payroll. This was not a lie. For two years, Cullen Curlee closely followed the pro-Truman Democrats in the state, and he received a salary from the federal government as Eastland's assistant.[86]

Moreover, both Eastland and Stennis did not need middlemen to gain access to federal departments and important people on the DNC. As soon as Eastland made his first allegations in the Senate about fraudulent practices in Mississippi, Chairman Boyle relieved Hood of his position as national committeeman. Before Eastland made his statements, he had already contacted Postmaster General Jesse Donaldson and provided him with evidence of the job sales. For Donaldson, this was enough reason to start an investigation and immediately return patronage to the members of the Mississippi delegation in Congress.[87] On top of that, U.S. senators have the power to pass resolutions and call for congressional hearings, which are financed by substantial government funds. Finally, the three senators who traveled to Jackson to conduct the hearings were closer to Eastland than to Truman; Hoey and McClellan were both conservative southern Democrats, and Karl Mundt was a Republican from South Dakota who openly advocated an alliance between northern Republicans and southern adherents of states' rights.[88] Once Eastland and his allies mobilized the power of the federal government against the Mississippi Loyalists, the Loyalists' cause was lost.

In February, Hood and Mize had claimed that Eastland's accusations of fraud served only one purpose: to prevent the Loyalists from running a candidate in the 1951 gubernatorial race. But in the campaign for governor, Eastland openly backed Paul B. Johnson Jr., who remained loyal to Truman in the 1948 election. Eastland aide Frank Barber explained that behind the scenes Johnson was in fact the real patronage dispenser during the Truman presidency. Johnson benefitted from his association with both Eastland and the Truman camp: Eastland recommended him for assistant federal attorney and the president carried out this recommendation. But during the 1951 campaign, Johnson's connection with the Truman administration became a liability.[89] "The Trumanites continue their love, friendship, and political influence for

Paul," Cullen Curlee wrote Eastland in February 1951, shortly before the senator made his statements concerning the job sales in Mississippi. "Of course, their influence and vote will be counted, not only for Paul, but it will also be a millstone around his neck and there will be no doubt about that."[90]

Johnson's main opponent was Hugh Lawson White, a strong states' righter who had led the walkout in Philadelphia in 1948. White had been governor of Mississippi from 1936 until 1940. During his tenure he introduced the Balance Agriculture With Industry (BAWI) program, an effort to attract manufacturers to the state. Johnson needed a Dixiecrat like Eastland to convince the electorate that he was not a Truman crony. Reporter Kenneth Toler of the *Memphis Commercial Appeal* understood the role Eastland could play in the upcoming campaign. "If Senator Eastland follows through as he is quoted as planning to do, he will carry weight in taking the Truman-backed label from Mr. Johnson."[91]

No less than eight contenders participated in the first primary for the Democratic nomination, including Ross Barnett and newspaper editor Mary Cain, the first woman in the history of Mississippi to run for governor. Hugh White and Paul Johnson received the highest number of votes and proceeded to the runoff election. In the contest between these two men, race became the predominant issue. White used Johnson's support of Truman in 1948 and his affiliation with the Trumancrats in the state to depict his opponent as weak on segregation. He charged that with Johnson in the governor's mansion, the national Democratic Party and civil rights activists would rule Mississippi.

In the all-black towns of Mound Bayou and Mount Carmel, the vote went overwhelmingly to Johnson, which served as ammunition for the White camp. According to White's campaign manager, C. D. Fair, Paul Johnson endorsed everything Truman stood for, including the FEPC and the anti-lynching bill. White stated that the 1951 election was the most important event since Reconstruction and that a victory for his opponent meant the defeat of white supremacy in Mississippi. Newspapers that supported White took aim at Johnson for his closeness to the main culprits in the job-selling scandal. The *Jackson Daily News*, a longtime enemy of the Johnson family, was particularly vehement in its attacks on "Little Paul."[92] Frank Barber declared the White campaign had even paid a black newspaper editor to endorse Johnson in a statewide radio broadcast the weekend before the election.[93]

Paul Johnson tried to counter these allegations by accusing White of supporting the repeal of the two-thirds rule at the 1936 Democratic National

Convention. Johnson also pledged to lead another walkout if Truman were nominated at the 1952 convention. Johnson campaigned on a neopopulist platform, which called for labor rights, higher teacher salaries, improved healthcare, and better farm-to-market roads. He portrayed himself as the people's candidate, while his opponent presented the moneyed interests. Johnson obviously opposed desegregation, but he was more moderate in his racism than White and refused to make it the centerpiece of his campaign.[94]

Eastland's open endorsement of Johnson was controversial in Mississippi. Across the state, newspapers supporting White called for Eastland's resignation. "If Senator Eastland should be able to name the next governor of Mississippi, then that governor would be 'obligated' to use his office to elect a junior senator acceptable to Senator Eastland . . . and on and on," the editor of the *Brandon News* predicted. "We do not believe that Mississippians want such a dictatorship established."[95] Eastland made clear that as an American and a citizen of Mississippi, he had a right to make his position known. He did not intend to impose his will on the voters, however. "Let me make this clear: I am not attempting to dictate or control the vote of anyone . . . I have never thought the Senatorship or Governorship should be used in an attempt to control any election."[96]

Eastland nonetheless went on the campaign trail for his friend, and Johnson gratefully used the senator's endorsement. At an appearance in Waynesboro, Johnson tried to discredit the claim made by Hugh White that he was not a strong advocate of state sovereignty. "Why if there were anything about me even close to Truman or his beliefs, Jim Eastland, the daddy of States' Rights, wouldn't be for me," Johnson said. "If they [the White camp] thought they could get away with it, they'd say I'm trying to put cut worms and boll weevils in the cotton crop."[97] Eastland certified Johnson's statement on his belief in states' rights at a rally in Ruleville, near the senator's plantation. "If I did not know that Paul Johnson would carry on the States' Rights movement I would not vote for him. In my judgment Paul Johnson's States' Rights allegiance is unquestionable."[98]

The Johnson stock was particularly low in the Delta. Paul Johnson Sr. never carried the region, and Johnson Jr. recalled that his father was often depicted as "a demon with horns" in the area along the Mississippi River.[99] By 1951 these hostile feelings toward the Johnson family still had not subsided in the Delta. Joseph Ellis of Clarksdale could not believe Eastland endorsed "that rank demigogue [sic] Paul Johnson for Governor. . . . You know of course, and you knew when you endorsed his candidacy, that his election would mean returning affairs at Jackson to that same low standard that characterized Bilbo's loathsome and infamous tenancy." Ellis promised to oppose Eastland to "the fullest extent of my ability and resources."[100] Another resident of Clarksdale concurred with Ellis that Eastland's alliance with Johnson was detrimental to the state. "Paul Johnson, Jr., with his wild promises of something for nothing, is not what we need in our government during these days of trial," he told Eastland. "I am very sorry you intervened in his behalf."[101]

But why did Eastland support a candidate who advocated a populist agenda? Loyalty to the Johnson family was the main reason. Thanks to Paul Johnson Sr., Eastland became U.S. senator when Pat Harrison died in 1941. Eastland revealed that Paul Johnson Sr. actually wanted him as his successor to the governorship. When Eastland said he would rather continue in the Senate, Governor Johnson gave his full support. "I think that I would have been ingrate had I not supported his son in this campaign," the senator explained. "In fact, if I had been neutral I would have always regretted it. . . . I am proud of the race he made and I think he has a future in Mississippi politics."[102] Eastland described Paul Johnson Sr. as a conservative governor, despite the reputation he had in the Delta as a profligate spender.[103]

Prominent Dixiecrats backed different candidates during the 1951 election. For example, Eastland campaigned for Johnson, while Fielding Wright endorsed White. Ideologically, Eastland was probably closer to the White camp. The former governor was a wealthy industrialist and lumberman, had been active in the states' rights movement, and represented the business interests. But in 1951, just like in 1947, indebtedness to Johnson Sr. made Eastland decide to support his son. The *Jackson Daily News* had little appreciation for Eastland's endorsement. In an editorial titled "A Foolish Extreme of Gratitude," the newspaper professed that "Jim Eastland does not owe a never-ending debt of gratitude to the Paul Johnson family." As a matter of fact, the *Daily News* believed the debt between the Johnsons and the Eastlands had been settled a long time before, when James Eastland received his nomination to the Senate. Thanks to his financial and personal support, "Woods Eastland placed Paul B. Johnson in the Governor's chair and Gov. Johnson in turn placed the son of Woods Eastland in the United States Senate. It was a complete cancellation of indebtedness on both sides."[104]

The support of Senator Eastland and his political network did not deliver victory to Paul B. Johnson Jr. Hugh White exploited the race issue to his advantage and won the runoff primary with 51.2 percent of the votes.[105] According to Cullen Curlee, the voters "didn't want any part of Truman or Trumanism in Mississippi."[106] In the end, Eastland was unable to remove the Trumancrat stigma from Johnson, even though the senator's call for a federal inquiry into the activities of the Loyalist Democrats delivered a major blow to this group.[107] Johnson's defeat clearly signified the unpopularity of the president in the Magnolia State. Only one year remained until the presidential election. Truman had sufficient reason to be worried about his standing in the southern states and about his chances of reelection. Could he repeat the 1948 race and win the White House without the backing of the Solid South?

As a matter of fact, Truman's 1948 campaign strategy had counted on the unwavering support of the old Confederacy. In November 1947, political strategist Clark Clifford had written a confidential memorandum for Truman with several suggestions about the upcoming contest for the presidency. Clifford described the Democratic Party as "an unhappy alliance of Southern conservatives, Western progressives, and Big City Labor." He anticipated a Truman victory if the administration relied on the traditional Democratic alliance of the South and West. Clifford assumed the South did not need much attention, because the region voted Democratic under all circumstances. "It is inconceivable that any policies initiated by the Truman Administration no matter how 'liberal' could so alienate the South in the next year that it would revolt. As always, the South can be considered safely Democratic. And in formulating national policy, it can be safely ignored."[108]

Clifford recommended Truman focus on the western states, labor, and particularly the black vote, because these constituencies had a decisive influence on the outcome of presidential contests. "A theory of many professional politicians is that the northern Negro voter today holds the balance of power in Presidential elections for the simple arithmetical reason that the Negroes not only vote in a bloc but are geographically concentrated in the pivotal, large, and closely contested electoral states such as New York, Illinois, Pennsylvania, Ohio, and Michigan," Clifford asserted. He did not foresee that such a focus on labor and northern blacks might lead to a southern bolt.[109]

Clifford made an interesting observation about possible motives to appease the southern states. "The only pragmatic reason for conciliating the South in normal times is because of its tremendous strength in Congress." In 1947, such a rationale did not exist. The Republicans were the majority party, which meant the president did not have a chance to get much of his legislative program passed anyway. Clifford therefore saw no reason to negotiate with southern conservatives, who often sided with the Republicans to scuttle Democratic initiatives.[110]

After the Democratic takeover of Congress in 1948, "normal times" returned, and the president again had to take the wishes of the South into consideration. Moreover, the presidential race proved that southern loyalty to the national party was not as natural as Clifford and other strategists assumed it to be. The Democratic leadership eventually decided to keep southern Democrats on Capitol Hill content and white southern voters within party ranks. Such a stand diminished the chances of enacting the more liberal pledges in the platform of the national party.

The leaders of the Democratic Party saw few possibilities to effectively discipline Dixiecrats such as James Eastland. The president and the National Democratic Committee initially tried to do so by taking away the federal patronage of states' righters. But this policy did not curb Eastland's growing power in the Senate, nor did it change his conservative voting behavior. Through his alliance with Pat McCarran, the powerful chairman of the Judiciary Committee, and through the system of seniority, Eastland received important committee assignments and the chairmanship of the Civil Rights Subcommittee, where he could cause great damage to the civil rights agenda of the national Democratic Party. During debates on immigration and internal security, the Mississippi senator articulated his vision of an ideal America and he identified its enemies. As a politician on the national stage, Eastland had real power to put this vision into legislative practice. He sponsored tighter immigration laws and stronger measures against subversion and he barred debate on civil rights as subcommittee chair. Eastland's position in the U.S. Senate enabled him to protect the traditionalist order in the South and mold national policy based on his white supremacist ideology.

Eastland's effectiveness in Congress impeded the progress of the States' Rights Party and the southern Republicans in the years following the Dixiecrat Revolt. The Dixiecrats wanted to convince the white southern electorate that a continued allegiance with the national Democratic Party would lead to the destruction of the southern way of life, but Eastland proved the opposite was true. The Republicans in the South faced a similar dilemma. They benefitted from the Dixiecrat Revolt, but at the same time the successful conservative record of southern Democratic politicians limited Republican support to areas where displeasure with the national Democrats was highest: the Black Belt counties.

The states' righters never found a persuasive response to the southern Democrats' argument that for now the white South was better off in the national party. Without grassroots support and the endorsement of prominent segregationists such as James Eastland and Strom Thurmond, and without money, the states' rights movement closed its Washington office in August 1952 and disappeared from the national political stage.[111] The Dixiecrat Revolt thus came to an end, but southern Republicans and southern Democrats carried on its ideological message of minimizing federal influence on the South's hierarchic social and economic structure.

In Mississippi, the Loyalists formed the only viable alternative to the Regular Democrats, who had been closely associated with the States' Rights cause. The Loyalists were just as segregationist as the Regulars, but their economic agenda was more in line with the liberal ideas of the national party. Theodore Bilbo was a guiding light for the Truman Democrats in Mississippi. The race-baiting governor and senator was a champion of the poor whites and advocated a progressive economic agenda that benefitted this group of voters. Although the Loyalists did not challenge the color line, their pro–New Deal stance posed a threat to the economic elite in the state, which profited from cheap labor and weak unions. Eastland and other states' rights veterans launched a propaganda war to stop the Trumanites. These neobourbons labeled the liberal initiatives of the Loyalists as part of a communist plot to destroy the white South. Eastland equated liberalism with socialism and communism, and he associated left-wing groups with desegregation. Based on this logic, the Loyalists ultimately aimed to integrate the South, although they did not speak out in favor of desegregation. The Regulars' publicity drive against the Truman Democrats formed the opening salvo in a campaign that eventually brought down the Loyalist faction in the state.

The almost simultaneous downfall of the States' Rights Party and the Mississippi Loyalists followed a repositioning of the national Democratic Party toward its conservative southern wing. The appeasement of former Dixiecrats by the national party leadership cut both ways: it made the states' rights movement superfluous, and it diminished the chances of economically liberal Loyalist groups in the South. The failure of the Truman Democrats in Mississippi was partly caused by political amateurism and questionable methods to gain monetary funds. But did the Loyalists have other options to finance their operations in the states' rights stronghold of Mississippi? The Democratic National Committee was reluctant to support its branch in the Magnolia State because it did not want to anger Eastland and other Dixiecrats in Congress, and the Mississippi Regulars still possessed enough power to thwart any challenges to their dominance. The result was a return to the status quo, which was exactly what Eastland and the neobourbons wanted. The planter-politician was back in the Democratic ranks and he was there to stay. During the following years he used his position in the Senate to increase his influence on national and state politics.

CHAPTER 4

DEMOCRATIC UNITY AFTER THE DIXIECRAT REVOLT

THE NATIONAL DEMOCRATIC PARTY could no longer take the South for granted in the 1952 presidential election. The Dixiecrat Revolt had taught southern voters that loyalty to the Democratic candidate was no longer an established fact and served as a warning for the national Democrats to take the South's demands into consideration if they wanted to keep the region on their side. Southern Democrats employed a variety of strategies to reclaim their position in the national party. Moderate segregationists like John Stennis and Mississippi's Attorney General James Coleman dropped the hardline approach of the states' rights Democrats and instead sought to enhance the South's standing in the Democratic Party through negotiation and compromise. While the moderates argued that their conciliatory course formed the best defense of states' rights, other southern Democrats backed the Republican ticket. They set up Democrats for Eisenhower groups, which were popular in the plantation counties.

Black Belt planter James Eastland did not join the southern Eisenhower movement, however. He realized that the political power flowing from his connection with the national Democratic Party was a better safeguard for Jim Crow than ideological purity and maverick campaigns. When Harry Truman decided not to seek reelection because of personal and political reasons, Eastland's choice to remain in the national party became less complicated. He also made sure to gain influence on Republican activities in Mississippi. Through Eisenhower Democrats like Ernest Spencer, the senator exerted control on the distribution of patronage, even during a Republican administration. Some Republicans saw opportunities for their party in the former Confederacy, but with conservative Democrats like James Eastland campaigning for the Democratic ticket, they needed to display patience before their dream of a Republican South became reality.

The Mississippi Democratic Party convened on June 26, 1952, to set out a strategy for the national convention in Chicago. During the weeks preceding the state convention, moderates such as John Stennis and James Coleman conferred to prevent a repetition of the events that transpired in 1948. William Winter, a state representative who had served on Stennis's staff as legislative assistant, kept his old boss informed about political developments in Mississippi during the spring of 1952. Winter feared that radical states' righters like Wallace Wright were going to dominate the state convention and bind the delegates to an uncompromising stand on civil rights matters, which would jeopardize the position of Mississippi in the national party. Winter wanted to prevent the political isolation of his state at all costs. He consulted with James Coleman, who subsequently discussed the situation with former governor Fielding Wright. Coleman and Wright agreed that solitary hardline action by the Mississippi delegates would not lead to any tangible results and they eventually managed to convince Wallace Wright of their point.[1]

Around the same time, John Stennis invited Governor White to his office in Washington to come up with a strategy for the state convention. Stennis flatly told White that he needed to take command of the situation in Mississippi as leader of the Democratic Party in order to ward off a takeover by forces that were unfriendly to him. White agreed with Stennis and told the senator that in his keynote address at the state convention he would not include rhetoric to which the national Democrats could object. Stennis's main objective was to remove the Dixiecrats from power. "I think that unless the Wally Wright-Tom Tubb axis is fully put out of command, there is a good chance that a new group will take over in Mississippi," he wrote Winter. Stennis thought that a faction headed by Paul B. Johnson Jr. "might be able to furnish the spark and leadership and thus those who supported Governor White will find themselves definitely second-fiddle in the state."[2] Instead of following the course set out by the Dixiecrats in 1948, Stennis thought that the interests of Mississippi and the South were best protected by taking a moderate approach and staying within the national party structure.

Hugh White's speech at the Democratic State Convention was defiant, but did not call for a dissident campaign by the Mississippi Democrats. To the applause of the audience, White declared that "never in the history of our state have our people ever surrendered their principles or compromised on issues of honor—and we will never change that proud heritage in the state of Mississippi." But he also expressed the hope that the upcoming national convention would result in an acceptable candidate and platform. White did not want to make a stand before that time, but instead preferred to make a decision after Chicago. He outlined three steps Mississippi could follow if the national Democrats refused to listen to the South: surrender to an anti-southern program; join the Republicans; or, like in 1948, vote for a "Jeffersonian Democrat." If the national Democratic Party again refused "to recognize the sound requests of the south—for recognition in party affairs— then we can only take step three and join our fellow southerners in appropriate action," White said.[3]

The state convention passed resolutions that endorsed U.S. senator Richard Russell of Georgia as presidential candidate and called for a national party platform that safeguarded "States' Rights, Free Enterprise and Private Initiative." The Mississippi Democrats also resolved that they did not adjourn, but recessed until August 5. On this date, they would decide on the outcome of the national convention. The state convention was extremely critical of President Truman. In a clear reference to his administration, one of the resolutions maintained that "Disloyalty, dishonesty, corruption, graft, influence peddling, loose morals and plain ordinary thievery which has been exposed in our governmental affairs, and those responsible therefor, must go and none such shall be countenanced or tolerated under any circumstances."[4] A surprise awaited the delegates when they entered the convention hall in Jackson. Although Hugh White denied he wanted to lead Mississippi into the Republican column, unsigned circulars claiming that the governor was in fact a Republican in disguise had been placed on the chairs in the hall.[5]

The Loyalist Democrats also organized a convention, where they picked Mrs. John Clark and Jimmie Walker as their representatives on the DNC. Walker called the Regulars "termites in the house of the solid South" and asserted that they "knowingly" tried to turn the southern states to the Republican Party.[6]

While the Loyalists depicted their opponents as Republican sympathizers, others interpreted White's keynote address as a call for another states' rights bolt. The governor vehemently repudiated these charges, telling journalists he "never once mentioned the word bolt" in his speech. "I can't understand how my speech could have been so misinterpreted outside of the state," he continued. "I will always be a Democrat and will always vote Democratic." The misinterpretation of White's speech by "several newspapers in the East" probably rested on his call for southern cooperation and his preference for a recess of the state convention, instead of an adjournment.[7] But these measures were only meant as a final escape route in case the national convention would follow the course set out in 1948. White preferred to work things out in the party first.

James Coleman did not relent in his efforts to keep Mississippi from bolting the convention. At the beginning of July he had lunch with Fielding Wright, Strom Thurmond's running mate in the Dixiecrat campaign. Wright told Coleman he did not object to Governor Adlai Stevenson of Illinois as Democratic presidential candidate. The former governor also realized that if Mississippi continued on its course of no compromise, the state lost "its standing with everybody throughout the nation." Coleman considered Wright the key person to keep the Mississippi Democrats in the national party, because of his role in the states' rights movement. Nobody could challenge his credentials as a true defender of state sovereignty. James Coleman asked his friend John Stennis to notify Chairman Frank McKinney of the DNC that he was "working like a steam engine to try to bring this situation down here under control." He also hoped "the National Committee will not jerk the rug from under me in my efforts to do so."[8]

Three weeks before the Democratic National Convention started, James Eastland already had a fairly accurate idea of what was going to happen in Chicago. Eastland was part of the Mississippi delegation, which was uninstructed, but in support of Russell. The Mississippi senator believed Stevenson was the foreseeable candidate. If he refused, Harry Truman was next in line. The reason why Truman was still in the picture was the candidacy of U.S. senator Estes Kefauver of Tennessee. With Stevenson gone, he might receive the nomination, which was clearly objectionable to the president, who detested Kefauver. Some of Stevenson's friends actually had already talked to Eastland about an eligible southerner for the vice presidency. They preferred Senator John Sparkman of Alabama, but Eastland advised them to consult with William Fulbright first to see if he was interested. Eastland expected that the national convention was going to adopt the 1944 civil rights plank, which "was written by Jimmy Byrnes and the party leadership." It was impossible for Byrnes to bolt the convention if this plank was adopted, but at the same time Eastland realized that Senator Hubert Humphrey "and the left-wingers" opposed such a toned-down civil rights program.[9] The same themes that had dominated the 1948 convention (and that had led to the southern walkout) were again high on the agenda in 1952. This time, however, more pragmatic politicians such as White and Coleman were prominent in the Mississippi delegation.

In Chicago, the first issue that confronted the group led by White was a fight in the credentials committee over which delegation from Mississippi was to be seated at the convention: the Regulars or the Loyalists. James Eastland together with Thomas Tubb prepared a brief to demonstrate that the Regulars were the only legitimate Democratic Party in the state and that the Loyalist faction violated state laws and represented just a small percentage of Mississippi Democrats. Eastland and Tubb argued that under Mississippi law the Loyalists did not have the authority to call for a state convention. Only 110 delegates had attended the Loyalist conference, which was not enough for a quorum. On top of that, the leaders of the Loyalists were mostly failed politicians: Jimmie Walker, for instance, received only 1.5 percent of the total vote in the 1951 gubernatorial primary campaign and had won these votes in the election organized by the Regulars. "It is indeed strange that these men, less than twelve months ago were candidates in the regular Democratic primary, claiming to be members of the regular Democratic Party, and now are seeking to hoodwink the National Democratic Party into seating them in the 1952 convention as the true and lawful representatives of the Democrats of Mississippi," Eastland and Tubb concluded their brief.[10]

The final decision of the credentials committee showed that the national party was more conciliatory to states' rights southerners than it had been in 1948: the committee acknowledged the Regulars as the official representatives of the Mississippi Democrats, thus ending the aspirations of the Loyalist group. "The delegates from the Magnolia state have shown an admirable self-restraint throughout what has been a trying ordeal," the *Jackson Daily News* commented on the attitude of the Regulars at the convention. The White group had nonetheless requested that a special train stand ready to take them back to Mississippi if things went wrong. Some of the delegates had not even unpacked their baggage.[11]

At the Monday evening session of the convention, Senator Blair Moody of Michigan introduced a motion that obliged the delegates to exert "every honorable means" to place the nominees elected at the convention under the Democratic Party heading in their respective states. Adoption of such a loyalty pledge would mean that a repetition of 1948—when Strom Thurmond appeared as the Democratic candidate in a number of southern states—would be impossible. The southerners were adamant. Governor Herman Talmadge of Georgia took the floor to declare that Moody's proposal was against the laws of his state and the state Democratic Party. Lister Hill and John Sparkman decided to take on the role of mediator and managed to add a clause to the Moody resolution which stated that the pledge "shall not be in contravention of the existing law of the state, nor of the instructions of the state Democratic governing bodies." This revised motion was accepted by forty-five states, including Mississippi. Virginia, South Carolina, and Louisiana were against the loyalty oath, but survived a vote on their dismissal from the convention.[12] Like the verdict of the credentials committee on the seating of the Mississippi Regulars, the modification of the Moody resolution and the refusal to expel "disloyal" southern states such as Virginia again demonstrated that the demands of the South were taken more seriously at the 1952 convention.

In contrast with four years earlier, the 1952 platform had one major objective: to keep the Democratic Party together. Senator Sparkman's work on the platform committee was instrumental in drafting a program that was not objectionable to the great majority of Democrats. As a southern Democrat, Sparkman was a states' rights supporter and opposed federally mandated desegregation. But he was no firebrand on the issue of civil rights and he had a great dislike for the Dixiecrats. His goals were to find a middle position between extremes and to avoid explicit references to civil rights legislation, in particular regarding the FEPC. The program drafted by the platform committee contained all these characteristics. It called for the improvement of congressional procedures to comply with majority rule after "reasonable debate" (an obvious attack on the southern use of the filibuster) and a combined effort by individuals, state governments, and the federal government to secure equal rights for all Americans. Yet the text did not mention the FEPC, nor did it ask for any mandatory measures to initiate desegregation. Civil rights proponents and states' righters objected to the party program; when the platform came up for a voice vote on the convention floor, Hugh White and Herman Talmadge sounded their protest against it. Hubert Humphrey was pleased with the final result, however, especially with the plank on reform in

Congress. The delegates eventually accepted the platform in relative harmony. The introduction of the loyalty pledge was actually more controversial than the contents of the civil rights paragraph.[13]

When the balloting for the presidential candidacy began, Estes Kefauver received 340 votes, Adlai Stevenson 272, and Richard Russell 268 (only five more than he obtained in 1948, when he did not campaign at all). Stevenson started to gain ground on the second ballot and finally won the nomination on the third, with 617.5 votes. By then, the number of Russell delegates had decreased to 261. Truman's prediction, that Russell was a great Democrat but that his southern roots blocked the path to the White House, had become reality. Left-wing groups in the big cities were essential for a Democratic victory, the president had told him, so it was impossible for a conservative from the South to become the party's presidential candidate. Even the nomination of moderate southerner John Sparkman as Stevenson's running mate led to protest from civil rights activists and liberals. In the end, Russell instructed the delegates who supported him to give their votes to Stevenson.[14] Did Russell's defeat exemplify the decline of the South's role in national party affairs? The Russell campaign ended in failure, but Sparkman's selection as vice presidential candidate was an indication that the former Confederate states still had a place under the Democratic umbrella.

After the convention, James Eastland traveled back to Mississippi to campaign for Adlai Stevenson. Voters there were confused about whom to support in the upcoming election. Their senator supported the Democratic ticket, but what about the Republican candidate, Dwight Eisenhower? The general was popular in the South and white Mississippians had trouble believing that Stevenson and "his Fair-Deal running mate" John Sparkman were true Democrats who honored the political legacy of Thomas Jefferson and Woodrow Wilson. Some thought the Republican platform looked more Jeffersonian.[15] Eastland did not offer much assistance. He told constituents the Mississippi delegation had tried to get another states' rights ticket together at the convention. The other delegates from the South had not been very cooperative, however. Eastland thought solitary action by Mississippi would lead to political isolation of the state. "Our people now have a choice between Stevenson and Eisenhower, and I think they are both good men," he answered.[16] Eastland maintained this pragmatic attitude during the remainder of the campaign.

At the beginning of August, Governor White and Fielding Wright conferred with Adlai Stevenson about his stand on civil rights and other sectional matters. Stevenson pleased White when he told him the states should be responsible for the enactment of civil rights measures.[17] At the reassembled state convention of August 18, Hugh White emphasized that the national party was more receptive to the demands of the South in 1952 than in preceding years. The convention decided to follow the governor's lead. Instead of forming a states' rights ticket under the Democratic label, the delegates chose presidential electors pledged to Adlai Stevenson and John Sparkman.[18]

Speaking before the Jackson Kiwanis Club in the Edwards Hotel, James Eastland predicted that Stevenson would "overwhelmingly" win the presidential election. Eastland described the Democratic candidate as "an outstanding American, honest, moderate and sincere with no taint [of] socialism in his body." He then gave his audience an interpretation of what had happened at the Democratic National Convention in Chicago. Eastland thought Mississippi did the right thing by staying in the national party this time. The Democratic Party had two large factions, he said, which were both striving for complete control of the organization. The national leadership, consisting of "professional politicians" and the big city bosses, strove to keep both sides in balance to prevent the destruction of the party. The two blocs Eastland referred to were the conservatives (the South, farmers, and city machines) and the liberals (organized labor, minority groups, and "socialists"). "Some day one of these groups will get the upper hand and put the other group out," Eastland wrote in the draft of his speech, "this is the one thing the machine bosses fear."[19]

To prevent this from happening, the Democratic leaders attempted to please both factions by giving them something they desired. For the national Democrats, it was impossible to ignore the demands of African Americans, because of their voting strength in the North. Simultaneously, southern whites still formed an important electorate for the Democratic Party. Eastland used Harry Truman's civil rights initiatives as an example of this balancing act. According to the senator, the president never made "an earnest attempt" to pass a comprehensive civil rights program. Truman knew that the strong civil rights bills he proposed would never pass Congress. At the same time, he warned that he intended to veto a watered-down proposal. This strategy led to the desired result, Eastland explained: "give the northern liberals a civil rights bill to make them happy, and to keep it from passing to make the South happy."

By staying in Chicago, the southerners had forced the national leadership to make concessions to them, and their presence prevented the nomination of Kefauver, who was a moderate on civil rights. "We stayed in the convention which was exactly the right thing," Eastland argued. "We sacrificed nothing. We made it impossible for a socialist to be nominated for president. Had we left the convention, we would have played in Kefauver's hands. The convention had to stay intact."[20]

Although James Eastland was back in the Democratic Party, his Dixiecrat past haunted him during the entire election season. A citizen from McComb, Mississippi, uttered her complete disbelief about Eastland's renewed allegiance to the national Democrats. "Every Mississippian knows that you bolted the party in 1948 because you claimed to be a States Rights man," she wrote the senator. "At that time we were proud of you, but every real States Righter has no respect for a 'Turncoat. . . .' You know Eisenhower is the lesser of the two evils and we could have shown the democrats that they could not cram just anything down our throats. What little patronage we may receive by sticking to the party is not anything compared to lost prestige and principal and the devaluation of our money."[21]

During the campaign, supporters of Eisenhower in Mississippi used rhetoric reminiscent of the Dixiecrat Party to undermine the Democratic ticket. In a radio address, renegade Democrat Ernest O. Spencer, the state chairman of the Citizens for Eisenhower-Nixon movement, told his listeners about the helplessness of the Mississippi delegation at the National Democratic Convention. "The most obnoxious Civil Rights, F.E.P.C., platform ever written by any Democratic Convention was adopted over the strenuous opposition of the Delegation's from Mississippi and the South," he said. Now that the political clout of the South in the Democratic Party was broken, the time had come to turn to the GOP, Spencer argued. According to him, Governor Stevenson "embraced and endorsed every phase and philosophy of the Truman Socialistic form of Government." The Democrats had therefore "abandoned our Jeffersonian Standard of Government by the people and are leading us down to disaster in absolute Socialism."[22]

Voters across Mississippi agreed with Spencer, and some of them even tried to get Eastland into the Republican camp. In a confidential letter, M. W. Swartz, president of the Peoples Bank of Indianola, warned that the nation was in great peril and that party loyalty had to be subordinated for a greater cause, an America based on white supremacy. "I believe that you cannot endure Stevenson's speech in Richmond and his advocacy of a Federal F.E.P.C. and his drive for limitation of cloture and all the other stuff he stands for," Swartz wrote Eastland. "Won't you come out for Eisenhower?"[23]

The Mississippi Democrats worried about the efforts by the Eisenhower supporters in the state. "It is my considered opinion that this State can easily be lost to Eisenhower in November," Thomas Tubb wrote Stephen Mitchell, the new chairman of the DNC. "The Democrats for Eisenhower group has all the moneyed interest in this State backing them." The Democratic Party in Mississippi was short on money, and although Governor White, Senators Eastland and Stennis, and six congressmen endorsed the national ticket, many Mississippians doubted that they should vote for Adlai Stevenson. The white voters in the state were still reluctant to go Republican, but at the same time they saw Stevenson as a candidate handpicked by Truman, a liberal controlled by former leaders of the ADA, and an opponent of state ownership of tidelands oil. Moreover, he gave the impression he did not need the South to win the election, catering instead to the demands of the extreme left wing of the Democratic Party and minority groups.

Another problem was the endorsement of Eisenhower by prominent southern politicians such as Governor Allan Shivers of Texas and Governor James Byrnes of South Carolina. Tubb stressed that the Democratic Party in Mississippi needed all the resources possible to get out the votes of the farmers, who usually followed the straight party line. The emphasis on party loyalty was important, because the Democrats for Eisenhower were making a strong case across the state that a vote for their ticket was in fact not a vote for the Republican Party.[24] William M. Whittington, who represented the third—or Delta—congressional district in the U.S. House, was "alarmed at the reports that come to me covering the thorough organization in behalf of Eisenhower not only in the Delta but in other parts of the State of Mississippi." Whittington believed the Mississippi congressional delegation needed to take the lead in the campaign to keep the state in the Democratic column.[25]

Eastland went on the campaign trail for Stevenson, but he declared that as senator, he was "not obligated to support any provisions of any platform of any political party."[26] At a rally in Alcorn, Mississippi, Eastland referred to Stevenson only once. He said that if the Democratic candidate were to win the election and attempt to pass civil rights legislation, southern congressmen would treat him the same way they dealt with Truman. It was critical, however, that the Democrats remained in power in Washington. The chairmanships of committees important to the South depended on Democratic majorities in Congress, and Republicans were opposed to vital federal programs, such as the Tennessee Valley Authority and farm subsidies. Speaking from the bed of a pickup truck in front of the Alcorn Court House, Senator Eastland said that since the end of the Civil War, the Republican Party had systematically fought southern progress. "My friends, the Democratic party is the party of the South. Why, the Republicans have only passed two farm bills in history and one of those cut support prices."[27]

In October, Eastland released a statement to take away all doubts about his support for the Stevenson-Sparkman ticket. Rumors had started to circulate that the senator's reticence to conduct an all-out campaign for the Democratic candidate was caused by Eastland's distrust about Stevenson's ideological course, in particular his disputed allegiance to states' rights principles. "Gov. Adlai Stevenson has done nothing to cause me to withdraw my endorsement of him," Eastland announced in a press release. "I have made several speeches for the Democratic nominees and shall continue to do so as the opportunity presents itself." With these words, Eastland distanced himself from Fielding Wright, who withheld his endorsement of Stevenson until he was sure of the candidate's political leanings.[28]

Adlai Stevenson made a real effort to convince southern voters that their political home was the national Democratic Party. "The genius of the Democratic Party lies in its ability to adjust conflicting viewpoints and arrive finally at programs and policies that meet the highest aspirations of all Americans," Stevenson said in a campaign speech in Nashville, Tennessee. He considered the issue of civil rights to be a minor quarrel within the party over how to achieve a common end. Moreover, the blind acceptance of any party line was contrary to American political tradition and therefore southerners had a right to criticize certain parts of the Democratic platform. But these disagreements should not lead to the destruction of southern loyalty to the Democratic Party. Stevenson argued that "following those embittered apostates who proclaim themselves Democrats while supporting the nominees of the Republican Party" would not lead to more political influence for the South.[29]

Like Eastland, Adlai Stevenson also discussed the influential position southerners had on congressional committees, influence that diminished if the Republicans won the elections. Stevenson explained that Democratic presidents could always count on southern politicians to formulate sound policy, especially in the field of foreign relations. The "glib men" sent into the South by the Republican Party tended to ignore the importance of the South when it came to foreign affairs. They preached a vague form of isolationism instead and tried to depict Stevenson as a socialist. "It is significant, I think, that in their March to the Sea the Republicans have tended to avoid discussion of what passes for Republican foreign policy," Stevenson said, clearly referring to General Sherman's infamous march through the South at the end of the Civil War. "Instead they have harped upon an alleged left-wing conspiracy of which I am supposed to be a helpless captive."[30]

As Election Day drew near, Stevenson appeared to gain the upper hand in Mississippi. The *New York Times* saw the influence of key political leaders such as Governor White and Senator Eastland as being decisive in keeping the state in the Democratic column. The states' rights movement that had dominated Mississippi in 1948 had scattered four years later. Eastland and White were Dixiecrats who endorsed the national party ticket, while their old brothers in arms—men such as former lieutenant governor Sam Lumpkin and Walter Sillers—campaigned for Eisenhower. The *New York Times* reported that "the Stevenson enthusiasts recognize the Eisenhower appeal as a real political threat and they are exercising a campaign vigilance that is believed to be without parallel in local elections since Reconstruction days." Republican strength was primarily located in urban areas and the Delta, while a Democratic victory depended on the rural vote.[31]

When the ballots were counted, the prediction of the *New York Times* came true: Adlai Stevenson carried Mississippi with 60 percent of the total vote. But Eisenhower won the 1952 presidential election, with the support of four former Confederate states: Virginia, Florida, Tennessee, and Texas. The Republican ticket also did surprisingly well in the Democratic heartland of the Deep South. Many Black Belt counties that had voted for the States' Rights Party in 1948 backed Eisenhower in 1952. In Mississippi, nine of the twenty counties with an African American population of 60 percent or more became the new frontier of presidential Republicanism. The Republican vote increased dramatically in the state, from a twenty-year high of 6.4 percent to 39.6 percent in 1952. The neobourbons of the former Dixiecrat Party (including Leander Perez) were some of the most vocal supporters of Eisenhower in the South.[32]

Although Mississippi went for the Stevenson-Sparkman ticket, the Democratic victory was rather narrow in comparison with previous years. William Winter noted that the number of votes for the Republicans (112,966) to those for the Democrats (172,553) was remarkable and that it signaled the beginning of the two-party system in the state.[33] General Eisenhower's popularity in the South undoubtedly contributed to the relatively good showing of the Republicans in the region, but widespread southern dissatisfaction with the political course of the national Democratic Party also played an important role. Shortly after the elections, Thomas Tubb thanked James Eastland for his assistance in the campaign. Tubb saw the results of the presidential election as proof that the South was still the backbone of the Democratic Party. He hoped that a well-organized team of southern senators and congressmen could again take control of the party and reinstall the two-thirds rule. If the national Democrats were more inclined to listen to liberals such as Senators Moody, Humphrey, and Lehman, Tubb expected one of two possible developments: the birth of a two-party system in the South, or the creation of a third party. Mississippi was not ready for competition between two parties, Tubb asserted, and he thought "the Nation should not have a Third Party."[34]

Eastland was pessimistic about the restoration of southern control over the Democratic Party and he rejected the idea of a two-party South, fearing that a split in the white vote would increase the power of African Americans. Surprisingly, he was more positive about another third-party attempt. "I believe the States-Rights movement in 48 was constructive and was one of the finest things we ever did," the senator replied to Tubb. "If the need arises, we might have to do this in the future." Eastland thought that the Dixiecrat victory in four southern states had scared Truman and that it had rebuffed his civil rights program.[35] The power of the southern bloc in Congress probably had more to do with Truman's reticence to make an all-out fight for desegregation than the election results, but Eastland had a point that the national Democratic Party was more careful in the approach to its southern members in 1952. The Stevenson campaign indicated that as long as the national Democrats took a moderate civil rights course, even a former Dixiecrat like Senator Eastland agreed to take a stand for the national party, although this support was limited.

The Republicans took control of the White House and Congress in 1952. This shift in power had consequences for the disbursement of patronage. In Mississippi, the Republicans were still divided into two factions: Perry

Howard's Black and Tan group and the Lily-Whites. The Republican National Convention had accepted the Black and Tans as the official delegates from Mississippi, but during the following months an organization called Citizens for Eisenhower-Nixon took control of the Republican campaign in the state, with the assistance of the Democrats for Eisenhower. Democrat Ernest Spencer was in charge of the Citizens for Eisenhower group. Besides his role in the Republican campaign, he was also the manager of the Walthall Hotel in Jackson and had served as Eastland's campaign finance chairman in 1942.[36]

After the elections, Spencer came up with a plan to manage federal patronage in the state. By giving all the pro-Eisenhower groups in Mississippi a voice in the matter, Spencer hoped to prevent scandals like the job sales fraud perpetrated by the Loyalist Democrats under Clarence Hood. He discussed his proposal with his old friend James Eastland, because it was the senator's "responsibility to confirm all major appointments."[37] During the early stage of the Republican rise in Mississippi, the partisan boundaries between states' rights Democrats and Eisenhower supporters were vague. Spencer's discussions with Eastland were an example of such political cooperation that crossed party lines. The Spencer faction was not really Republican in sentiment. The founders and leaders of this group were in fact "Eastland Democrats" who realized early on that Stevenson was not going to win the election. By choosing the side of Eisenhower, they wanted to "broker Eastland's influence over patronage with the new president, especially in the area of judicial nominations." This strategy seemed to work: during the Eisenhower administration, no changes occurred in judicial patronage in the state.[38]

Despite Eastland's growing power, he began to have doubts about continuing his career in national politics. At the beginning of 1953, rumors started to circulate that Eastland was thinking about retirement. He was telling people close to him that he wanted to spend more time on his plantation, and health issues also became more of a problem. Eastland did not like to participate in the social life of Washington politics. He preferred to stay at home instead and read detective novels. He stopped giving speeches in the Senate, which gave fodder to potential opponents in the upcoming Senate race of 1954.[39] In February, State Senator Brinkley Morton of Senatobia reported that Eastland had informed him he would not seek reelection "under any circumstances."[40] But Eastland's friends in the state wanted him to stay in national politics. "Should you change your mind about not running for reelection, you would have very little opposition, if any," Curlee wrote, trying to convince Eastland. "The people of Mississippi want you."[41] In August, at a meeting of the Touchdown Club at the Heidelberg Hotel in Jackson, the senator finally announced that he planned to make a statement about his career in a few weeks. Before speaking at the Touchdown Club gathering, Eastland met with Fielding Wright and Eisenhower Democrat Ernest Spencer. The *Jackson Daily News* described Spencer and Eastland as the "key men in the state's patronage picture."[42]

On August 15, after more than half a year of speculations, Eastland finally declared his intentions. He sent his administrative assistant Courtney Pace to Jackson to tell reporters that the senator was going to run for reelection in 1954 and that he also intended to remain neutral in the 1955 gubernatorial race. In the election of 1951, politicians, press, and voters had disapproved of his interference. Although Eastland stated it was his goal to stay out of the campaign for governor, he also declared that he intended to "follow in the future the same policies which I have pursued in the past."[43]

Hugh White encouraged his lieutenant, Carroll Gartin, to run against Eastland and promised him gubernatorial support. Keeping the 1951 race in mind, White said the governor's office "owes Jim Eastland nothing." Gartin and other possible opponents of Eastland faced an intense campaign against a powerful politician; the senior senator had plenty of experience on the stump and his influence in Washington was growing, both on the Judiciary Committee and the Agriculture Committee. Kenneth Toler of the *Memphis Commercial Appeal* considered Eastland's work for the farmers (especially cotton farmers) to be his most important asset for winning reelection.[44]

Eastland's political network in Washington undoubtedly enhanced his chances to retain his Senate seat. Shortly after Eisenhower's inauguration, he contacted the new secretary of agriculture, Ezra Taft Benson. Benson shared Eastland's antipathy to communism and Big Government. In Benson's case, this laissez-faire approach also meant he was opposed to government price supports for farmers, a form of federal interference Eastland actually approved of. In a long talk with the secretary, the Mississippi senator told him "that the Southern farmer is afraid of the Republican Party and was afraid that he [Benson] would 'pull the rug' from under us."[45]

Benson tried to reassure Eastland he was in favor of federal subsidies too and that he wanted to prevent a sharp decline in the price levels of agricultural commodities. Eastland believed Benson, but he was "afraid of the big industrial group who seem to be in control." Benson's assistants were another problem. Although Eastland thought they were more talented than the men who had worked for Benson's predecessor, Charles Brannan, he did not like the fact that they advocated flexible support prices. In 1954, the old farm bill expired and Eastland believed enough votes could be gathered to renew the 90 percent price support level. The Republicans were afraid to block this bill. "There is one sure thing in American politics, as I see it, and that is the farmer will vote against any candidate who opposes high support prices," Eastland predicted.[46]

Besides his status as an influential defender of farming interests, James Eastland was also building up a reputation as a communist hunter. In March 1954, he traveled to New Orleans on behalf of the Senate Internal Security Subcommittee to hold hearings about communist control of the Southern Conference Educational Fund (SCEF), the educational branch of the Southern Conference for Human Welfare. The SCHW no longer existed, but the SCEF continued its work to encourage desegregation and fight racial discrimination in the South. It was no mere coincidence that Eastland's probe into the SCEF took place in the early spring of 1954. A Supreme Court ruling on school segregation was imminent and Eastland anticipated a reversal of the "separate but equal" clause that formed the basis of the southern educational system. Moreover, the SCHW had criticized Eastland bitterly for his statements on black soldiers in the 1945 debate about extension of the FEPC. Now the time had come to retaliate.

One of the people subpoenaed to testify was SCEF president Aubrey Williams, a New Dealer who had served as director of the National Youth Association and the Works Projects Administration. According to Williams, the Senate Internal Security Subcommittee "seemed to be concerned mostly with smearing the Roosevelt New Deal with which I was privileged to be connected."[47] Virginia Durr also received a subpoena. Durr was a former board member of the SCEF and had been a candidate for the U.S. Senate on the Progressive Party ticket in 1948. During the 1930s, she organized southern white women to oppose the poll tax. Durr was also the sister-in-law of Supreme Court Justice Hugo Black of Alabama, a liberal appointed by Franklin Roosevelt and a proponent of desegregation. If Eastland could somehow link Virginia Durr to communist activities, Black's standing would suffer too. In case the Supreme Court ruled against school segregation, Eastland was in a position to argue that the decision had a red tinge. Paul Crouch, a former communist who later turned out to be a paid informant for the subcommittee, actually claimed that Durr "plotted with the Communist leaders to exploit her relationship as sister-in-law of a Justice of the Supreme Court in the interests of the World Communist Conspiracy and interest of overthrowing our Government."[48]

Virginia Durr asserted that the hearings were in fact Eastland's opening salvo for his reelection campaign. "Jim Eastland was running for the Senate on the grounds that the Supreme Court was a communist-dominated outfit if it handed down this ruling that 'niggers' and white folks had to school together," said Durr. She called the Mississippi senator "the most disgusting character" she had ever known, a man filled with a wild fear of miscegenation. After Durr received the subpoena, she started calling journalists and politicians in Washington for help. Virginia Durr and her husband, Clifford Durr, were good friends with Senator Lyndon Baines Johnson, who then served as minority leader, and with Lady Bird Johnson. Durr wanted to make sure that no Democratic senator joined Eastland in New Orleans, and Lyndon Johnson was the right person to take care of such business. Johnson told Durr he was not aware of Eastland's plans. He pledged to make an effort to help his old friends, but he could not make any promises. Durr then got in touch with Republicans in Congress, particularly GOP politicians she had worked with in the anti-poll tax fight. She also contacted Senator William Langer of North Dakota (the Republican chairman of the Judiciary Committee), Estes Kefauver, and Lister Hill.[49]

Durr's strategy was based on limiting support in the Senate for the hearings in New Orleans. If Eastland showed up alone, without any other Democratic or Republican senators traveling with him, the Senate would feel less obliged to follow up on the outcome of the hearings. The plan worked: with the assistance of LBJ and other members of Congress, Durr managed to prevent an investigation by a full committee. Eastland was the only U.S. senator at the trial, none of the accused was convicted, and the SCEF was never listed as a communist front organization.[50] When the *Montgomery Advertiser* asked journalists who had covered the hearing which of the participants formed the greatest threat to the United States, half of them voted for James Eastland, closely followed by Paul Crouch.[51]

Two months after the SISS hearings in New Orleans, the Supreme Court handed down the verdict that boosted Eastland's faltering career. The

Brown v. Board of Education decision declared segregation in public schools unconstitutional and confirmed the worst fears of the white South: federal interference in the education of their children. Dwight Eisenhower understood that white southerners were afraid of school desegregation. "These are not bad people," the president told Chief Justice Earl Warren. "All they are concerned about is to see that their sweet little girls are not required to sit in school alongside some big overgrown bucks."[52]

James Eastland completely agreed with the Republican president. Ten days after *Brown*, on May 27, he mounted the rostrum in the Senate to demonstrate that the Supreme Court had "entered the social field in violation of the Constitution, the laws of nature, and the law of God." This was the first step toward the creation of a police state, where the Court "sits as a Constitutional Convention in judicial robes, and has arrogated unto itself the sovereign powers of the American people, speaking through their Congress and the State legislatures, to amend our Constitution." The senator quoted Thomas Jefferson and Alexis de Tocqueville to show he was not the first one who feared "the outcome of concentrated judicial power."[53]

Eastland was convinced communist front organizations were behind the *Brown* decision and that the Supreme Court justices were influenced by Marxist doctrine. "Everyone knows that the Negroes did not themselves instigate the agitation against segregation," he stated. "They were put up to it by radical busybodies who are intent upon overthrowing American institutions." Using the Civil War as a rhetorical framework, the senator concluded his speech by telling his audience Dixie would again rise to defend its social traditions against attacks from extremist groups in the North. "We, in the South, have seen the tides rise before; when we refuse to be engulfed, they recede," Eastland declared. "The present campaign against segregation is based upon illegality. The South will therefore prevail."[54]

The *Brown v. Board of Education* verdict became one of the most important topics of the 1954 Senate race in Mississippi. According to Erle Johnston, a campaign worker for Eastland, "the United States Supreme Court gave Senator James Oliver Eastland the only issue he needed to assure his re-election against his only but formidable opponent, Lieutenant Governor Carroll Gartin."[55] The defense of segregation was a central theme in Eastland's reelection bid. The senator had held the chairmanship of the Civil Rights Subcommittee for three years, from 1949 until 1952, when the Republicans became the majority party in the Senate. During the campaign he boasted that as chairman he did not call for any meetings of his subcommittee and that he had special pockets put in his pants where he kept civil rights bills.[56] His position on the Internal Security Subcommittee bolstered his image among Mississippi voters as a combatant of the communist menace and a defender of Americanism. Combined with his strong voting record on farming interests, the senator could fuse his influential positions on cotton, communism, and civil rights into a powerful campaign message. In a letter to Louis Gardner of Natchez, Eastland's campaign manager Arthur Sullivan stressed the importance of voting for the senator. "Mississippi and the South must keep Jim in the Senate. We have to go back to Reconstruction days to find a more perilous time in the life of our state. For twelve years Jim has been in the forefront of every fight against legislation that sought to destroy or change our traditional way of life. His record is a monument to courageous effort in a righteous cause."[57] The 1954 election contest foreshadowed the themes that dominated Eastland's campaigns in the 1960s and 1970s. In contrast with the race against Wall Doxey, the senator now presented himself as the experienced leader of an embattled South.

Frank Barber recalled that the 1954 campaign was "a very stiff election." Barber was one of Eastland's field men in the race against Gartin. He coordinated the campaign in five counties in south Mississippi. "The election was the first he'd really been seriously contested for his senator's seat," Barber said about Eastland's reelection bid, "and Gartin had the support of the administration up here, Gov. Hugh White." Since Gartin was from Laurel, the lieutenant governor had many connections in that region and Barber's area of operation became a battleground for votes.[58]

Gartin's real challenge was to deconstruct the image of Eastland as the accomplished political expert in the fields of segregation, agriculture, and anticommunism. Gartin opened his campaign on the night of June 15 in his hometown of Laurel. "A holiday spirit was in the air," the *Laurel Leader-Call* reported, and artists such the gospel singing Hurt Family, the Laurel Melody Boys, and the Bob Scott Quartet entertained the audience at the rally. Around 8 pm, Gartin appeared on stage to deliver his opening address.[59]

The three main themes he used against his opponent were Eastland's attendance record in the Senate, his neglect of small southern farmers, and surprisingly, his civil rights record. Gartin called Eastland the "man who's seldom there," a wealthy planter-politician who preferred to pay "much greater attention to the operation of his 6000-acre plantation than he has to the business of the people of this state." He charged that the senior senator had neglected his duty to Mississippi when he served as a member of the Agriculture Subcommittee responsible for the division of acreage allotments between the South and the West. Because Eastland had not stood up for his state, western cotton states such as New Mexico and California almost doubled their acreage, while the allocations for Mississippi had actually decreased. The revised allotments were the result of new policies initiated by Ezra Taft Benson, who ordered a drastic cotton acreage reduction of almost 18 million acres. Eastland and the other members of the subcommittee had failed to draft alternative legislation and, on top of that, Eastland had not defended the interests of southern agriculture. The new law was "an injustice to the man least able to afford it," Gartin said, "the hardships which this steal has caused has been borne largely by the small hill farmers." While Eastland was neglecting his work on Capitol Hill, he used his position as U.S. senator to send a great amount of campaign letters to voters in Mississippi without paying postage. According to Gartin, Eastland was "guilty of one of the most flagrant violations of the franking privilege ever committed by a member of the Senate."[60]

Gartin promised he was a different politician, a representative of all the sections in the state, a senator who would be on the job full time. Reminding the audience of Eastland's indecisiveness the year before, Gartin said a senator must "want to be a senator, and it is not reasonable to believe that he will be of much value to you in Washington if he dislikes the job and is constantly threatening to quit it." On the topic of civil rights, he held Eastland partly responsible for the Supreme Court decision in *Brown v. Board of Education*. Gartin believed his opponent had not made an all-out effort to prevent the nomination of Chief Justice Earl Warren and other liberal members of the court. "He now says they are 'political hacks' but he did not say so and fight their appointments," Gartin stated. The lieutenant governor said he was just as strongly opposed to desegregation as Eastland proclaimed to be, and he pledged to make sure the southern "segregated way of life" remained intact. Gartin did not doubt Mississippi political legends John Sharp Williams, Pat Harrison, and Theodore Bilbo would have made every effort to block the appointment of men like Warren to the Supreme Court. But Eastland personally disliked Bilbo, and he had only halfheartedly defended his colleague, already ill with cancer, when his seating was challenged in 1947. Gartin wanted to continue the fight for Jim

Crow on all fronts, but he also thought all Mississippi children—white and black—were entitled to a good education within the system of segregation.[61] Carroll Gartin maneuvered himself in the underdog position, a defender of the small farmer who took on the senior senator of Mississippi. Gartin's strategy was based on the premise that despite Eastland's seniority and power in the Senate, he had not done enough to protect southern agriculture and segregation.

James Eastland retorted Gartin's charges in his opening speech of June 26, in his hometown of Forest. Standing in the blazing sun, Eastland outlined a radical plan to protect southern apartheid. Because of the Supreme Court decision, the South again faced the same conditions as during Reconstruction. He called for all-out resistance to desegregation. "At all costs, and regardless of the consequences, we must protect our schools, our racial heritage, our culture, and our Southern way of life." He believed the southern states needed a consistent plan, "cohesion and unity" to fight the Supreme Court, which had become an instrument of left-wing organizations and "racial pressure groups."[62]

While the South should devise an overall strategy to combat the decrees passed by this court, its people needed to turn to temporary measures as a delaying tactic. Eastland did not eschew hard action; he thought southerners "would be on sound ground to make this fight through the use of the police power inherent in every state predicated upon the hard realities of the situation." These hard realities consisted of powerful enemies arrayed against the South, with plenty of financial resources and under the guidance of "ruthless and ambitious men." According to Eastland, the CIO and the NAACP were the main culprits. Earlier, on May 26, Eastland had introduced a constitutional amendment in the Senate to ensure "that there shall be no limitation on the power of any state to regulate health, morals, education, marriage and good order within the state." In order to ensure passage of this amendment, Eastland proposed the formation of a national organization "to fight the Court, to fight the C.I.O., to fight the N.A.A.C.P., and to fight all the conscienceless pressure groups who are attempting our destruction."[63]

Another goal of this organization would be the mobilization of public opinion, particularly in the North. The speech Eastland delivered on May 27 led to a "stupendous and nationwide" response, the senator said. His office received a great amount of letters from across the United States. "The vast majority of the people of both races favor segregation. The average Northerner feels just as strongly on this issue as we do." For James Eastland, the defense of Jim Crow was not just a southern fight, but also a national fight based on beliefs shared by southern and northern whites. Moreover, these beliefs were not limited to racial issues. Eastland talked about a "crusade to restore Americanism," to return political power to the people, and to promote free enterprise. This fusion of segregation, states' rights, traditional values, and capitalism "will give us recruits and add to our support in the North and West." Eastland predicted that defeat meant death, the end of "Southern culture and our aspirations as an Anglo-Saxon people." He concluded his speech by pointing to the freedom fight of Ireland against Great Britain, and how Mahatma Gandhi "mobilized the sentiment of his people," which eventually drove the British Empire from India.[64] Eastland saw little discrepancy between linking Gandhi's nonviolent protest with the use of police power by southern states to uphold segregation. From Eastland's point of view, the Indian struggle for independence and the South's fight to protect Jim Crow shared an important similarity: they were both engaged in a crusade for freedom against a powerful imperialist regime.

Eastland devoted most of his opening address to the segregation issue, but at the end of his speech he promised that during the remainder of the campaign he would also discuss other subjects, such as the completion of the Natchez Trace Parkway, the development of the tourism industry on the Gulf Coast, flood control, and soil conservation.[65] The senator did not forget to talk about farm interests at the rally in Forest and he managed to connect this topic with the threat of communism. Eastland charged that the CIO was trying to unseat him and Senator Allen Ellender of Louisiana. Their removal would have disastrous effects on maintaining price support for agricultural products. The Senate Agriculture Committee was divided eight to seven in favor of price support, with Eastland and Ellender belonging to the group advocating such measures. Eastland saw himself as one of the fifteen senators who designed agricultural policy in the country. He was therefore in a key position to help southern farmers. If the Democrats returned to power in Congress, his seniority increased his influence in the Senate. In combination with his knowledge of the subject, "no man in the government of the United States will have more power to aid agriculture." Eastland repudiated Carroll Gartin's charge that he was responsible for reduced acreage allotments for Mississippi farmers while cotton growers in the West had gained higher allocations. Gartin's statement was based on false calculations, Eastland said, describing his input into the drafting of new acreage legislation and his resisting Republican senators from western states as "a life saver for thousands of our farmers and they know it." Eastland was able to do such work for southern agriculture because of his years in the Senate; he ranked fourteenth in seniority, while his opponent—if elected—would be ninety-sixth.[66]

Geography played an important role in the Senate race. The Delta was Eastland country and the senator did not even bother to appoint a campaign leader in that area.[67] Eastland had a trusted political cadre of field men in other parts of Mississippi who worked hard to get their candidate reelected. They also reported on the activities of the opposition. Gartin campaigned vigorously during the hot summer months of 1954, closely followed by Eastland's trustees. Like Wall Doxey before him, Carroll Gartin attempted to get the voters in the Mississippi Hills behind him in his fight against Delta planter Jim Eastland.[68] Hugh Allan Boren, an attorney from Tupelo, urged the people in the Gartin camp to focus on the area north of Highway 80 and east of Highway 51, primarily the Hills and Prairie counties in northeast Mississippi. Boren also suggested they concentrate on women voters and draw away attention from Eastland's position in the Senate. "Something has got to be done to over-come this 'Agriculture Committee' and 'Seniority' talk."[69]

Gartin's allegations about Eastland's absenteeism and voting record were not the only matters that plagued the senator. His alcohol consumption also loomed as a possible point of discussion in the campaign. H. A. Womack, who lived in the Hill Country town of Mantee, contacted Eastland to tell him that Gartin was going to use the alcohol issue to explain why the senator was not in the Senate often. "I understand that he will tell the people that why you were absent on so many roll calls that you were at your Delta home drunk," Womack wrote.[70] Eastland immediately replied with a long letter. He insisted that the people who were close to him knew him as a sober man. "They know that my home is a home where no whisky or any other kind of liquor is ever brought or served," he stated. "They know I do not fool with whisky and never have." Eastland said he had a reputation "of sobriety and hard work," both in Washington and in Mississippi.[71]

Eastland's allies offered help in challenging the rumors about his inebriation and his political conduct. On August 17, State Representative Wilma Sledge of Sunflower County appeared on the Jackson-based television station WLBT to stand up for her friend and neighbor. Sledge had known the Eastland family for twenty years and had a deep respect for the senator's accomplishments. She argued that with such an "outstanding" record, it was inevitable "gossips and scandal mongers will spread lies and filth about his private life." Sledge called Eastland the accepted national leader in the battle against desegregation, not only for his own state, but for the entire South and the nation. She argued that his work for southern farmers, especially cotton growers, was beyond question. Gartin's campaign was based on the "political truism that when the individual has no record of his own to run on he attempts to run on the demerits of his opponent." She knew Gartin from her work in the state legislature, where he chaired the upper chamber as lieutenant governor. Although Gartin had pledged that he would uphold segregation, he was not present when the Sillers Resolution came up for a vote. This resolution, drafted by Walter Sillers, would have permitted a referendum to give the legislature the power to abolish the public school system in case of desegregation. Because the votes were equally divided on the resolution, Gartin was supposed to cast the decisive ballot. But the lieutenant governor was absent, Sledge stated, and therefore the resolution was not adopted. "Yes, Carroll refused to vote, so the people of Mississippi have not had the opportunity of going to the polls to express themselves on segregation," she declared.[72] A similar resolution was again introduced later that year. This time, the state legislature accepted Sillers's proposal for a referendum on public education. In December 1954, only one-third of qualified voters showed up to participate in the plebiscite. These voters gave the legislature full authority to close down public schools if necessary.[73]

Editor Hodding Carter III of the *Delta Democrat-Times* argued that especially the Delta was in favor of abolishing the public school system. If the state legislature were to undertake an equalization program for black schools to ward off desegregation, the Delta would feel the economic brunt, because the majority of blacks lived in this area. Carter wrote that the debate over the Sillers Resolution highlighted "the traditional political split in Mississippi between the plantation Delta, with its high proportion of Negroes, and the 'Hills,' an all-embracing term for the rest of the state characterized primarily by white farmers of small plots of land."[74]

Gartin was the Hill Country candidate, the representative of the small farmers and the working class. This reputation earned him the endorsement of several labor organizations. For instance, the Mississippi chapter of the

Brotherhood of Locomotive Firemen and Enginemen advised its members to vote for Gartin. According to Chairman A. F. McDaniel, Eastland's voting record spoke for itself; during his entire career, he had cast votes that were detrimental to laborers. "Big business is already active and will spend tremendous sums of money to keep Senator Eastland in office," McDaniel wrote, "we do not have the money, but we do have the votes." These votes should be cast for Carroll Gartin, who understood the problems of "the average citizen of Mississippi" and who had "the interest of the common people at heart."[75]

Wilma Sledge also mentioned labor's approval of Gartin, but to her this was a sign the lieutenant governor was a pawn of the CIO. "Whether [Gartin] is a willing or a captive candidate of the C.I.O. perhaps only he and they know," Sledge said. "Certain it is that they must be for him as they have declared themselves against Eastland." Eastland was a well-known opponent of organized labor and an advocate of the Taft-Hartley Act, which limited the power of unions. Sledge recalled a debate in the state legislature on a right-to-work bill, legislation that prohibited mandatory membership in a union for employees. Passage of such a bill seriously weakened the bargaining position of labor unions. Business interests therefore favored enactment. During the debate, "labor bosses and their lobbyists" gathered on the balconies of the State Senate chamber to make sure that the right-to-work bill did not pass. Sledge criticized Gartin (who chaired the Senate meeting) for giving the labor representatives the opportunity to disrupt the debate. "Whether this indulgence stemmed from the fact that he was one of them, or whether he was inept in his duties as presiding officer is matter for conjecture," Sledge stated. She also noticed Gartin was not in the chamber when the decisive vote was taken and asked: "Did he run out on labor when the going got rough?" No matter what his intentions were, Sledge was sure the Congress of Industrial Organizations supported Gartin and she quoted CIO regional director R. W. Starnes to substantiate her claim.[76] If Eastland's opponent could somehow be linked with the CIO, he could then be branded as a fellow traveler and an enemy of the southern way of life.

Eastland ran as the establishment candidate and major newspapers such as the *Jackson Daily News* supported him, despite his aid to Paul B. Johnson Jr. in the 1951 gubernatorial election. Editor Fred Sullens pointed at Eastland's experience in the Senate as the main reason to endorse him.[77] The *Delta*

Democrat-Times backed Carroll Gartin. Hodding Carter described Gartin as "young, energetic, and anxious to serve in the Senate," a great contrast to James Eastland. "If, as his supporters say, [Senator Eastland] is ill, and thus unable to attend many sessions of the Senate, he isn't being fair to himself by staying in Washington," Carter wrote. Another problem was Eastland's preoccupation with large-scale farming. Carter asserted that this focus on agriculture had impaired the development of business and industry in the state. The other two themes of Eastland's campaign, communism and segregation, did not make the senator the most qualified candidate according to the *Democrat-Times*. Carter called the hearings in New Orleans disgraceful, reminiscent of Joe McCarthy, and merely an attempt to draw attention. The editor did not believe "Gartin would ever revert to the tactics employed by Jim Eastland in searching throughout the South for a communist in an obvious effort to capture headlines in his own bailiwick." He also considered Eastland's most important campaign subject, the defense of segregation, obvious in a state like Mississippi, where all people running for public office had to pledge their allegiance to Jim Crow. Although Gartin promised to fight desegregation, he was more pragmatic in his approach and opposed the closing of public schools in Mississippi. In addition, the lieutenant governor had served overseas during World War II, while Eastland had no military experience. For all these reasons, the *Delta Democrat-Times* thought Carroll Gartin would "make a better Senator than has Jim Eastland."[78]

Despite the initial fears of the Eastland camp about the popularity of Carroll Gartin, the senator coasted to victory rather easily. During the campaign, the lieutenant governor had been the slightly more liberal candidate. Together with Governor White, he rejected the hardline approach to the maintenance of school segregation initiated by Walter Sillers and his allies. In the year of *Brown v. Board Education*, such a decision was not a real political asset in a campaign for U.S. senator of Mississippi. To a certain degree, the 1954 primary campaign reflected the old political division between Delta and Hills. But even in the nonplantation counties, Eastland had plenty of supporters. Gartin received the support of a few counties in the eastern part of the state, but Eastland won with decisive numbers. He defeated his opponent by roughly 140,000 votes to 82,000.

The 1954 election demonstrated how hard it was for even a young and popular challenger like Carroll Gartin to defeat incumbent candidate James

Eastland. The senator used the full force of his political network to get reelected, which cost him a considerable sum of money. After the election, he contacted Ernest Spencer to see if the Democrats for Eisenhower would be willing to help him make up his deficit. "I am greatly disappointed at the lack of interest and assistance from those whom I have helped through the years with every problem they have had in Washington," Eastland complained to Spencer. "I wish you would contact our friends who have not helped in the campaign and ask them to help share this burden."[79]

Besides a strong organization, Eastland's road to victory was paved with attacks on the Supreme Court. The desegregation verdict of the Warren Court reignited the senator's career and fueled his reelection bid. Now that the biggest threat to the system of segregation came from the Supreme Court, the *Brown* decision also offered the opportunity to move attention away from the liberal tendencies of the national Democrats to the activities of the judicial branch. Particularly in later years and later campaigns, Eastland used this approach as an escape route to avoid discussions about his membership in the Democratic Party.

The campaign between Eastland and Gartin was a contest between two different strategies for the defense of segregation. While the senator proposed an all-out battle of massive resistance against the *Brown* ruling and desegregation, his opponent chose a more pragmatic approach to defending Jim Crow. In the years after *Brown*, these strains of opposition to racial integration crystallized and led to the development of two camps that had a common goal, but different visions of how to achieve that goal. The massive resistance forces saw segregation as a "positive good" and had no inhibitions about climbing the barricades in defense of their way of life. They also wanted to spread their gospel northward, through public relations campaigns and propaganda bureaus. Pragmatic or practical segregationists like Gartin were less inclined to place segregation above all other concerns (for example, the preservation of public education) and they thought it was better to draw attention away from the racial caste system in the South. Although these two blocs were often at odds with each other, the boundaries between them were not clearly drawn. Massive resisters could also be pragmatic, and vice versa.

The 1954 Senate race established James Eastland as a leader of massive resistance in Mississippi. Only two years before, the senator had contemplated retirement. Under pressure from his friends in the state, Eastland decided to seek reelection and subsequently initiated a drive to back up his credentials as a fighter for the southern and American way of life. The hearings in New Orleans, merged with Eastland's opposition to *Brown*, reinforced his image as a strong combatant of leftist subversives trying to bring down state sovereignty, segregation, and the American system of government. Eastland's position on the Senate Agriculture Committee bolstered his reputation as an advocate of the farmer, in particular large cotton planters. Eastland's seniority, committee assignments, and public image, combined with a statewide nexus of loyal women and men that campaigned for him and kept track of his rival, made the planter-politician practically unbeatable. The senator's team successfully depicted Gartin as young and inexperienced, weak on segregation, and a pawn of organized labor. These credentials led to Gartin's defeat despite his erstwhile popularity among the electorate.

Conservative Democrats like James Eastland slowed down the pace of partisan realignment in the former Confederacy and kept the Democratic Party competitive in the Deep South state of Mississippi. A symbiosis existed between southern members of Congress and the national party. This symbiosis manifested itself in the 1952 presidential election and the 1954 Senate campaign. Eastland built up seniority and authority through his affiliation with the Democratic Party, which he used as campaign tools against Gartin. The national Democrats adopted a more conciliatory tone toward the white South at the 1952 national convention, where the credentials committee accepted the Regular faction as the official Democrats of Mississippi. Although the loyalty oath created controversy, moderate southerners such as Alabama senator John Sparkman managed to find consensus between the liberal and southern wings of the party. In return, former Dixiecrat James Eastland campaigned for Adlai Stevenson and the state party, led by Governor Hugh White, remained loyal to the national presidential ticket. Behind the scenes, John Stennis and James Coleman masterminded a centrist course that sustained segregation and the bonds with the national party and that undermined the control of the states' righters. Coleman continued this strategy of moderation when he won the governorship in 1955, thus safeguarding Mississippi's position within the national party structure.

The Dixiecrats initially placed their hopes on Richard Russell's bid for the presidential nomination, but when his attempt failed, Walter Sillers and other radical segregationists flocked to the Republican Party. They set up Democrats for Eisenhower groups, which tapped into the popularity of the war hero below the Mason-Dixon Line, without taking on the official GOP label. Eastland did not join their exodus from the Democratic Party, but he gained influence on the southern Eisenhower movement through his friends, and thus continued to shape the disbursement of federal patronage under a Republican president. Because Senator Eastland and his allies exercised control over Democratic and Republican politics in Mississippi, the one-party system in the state was not seriously threatened during the 1950s. As long as the battle lines between Democrats and Republicans remained foggy, Democratic hegemony in Mississippi was assured.

CHAPTER 5

THE POLITICS OF COMPROMISE

“**Y**OUR RE-ELECTION PROVES beyond doubt that the people of Mississippi recognize and appreciate a leader who has rendered loyal and capable services to his people,” Walter Sillers wrote James Eastland on August 26, 1954. “Your record of outstanding service—courage to take a stand and speak out for what you believe in regardless of the political results or whether it be popular or not—appealed to all the people and they registered their approval and confidence in you.” Sillers interpreted Eastland’s victory over Gartin as white Mississippi’s endorsement of massive resistance to federal interference in southern race relations.[1] The term “massive resistance” denotes the hardline opposition that emerged in the South after the *Brown v. Board of Education* decision. Advocates of massive resistance wanted to protect segregation at all costs, including the abolition of public schools. The Citizens’ Councils formed the more visible exponent of this intransigent movement. Eastland regularly spoke at Council meetings.

Numan Bartley was one of the first scholars who studied massive resistance. He called the leaders of the movement neobourbons, a group of upper-class whites from the Black Belt regions in the South. This reactionary leadership also had support in other rural areas below the Mason-Dixon Line. “Fundamentally, proponents of this doctrine sought to suppress the social and ideological aspects of southern change,” Bartley wrote.[2] More recent studies of massive resistance call for a closer examination of the different elements that made up southern white opposition to desegregation. The authors of these works argue that massive resistance was not a monolith and that much can be learned from studying its grassroots components.[3]

One of the strands in the campaign to resist desegregation were the proponents of practical segregation. Practical segregationists did not differ in their commitment to racial separation from the massive resisters, but they did use a different strategy to achieve their goal. Instead of outright defiance, practical segregationists preferred to soft-pedal the race issue. By luring attention away from Jim Crow, they intended to maintain the status quo and social tranquility, which would hopefully attract business and industry to the South.[4] Practical segregationists did not mind compromising if it served the higher goal of keeping traditional southern race relations intact; massive resisters were much more adamant about that matter. Mississippi circuit judge M. M. McGowan, Council activist and states' rights partisan, for example declared that "compromises are our most deadly enemies."[5]

Most historians place James Eastland in the massive resistance camp. "Eastland was the voice of the neobourbon South, and he epitomized the contradictions, paranoia, and indignant belligerence of the resistance itself," argued Bartley.[6] John Stennis on the other hand embodied the principles of practical segregation.[7] Although these two factions often fought each other over strategy, they were not mutually exclusive; the figureheads of the massive resistance forces were not always as uncompromising as they sounded. Eastland is a clear example. When he delivered a speech at a Citizens' Council rally, he frequently called for outright defiance against the federal government. But as U.S. senator, he was also a master in the politics of compromise. In contrast with the picture scholars have painted of him, Eastland moved between the boundaries of massive resistance and practical segregation. He knew that these two approaches to the defense of segregation actually reinforced each other and he also knew that when the political environment changed, the approach changed with it. James Eastland demonstrated that the rhetoric and ideology of massive resistance could go hand in hand with a pragmatic strategy to ensure the survival of Jim Crow.

The leaders of the national Democratic Party preferred to work with practical segregationists, but they did not want to offend massive resisters either. After the 1952 election, they attempted to accommodate both camps while simultaneously trying to placate the black electorate. This wavering stance only led to growing resentment among southern segregationists and African American voters, both of whom wanted a clear (albeit diametrically opposed) answer to the race question. Although the issue of segregation troubled the electoral politics of the national Republicans less during the

1950s, they also had to engineer an efficient race strategy if the party wanted to expand its southern base in the future.

While Eastland and Gartin were stumping the state during the summer of 1954, a small group of men formed the first Citizens' Council in Indianola, a town located a few miles south of Eastland's farm. The main objective of the Council was the organization of southern whites in opposition to the verdict in *Brown v. Board of Education*. World War II veteran and plantation owner Robert Patterson was one of the key movers in organizing the gathering in Indianola. Circuit Judge Thomas Brady from Brookhaven, Mississippi, inspired Patterson to call for such a meeting. Shortly after the Supreme Court ruled segregation in public education unconstitutional, Brady delivered a speech before the Greenwood chapter of the Sons of the American Revolution. In his address, he labeled May 17 (the day of the *Brown* decision) "Black Monday," a term used earlier by Mississippi congressman John Bell Williams. Brady turned his speech into a book, which soon became the ideological and organizational manual for the Citizens' Councils.

The main theme of the book was the denunciation of the *Brown* ruling as a decision based on false principles and a danger to the Republic. Brady proposed different strategies to uphold the system of segregation; among other things, he suggested the election of Supreme Court judges by the people, the institution of an education program to teach young Americans the truth about communism and the logic behind racial separation, and finally, if all else failed, the shutdown of public schools. In order to effectively mobilize resistance, Brady advocated the organization of southern whites in groups at the state level. These groups were supposed to abide by the law, which meant they should not copy the tactics of the Ku Klux Klan. Instead of night riders engaged in open violence, Brady envisioned a regional network that resisted desegregation through legal means and informed the nation about the dangers of federal interference in (what he considered) state matters. If necessary, this movement could be turned into a political party aimed at the protection of state sovereignty.[8]

By using the Klan as contrast, the leadership of the Citizens' Councils wanted to portray their organization as a lawful, middle-class association. Although he was not a member, Walter Sillers described the people who had joined the Councils as "outstanding, upright white citizens of Mississippi and they have the interest and welfare of the white people at heart." Sillers emphasized these white Mississippians did not mean to harm anybody. They had merely organized themselves to counter "the vicious attacks and forced integration" by civil rights organizations and the federal government.[9] Southern unity was essential in making the Councils successful. "Like the bundle of sticks the father gave to his sons to break, we cannot be broken if we are bound together, united in certain basic fundamental causes," Brady wrote Sillers on the day of the *Brown* decision. "If we operate separately, the Southern States one by one will be destroyed."[10]

The men who heeded Robert Patterson's call exemplified the class structure of the Council movement. Present at the first meeting in Indianola were the town's mayor, a banker, and the city attorney. Together with plantation owner Patterson, these men represented the political and economic establishment of the Delta. The Councils were particularly popular in black majority regions such as the Delta, but the organization soon began to spread across the state and the South. The Citizens' Councils were able to refrain from violence to implement their agenda because leaders and members belonged to the middle and upper classes. As such, they could use economic measures like boycotts and the firing of employees who opposed the racial status quo. In combination with other forms of intimidation, the Councils stifled the quest for civil rights. And although they did not openly advocate violence, their course of action created an atmosphere that encouraged the use of force by segregationists who were less concerned with the rule of law.[11]

The Council leaders emphasized that political involvement was not the primary aim of their organization. In September 1954, State Representative Wilma Sledge declared that "it is not the intent or purpose of the Citizens' Councils to be used as a political machine."[12] The Councils nonetheless claimed credit for the passage of two amendments to the state constitution that bolstered segregation: one amendment authorized the legislature to abolish the public school system, the other raised voter qualifications. Moreover, the movement had strong political allies, including Walter Sillers and James Eastland.

Since the founding of the first Citizens' Council, Eastland delivered speeches at numerous Council gatherings across the South. On August 16, 1955, he addressed the Mississippi Association of Citizens' Councils, lauding its members for "spear-heading the hard core of resistance to the forces and influences bent upon the destruction of our Southern institutions, traditions, and culture." Eastland then discussed developments across the nation that had occurred after the passage of *Brown*. The picture the senator painted was not rosy for supporters of segregation. "The social life in high schools has been completely disrupted," Eastland explained. But "the greatest tragedy" was the "lowering of educational standards. The intelligence level of the White child must be geared to what the Negro can absorb." Eastland considered it necessary to muster recruits outside the South in the struggle to maintain "the identity and integrity of the White race" against what he deemed a communist-inspired political Court and subversive organizations. He was hopeful that whites in other parts of the country would eventually rally around the southern cause. His office had already distributed 250,000 transcripts of "The Supreme Court's 'Modern Scientific Authorities' in the Segregation Cases" speech, and requests for more copies kept coming in, even from the West Coast. Eastland predicted that the national tide would eventually turn in favor of the white South, but he also stressed the importance of regional unity and organization. The senator ended his speech with one of his trademark statements: "Resistance to tyranny is obedience to God."[13] Despite the fervor he put in his speeches, Senator Eastland never joined the Citizens' Council, and he advised his staff workers against becoming a member if they aspired to a career at the federal level. "I wouldn't join that thing if I were you," Eastland once told his legislative assistant Frank Barber. "You might be up for a federal appointment sometime."[14]

Eastland, Sillers, and the Citizens' Councils represented the massive resistance movement in Mississippi. Although they did not propose outright violence, the proponents of massive resistance went far in their defense of segregation, arguing that the destruction of the public school system was a real possibility. Practical segregationists opposed the radical strategies of the massive resistance forces. In general, they were just as committed to the maintenance of Jim Crow as their more extremist counterparts, but they chose moderation over zealotry to fight desegregation. James P. Coleman was one of these practical segregationists. In 1955, he ran against Paul B. Johnson Jr. in the race for governor. Coleman was from the Hill town of Ackerman and he concentrated his campaign during the first primary in this part of the state. Thanks to his association with former governor Hugh White, he also received considerable support from the Delta, and the law and order image he had built up as attorney general made him particularly popular on the coast, where he had focused his crime-fighting activities. Coleman never denied he was a loyal Democrat, but he also did not forget to mention his successful defense of Jim Crow laws and the work he did for the Mississippi delegation at the 1952 national convention. Johnson's attempts to ridicule Coleman as "Constable Coleman" and "Dick Tracy Coleman" failed miserably, and the departure from his neopopulist principles also backfired. Johnson tried to brand his opponent as a pawn of left-wingers and labor and as soft on segregation, but Coleman could counter these accusations by pointing at his past experience as attorney general. Eastland again supported Paul Johnson, while John Stennis backed his friend James Coleman. The latter won the second primary with almost 56 percent of the vote.[15] Carroll Gartin was reelected as lieutenant governor.

James Eastland and his allies had already challenged Coleman's approach to segregation before his inauguration. At the end of 1955, Eastland, John Bell Williams, and Thomas Brady urged the state legislature to adopt a resolution of interposition. Following John Calhoun's theory of nullification, the advocates of interposition argued that the states had the right to reject decrees coming from the Supreme Court which they deemed dangerous and unconstitutional.[16]

Around the same time Eastland introduced his philosophy of interposition, the senator was involved in the formation of a region-wide association to protect segregation. Setting up such a coordinating group had been on Eastland's wish list for a long time; at various segregationist gatherings he had called for the establishment of a regional commission promoting the southern cause. On October 29, 1955, the Eastland office issued a press release calling for the formation of an organization aimed at combating "the rising crescendo of vicious propaganda against the South and its institutions, much of it inspired by Communist front and race minded groups."[17] Two months later, a group of high-profile segregationists convened in the Peabody Hotel in Memphis and officially founded the Federation for Constitutional Government (FCG). Its goal was to fuse the neobourbon leadership in the South with white supremacy groups like the Citizens' Council, which were rapidly growing. The Federation was supposed to be the central institution in a broad states' rights movement. The FCG would coordinate massive resistance in the South and spread this message to the North.[18] Eastland's ideas about southern unity and the universal nature of white racism were clearly incorporated in the agenda of the FCG.

Preparations for the establishment of the Federation had been underway since January 1955, under the supervision of New Orleans industrialist and states' righter John U. Barr. The charter of incorporation of the FCG did not mention the defense of segregation. Instead, the organization was described as an instrument to teach Americans their civic duties and liberties and to warn them about the dangers of socialism and communism. In order to protect and promote the "Democratic" and "American Way of Life," the founders of the FCG wanted to acquire different media outlets (including newspapers and television stations), institute chairs and departments at universities to educate students about their responsibilities as citizens, conduct research on the preservation of state sovereignty, and cooperate with religious organizations that were strongly opposed to left-wing ideology. Article I.7 of the charter declared that the distribution of political propaganda or attempts to influence legislation and campaigns for public office should not be the primary aim of the Federation.[19]

Judging from the founding text of the FCG, the organization appeared to be a group primarily concerned with the conservation of the basic tenets of classic republicanism. One look at the names on the Federation's advisory board and executive committee reveals, however, that the perpetuation of constitutional government was not the true objective of the association. Champions of segregation such as Leander Perez of Louisiana, Walter Sillers of Mississippi, and Gessner McCorvey of Alabama were all affiliated with the FCG. Federation supporters primarily represented the neobourbon factions in the various southern states. Moderate and practical segregationists like James Coleman and Jim Folsom were conspicuously absent.[20]

James Eastland articulated the fusion of segregation, laissez-faire capitalism, and limited government interference that marked the FCG in a speech handed out at the meeting in the Peabody Hotel.[21] He called the mission of the Federation a crusade to restore Americanism and return government to the people. Eastland added that "our organization will carry on its banner the slogan of free enterprise and we will fight those organizations who attempt with much success to socialize industry, and the great medical profession of this country." He thought that this economic component would resonate in the North and the West. Although the Mississippi senator wanted to portray the FCG as a truly national organization, he specifically addressed his southern followers in the last part of the speech: "Generations of Southerners yet unborn will cherish our memory because they will realize that the fight we now wage, will have preserved for them their untainted racial heritage, their culture, and the institutions of the Anglo-Saxon race." These words left little doubt about the true intentions of the Federation. Moreover, by December 1955 the FCG had abandoned its nonpolitical stance. The purposes of the group now included the promotion of politicians who subscribed to the Federation's objectives and resistance to leftist candidates who ran for public office, including the presidency and vice presidency.[22]

After Eastland announced in October that he encouraged the formation of a regional council to protect segregation and state sovereignty, letters from the South and other parts of the country started to pour into the senator's office. T. R. Waring, the editor of the *Charleston News and Courier* in South Carolina, supported the initiative, and so did Lee Guice, a lawyer from Biloxi, Mississippi. "Yesterday I read the statement you issued on Saturday, calling for a Southern Commission to combat the northern propaganda which has now reached a crescendo in its efforts to injure the south," Guice wrote Eastland. He approved of this plan and he hoped all southern states would adopt it.[23]

Some of Eastland's constituents feared the opposition of the FCG to organized labor, however. C. E. Browning of Starkville was a member of the local Citizens' Council and active in the Order of Railroad Telegraphers. "I feel that it would be a grave mistake for the citizens council to go to fighting labor unions, we have all we can do to fight for segregation and to maintain segregation without taking on another issue on the side," Browning argued. Another union member from Long Beach, Mississippi, requested the senator stop his attacks on the CIO. He was not a supporter of the CIO, but he thought Eastland's anti-labor stance would hurt the fight for the maintenance of segregation and result in the loss of support from the white working class in the South. Eastland could only win their trust if he directed his criticism of organized labor at the union leadership: "if you will refrain from attacking the CIO, as an organization, and attack ONLY some of their LEADERS, making it PLAIN EVERY TIME that their actions are against the interests of the members, you will gain much support from the average union man." Eastland tried to assure the letter writer, R. K. Daniel, that he did not mean to denounce common laborers. "I have always been a friend of organized labor and will be the same in the future, but I will also oppose the political and social activities of the labor leaders in attempting to integrate and destroy the white race," Eastland replied. "The issue is much bigger and broader than Mississippi."[24]

But the men who were present at the FCG meeting in Memphis were not known for their support of union members or the working class in general; they were plantation owners, business leaders, and oilmen.[25] The Federation for Constitutional Government did not only want to preserve the Jim Crow South, but also the economic status quo in the region. Eastland intended the FCG to be a grassroots movement, a "people's organization" free from the influence of "fawning politicians who cater to organized racial groups."[26] That idea never materialized, however. The Federation was a collective of leaders, a reflection of the segregationist establishment in the South. Although the FCG was supposed to be a nonpolitical entity, its strategy and outlook closely resembled the Dixiecrat Party, whose standard-bearers (Strom Thurmond and Fielding Wright) were Federation members.

The FCG never took off. Eastland's brainchild quietly died a slow death because of lack of funding and the success of the Citizens' Councils, which formed their own national organization less than four months after the founding of the Federation for Constitutional Government. Council members, often provincial in outlook and wary of the professional politicians that dominated the FCG, preferred to focus on fighting for segregation at the local level. Moreover, some of them did not subscribe to the broad agenda of the Federation, which combined the defense of Jim Crow with assaults on organized labor and on government activism. Average Council members simply wanted to maintain racial customs in their own town and often recoiled from "Eastland's epic fantasies," Bartley stated.[27] The rapid eclipse of the Federation did not diminish its importance, however. The founding of the FCG was a clear signal that a significant segment of the southern political elite was ready to commit itself to massive resistance.[28]

Governor Coleman's brand of practical segregation often provoked the ire of the Citizens' Council crowd. "Ever since the second primary the governor had been making statements designed to soft-pedal the race issue and to calm the people's fears about immediate integration, a policy at direct variance with that of the Citizens' Councils," Hodding Carter III wrote.[29] Instead of trying to mobilize whites in a united front through extremist rhetoric and actions, the practical segregationists chose realism and self-restraint to defend southern apartheid. By following such a pragmatic course, they hoped to draw attention away from southern racism, limit federal interference, and lure businesses and industry to the region.

Coleman's reputation as *realpolitiker* had surfaced in the months before his inauguration. At a meeting of the state's Legal Education Advisory Committee (LEAC) in December 1955, the governor-elect called Eastland's interposition resolution "legal poppycock." Coleman argued that segregation could not be protected by defying the federal government and that nullification would only be successful if Mississippi seceded from the Union, which was not a realistic option. "I don't have one iota of fear that we will not have segregation continued in this state," Coleman said, and he proposed that the legislature pass seven stringent measures to put even more safeguards around the system of Jim Crow.

In addition to Coleman's suggestions (which included the repeal of the compulsory school attendance law), state senator and Council supporter Earl Evans submitted a plan to form a state-sponsored committee to investigate subversive activities in Mississippi. Like Eastland, Coleman wanted to initiate a nationwide propaganda offensive to teach Americans about segregation. "The rest of the nation ought to know that we in Mississippi don't kill and fry Negroes and eat them for breakfast," he said. "As a matter of record, 252 of the 272 Negroes killed in Mississippi last year were killed by other Negroes." The Mississippi State Sovereignty Commission, the successor to LEAC, would fulfill this public relations function during the Coleman administration.[30]

On January 17, 1956, James Coleman was inaugurated as governor of Mississippi. In his inaugural speech, Coleman reiterated that he did not have "the slightest fear that four years hence when my successor stands on this same spot to assume his official oath, the separation of the races in Mississippi will be left intact and will still be in full force and effect in exactly the same manner and form as we know it today." Coleman promised he would defend "Mississippi's way of life," but he also cautioned against radical measures to prevent desegregation. Following the course of the "amateur or the hothead" would only lead to detrimental results; according to Coleman, the citizens of Mississippi "must keep cool heads and calm judgment," particularly now that segregation was under direct assault from different directions. The state legislature subsequently passed most of the legislation Coleman had proposed at the LEAC meeting and also enacted an interposition resolution, which was praised by Lieutenant Governor Gartin and signed into law by the new governor.[31]

Later that year, the State Sovereignty Commission was created as a counter agency to the NAACP and to protect states' rights against federal encroachment. Although the Sovereignty Commission later gained the reputation as the southern version of the KGB, during Coleman's tenure it was primarily a propaganda organization.[32] The Citizens' Councils and other exponents of massive resistance seemed to have little to complain about Coleman's stand on the race question during the first months of his governorship, but that would soon change as the state and the nation geared for the 1956 presidential campaign.

By the time the Mississippi State Sovereignty Commission came into being, James Eastland already occupied the chair of the influential Senate Judiciary Committee. During the preceding two years, his leverage on the committee had steadily grown. The death of more senior committee members was one reason for Eastland's rise to power. When Eastland thought about retiring from national politics in 1953, Pat McCarran, the former chair of the Judiciary Committee, told his friend from Mississippi that he should continue his career. "You're a young man, and I'm an old man; you're going to be chairman of the committee," McCarran predicted.[33] On September 28, 1954, little over a month after Eastland beat Gartin in the Democratic primary, McCarran died. When the Senate eulogized him on November 8, eighteen Republican senators, including Joseph McCarthy, paid tribute to their deceased colleague. Only eleven Democrats, mostly from the South, followed their example.[34] The Democrats regained control of the Senate after the 1954 elections and Senator Harley Kilgore of West Virginia became the new chair of the Judiciary Committee. James Eastland succeeded McCarran as chairman of the Internal Security Subcommittee.

William Rusher, who served as special counsel to the Internal Security Subcommittee for a year, described Eastland's conduct as chairman of SISS and the bipartisan harmony that characterized the subcommittee, a "tradition which had been handed down from the date of its founding." James Eastland got along extremely well with Republican William Jenner of Indiana, the ranking member of the committee. Party labels seemed to be of little consequence in the hiring of staff. Rusher was from Chicago and no supporter of the segregationist system in the South. He nonetheless did not doubt communists and fellow travelers used the civil rights issue to depict Eastland as the embodiment of evil, while other southern senators with similar racist views escaped the same kind of scathing criticism. "The Communists would have attacked *any* chairman of the hated Subcommittee with any stick that came at hand," Rusher claimed. "Certainly there was nothing very offensive about Eastland personally."[35]

Rusher depicted the Mississippi senator as a taciturn and gruff man, whose stare even unnerved his own staff. Eastland was constantly smoking cigars and did not seem to care where the ashes fell. A permanent circle of stale cigar ashes ringed the swivel chair in his office. Although Eastland was a well-known member of the southern bloc in the Senate, Rusher did not consider him a leading character of the group. Most of the time, the Mississippi senator followed the instructions or advice coming from his colleagues, in particular Lyndon Baines Johnson. "As an investigator of domestic Communism Eastland must be relegated distinctly to the middle rank," Rusher assessed. He was "not nearly so competent or venturesome as his predecessor, Senator Pat McCarran."[36] McCarran, the architect of the Internal Security Subcommittee, served as an example for the new chairman.

While Eastland continued the hardline approach of his predecessor as head of SISS, outspoken liberal Harley Kilgore took control of the entire Judiciary Committee. One of the first issues that came before Kilgore's committee was the nomination of John Marshall Harlan to the Supreme Court. Eastland initially objected to Harlan's appointment because of the judge's position on desegregation, but during the hearings the Mississippi senator primarily focused on the foreign policy views of the nominee. Eastland feared that Harlan supported a "one-world" agenda and would place United Nations charters over domestic law. Eastland told a journalist from the *Clarion-Ledger* that Harlan's position on segregation was not the main reason to block his nomination. "I'm sure that John Marshall Harlan is a good judge and a honorable man," he said. "But a vote to seat Judge Harlan is a vote to compromise the sovereignty of this country—and that I will not do."[37]

Even if Harlan joined the Supreme Court and supported its decision on desegregation, Eastland thought the decree would not have much influence. He argued that as long as southern governors employed their police power to promote "peace and good order" and "insure public health" in separated schools, the race question could be avoided, and the schools would not violate the Supreme Court decree. The *Clarion-Ledger* reporter nonetheless did not forget to mention that the NAACP fully endorsed Harlan.[38] Eastland said his opposition to the nomination was not based on the judge's views of Jim Crow laws, but the issue of segregation, the protection of state and national sovereignty, and the threat of foreign control were closely intertwined. Despite Eastland's misgivings, the Senate confirmed Harlan by a vote of 71–11.

Harley Kilgore's tenure as chair of the Judiciary Committee was primarily characterized by efforts to rewrite the antitrust laws of the United States. One of his last statements as chairman concerned civil rights, however. On February 6, 1956, a black student named Autherine Lucy met a hostile mob that pelted her with rotten eggs during her first week of class at the University of Alabama. The university decided it could not guarantee Lucy's safety and expelled her. Kilgore was enraged. He contacted Attorney General Herbert Brownell and requested a federal investigation into the matter. In an official statement, Kilgore declared: "if the government stands by and permits individuals to take the law into their own hands it can only lead to national disrespect for the basic concepts of our nation." The press release was a clear demonstration of Kilgore's stand on civil rights, but he did not succeed in putting the issue high on the agenda of his committee. On February 28, after a chairmanship of only one year, Kilgore died of a cerebral hemorrhage.[39] His successor would have less liberal views on racial equality.

A few days after Kilgore's death, the Senate Democratic Steering Committee met in a room of the U.S. Capitol to discuss who would be the new chairman of the Judiciary Committee. Majority Leader Lyndon Baines Johnson normally chaired the meetings of the steering committee, but he was in Texas that day. He had urged the committee to choose a successor to Kilgore, but to wait until his return to fill a vacancy on Appropriations. Johnson picked the right time to leave Washington, because the steering committee faced a controversial nomination: based on seniority, James Eastland was next in line for the chairmanship. Yet the members of the steering committee also realized that his appointment might cause considerable resentment among liberal Democrats in the Senate, in the progressive wing of the Democratic Party, and with important blocs of voters. Surprisingly, Senator Dennis Chavez of New Mexico eventually made the motion to give Eastland the chairmanship. Chavez had been elected to the Senate in 1936 as the first Hispanic to serve in that body. He was a strong New Dealer and supported Roosevelt's ill-fated Supreme Court reform plan. On top of that, Chavez sponsored the creation of a permanent FEPC, for which he fought a long and hard battle in the Senate. Because of the opposition coming from Eastland and other southern Democrats, that legislation did not pass.

Chavez told the other members of the steering committee it was obvious he did not always agree with Eastland's views, but that his colleague from Mississippi was entitled to the chairmanship because of seniority. Senator John Pastore of Rhode Island, a liberal who had opposed the McCarran-Walter Immigration Act of 1952, agreed with Chavez and called the seniority rule "the only safe rule." He understood that Eastland's nomination was politically explosive, however. "Some people feel that statements about the Supreme Court, its decisions, and other statements made by Senator Eastland are harmful to our country," Pastore said. Senators Lehman and Morse—two liberal Democrats who were not on the steering committee—were particularly opposed to Eastland becoming chairman of Judiciary. Pastore asked Senator Earle Clements of Kentucky if he had discussed the matter with them. Clements thought that the nomination of a new chair for Judiciary should not fester on too long; if Lehman and Morse could not accept Eastland now, they would not do so in the future. Moreover, he thought Eastland would be forced to tone down his rhetoric once he became chair. The Judiciary Committee was an important standing committee and its chairman was supposed to act in a responsible and dignified manner. Pastore hoped Lehman and Morse could be persuaded to give up their protest. "If this selection of Senator Eastland as Chairman of the Judiciary can be done without breaking our party wide open, it is my judgment that we should so proceed," he stated.[40]

The steering committee adopted the Chavez motion without objection, and Senator Clements declared that the committee had followed the Senate rule of seniority. Liberal organizations and civil rights activists were incredulous about the decision. Judiciary rules on legislation relating to civil rights, federal courts and judges, and constitutional amendments, and its chairman sets the agenda. How could the steering committee place one of the fiercest opponents of racial equality in a position were he was able to do the most damage? When Eastland's nomination came up for a vote on the Senate floor, Lehman and Morse openly voiced their opposition but did not call for a roll call vote. Eastland later said that this was Lyndon Johnson's "handiwork," and that he had the majority leader's backing "all the way."[41] Other liberal senators apparently also tried to convince Wayne Morse not to take a stand against Eastland. "Eastland's friends will retaliate against you by cutting appropriations for public works," they told him. Hubert Humphrey warned the Oregon senator that he put his reelection in the balance. Morse nevertheless made the speech, but he did not attack

Eastland personally. Democrats on the floor afterward commended him for keeping his rhetoric at a "high impersonal plane." At the end of the nomination debate, Eastland emerged from the cloakroom and slid into a chair next to Morse.[42]

After the vote, NAACP spokesman Clarence Mitchell strongly denounced the nomination. "The Senate of the United States has just voted to put an accessory to murder and treason in its most powerful judicial position," he declared. Senators were "looking the other way when a mad dog is loose in the streets of justice."[43] But Eastland's friends and supporters in Mississippi (and across the South) congratulated the senator on his appointment. Judge Talbot from Clarksdale was one of them. "I have known for many years that you are held in high esteem by your fellow-members of the Senate—both Democratic and Republican," Talbot wrote. "No doubt that esteem carried more weight than the NAACP represented by Senator Lehman from New York." Eastland thanked Talbot for his letter as he looked ahead to the many responsibilities of his new post. "This job is going to present a lot of headaches," he responded, "but I will do the very best I can with it."[44]

Majority Leader Johnson and the members of the steering committee all argued they had simply followed the seniority rule with the Eastland appointment, and that they had little choice in deviating from this policy. Senator Clements even stated that "up to this date, no better system than the seniority rule had been offered."[45] A year later, however, Lyndon Johnson took a different approach when Senator Estes Kefauver requested a seat on the Foreign Relations Committee based on his seniority. Ever since his 1948 election to the Senate, Kefauver had tried to become a member of the committee. When Senator Walter George of Georgia retired at the end of 1956, Kefauver thought he finally had a real chance to gain the coveted seat. Disillusionment soon set in, though. The steering committee decided to give the position to John Fitzgerald Kennedy, a young senator from Massachusetts who was elected to the Senate in 1952.

Kefauver was angry about the procedures followed by the steering committee. Why was he rebuffed in favor of somebody with four years less experience in the Senate? Kefauver first wanted to insert a statement about the matter in the *Congressional Record*, but eventually decided to write a letter to Lyndon Johnson. "I had four years seniority over Senator Kennedy and this action indicates that the Seniority Rule may or may not be applied according to personal or other considerations," he protested. "I have tried, Lyndon, to cooperate with you and be helpful to you. . . . Notwithstanding all of this, I have been turned aside on every request for Committees that I have made since you became the Democratic leader."[46]

Johnson replied that in addition to seniority, the steering committee took other factors into account, such as "geography, political philosophy, the current status of a member desiring a change, and sometimes the estimate of a man's own colleagues toward him." The vote to seat Kennedy instead of Kefauver was unanimous, LBJ explained. Moreover, it was the first time "that it was possible to accommodate Jack Kennedy with a Committee of his own choice." The majority leader reminded Kefauver that he had "already achieved a commanding position on two major Committees" and that Foreign Relations had reached its quota of southerners, with three of its members coming from below the Mason-Dixon Line.[47] According to political reporter Charles Fontenay, the nomination was decided during a meeting of party leaders at the LBJ Ranch in Texas. Among the people present was James Eastland, who had an intense dislike for Kefauver.[48] The Tennessee senator was a maverick who often refused to fall in line with the Southern Caucus, especially in the field of civil rights.

Besides personal animosity, presidential politics also played a role. Both Lyndon Johnson and John Kennedy were eyeing the 1960 nomination for president, and they were not likely to give a formidable opponent like Kefauver a position on Foreign Relations, a prestigious committee that often served as a platform for senators with presidential aspirations. In his letter to Johnson, Kefauver strongly denied he was going to run for the presidency again in 1960, but the Democratic leadership obviously did not want to take any bets. Kefauver was never part of the Senate establishment, and he had built up a reputation as a crusader against the party hierarchy.[49]

The fact that Kennedy was nominated to Foreign Relations instead of Kefauver demonstrates that seniority was not always the overriding factor in committee assignments, despite the claim by the steering committee that it had to follow the seniority rule when Eastland's nomination came up. In addition to the reasons named above, sectional appeasement also played a role. In contrast with Kefauver, James Eastland had been a loyal member of the southern bloc in the Senate, led by Richard Russell.[50] Denying Eastland the chairmanship of Judiciary might upset the powerful group of Democratic senators from the

South, and put even more strain on the already troubled relationship between the national Democratic Party and the Democratic Party in Mississippi. Finally, Johnson seemed to get along better with Eastland than Kefauver. When Johnson's candidacy for leader of the Senate Democrats came up at the end of 1952, John Stennis sent Eastland a letter of recommendation, describing LBJ as "trustworthy in every way . . . the most able and all-around man for our Floor Leader—and very definitely the best bet for us in our peculiar situation." Although Stennis realized Eastland already knew the Texas senator "quite well," he wanted to make sure Johnson had his support. Eastland needed just six words for his response: "I am strong for Lyndon Johnson."[51] The Kefauver episode thus indicates that besides seniority, many other factors—including party standing, presidential aspirations, political considerations, and personal friendships—could in fact be used to determine committee chairmanships.

Most southern Democrats in the Senate followed a similar career path pattern: get elected at a relatively early age, become a member of attractive committees, slowly build up seniority, and eventually obtain a committee chairmanship. Reelection was often not a big problem for southern Democrats. Voters in the South saw their representatives on Capitol Hill as long-term investments, whose efficiency would only increase as the years rolled on. Once these politicians attained a senior position in the House or the Senate, they had the power to tend to their districts or states in an even more effective way. Simultaneously, their positions of power dissuaded challengers in the Democratic primaries or Republicans in the general elections from running against the incumbent Democrats. Besides being patient and in good health, southern senators also had to be willing to "go along" in order to advance to a leadership position.[52]

Eastland followed these rules; Kefauver often did not. While the senator from Tennessee gained the reputation as an outsider, distrusted by his fellow southerners in the Senate, Eastland dutifully attended the meetings of the Southern Caucus, took his cues from more experienced members, and befriended powerful Democrats like Lyndon Johnson. As a result, Eastland received his preferred committee assignments without much trouble—with liberals such as Chavez and Pastore even arguing on his behalf. Once he was chairman, Eastland could set the agenda on issues that mattered to him and his constituents without much interference from the elected party leadership. At the same time, he respected the turf of his committee members, particularly in relation to federal appointments at the state level. This system of *quid pro quo* earned him the esteem of the other senators on Judiciary and gave him the authority to effectively deal with subjects he deemed important. Southern moderates such as Lyndon Johnson in the Senate and Sam Rayburn in the House could attain leadership roles within the party, while conservatives like Eastland were in a position to reap the benefits of their chairmanships without strict adherence to party discipline.[53]

The division between moderate and conservative southern Democrats surfaced clearly on March 12, 1956, when Walter George delivered the Declaration of Constitutional Principles in the chamber of the Senate. The signers of this text, better known as the Southern Manifesto, pledged themselves "to use all lawful means to bring about a reversal" of the *Brown* decision.[54] The Manifesto signaled the entry of massive resistance at the level of national politics. The strategies and goals embodied in the document had a decisively neobourbon character, and its introduction forced moderate southern politicians to endorse its basic premises even if they did not agree with them.[55]

As the massive resistance movement reached its height, Democrats from the South did not want to appear weak on segregation. New Dealer Lister Hill of Alabama, confronted with a primary challenge from a states' rights ideologue, apparently signed the Manifesto without reading it. But there were divisions in the southern ranks. The final text was a compromise between the massive resisters and the practical segregationists, and some of the southern members of Congress did not sign it. In the Senate, Kefauver and Al Gore Sr. of Tennessee and Johnson of Texas did not sign the document. As a matter of fact, the authors of the Manifesto did not even ask LBJ to endorse it. John Stennis, who was a member of the drafting committee, explained in an interview that they realized Johnson had a different responsibility as majority leader and possible presidential candidate. Johnson himself wanted to keep the confidence of his southern brethren, but at the same time he did not want sectionalism to tear the Democratic Party asunder, especially in an election year. He thus downplayed the Manifesto as a piece for home consumption and an attempt to help Walter George, whose reelection was in jeopardy.[56]

Most of the other senators from the former Confederacy were pragmatic enough to understand LBJ could not appear too southern. "The Southern dons of the Senate, the conservative men with seniority and power . . . regarded him with pride as their boy," Johnson's aide Booth Mooney said. "The southerners did not always agree with their Leader, but they wanted him to do well, and when it was necessary, were usually willing to stretch their own convictions to support him."[57]

Senator Eastland obviously did not refrain from signing the Manifesto, and he received praise from his constituents for doing so. In response to congratulations sent by three attorneys from Indianola, Eastland wrote: "I thought the Manifesto was a splendid showing of unity on the part of the Southern group in Congress and I believe that it will have a profound effect on the thinking of the people in the North. We must move on the offense."[58]

But while Eastland commended the southerners on Capitol Hill for their united action and started plotting yet another campaign up North, the governor of his own state urged for moderation. James Coleman continued his course of practical segregation and took a critical stand against massive resistance tactics, including the Southern Manifesto. "The greatest need of our time is for cool, clear thinking on racial problems," he said again on March 24, 1956. "This is no time to let hotheads make us lose our perspective and go beyond the point of no return."[59] The battle lines were clearly drawn in Mississippi, with the Democratic State Convention only a few months away.

Since the convention of 1952, the leadership of the national Democratic Party had taken small steps to regain the trust of its southern wing. In the fall of 1954, an advisory committee of the DNC met in New Orleans to discuss the loyalty oath. In 1952, the oath had almost resulted in another walkout of southern delegations. These delegates claimed the oath violated states' rights and was therefore unacceptable. At the meeting in New Orleans, Hubert Humphrey (who had supported the loyalty pledge in 1952) and Governor John Battle of Virginia (who had opposed it) joined with other members on a special committee to work out an agreement. Four southern states—Florida, Tennessee, Texas, and Virginia—went for Eisenhower in 1952, and the Democrats did not want to let that happen again in 1956. In order to pacify southern Democrats, the advisory committee decided not to force anyone to sign a pledge or take an oath of loyalty at upcoming conventions. Parting DNC chairman Stephen Mitchell attempted to limit questions of loyalty on an individual basis; he wanted to prevent Democratic Eisenhower supporters such as Governor Shivers of Texas from coming to the convention as Democrats and then campaigning for the Republican candidate in the general election. But even this proposal failed. Paul Butler, the new chairman of the Democratic National Committee, simply expressed the hope that the bolters of 1952 stayed loyal to the Democratic ticket in 1956.[60]

In Mississippi, the Eisenhower and Stevenson camps of the state Democratic Party tried to rediscover common ground at a dinner party in February 1955. Leaders of the DNC, Governor Hugh White, and Dixiecrat standard-bearer Fielding Wright were all present at the dinner. A newspaper reporting on the gathering noted that the strong support for Eisenhower in Mississippi during the 1952 campaign had rekindled the Democratic leadership's interest in the South. "No longer can they turn their backs on Southern problems and expect blind obedience and support," the paper announced. The fact that the national party again tried to woo Mississippi should be interpreted as "a promising situation, even if we do cluck our tongues and try to forget our grievances against the national Democrats in previous years."[61]

During the months preceding the Democratic State Convention in Mississippi, the Citizens' Council movement and Coleman's troops tried to gain the upper hand in organizing the delegation to Chicago, where the national convention took place. In May, the executive committee of the Councils distributed a resolution based on massive resistance philosophy to the county branches of the Democratic Party in Mississippi. The executive committee urged the local Democratic organizations to consider the resolution at their caucuses. If adopted, the Mississippi delegation was bound to vote only for candidates who acknowledged the right of interposition. In addition, the resolution asked to reconvene the state convention after the national convention to evaluate its results. Governor Coleman did not have problems with a declaration stating the principles of Mississippi, but he opposed a resolution that limited the freedom of the delegates. Thomas Tubb, chairman of the Democratic State Executive Committee, chose Coleman's side and declared that the Citizens' Councils were "endangering the fight for segregation" by getting politically involved. In the end, the governor emerged victorious, with only ten county groups adopting the resolution.[62]

James Eastland went on a business trip to Mississippi a few days before the state convention. Reporters who wanted to know the senator's preference for a Democratic presidential nominee greeted him at the Jackson airport. Eastland was cautious in his remarks. He thought Eisenhower's chances for victory had diminished since 1952, but he did not make any straightforward comments about who would be his opponent. "My attitude is to wait and see," Eastland said. "I don't know what's going to happen." Neither did he want to reveal his thoughts on reconvening the state convention after Chicago. Eastland did not attend the state convention, because he had to be in Washington to chair his committee.[63]

Before the opening of the convention, Coleman and his supporters had gathered in the executive mansion to discuss strategy, while their opponents organized a meeting in the Edwards Hotel. On the day of the state Democratic gathering, the governor again defeated the massive resisters. Although the assembly held open the possibility to reconvene, the delegates voted down a motion to set a fixed date. Walter Sillers and State Attorney General Joe Patterson supported the idea of a set date, but Coleman did not give in to their demands. If the state Democratic Party adopted such a motion, northern Democrats would undoubtedly demand "that Mississippi be thrown out of the national convention," the governor said. He reached a compromise with the opposition on resolutions concerning segregation and states' rights, but the delegation to Chicago was uninstructed, which was a victory for the moderates. Coleman promised that "if we don't get the treatment we deserve in Chicago, I'll be the first to call a 'recess' convention."[64]

Witnessing the proceedings on the floor, an editor of the *Clarion-Ledger* called the governor an "expert on power politics" and compared the conference with a Broadway show, containing "much of the suspense of a mystery thriller."[65] As a master politician, James Coleman already had a strategy prepared before the state convention assembled. He outlined his plans in early July to editor Frederick Sullens of the *Jackson Daily News*. In direct opposition to massive resistance tactics, Coleman wrote Sullens that it was in the best interest of Mississippi to keep calm. Radical standpoints only furnished opponents of segregation with fodder to attack the state delegation at the Democratic National Convention. "I know we have many strong friends in the North, who really wish to help us," Coleman told Sullens. "They cannot do it, however, if we say or do things which lay them victims to those who hate us and in any possible way render their position untenable as they go about trying to help us."[66]

The governor did not consider it necessary to prepare a detailed plan for the proceedings in Chicago; like Eastland, he proposed a wait-and-see attitude and formed responses to events as they occurred. Delegates had the opportunity to express their views fully. "I do not think I could dictate to men like Jim Eastland, who will be on the delegation, even if I wanted to do so," Coleman observed. Instead of following rigid massive resistance tactics, tactics based on a bound delegation, uncompromising principles, and a fixed date for a recess convention, Coleman desired a strategy that gave as much leeway to the delegates as possible, while taking their different viewpoints into account. "This is just strategy, but the right strategy made Chancellorsville a great victory, and the wrong strategy made Vicksburg a paralyzing defeat," Coleman explained to Sullens, using the framework of the Civil War to clarify his point.[67]

Coleman was a member of the national party's platform committee, which had to work out a civil rights plank acceptable to both the North and the South. The Mississippi governor believed this job could be accomplished, but presidential candidate and frontrunner Adlai Stevenson (who had Coleman's support) complicated things when he called for unequivocal acceptance of the Supreme Court decision in *Brown v. Board of Education*. Coleman responded to Stevenson's statement in usual fashion. "I feel right now is the time for all of us who want harmony in the Democratic party to stay quiet," he said on August 8, almost a week before the opening of the national convention. "What the platform contains is far more serious than what any candidate says. The South believes that the remainder of the country will give us more consideration and fair treatment than it has in the past." According to Coleman, Stevenson still stood out among the other candidates as "the best friend of the South."[68]

Up until the national convention, James Eastland kept quiet about his preference for a Democratic nominee. At a Citizens' Council rally, he proclaimed that his endorsement would be "a kiss of death" for the candidate he preferred, because of his stand on segregation.[69] Even after Stevenson's statements on *Brown*, Eastland did not attack the former Illinois governor, perhaps because the other candidates for the nomination—Estes Kefauver and Governor Averell Harriman of New York—were even more distasteful to him. At the Neshoba County Fair, Senator Eastland instead talked about the importance of selecting a suitable politician for the vice presidency. As president of the Senate, the vice president administered the rules of the upper chamber, he said. It was therefore critical somebody friendly to the South occupied this post. Eastland also stressed "the tremendous importance" of keeping southern control over Congress. With the White House and the

Supreme Court in the hands of the opposition, he argued, southern leadership in the House and the Senate was the only safeguard against increased federal interference. "Eastland's statements were interpreted by some as a bid for continued party solidarity as a protection for the seats of the southern Democrats in Congress," a journalist observed.[70]

Eastland's political style had slowly changed since his entry on the national political scene in 1941. Race remained the underlying motive, but Eastland managed to couch this motive in language that emphasized anticommunism and constitutional government. He hoped that a turn to colorblind rhetoric would attract a national audience to his agenda.[71] The speech at the Neshoba County Fair demonstrated that Eastland also took a more cautious approach to Democratic Party politics. While Jackson attorney and gubernatorial candidate Ross Barnett railed against Stevenson and criticized James Coleman for not furnishing the state delegation with "positive, forcible, straightforward leadership," Eastland talked about the importance of southern Democratic unity and the deleterious effects of foreign aid on the American farmer.[72]

Perhaps a letter from W. C. Neill influenced the senator's newfound moderate tone. Neill, the vice president of the Leflore Bank and Trust Company in Greenwood, wrote Eastland and Coleman shortly after the latter had called the idea of interposition complete nonsense. "Since I have known both of you boys since your salad days, and since I have a reasonable amount of affection for both of you, and each of you," Neill wrote, "it gripes the Hell out of me to have you busting out in the newspapers with 'nullification' and 'legal poppycock' in connection with *THE* matter that should be handled and talked about in the most judicious, careful, cautious and temperate manner." The Greenwood banker did not give "a damn" about what Eastland and Coleman thought about each other personally, but he deemed it extremely unwise to divide over the protection of segregation. "The Russians must be rejoicing on account of your unwitting remarks," Neill warned, "what they want is a split." Contemplation and unity, not internal schisms, was what the white South needed to effectively defend its social system.[73]

Although Eastland refrained from publicly discussing his choice for a Democratic presidential candidate, he had already made up his mind by the time of the Neshoba County Fair. Lyndon Baines Johnson was his man. On August 3, the majority leader sent his friend from Mississippi a thank-you note. "Jim, you have helped me over many a rough spot during the last seven months," Johnson wrote from his ranch. "I did not want too much time to go by before I told you that I know it." Eastland responded three days later: "You have certainly made the best Majority Leader we have ever had. I think the world of you personally and was certainly glad to cooperate." He concluded his letter by telling LBJ that he was "leaving tomorrow for the Convention and will vote for you for President."[74] Lyndon Johnson had helped James Eastland get the chairmanship of Judiciary; in return, Eastland promised his support in Johnson's attempt to become president of the United States.

One day before the start of the national convention, Johnson announced his candidacy, but by then it was already too late. Like his mentor Richard Russell, LBJ was a master of Senate politics, but he had difficulty controlling the unruly delegates at the convention. The Mississippi delegation, after surviving yet another seating challenge in the credentials committee, voted for Johnson on the first ballot. By voting for LBJ instead of Stevenson on the first ballot, Mississippi followed Eastland's preference. At the morning caucus of the delegation, the senator had introduced a motion to support Johnson. The Mississippi vote for the majority leader was an acknowledgment of the work he had done to get Eastland the chairmanship of the Judiciary Committee. In case Johnson's bid for the candidacy failed, the delegates would turn to Adlai Stevenson, Coleman's preference. Walter Sillers, who was in Chicago as a delegate, backed this proposal. He explained that his vote was not an endorsement of Stevenson's politics, but a tribute to Coleman, who had successfully fought for a mild civil rights plank as member of the platform committee. Senator Eastland did not want to vote for Stevenson, but since the majority of the Mississippi delegates endorsed the plan and the delegation was under unit rule, the votes of the state would automatically switch to Stevenson if LBJ failed to win the nomination on the first ballot.[75]

John Stennis delivered a seconding speech for Lyndon Johnson's candidacy and the delegates from Mississippi were part of a parade in support of LBJ. Lieutenant Governor Carroll Gartin wore a cap proclaiming "Love that Lyndon," and the backers of the Texas senator marched down the aisles to the tunes of "Yellow Rose of Texas," "Old Cow Hand from the Rio Grande," and of course "Dixie."[76] But all these demonstrations were to no avail. Stevenson won overwhelmingly on the first ballot. Like Russell in 1952, LBJ's status as a southerner and his inability to adapt his skills as Senate majority leader to the politics of a national convention caused his defeat in Chicago.[77]

Stevenson was again going to be the Democratic presidential candidate. He left it up to the convention to choose his running mate. Estes Kefauver eventually won the vice presidential nomination on the second ballot, but it was a close race against John Kennedy. JFK received broad regional support, with particularly strong backing from southern states, including Mississippi. "I'll be singing 'Dixie' for the rest of my life," the Massachusetts senator told journalist Arthur Krock afterward.[78] He sent a note to Eastland after the convention, thanking him for his aid in Chicago. "Mississippi was of the greatest possible assistance, and Frank Smith and others have told me how helpful you were," Kennedy wrote. "I am most appreciative. We almost made it!"[79] At the closing session of the convention, with Truman, Stevenson, and Kefauver holding pep talks, only two out of forty-four Mississippi delegates were still on the floor. When Hugh Wall and Harris Gholson put the state standard into the Stevenson demonstration, they received a thunderous applause. Support for the Stevenson-Kefauver ticket among Mississippi Democrats was far from unanimous, however.[80]

James Coleman proudly declared the Democratic program did not include an official endorsement of the *Brown* decision, despite pressure from liberals such as Senator Lehman, Walter Reuther of the AFL-CIO, and Roy Wilkins of the NAACP. According to Coleman, the voice of the South in the Democratic Party had been restored. "It is obvious that the Democratic plank on Civil Rights is less objectionable to the South than will be the Republican plank," the governor said at a press conference. "Our platform contains better programs for agriculture and in the field of States Rights than will the GOP document."[81] The compromise on civil rights reached in the platform committee might have been acceptable to Mississippi Democrats, but the presence of Senator Kefauver on the Democratic ticket was problematic to them. "I am sick over the nomination of Kefauver," Carroll Gartin declared.[82]

Some Mississippians had trouble with Coleman's positive assessment. Jackson lawyer Archibald Coody, a vitriolic racist who had been friends with the Eastland family for years, wrote the senator that he preferred to "die and go to hell" before he would vote for either the Democrats or the Republicans. "If we don't fight to the finish now, we may as well arrange for our mullatto [sic] grandchildren," he continued his letter. "In less than a year we will have niggers and whites in the same school and nigger teachers for white children." Coody called himself "The Lone Eagle" and was the author of *The White Chief,* a biography of James K. Vardaman. While his father had redeemed Mississippi as member of the Klan, Coody was shocked to learn that the state leadership (including Walter Sillers) now seemed to go along with the Democratic platform. "We have the worst plank we ever had on 'civil rights,' and one for wide open immigration, so that 15 million jews can come in," he fumed. "Before many years, the Federal Government will confiscate your farm," he warned Eastland, "and sell it on 40 years time to the tenants, and kick your kids into the sunflower [sic] river."[83] Archibald Coody was extreme in his racist views and rhetoric, but his letter did demonstrate the fear of federal interference in southern race relations that many segregationists shared and the alienation they felt from the American two-party system.

Mississippi segregationists who no longer considered the national Democratic Party their home had two other options in the 1956 election: an unpledged states' rights ticket and the Lily-White Republican Party. Ernest Spencer's Citizens for Eisenhower group—founded in 1952 by disaffected Democrats—and the Young Republicans under Wirt Yerger had taken control of the Lily-Whites, and they went to the Republican National Convention in Chicago to challenge the seating of Perry Howard's Black and Tan faction. Howard, by then already seventy-nine years old, was not planning to give up his influence on Republican politics in Mississippi easily. He threatened to mobilize northern black voters to campaign against Eisenhower if his delegation was not seated.

The Eisenhower camp came up with a compromise: the Black and Tans would receive eight votes at the convention, the Lily-Whites seven, and at the 1960 convention the Yerger-Spencer group would be recognized as the official representation of the Mississippi Republicans.[84] Yerger did not want to be near the Howard faction at the convention and also desired to split the vote, but when the convention opened the Republican delegates from Mississippi were all sitting together. Wirt Yerger was nowhere to be seen, however. One of the state's delegates thought he was probably somewhere else in the hall.[85]

A few days before, Chairman Bidwell Adam of the Mississippi Democratic Committee had already sent a letter to Eastland's old friend Ernest Spencer, urging him and his "patriotic followers" to rejoin the Democrats. "Now that Perry Howard has been recognized as the Republican party head of the State of Mississippi and this party has demonstrated that your effort, labor and work are not appreciated, may I suggest that you come back home, hang your coat and hat on a Democratic rack and join with the political forces of democracy in administering a thorough repudiation of the Howard forces," Adam advised. "You belong in the Democratic party and I believe this is a golden opportunity to pay off the crowd of Republicans who thought more of Howard than they did you when they placed him in power and designated him as their standard bearer in Mississippi."[86] Spencer and his Republican friends did not return to the Democratic Party, however. They introduced their own slate of GOP electors instead, in addition to a Black and Tan slate. Both Republican factions were pledged to Eisenhower.

States' rights Democrats assembled on August 21 in the Heidelberg Hotel in Jackson to select a slate of presidential electors. Attorney W. B. Fontaine, chairman of the convention, told the press that his group could neither vote for the Republican candidates nor for the Democrats because of "their open stand against the South." The candidates of both parties were objectionable to Fontaine, but the issue that really bothered him were the Democratic and Republican positions on civil rights. The states' righters were not afraid they would be thrown out of the Democratic Party. "We are as good Democrats as Gov. Coleman," a spokesman for the states' rights group said. "We stand for constitutional government as the old Democratic Party stood."[87]

Earl Evans, the president pro tem of the State Senate, resigned as Democratic elector and joined the states' rights cause. Four years before, he had served as an elector for Eisenhower. Evans believed in the principles of the Mississippi Democratic Party, but he could not campaign for the candidates and the platform of the national Democrats. He denied that the state's representatives in Congress would suffer if they did not support the national ticket. Evans used Senator Eastland as the main example to support his claim. Did he lose his seniority when he campaigned for Thurmond in 1948? The states' righters issued advertisements warning voters that professional politicians tried to take away their right to vote. "You can vote for a free and independent way of life—the Mississippi way," the states' rights faction announced. "Thousands of men and women, by signing petitions, have told the would-be political bosses of our state, they cannot force us to support the NAACP, the ADA, Eleanor Roosevelt, [Carmine] DeSapio, and their front men, Stevenson and Kefauver." Fontaine, Evans, and their followers claimed that voting for a man who advocated integration meant nothing else but an endorsement of integration itself.[88]

The Mississippi Democrats pledged to the Stevenson-Kefauver ticket responded in kind. Pictures of Senators Eastland and Stennis and five of the state's six congressmen—John Bell Williams joined the states' righters—appeared in newspapers. The following words were printed above the pictures: "DO YOU BELIEVE THESE MEN WOULD BETRAY MISSISSIPPI?" The advertisement reminded voters that their congressional delegation was "on the firing line in Washington," defending the interests of the state. Not voting Democratic would be detrimental to the fight they were waging on Capitol Hill: "Do you want to make them serve four more years with a Republican president and with Ezra Benson and Herbert Brownell?"[89] It was no coincidence the advertisement mentioned these two members of Eisenhower's cabinet. Brownell was responsible for civil rights policy as attorney general, and the programs of Secretary of Agriculture Benson had a major influence on the economy of Mississippi.

Other Democratic officials in Mississippi echoed the advice of protecting the state's congressmen and senators. Chairman Bidwell Adam said it was important that Eastland and his colleagues retained their seniority, and he advised against a recall of the state convention. Secretary of State Heber Ladner and Attorney General Patterson expressed a similar message. Patterson dispelled the idea that the vice president had any real power in the Senate, thus contradicting Eastland's statements at the Neshoba County Fair.[90] The Democratic campaign in Mississippi was not about winning votes for Stevenson and Kefauver, but a contest to keep the state's members of Congress in power.

From his home in Ruleville, James Eastland declared on August 22 he would support Stevenson and Kefauver.[91] But he again adopted a rather lackluster attitude toward the campaign and thought there was little difference between the Republicans and the Democrats. "It is a sad but true commentary that principles have little or no meaning in the platform of either the Democratic or the Republican Party," he noted. "Insofar as the platforms are concerned, there is little or nothing to choose from between them." Eisenhower had not shown a passionate commitment to civil rights during his first four years in office, but Eastland believed that the president had been largely responsible for the desegregation of public facilities. Stevenson was perhaps just as militant on racial equality as Eisenhower, Eastland argued, but at least the Democratic candidate had to deal with the powerful bloc of southern states in his party.

"We are engaged in a long range struggle that will require all the courage, fight and determination that is at our command," the senator observed. "The path we have to follow will not always be easy but you may rest assured that our eyes should always be directed to the main purpose of preserving our way of life and the integrity and sovereignty of the States."[92]

With both major parties committed to some form of civil rights legislation, white southerners began to realize that their representatives in Congress were the only politicians they could count on. These voters found themselves between Scylla and Charybdis and they wanted to make sure they made the right decision in the election. As "an advocate of true Jeffersonian principles of democracy," the owner of the Rebel Oil Company in Jackson was inclined to vote for the states' rights electors. "The only problem facing me is to find out if I can what effect, if any, would it have on the chairmanships of the various committees and commissions that our Senators and Representatives now hold should the state of Mississippi be carried by the State Right ticket," he inquired in a letter to Eastland. "If a vote for the States Rights [Party] would impair our wonderful position, especially on the Judiciary Committee, then I feel that possibly the end would not justify the means."[93]

Adlai Stevenson carried Mississippi with 60 percent of the vote. The two Republican tickets received 24 percent, with 56,372 voters casting their ballot for the Lily-Whites, and 4,311 supporting the Black and Tans. Sixteen percent of the electorate went to the States' Rights ticket.[94] The Democratic vote in Mississippi was almost identical to 1952, while the combined vote of the states' righters and the Republicans equaled the Republican result of four years earlier. Stevenson would be the last Democratic presidential candidate to carry Mississippi for twenty years. Senator Eastland was ambiguous about Eisenhower's national victory over Stevenson. "I'm like the little boy who was run over and trampled by a bull calf," he told a reporter. "I ain't cryin' and I ain't laughin.' I just ain't got nothing to say."[95]

Northern Democrats were more outspoken about the election results, however. They blamed the loss of six Senate seats on the appeasement policy toward the South initiated by the party leadership after the 1952 convention. Moreover, Stevenson did not profit from the conciliatory stance taken toward the old Confederacy. The Democratic candidate lost another three southern states in 1956. In addition to Florida, Virginia, Tennessee, and Texas, Eisenhower carried Louisiana and the border states of Kentucky and West

Virginia. Important urban areas in the North, the Midwest, California, and the Border South—key to Democratic victories in presidential elections—also moved to the Republican ticket in 1956. According to columnist Doris Fleeson, embittered northern Democrats warned that "when the cities break from the Democrats, their presidential cause must fail because such elections are won and lost in the big States."[96]

Spokesmen of the NAACP concurred with this view and had little trouble naming the main culprit: James Eastland. Thurgood Marshall explained that he was inclined to support Adlai Stevenson, but that he had great difficulty separating Stevenson's Democratic Party from Eastland's Democratic Party.[97] Clarence Mitchell was more direct in denouncing Eastland and the Democrats. "Tell those Democrats if they keep a stinking albatross like Senator Eastland around their necks they can kiss our votes goodbye," Mitchell said.[98] These statements by NAACP officials illustrate the dilemma the national Democrats faced as they entered the 1960s: could the Democratic Party be an organization where southern segregationists like Eastland *and* civil rights activists like Marshall and Mitchell found their political home?

Although Stevenson still received the majority of the black electorate in 1956, the Republicans' stock among African American voters was rising. Eisenhower faced a dilemma: he wanted to expand the inroads he had made into the South, but at the same time he hoped to solidify black support for the GOP. The president was ready to move on civil rights after his second victory over Stevenson, but it had to be a moderate initiative that would not upset white southerners too much. In late 1955, Attorney General Herbert Brownell had already suggested a civil rights plan during a cabinet meeting. Brownell's proposal entailed a comprehensive approach to fight racial inequality. He wanted to organize a civil rights commission which was authorized to examine voter discrimination, institute a civil rights division in the Justice Department under the command of an assistant attorney general, and give the attorney general a broad mandate to file civil suits and enforce constitutional rights, including school desegregation.[99]

Eisenhower had doubts about the sweeping character of Brownell's plan. FBI Director J. Edgar Hoover had warned him about communist influences in the civil rights movement, and the president preferred to limit federal interference to the protection of voting rights. Eisenhower considered the suffrage a fundamental constitutional right, but he was more ambivalent about the role of the national government in matters of education. Moreover, he did not want to offend his white southern base. The president therefore endorsed federal protection of voting rights, and he also backed Brownell's suggestion to set up a civil rights commission and a special division in the Justice Department. The administration needed bipartisan support in Congress to ensure enactment of Brownell's initiative.[100]

So far, a coalition of conservative Republicans and southern Democrats had been able to prevent any significant progress on desegregation. Now that a Republican administration openly sponsored a civil rights bill, that pact started to fracture. Majority Leader Johnson was not averse to the enactment of civil rights legislation either. As a southerner with national ambitions, LBJ needed some sort of legislative achievement in the field of civil rights. At the same time, he did not want to betray his southern friends. Like Eisenhower, Lyndon Johnson wanted a compromise, a limited bill that was acceptable to the white South and the liberals from the North. Johnson hoped adoption of such a moderate law would move the discussion about civil rights to the background and reunite the Democratic Party.

Confronted with this new reality, southern bloc leader Richard Russell decided to give LBJ a chance. Previous efforts to pass civil rights bills had foundered in Jim Eastland's Judiciary Committee. The last attempt to enact such legislation took place in the summer of 1956, when Lyndon Johnson stalled debate on a civil rights resolution from the House through close cooperation with Speaker Sam Rayburn. Rayburn managed to get a quick vote on the resolution and then handed the bill to one of Johnson's aides, who rushed it to the Senate. This move caught civil rights advocates in the upper chamber by surprise; without any liberal opposition on the floor, the resolution was referred to Eastland's committee, where it died when the 84th Congress expired. The Democratic leadership, eager to maintain party unity in an election year, did not want discussion on the divisive issue of racial equality. A year later, circumstances had changed.[101]

In 1957, civil rights supporters finally managed to bypass Eastland's committee. Vice President Nixon ruled that the Senate needed to vote on the question of whether House Resolution 6127—Brownell's civil rights bill—should go to Judiciary or straight on the calendar for floor debate. The division of votes was interesting; although the southerners were defeated, 45 to 39, four liberal western senators joined their colleagues from the South by favoring study of H.R. 6127 in the Judiciary Committee. In return, five southerners (including James Eastland) changed their vote on the Hells Canyon Dam, a water power project on the Snake River in Idaho. These five southern senators initially opposed the use of public money to finance the dam, but they agreed to alter their position if westerners who profited from the venture would come to their aid in the civil rights fight.

Wayne Morse, the senator from Oregon who had spoken against Eastland's nomination as chairman of Judiciary, was one of them. Morse vehemently denied the allegations; he claimed to have voted for referral to Eastland's committee because of procedural considerations, not to ensure government financing of the dam. Notwithstanding Morse's remarks, the Hells Canyon bill was adopted on June 21, with crucial southern support. Lyndon Johnson would use this gentleman's agreement between the South and the West to moderate Brownell's civil rights package.[102]

Johnson would not get anywhere without the tacit approval of Richard Russell, however. As leader of the Southern Caucus, Russell held extraordinary power to thwart any form of legislation that undermined Jim Crow. The filibuster used to be the South's weapon of choice and under normal circumstances Russell would probably have instructed his senators to talk Brownell's initiative to death. But in 1957 the situation was different. The South's old Republican friends were rallying around the administration's civil rights proposal. "Frankly, the outlook for our success on these Civil Rights Bills is not as good as it was in the past," James Eastland wrote one of his constituents, "because of the lack of support from some of our former Republican allies, who will probably follow the President this time."[103]

As a result, a real possibility existed that supporters of H.R. 6127 could muster enough votes to invoke cloture and end debate on the bill. Cloture not only put the future use of the filibuster at risk, but it might also arouse the ire of moderates who were willing to find a compromise. If these moderates chose the wing of northern "extremists" because of intransigent southern opposition, the senators from the former Confederacy were really in dire straits, Johnson warned. Russell thus decided to follow a course of moderation instead of massive resistance and was able to convince most members of the Southern Caucus. These men realized that passage of a civil rights bill was now inevitable and that it was in their interest to negotiate about its content. They hoped that by assuming a pragmatic attitude toward the matter, the Senate would engineer a law which was more symbol than substance. Johnson had picked up promising signals from the GOP camp; although Republican senators generally voiced their approval of the civil rights bill, many of them were in fact not very enthusiastic about Brownell's activist ideas. With the help of these Republicans and the proponents of the Hells Canyon project, the South was in a good bargaining position to remove the more profound elements of the legislation.[104]

The outcome of the debate on the 1957 civil rights bill constituted a defeat for supporters of segregation and advocates of racial equality. For the southern senators, the fact that a civil rights bill passed Congress was already a setback by itself, but in the end they carried the day because the Senate stripped the law of its most far-reaching clauses. In order to prevent a southern filibuster, Democratic senator Clinton Anderson of New Mexico came to Johnson's help and proposed an amendment that gutted Section III of Brownell's plan, the part that enabled the attorney general to prevent violations of voting rights and other civil rights. Section III gave the federal government new (and broad) powers to break down Jim Crow laws, which was of course completely anathema to the white South. Anderson, no enemy of the civil rights movement, desired passage of H.R. 6127 above all, however, and he teamed up with two moderate Republicans to submit an amendment that weakened Section III. Johnson managed to round up enough votes for Anderson's motion, and the amendment passed 52–38.

In addition, the southern bloc succeeded in making a jury trial provision part of the civil rights bill. The inclusion of this clause meant that a jury would judge violators of voting rights. These juries were all-white in the South, however. Eisenhower was furious. He had initially preferred more limited legislation that dealt with voting rights only, but now that the Senate had basically derailed the entire civil rights bill, he considered vetoing it. That did not happen; after Congress made some minor alterations to the bill, the president signed it into law on September 9, 1957. Liberal senators blamed Eisenhower for not providing enough leadership in the debate, while the president criticized Lyndon Johnson for destroying the original plan submitted by Brownell. The majority leader nonetheless received praise for guiding the first civil rights law since Reconstruction through the Senate. LBJ had achieved the civil rights victory he wanted without completely estranging the Southern Caucus.[105]

Eastland's correspondence during the civil rights bill debate clarifies how he perceived the Senate battle to block this legislation. These letters also provide information about the strategy Russell's troops followed. The senator anticipated a tough fight for the southern bloc early on. "It appears that they will pass a Civil Rights Bill this time," he told Eugene Morse, a lawyer from Jackson, in February 1957. "I do not believe there is any way for us to beat it, but we will certainly stand our ground and do the very best that we can."[106] At the beginning of March, Walter Sillers complimented Eastland for the jury trial amendment he introduced, but Sillers warned him to refrain from making passage of the amendment a sectional issue. Eastland's statement could be interpreted as an "appeal for help to the South only in its controversy with the negroes on segregation and integration," said Sillers, "when as a matter of fact the great danger you are attempting to guard against is one which will affect the nation over." Walter Sillers encouraged Eastland to convince a national audience that the jury trial motion was in the interest of the entire country as a safeguard against federal encroachment, and he also deemed it wise to find "a good friend from the North" who would support the amendment.[107]

Eastland was in fact a step ahead of Sillers; he had already asked Democrat Joseph O'Mahoney of Wyoming to offer the amendment. O'Mahoney had been in the Senate since 1934 and used to be a staunch New Dealer. Eastland called him "one of the real liberals in our country." The Wyoming senator thought Brownell's bill was in violation of the Constitution because it did not guarantee a jury trial.[108] The cooperation between O'Mahoney and Eastland was the new South-West alliance in action. O'Mahoney voted against putting the civil rights bill on the calendar and introduced the jury trial amendment, while Eastland changed his vote on the Hells Canyon Dam. Because the jury trial motion came from a westerner and not from a southerner, senators from outside the South had less trouble voting for it.

During the following months, James Eastland kept Walter Sillers abreast of developments in the civil rights battle. In June, Eastland explained that proponents of the bill would probably be able to bypass his committee. Sillers wanted to know whether a filibuster could kill the bill or merely delay its enactment. If the latter was the case, he suggested adding amendments to the legislation "which will lessen its viciousness." Otherwise, Sillers advised to "filibuster the h—ll out of it."[109] Besides discussing these strategic considerations, Eastland also expected relief would come from outside the South, particularly if the Warren Court kept its activist attitude. "I am hopeful that these recent decisions will arouse other areas of the country and that we can get some non-southerners to lead an effort to bridle this Court," the senator wrote. "Of course, as long as it was only the integration decision, southern comments on it were considered sectional and we were at a great disadvantage. Now, I hope these recent events will turn the tide."[110]

Eastland saw the rest of the nation moving to the side of the South, a perception he mentioned multiple times in his correspondence. Based on the "thousands of letters" his office received from all over the United States, he concluded that "the country is up in arms over the recent actions of the Supreme Court."[111] By adjusting their rhetoric to colorblind constitutional arguments, southern senators—including Eastland—understood they could gain allies outside the region. They also used the media to accomplish this goal. The Southern Caucus decided its members should accept all invitations coming from television stations to explain the "inequities" of the civil rights bill to the rest of the country. Eastland did an interview on the *Mike Wallace Show* and was surprised that so many Americans reflected favorably on his appearance. He received over twelve hundred letters, "most of it from non-southern sources," and according to the senator only three of these letters were critical about the standpoints he expressed during the show.[112]

By mid-July, Eastland thought the South would be able to take "some of the most vicious parts" out of the bill and perhaps initiate a filibuster. "The chances are that they will whip us but I believe those provisions that deal in school integration and segregation matters will be stricken from the bill," he wrote his friend Si Breland.[113] In order to ensure adoption of the jury trial amendment, O'Mahoney had requested that his southern colleagues provide him with information about blacks serving on juries in the South. Among others, Eastland contacted Sidney Mize and Allen Cox, two U.S. district judges in Mississippi, and asked them about discriminatory practices in the selection procedure for jury duty. The senator specifically wanted to know whether a policy existed that excluded African Americans from jury service.[114] In general, the response coming from southern federal judges to such queries was that "blacks had served on their juries for years." By inserting these answers into the *Congressional Record*, O'Mahoney's motion gained crucial support from outside the South, Eastland claimed. "Most of the Senators were actually amazed, and I think these telegrams did a great deal in our success in passing a Jury Trial Amendment."[115]

Although the southern senators managed to severely weaken Brownell's original proposal, the fact remained that Congress eventually passed a civil rights law. After passage of the act, James Eastland and his Senate colleagues from the South had to explain their strategy to the home front. White southerners needed to be reassured that their senators were still committed to Jim Crow.[116] Senator Strom Thurmond complicated this task. In defiance of caucus agreements, he mounted the rostrum on August 28, 1957, and launched into an oration against the civil rights bill that lasted more than twenty-four hours. Thurmond obviously received praise from white southerners for the stand he took, but it reflected badly on the other southern senators. Why had they not joined Thurmond in his lone defense of the South?

James Eastland and John Stennis issued a joint press release two days after Thurmond's speech to tell their constituents that an organized filibuster would have been hopeless because the southerners only had eighteen votes, which was not enough to prevent cloture. If southern senators had followed Thurmond in his maverick enterprise, Eastland and Stennis expected that the opposition would retaliate by adding amendments on school integration to the bill. The two Mississippi senators were certain the filibuster could still be used in cases of forced integration of schools, swimming pools, and other public places. Senators from other parts of the country had helped the South in weakening the bill, but they had only done so because the Southern Caucus had promised not to engage in a filibuster. Breaking this agreement would have increased opposition to southern interests, not only during the 1957 debate, but also in the future. "There was absolutely no way left to prevent passage of this bill," Eastland and Stennis concluded. "Had there been, we would have followed this course to a man."[117] A rational approach this time prevailed over an unyielding stand.

Since 1932, the southern bloc in the Senate had counted on the Taft wing of the Republican Party. Because Democratic administrations proposed civil rights legislation, southern Democrats were always able to find enough conservative Republican allies to block these initiatives. But in 1957 the situation was different. A Republican president now endorsed a civil rights bill, which "completely demolished and destroyed" the old GOP-South coalition. "Fully appreciating what a box we were in, the Southern Senators unanimously decided that the first line of defense in the Senate was to fight the bill on its merits and attempt to gain enough support from both Northern Democrats and Republicans to delete as many of the most obnoxious features as was humanly possible," Eastland remarked. He claimed that the final version of the bill was in fact a victory for the South. The Mississippi senator nonetheless had a hard time determining what course to follow when the bill came up for a vote. He could have taken the easy road of the filibuster, "the course that would be popular and win me acclaim and applause throughout all of the South." But in the end, he decided to back down. The "headlong and heedless course" of a filibuster "would be the equivalent of treason to my people," because this would eventually have led to much more radical legislation.[118]

In some ways, the debate on the civil rights bill had helped the South. Through the media, the southern senators spread the message that their fight was not just about segregation, but a struggle for the preservation of constitutional government. Eastland was confident that the Civil Rights Act of 1957 was the last one of its kind that would be enacted in the foreseeable future. He predicted that the opponents of the southern cause were "going to find that the white people of the United States are not going to tolerate dictation and subservience to the vocal and potent minority groups that forced the Eisenhower Administration to adopt the course of action it pursued during this last Congress."[119] As always, James Eastland had faith that white America thought the same way as the white South and that the country would eventually turn to the side of the old Confederacy.

When President Eisenhower federalized the Arkansas National Guard and sent in regular army units to ensure the desegregation of Central High School in Little Rock during late September 1957, Senator Eastland's argument that the difference between Republicans and Democrats on civil rights issues was negligible all of a sudden sounded very plausible. Earl Warren, appointed by Eisenhower, ruled over the *Brown* decision; a Republican president had signed the first civil rights bill since Reconstruction into law; and that same president appeared more than willing to reenact Reconstruction by sending federal troops down South. "In fact, the Court and the Executive are changing the form of our Federal system," Eastland responded to an inquiry about the situation in Little Rock from one of his constituents. "You can count upon me to oppose the Court and the Executive at every turn. If our people stand firm in opposition, I think we will be victorious."[120] Political parties no longer seemed to matter; the greatest threat to segregation now emanated from federal institutions, in particular the Supreme Court. This argument enabled Eastland to draw attention away from his status as a Democrat and instead focus on the alleged communist sympathies of, for instance, Supreme Court justices. At the level of national politics, the only wall of defense for the southern way of life was the region's Democratic representatives in Congress.

The southern Republicans were on the rise, however, even in the Deep South state of Mississippi. Republican growth below the Mason-Dixon Line was a halting process, stymied by Eisenhower's interference in Little Rock. As the crisis unfolded in Arkansas, segregationists menaced Chairman Wirt Yerger of the Mississippi GOP for his links with the Republican administration.[121] Yerger had nevertheless made important strides toward forcing Perry Howard out of power and had establish the Lily-Whites as the official Republican Party in the state.

Since Eisenhower's entry into the White House in 1952, Ernest Spencer had been the chief dispenser of federal patronage in Mississippi. Yet Spencer's loyalty to Ike had its limits. He renounced his party membership in October 1957 because of the White House decision to send the army to Arkansas. "Your unwarranted act in ordering military force has completely destroyed our Eisenhower organization and everything accomplished in Mississippi during the past five years," he dramatically announced to the president. Other party members followed Spencer's lead and resigned from the state Republican Party. "The followers of Eisenhower in Mississippi have departed faster than the Israelites out of Egypt," the *Jackson Daily News* noted. But Wirt Yerger stayed, took over federal patronage, and continued to build on the groundwork the National Republican Roundup Committee and Spencer's Citizens for Eisenhower had laid in the state. Yerger and his Loyalists formed the hardcore of the new Mississippi GOP, whose base was the white voter.[122]

Despite the attempts by Yerger and his fellow Republicans to construct a viable party in the state, and despite the growing resentment of white voters toward the national Democrats, the Mississippi Democratic Party still retained near hegemonic status at the end of the 1950s. Governor Coleman, by keeping the state party in the national party structure, improved the reputation of Mississippi while maintaining segregation. "I don't think there is any question but what Coleman brought tremendous prestige to Mississippi, and the manner in which we conducted ourselves has helped us to gain a lot of friends for our cause," Carroll Gartin explained to Beby Turnage, an attorney from Monticello, Mississippi. "You can't do it by 'cussing' and the new approach of friendship and understanding, in my opinion, will finally win this battle for us."[123]

Coleman's "new approach" of practical segregation proved to be much more effective in sustaining the system of Jim Crow than the radical strategies of, for example, the Dixiecrats in 1948 and the Citizens' Councils during the 1950s. Even James Eastland realized that pragmatism often yielded more results than outright defiance, although he preached the latter message multiple times on the Senate floor and at Council gatherings across the South. Eastland could have followed John Bell Williams's example and supported the States' Rights ticket in 1956. Instead, he stayed loyal to the candidates of the national Democratic Party. When Eastland's appointment to the chairmanship of the Judiciary Committee came up, Earle Clements already predicted that "Senator Eastland would be less controversial in the future as a consequence of this important position and the responsibility entailed by such a position."[124] As chairman, Eastland's authority to protect southern traditions grew. Simultaneously, it reinforced his ties to the national Democratic Party, an organization viewed with growing suspicion by many white southerners.

The policies of the Democratic Steering Committee indicated that political expediency sometimes prevailed over staying true to the party line. A southern Democrat like Estes Kefauver was much closer to the national Democrats' attitude toward civil rights, yet he was denied his committee requests, while a reactionary segregationist like James Eastland was elevated to the chairmanship of one of the most important committees in the Senate. Different considerations influenced the decision of the steering committee to nominate Eastland. If its members bypassed the senator from Mississippi, tensions between the northern and the southern wing of the Democratic Party most likely would be exacerbated. The party leadership preferred to prevent such developments, especially in an election year. At the 1954 meeting in New Orleans, the national leaders of the Democrats had already jettisoned the loyalty oath to placate the South. Denying Eastland the chairmanship meant providing the massive resisters and the southern Republicans fuel to attack the national Democrats, and it also complicated the work practical segregationists such as Coleman were doing on behalf of the national party.

Personal considerations and the politics of reciprocity also played a role. Eastland knew how to barter and he got along with most of his colleagues in the Senate.[125] "I just want to express my very deep thanks to a Senator who has been a gentleman, an able legislator, and a real friend, even under the most difficult circumstances," Lyndon Johnson wrote Eastland on the day

President Eisenhower signed the 1957 Civil Rights Act.[126] Finally, one more factor might have caused the steering committee to make Eastland head of Judiciary: based on seniority, none other than Estes Kefauver was next in line for the chairmanship.[127]

The politics of Democratic consensus was perhaps most evident in the debate on the civil rights bill. Democrats from different sections of the country pulled together to engineer a compromise. The outcome was a weak voting rights law which gave the Democratic Party at least the semblance it was committed to racial equality. Such a commitment was important for majority leader and White House aspirant Lyndon Johnson, who wanted a civil rights victory without tearing the national party apart. James Eastland and other Southern Caucus members claimed they had found victory in defeat. Eastland could have followed Thurmond and made a symbolic stand for the South, a stand that would have done his defiant rhetoric of massive resistance justice. Yet he chose the path of pragmatism. "The bitter experience of the War Between the States was that we won many battles but lost the war," Eastland wrote Jesse Shanks. "I am convinced that at this present time in our history, while we did admittedly lose a battle on the present Civil Rights legislation, we are following a course of action which is going to result in our ultimately winning the war."[128]

Senator Eastland, compared by his admirers with dashing Confederate generals like Robert E. Lee, Stonewall Jackson, and Nathan Bedford Forrest, now sounded a tactical retreat. The course of action Eastland referred to in his letter could only be sustained as long as the national party accommodated southern segregationists, however, and as long as white southerners kept voting Democratic. Senator Eastland compared the struggle over civil rights with the Civil War, but he predicted a different outcome than occurred in the War Between the States. Instead of southern defeat, he expected that the North eventually would join the South in its defense of local control and segregation.

CHAPTER 6

THE ERA OF POWER POLITICS

Kennedy and Eastland

I N SEPTEMBER 1956, an editorial titled "Whither Goest Thou, Senator?" appeared in the *Simpson County News*. This newspaper from the Mississippi Hill Country clearly was no ally of Senator Eastland. The editors wrote it as a response to a letter by C. C. Jones, who objected to Eastland's endorsement of the national Democratic ticket. "To deny that the Democratic Party has been drifting toward socialism, which endangers democracy and individual freedom would be stupid, and contrary to all known facts. Such drifting lays the foundation for Communism, or a ruthless dictatorship," declared Jones, a retired Baptist pastor and president of the Citizens' Council in Simpson County. He then stated that he could not vote for the Democratic ticket. Eastland expressed his approval of the pastor's views and congratulated him on the soundness of his position. The editors of the *Simpson County News* were astonished. They printed both letters in their newspaper and asked whether Eastland was still going to vote for Stevenson and Kefauver, despite the words he wrote to Jones. Was the senator a Democrat, or a Republican in disguise (something he had been accused of before)? "Evidently Senator Eastland has dropped his cigar and is talking out of both sides of his mouth," the newspaper wryly noted. The editors warned Eastland not to play both sides of the fence but to stick to one statement. They thought the Democratic Party was actually better off without the Delta planter in its ranks. "Bro. Jones plans to go fishing on Presidential Election Day, and the Editors of your Simpson County News will vote the Democratic ticket," the editorial concluded. "Wonder what 'Squire' Jim will do? Buy a saddle for fence straddling?"[1]

As the civil rights struggle intensified during the 1960s, the issue of

Democratic "fence straddling" moved to the foreground. James Eastland was not the only Democrat who faced such allegations; in a party that housed southern segregationists as well as northern liberals, Democratic politicians often had to find an agreement that was acceptable to both wings of the party. Particularly Democrats with national ambitions could not escape this reality. The politics that surrounded the Civil Rights Act of 1957 demonstrated how difficult it was to formulate meaningful legislation that did not offend any of the major sections in the Democratic Party. The compromise forged by Lyndon Johnson required the support of Democrats from all regions of the nation. The final result boosted LBJ's chances for the presidency, but it also benefitted another Democrat who had his eyes on the White House: John F. Kennedy. During the 1957 debate, Kennedy supported both Section III (which pleased African Americans) and the jury trial amendment (which pleased white southerners). His cautious and moderate approach to the civil rights question "reflected the racial dilemma of a would-be Democratic presidential nominee who needed southern support for that aspiration to be realized and a Massachusetts senator facing reelection who needed support in a liberally inclined home state," one historian noted. "Satisfying both constituencies on the civil rights issue was almost impossible. His straddling was bound to attract a reaction from those who felt strongly about the issue."[2]

Despite the conflicting interests of white southerners and African Americans, Kennedy nonetheless set out to recruit both groups in his race for the presidency. The Democratic National Convention of 1956 revealed that Kennedy could count on substantial support from the South, but he also needed a significant number of black voters to win the election. During the four years between the two conventions, JFK attempted to court white southerners without estranging the black electorate. As president, he continued this approach. Kennedy's razor-thin victory over Richard Nixon made him even warier to propose far-reaching civil rights legislation that would offend the powerful southerners on Capitol Hill. JFK was a gradualist on civil rights matters.[3] Instead of formulating bold New Frontier programs to end southern apartheid, Kennedy initially decided to focus on foreign policy and to keep the South on his good side. In the end, developments beyond the president's control forced him to confront the issue of segregation more directly. But even in this confrontation he relied on southern politicians such as James Eastland to help him solve the crises caused by increased civil rights activities.

Kennedy's indebtedness to the South was partly the result of his forays into the region to gather support for his 1960 presidential bid. He "approached Southern states with some caution," Kennedy's advisor Theodore Sorensen recalled. "He wanted to acknowledge their support for him at the 1956 convention and to demonstrate that his religion would not frighten Southern voters away." At the same time, JFK did not want give the impression he supported segregation.[4]

Mississippi voted for Kennedy's vice presidential candidacy at the convention in Chicago. Although the delegates at first wanted to back Lyndon Johnson, they switched their votes to Kennedy when the majority leader made it clear he did not want the second spot. State Representative Edgar J. Stephens Jr. was in the Governors' Suite in Chicago with James Coleman and James Eastland when the decision was made to support JFK in an effort to prevent Kefauver from getting on the ticket. Stephens remembered it did not take much time to convince the other members of the Mississippi delegation to get in line behind Kennedy. "Of course questions were asked about your stand on farm price supports and similar matters dear to the heart of the South but it was generally agreed that you were a level-headed, able and honest man who could be trusted," he wrote JFK a year after the convention. "Senator Eastland spoke of the esteem with which you were held by the other Senators." Edwards was therefore delighted to hear Kennedy would come to Mississippi on October 17, 1957, to address a meeting of the state's Young Democrats in Jackson.[5]

"As you can well understand, our fingers are still crossed on this whole event—and we are particularly hopeful that there will be no out-of-state publicity before or after Jack's arrival," Ted Sorensen wrote to Congressman Frank Smith, a moderate from the Mississippi Delta.[6] Sorensen feared negative feedback from the press on their visit to the segregationist stronghold of Mississippi. Journalists were undoubtedly going to ask questions about Kennedy's position on segregation, which might cause embarrassment in front of a southern audience and would most likely hurt his chances to get substantial support from white southerners and African Americans in his quest for the presidency. Like the South's practical segregationists, Sorensen preferred to ignore the race question for now and instead stress broad themes, such as economic growth.[7]

Not the press, but the Mississippi Republican Party forced Kennedy to address the issue of Jim Crow. Right before his arrival in the state, Wirt Yerger called attention to JFK's support of Section III of the 1957 Civil Rights Act. Yerger also wanted to know Kennedy's views on the developments in Little Rock. By asking the Massachusetts senator to clarify his position on segregation, the chairman of the Mississippi GOP attempted to disrupt his visit to Jackson. Kennedy kept calm and instructed Sorensen to insert a statement about civil rights in the speech he was about to deliver.

In the Victory Room of the Heidelberg Hotel, in front of two thousand people, Kennedy began his address by invoking the spirit of L.Q.C. Lamar, the Mississippi statesman who had called for sectional reconciliation after Reconstruction. JFK devoted a chapter to Lamar in his Pulitzer Prize-winning book *Profiles in Courage* and he frequently mentioned him at speaking engagements in the South. Obvious reasons governed this choice: Lamar was the first Mississippi Democrat to be elected to Congress after Reconstruction, and he preached the gospel of national unity after an era marked by intense regional conflict. Kennedy told his audience he accepted the Supreme Court decision on school desegregation as the law of the land. "I know that we do not agree on that issue," he said, "but I think most of us do agree on the necessity to uphold law and order in every part of the land." He then turned to Wirt Yerger's challenge. "And now I invite Mr. [Yerger] to tell us his views on Eisenhower and Nixon," Kennedy declared, directing the attention to the Republican role in the enactment of the Civil Rights Act—specifically the bypassing of Eastland's committee—and the Little Rock crisis.[8]

Kennedy's reference to Redeemer Democrat Lamar and Republican involvement in federally mandated desegregation had the desired effect. Sorensen expected that the guests would not respond well to JFK's remarks on the *Brown* decision, but instead they applauded his candor and, above all, his attack on the GOP. "The crowd came to its feet, alive, roaring and stomping its approval: Jack Kennedy had won it by his own display of courage and by turning all good Democrats against the odious Republicans," *Time* reported.[9] Kennedy convinced his listeners that the battle was not between North and South, but between Democrats and Republicans. This appeal to partisan spirit apparently still worked in Mississippi, especially following Eisenhower's dispatch of troops to Arkansas. When the reception in the Heidelberg Hotel came to an end, Kennedy went to the governor's mansion, where he spent the night. Senators Eastland and Stennis also stayed at Coleman's residence, and the three Mississippi politicians talked with JFK into the early hours. Kennedy considered the South a strong base of support for the 1960 campaign.[10]

Right after the journey to Mississippi, Sorensen reflected optimistically on Kennedy's performance in the state capital.[11] Mississippi Democrats shared Sorensen's satisfaction about JFK's appearance at the Heidelberg Hotel. They expected that his trip to the South would have a beneficial effect on Democratic unity. State Attorney General Joe Patterson called JFK's visit "a treat and a pleasure," and he considered Kennedy a friend of the South. Patterson argued that if the national Democrats adopted "a conservative, and at the same time progressive, program" and a conservative presidential ticket, the Democratic Party could win the upcoming national race without "the aid of the radicals." Patterson wanted to quell the influence that left-wing minority organizations had on the outcome of elections. "I think their strength is wholly exaggerated, and it remains for some strong party candidate to show this group that they do not control the destiny of this country."[12] These Mississippians saw John Kennedy as a politician who understood southern concerns and who could keep the national party together.

Prominent Deep South segregationists such as Governor John Patterson and Citizens' Council leader Sam Engelhardt from Alabama and Joe Patterson from Mississippi flocked to Kennedy's banner. James Eastland was also positive about the young politician from Massachusetts. During his time in the Senate, Kennedy had developed a good working relationship with his colleagues from the South and he shared Eastland's firm anticommunist views. In a 1959 interview with CBS radio program *Capitol Cloakroom*, Eastland said he would "support any reasonable Democratic candidate" at the party's convention next year, expressing his early preference for John Kennedy and Lyndon Johnson. But many of Eastland's constituents objected to this choice. "How could you support Kennedy? We all know his stand on so called 'civil rights,'" a citizen from Biloxi asked Eastland in July 1959. The letter was an early indication of the political storm that loomed on the horizon.[13]

By the spring of 1958, ominous signs had already begun to emanate from below the Mason-Dixon Line. In mid-May, Sam Wilhite submitted a confidential report on Democratic prospects in the South to Drexel Sprecher, deputy chairman for political organization of the Democratic National Committee. Wilhite wanted to call the attention of the DNC to the worsening position of the Democratic Party in the southern states. He noticed that an unpledged elector movement had begun to gain a foothold in the five states of the Deep South, and that it might spread to Virginia if the school desegregation matter "exploded" in the Old Dominion. "I consider this question much more serious than the 1948 bolt," Wilhite remarked. "Practically the same leadership in 1948 is behind this movement now, but with a much more volatile and emotional issue to rally the people to such a movement, which is causing other outstanding leaders to be swept up into this movement that otherwise would not be." Liberals and moderates no longer dared to speak up. States' rights gains in peripheral southern states such as Tennessee, Florida, and North Carolina could set off Republican victories there. In a follow-up, Wilhite indicated that the Democratic leadership in the South did not necessarily favor a bolt from the national party or a third-party campaign, but the furor at the grassroots was so intense that they had to come up with an adequate response soon. "There is much unrest and dissatisfaction in the over all picture in this area," he warned.[14]

In the meantime, John Kennedy had begun to pursue the black vote more vigorously. Fearing the nationwide appeal of his opponents in the primaries, he decided to come out for a strong civil rights plank and openly endorsed the sit-in movement that had started at a lunch counter in Greensboro, North Carolina. In the quest for votes, Kennedy even declared privately that he no longer cared about his Deep South base. "I want to be nominated by the liberals," he told Arthur Schlesinger, "I don't want to go screwing around with all those Southern bastards." But Kennedy's sudden denial of his southern friends knew its limits. When some of his staff suggested asking for Eastland's removal as chair of the Judiciary Committee and thus buttressing his newfound commitment to civil rights, JFK demurred. "After all, the Senate is a body where you have to get along with people regardless how much you disagree," he explained. "I've always got along pretty well with old Eastland."[15]

The outcome of the 1959 gubernatorial race had a major influence on Mississippi's role in the presidential election the following year. Jackson lawyer Ross Barnett, Lieutenant Governor Carroll Gartin, and District Attorney Charles Sullivan of Clarksdale competed against each other in the first primary. The young and attractive Gartin had a good chance of winning the election, thus ensuring the continuation of the politics of practical segregation observed by Governor Coleman, who backed his lieutenant. Coleman's enemies—the massive resisters in the Citizens' Councils and the Eastland camp—desired a strong opponent of the governor's policies and eventually settled on Barnett.

Eastland himself aided fellow Mississippi Deltan Sullivan. Without a third candidate to split the vote, the senator feared his old adversary Gartin would win in the first primary.

But even with Eastland's help, Sullivan ended third in the election. Carroll Gartin and Ross Barnett proceeded to the run-off primary. The contest between Gartin and Barnett exemplified the competition between practical segregationists and massive resisters for control of the state. After continuous rumors that James Coleman planned to challenge Eastland in the 1960 Senate election, the governor finally unveiled his political plans: he was going to run, but for a seat in the state legislature. This announcement did not diminish anxiety in the massive resistance ranks, however. Coleman wanted to take over Walter Sillers's position as House Speaker, one of the more powerful positions in Mississippi politics. If Coleman managed to defeat Sillers and Gartin won the gubernatorial campaign, the practical segregationists would achieve an almost complete victory. The Citizens' Council crowd used the looming establishment of a White-Coleman-Gartin dynasty as a campaign tool, and they tried to link the Gartin camp with organized labor. James Eastland silently switched his support to Barnett, followed by other allies of Charles Sullivan. Besides ideological considerations, Eastland had not forgotten Gartin's opposition in 1954. In the run-off primary, Barnett successfully painted his opponent as a pawn of the AFL-CIO and weak on segregation. "The C.I.O. plays 'footsie' with the NAACP, the ADA and other radical organizations," the Barnett campaign warned. "In line with the C.I.O. policy, Carroll Gartin is beginning to unfold his plans for a welfare state in the State of Mississippi."[16]

Gartin never found an adequate answer to his rival's charges that he was a racial moderate. Barnett won the election with 54 percent of the vote, while Eastland's friend Paul B. Johnson Jr. became the new lieutenant governor. Many of Barnett's supporters in 1959 planned to support Johnson for the governorship in 1963. Although Coleman got elected to the state legislature, Walter Sillers remained Speaker of the Mississippi House of Representatives. With Sillers retaining his commanding position in the House and Barnett in the governor's mansion, the Citizens' Councils could claim a resounding triumph over the practical segregationists. The days of moderation were over; Barnett and the forces of massive resistance in Mississippi prepared themselves for an all-out fight to save Jim Crow.[17]

A plethora of Eastland men kept Kennedy and his aides abreast of the political situation in Mississippi. Frank Barber, Eastland's former assistant, was close to Sorensen and John Kennedy and he volunteered to become active on Kennedy's southern staff if he planned to enter the Florida primary. Barber expected that Governor-elect Barnett would not have much influence on issues concerning national politics and that he would follow Eastland's directions. "I am not ready to concede, as some Mississippi democrats have, that Governor Barnett is a bolter, states righter or third party man," he explained to Mayor John Hynes of Boston. "I believe that with the proper coaching from our Senatorial and Congressional delegations that Governor Barnett will be loyal to the party and to its nominees." Since Eastland had already indicated he favored Johnson and Kennedy, Barber thought the situation was under control.[18]

Sam Wilhite was less optimistic. He thought the defeat of the Coleman forces called for "an agonizing reappraisal" of the political situation in Mississippi. Wilhite expected that the extreme segregationists—people like Congressman John Bell Williams—were going to have significant influence on the Barnett administration. Prospects for the national convention did not look good either. "I think there is going to be a very antagonistic attitude taken by Governor Barnett and his people at the National Convention, which may result in their being unseated by the National Party," Wilhite told Kennedy. "In other words, I think that in Mississippi the seeds of revolt have been well-planted."[19]

Barnett expressed his uncompromising attitude toward the Democratic Party at a Citizens' Council rally in New Orleans on March 7, 1960. He stated that in the first place, he was a Mississippi Democrat, and that he was going to conduct himself as a Mississippi Democrat at the national convention in Los Angeles. Barnett declared that the preservation of Mississippi's "racial integrity" was his first priority. "Where the principles of the people of Mississippi are involved, there can be no compromise," he shouted. "The people did not elect me Governor of Mississippi to bargain their heritage away in a smoke-filled room!" Barnett displayed his Dixiecrat credentials when he called for a collective South-wide movement of independent electors that could force the election of the president into the House. He felt that the southern states were more united than in 1948, when the States' Rights Democrats only needed two more states to accomplish their goal.[20] Barnett's allegiance to the Democratic Party obviously had its limits, and the hardline plan he proposed sounded exactly like the predictions Wilhite had made in his 1958 report to Sprecher.

Shortly after leaving office and taking his seat in the legislature, James Coleman talked to Eastland's staff assistant Wilburn Buckley. Sitting in the House chamber, Coleman asked Buckley to convey his deep appreciation for the senator. "He stated that during [his time as governor] had you desired to do so you could have hurt his administration," Buckley wrote Eastland. "This you declined to do and he certainly did appreciate your attitude toward him." Considering the upcoming national convention, the former governor hoped the states' righters did not stage a walk-out. A bolt would no longer hurt Coleman politically, but he expected that Eastland's chairmanship might be at peril if the delegation left the convention. Such a development—Eastland losing command of the Judiciary Committee—would not only be detrimental to Mississippi, but to the entire South, Coleman argued.[21] James Coleman and James Eastland: the former a practical segregationist, the latter a figurehead of the massive resisters. In public they fought each other, but behind the scenes these two Mississippians worked together to protect the southern way of life.

Despite the pledges of Loyalist Mississippi Democrats that the state would go for Kennedy, nobody knew exactly how its delegates would behave at the national convention. "Mississippi does not desire to leave the party of her forefathers," State Representative Frank Shanahan of Vicksburg wrote Kennedy's campaign headquarters, "but we will most certainly do so before we give up her traditions and self-respect."[22] A rebellious delegation under the leadership of Ross Barnett traveled to Los Angeles in July 1960 to attend the Democratic National Convention. It was the last national convention James Eastland participated in. As member of the platform committee, the Mississippi senator was unable to prevent the adoption of the strongest civil rights plank in the history of the Democratic Party.[23] Neither could he persuade Barnett to make the state delegation vote for Lyndon Johnson on the first ballot.

Eastland and Stennis eventually decided to take Barnett to Johnson's hotel room, in an attempt to change the governor's mind. Before the three men departed for the hotel, Barnett had already stated he could not support the Senate majority leader because of his liberal standpoints. Eastland and Stennis tried to temper the governor, telling him that LBJ was "just like you are. He's not a liberal." At the hotel, Johnson voiced a similar message, telling Barnett he was far from progressive. But the chief executive of Mississippi came prepared; he confronted LBJ with an article in *Reader's Digest* where the Texas senator described himself as "a rancher, and a liberal."[24]

Johnson tried to convince Barnett that he was talking about being liberal in granting jury trials, but it was to no avail. Judge Tom Brady, acting on behalf of the Mississippi delegates, nominated Governor Ross Barnett as presidential candidate for the Democratic Party. The delegation from Mississippi almost bolted when the convention booed Brady for stating that communists were behind many of the civil rights activities across the country. Kennedy eventually won the nomination by acclamation, but the Mississippians did not want to be part of it. Barnett, Eastland, and Stennis pulled out all the stops to make sure the convention minutes showed they shifted their votes from Barnett to LBJ instead of JFK. "We protest vigorously and we insist that the record show the full facts and that the 23 votes [of Mississippi] be recorded in your official record for Sen. Lyndon Johnson," the triumvirate wrote in a telegram. An earlier attempt by Eastland, Stennis, and the governor to convince LeRoy Collins, the chairman of the convention, to change the minutes had failed. "Who's going to campaign for the ticket in Mississippi if it isn't us?" Stennis had asked Collins in desperation. "Who's going to campaign? We can't campaign on that record in Mississippi."[25]

The Mississippi delegation left Los Angeles in disillusion. After casting their last votes for Lyndon Baines Johnson as vice presidential candidate, most of the delegates went home, not caring about the festivities on the last night of the convention. It was not a walkout, the *Clarion-Ledger* reported, "just a feeling that the show was over, most folks fed up with the congestion, confusion and radicalism of the convention." Congressman Thomas Abernethy criticized the national party's stance on civil rights, agriculture, and fiscal responsibility, which were all important issues in Mississippi. "If these were enacted into legislation it would carry the country to an extreme left socialist position such as never was dreamed of by most Americans," he said. Abernethy considered his state strongly Democratic, but with the current platform it was going to be difficult for Mississippians to vote for the national ticket.[26]

On August 16, one month after Los Angeles, the state Democratic Party reassembled in convention and drafted a resolution that rejected and opposed "the platforms of the national Democratic and Republican Parties and their candidates, so long as they are pledged to and running on said platforms in their present forms." Walter Sillers, chairman of the Mississippi Democrats' resolution committee, sent a telegram to James Eastland with the request to show his support for a slate of independent electors "dedicated to segregation, states' rights, and constitutional government." In Sillers's opinion, only independent action based on southern unity could prevent the destruction of the South's society. "Speaking for the Democrats of Mississippi, we urge you to join us and others in this great effort to save this nation from totalitarianism," Sillers concluded his telegram. "This may be our last chance to salvage our freedoms from the selfish and ruthless hands of greedy politicians."[27]

But Eastland no longer lived in 1948. He was wary of yet another bolt from the Democrats. Based on his seniority and chairmanship of the Judiciary Committee, he had become a powerful figure in Congress and the Democratic Party and he was not willing to give up his influence for a volatile third-party effort that had little chance of success. On August 19, three days after Sillers sent his telegram, Eastland and Stennis issued a joint statement in which they pledged their support to the Kennedy-Johnson ticket. The senators "concluded that the plan for independent electors, even though prompted in good faith, will not have sufficient strength in the South to be effective." Although Eastland and Stennis would vote for the national candidates in 1960, they did not accept all the provisions in the party's platform. Through their influence in the Senate, Stennis and Eastland argued, they could prevent the enactment of these provisions into law: "We are now in an era of power politics, and we know from experience that the strongest and most effective way to protect or preserve the interests of our State and country at this time is with national party affiliation."[28]

Southern segregationists of course remembered Eastland's prominent role in the 1948 revolt against the national party. "It was Senator Jim Eastland who first urged Mississippi and the South to use their electoral votes to obtain concessions from the national Democratic party," recollected Erle Johnston. Johnston served as Eastland's publicity man in his first Senate campaign, but he worked for the unpledged electors in 1960. The irony of Eastland taking a stand in 1948 for an independent southern course and his advocacy of a Loyalist position twelve years later was not lost on Johnston: "But now, in the year of 1960 as Governor Ross Barnett was organizing an unpledged elector campaign—a first for Mississippi—Senator Eastland, who earlier said it was the South's best route, announced on television before a group of newspapermen that he would support the Democratic ticket."[29]

Mississippians lambasted Eastland's connection with John Kennedy, "the fair haired boy of Reuther, Hoffa and other Union bosses," and Lyndon Johnson, "the greatest scalawag the South has known since Reconstruction Days."[30] Eastland's constituents regularly charged Lyndon Johnson with treason to the South. After all, "Mr. 'Turncoat' Johnson" served as the running mate of a Catholic Yankee, ran on a platform that was detrimental to Jim Crow, and scorned his southern heritage.[31] In the eyes of many white southerners, Lyndon Johnson became the ultimate symbol of Democratic treason to the Southland, a modern-day Benedict Arnold who had abandoned the southern cause for political glory. The two Mississippi senators had to be careful not to receive a similar stigma. Such prospects loomed large for Eastland by the end of October, when former president Harry Truman visited Tupelo to campaign for the Kennedy-Johnson ticket. Eastland was present at the rally to introduce Truman. Twelve years before, the senator had gloated about his number one spot on Truman's unpopularity list. Now, he called the Missourian one of the greatest presidents in the history of the United States. One resident of Long Beach, Mississippi, had long idolized Eastland, but his appearance in Tupelo all but ended that admiration. Eastland's backing of the national ticket already thoroughly disgusted him, but he "never once dreamed that you would stoop to asking your people to support that gang of communists and their supporters in Washington, with Harry Truman just one of their chief spokesmen."[32]

Despite such negative feedback, the Democratic campaign picked up steam in Mississippi after Lyndon Johnson's train tour through the state with Eastland and Stennis on board. While the vice presidential candidate and the two senators traveled through southeast Mississippi, James Coleman spoke in other parts of the state, where he urged voters to get into "the mainstream of political action." Coleman argued Mississippi needed all the help it could get to protect its principles, and it would only get that help if Mississippians sat at the table where the decisions were made. According to the former governor, the Democrats were the only party that could offer such assistance.[33]

The voters did not reject Coleman's pleas outright. During the first weeks of the campaign, the unpledged elector movement barnstormed the state and seemed well on its way to winning an easy victory. But voters began to turn away from Barnett's crusade because it lacked a clear platform and a candidate. Besides these problems, Barnett also expected that the state's two U.S. senators would not enter the race, at least not on behalf of the Democratic ticket. The Mississippi press considered their participation during the last few weeks of the campaign significant in turning the tide of the unpledged electors. Many white voters did not like Kennedy and Johnson, but they would cast their ballot for them to protect the influence of Eastland and Stennis in Washington.[34]

In a statewide television appearance, Eastland himself admitted he would have supported the unpledged electors if the stakes were not that high. "I would be for the independents . . . if the South held the balance of power," the senator said. But with only Mississippi and parts of Alabama favoring an independent slate, political isolation might be the result if the endeavor failed. Popularity of the Democratic ticket was strongest in the sixth congressional district, an area with industrial centers such as Carroll Gartin's hometown of Laurel, where workers traditionally supported the Democratic Party. The unpledged electors had their greatest following in the Delta and around Jackson. The young and energized Republican Party, by 1960 completely under white control, also polled highest in this section of the state.[35]

In response to the many critical inquiries about Eastland's support of the Democratic ticket, his office drafted a series of form letters to outline his motives. The letters explained that a senator would not be able to do anything without affiliation to the Democratic or the Republican Party. In order to combat "the socialistic and unwise proposals which confront our country," Eastland needed to be associated with one of the two major national parties. Moreover, seniority was a party rule, not a Senate rule, and Eastland would lose his chairmanship of the Judiciary Committee to Estes Kefauver if he abandoned the Democrats, who held the majority in Congress. The office staff included a statement by none other than NAACP leader Clarence Mitchell, who confirmed in the *Washington Post* that parties could pass resolutions, but that only Congress could legislate. Eastland indicated he would never criticize anybody for voting their convictions, even if they cast their ballot for the Republicans.[36]

The unpledged electors won the race in Mississippi, but their victory was narrow: the independent slate received 39 percent of the vote, the Democrats 36.3, and the Republicans 24.7. Mississippi's electoral votes went to Senator Harry Byrd of Virginia.[37] After the election, James Coleman thanked Stennis for his contribution to the Democratic campaign. He was proud the South was still largely Democratic. "If you, Senator Eastland, and the rest of us had maintained a political silence, if we had gone away and hidden ourselves from the dirty political onslaughts that we had to stand up to, the regular Democratic ticket would not have polled 50,000 votes in this State," asserted Coleman.[38]

Frank Shanahan congratulated John Kennedy on defeating Richard Nixon and proudly notified the president-elect that his home county of Warren voted for the Democratic ticket. Democratic strength in Mississippi was primarily located in the northeastern part of the state, in some eastern counties, and on the Gulf Coast. "Were it not for the fact that Congressman John Bell Williams and Governor Ross Barnett and House Speaker Walter Sillers actively fought the Democratic pledged ticket, we would have carried the state easily," Shanahan informed Kennedy. According to the state legislator from Vicksburg, all was not lost yet for the national Democratic Party in Mississippi.[39]

James Eastland faced no opposition in the 1960 Senate election. The Sunday before the primary vote, the *Clarion-Ledger* published an op-ed piece about the many strengths of the senator and why the people of Mississippi should cast their ballots for him. As head of the Judiciary Committee, he had jurisdiction over more matters than any other chairman. His influence on civil rights, anticommunist measures, and immigration made him a "chief target for attacks and abuse by radical elements." The newspaper saw these attacks as a confirmation of Eastland's power in Washington. In combination with his seat on the Agriculture Committee, Mississippi's senior senator was in an excellent position to protect the state's social system and help its economy. "Senator Eastland is a dynamic leader, a successful planter-farmer, of proven ability, integrity, and sincerity," the *Clarion-Ledger* reported, "the South will need his effective leadership during the critical period ahead."[40]

The Jackson newspaper effectively summarized why the white citizens of Mississippi voted for James Eastland: although he was a Democrat, the South could ill afford to lose such a powerful politician. As long as southern voters made the distinction between the national Democrats and Eastland's brand of Democratic politics, and as long as Eastland could defend his position within the national party, his seat was secure. For the nascent Republican Party in the South, then, the challenge was to connect the Mississippi senator with the liberal initiatives of the Kennedy White House.

After Election Day, Eastland talked almost apologetically about his stand in the presidential election. He told one of his constituents from Smithdale that in light of the circumstances, supporting the Democratic candidates was the best thing to do. Most of the people in the unpledged elector movement were his friends, however, and Eastland shared their sentiments.[41] A resident of Starkville, Mississippi, asked Eastland to vote against foreign aid and to take a strong stand against Cuba and the "socialistic proposals" of Kennedy. "I cannot understand why you urged the people of Mississippi to vote for our socialist President John Kennedy," she expressed. Eastland sent a curious answer. "I announced definitely during the campaign that I was supporting Kennedy, and stood very much against the proposals he was enunciating," the senator replied. According to Eastland's logic, there was "nothing unusual about this." He argued that Nixon had similar views on southern problems and that there was no profit in bolting the party.[42]

The Democratic leadership and the Kennedy administration rewarded the senatorial duo from the Magnolia State in various ways for their loyalty to the ticket. First of all, James Eastland retained the chairmanship of the Judiciary Committee in the new Congress, despite protests from civil rights proponents who argued the committee "was stacked in advance against President-elect John F. Kennedy." Besides chairing Judiciary, he continued his work as head of the Internal Security Subcommittee and as a member of the Agriculture and Forestry Committee and the Joint Committee on Immigration and Nationality Policy.[43]

Eastland and Stennis also maintained their influence on the distribution of federal patronage in the state. Shortly after Kennedy's inauguration, Senator Stennis contacted Larry O'Brien, the White House legislative liaison and a chief administrator on patronage issues. Stennis worried about the president's plans to alter the membership and administration of the Agricultural Stabilization and Conservation Service committees (ASCS) in various states. For an agricultural state like Mississippi, appointment to the ASCS naturally was not a trivial matter. Stennis had discussed the case with Eastland, and the two senators wanted to make sure the White House was not going to change the system without consulting them first. "Our State Committeemen and State Administrative Officers have not been selected on a political basis," Stennis assured O'Brien. Instead, these officials were nominated to represent the agricultural interests of different sections in the state. After receiving Stennis's letter, O'Brien phoned the senator to talk about the handling of statewide patronage. He subsequently guaranteed Stennis that "you two [Eastland and Stennis] will recommend to us on matters affecting Mississippi."[44]

Eastland and Stennis probably remembered the patronage imbroglio during Harry Truman's presidency. Their decision to choose pragmatism over principle in the 1960 campaign now bore fruit, as the White House recognized them in the disbursement of federal largesse. By the end of March, Chairman John Bailey of the Democratic National Committee also agreed to follow the advice of Stennis and Eastland regarding statewide appointments and statewide patronage.[45] While the two senators secured their influence on the distribution of federal jobs in the state, the DNC and the administration decided to discipline Mississippi congressmen Thomas Abernethy, Bill Colmer, Jamie Whitten, and John Bell Williams for their refusal to endorse the presidential candidates of the Democratic Party. Like Harry Truman had done in 1949, the president and the national committee initially withheld patronage from disloyal Democrats.

Abernethy enlisted Stennis's help to restore patronage to the derelict House members from Mississippi. On March 1, Stennis and Eastland met with Larry O'Brien and John Bailey in a DNC office on Connecticut Avenue to discuss the matter. Bailey asked the two senators for suggestions about the nomination of postmasters and rural carriers in the four congressional districts represented by Abernethy and his fellow rebels. Eastland and Stennis both agreed that despite their behavior in the presidential election, the congressmen should be in charge of such appointments. Their constituents "were entitled to have these selections made by someone responsible to the people," assessed Stennis. He advised against consulting with the state Democratic Committee about federal patronage. Such a course had gone completely awry during the Truman administration. Moreover, with the massive resisters firmly entrenched in the upper echelons of the state party, Stennis deemed it wise to return patronage to the elected representatives of Mississippi. O'Brien and Bailey promised to take the recommendations made by Stennis and Eastland into consideration. "Bailey is sharp and keen," Stennis told Abernethy after the meeting with O'Brien and the new DNC chairman. "He does not seem to want to punish anyone, but to build. But at the same time he is a sharp shooter."[46] Eastland and Stennis had learned their lesson on patronage when Truman was president. The four Mississippi congressmen, including New Deal veterans like Bill Colmer and Thomas Abernethy, clearly had not.

In his attitude toward civil rights activists, Kennedy affirmed Eastland's views of the newly elected chief executive. "The fact of the business is, I don't think the President himself has ever been as radical as the group who wrote the platform in Los Angeles," Eastland told one of his fellow planters in Mississippi.[47] Although Eastland thought Kennedy was too liberal on federal spending and government centralization, he did not expect revolutionary initiatives from the administration in fields vital to the South, such as civil rights. The senator was right. On March 16, 1961, Lee White, assistant special counsel to the president, dispatched a memo to Larry O'Brien, who had a meeting scheduled with Eastland. White instructed O'Brien to commend Eastland for securing prompt action on the omnibus judgeship act, a bill creating 130 new judicial positions. He also advised to ignore the civil rights issue. "Presumably there is no good reason to discuss civil rights or civil rights legislation at this time," White noted. His memorandum shows the deference of the Kennedy team toward senior members of Congress, especially during the first year of the administration.[48] Thanks to Eastland's help, Kennedy could sign the judgeship bill into law on May 19. But in exchange for his assistance, the Mississippi senator demanded the right to appoint the first new federal judge to the bench. Eastland nominated his friend William Harold Cox, a successful attorney and the son of a Sunflower County sheriff. Moreover, Cox was a devoted segregationist.[49]

Cox was no stranger to John Kennedy. In May 1959, when he was still on his quest to get the support of southern racists for his presidential bid, Kennedy contacted Cox, explaining his contribution to the Kennedy-Ervin labor bill. Cox regretted that he did not have the opportunity to listen to Kennedy's speech in Jackson, but promised to visit his office when he was in Washington. Although the president appeared to have little qualms about Eastland's choice, Attorney General Robert Kennedy wanted to make sure Cox would be impartial in civil rights cases. In an interview, the nominee assured the attorney general he would uphold the Constitution as interpreted by the Supreme Court. Such promises took on a completely different meaning in the Deep South, however. Once Cox was appointed federal district judge, he enraged civil rights advocates with his outspoken racism. According to Clarence Mitchell, the Kennedy White House began to look "suspiciously like a dude ranch," with Jim Eastland as general manager.[50]

Eastland's influence on the Kennedy administration's approach to civil rights unrest became clear during the Freedom Rides of 1961. A year earlier, in *Boynton v. Virginia*, the Supreme Court had outlawed segregated terminals on interstate travel. During the spring of 1961, interracial groups of civil rights activists started traveling through the South by bus to test compliance with the verdict. The day President Kennedy signed the judgeship bill, a band of Freedom Riders affiliated with the Student Nonviolent Coordinating Committee (SNCC) boarded a Greyhound bus bound for Montgomery, Alabama. The trip had started on May 17 and went through Birmingham, where the group did not escape an encounter with Eugene "Bull" Connor, the city's commissioner of public safety. By the time Connor arrived, an angry crowd had already assembled at the bus station. The commissioner told the riders that they were not going to Montgomery, but to the city jail for their "own protection." The next morning, Robert Kennedy and Burke Marshall, assistant attorney general for civil rights, arranged an emergency meeting with the president to discuss the events in Alabama. John Kennedy, still in his pajamas, listened to his brother's dire briefing of the situation: another group of Freedom Riders was in jail in Birmingham, they were conducting a hunger strike, and the bus company refused to transport the travelers without police protection.[51]

When JFK tried to call John Patterson later that day, the receptionist said the governor had gone on a fishing trip in the Gulf of Mexico. Less than a year earlier, Patterson had promoted Kennedy in Alabama and in other southern states and raised money for him. By the spring of 1961, however, he had turned increasingly hostile toward the Kennedy administration because of its handling of the Freedom Riders. "The people of this country are so goddamn tired of this namby-pamby business in Washington where these Negroes are concerned, and I'm sick of it," Patterson told John Seigenthaler, a Justice Department official sent by RFK to negotiate with Alabama's chief executive. "I'm sick of these spineless people that I supported not standing up." Robert Kennedy's incessant demands to provide protection for the riders irritated Patterson. Seigenthaler and Patterson nonetheless hammered out a deal that would prevent the use of federal marshals and get the riders out of Alabama as soon as possible. State troopers were going to provide escort on the highways, and local police would be in charge of the operation in Birmingham and Montgomery.[52]

The Kennedy brothers were relieved that they did not have to dispatch the military to Alabama, but they were not out of the Deep South woods yet. Mob violence again broke out in Montgomery. Even Seigenthaler did not escape a beating by the hoodlums. When he tried to stop a group of men assaulting a black girl, one of the rioters knocked him unconscious with a lead pipe. In an attempt to prevent further escalation, Robert Kennedy sent in a contingent of U.S. marshals to protect the riders against the waves of vicious attacks. The arrival of civil rights leader Martin Luther King Jr. in Montgomery added more tension to an already explosive situation. A large group of whites surrounded the church where he was delivering a sermon, and they were ready to attack. At that point the White House seriously started to contemplate the use of federal troops to reinforce the outnumbered marshals and stave off a bloodbath.

Deliverance came from an old ally. John Patterson, refusing to take phone calls from the attorney general, finally mobilized the National Guard to restore order in the downtown area. The Alabama governor contacted Robert Kennedy later that evening, after a two-day silence between the two Democrats. "You got yourself a fight," Patterson yelled. "You got yourself what you wanted. And you've got the National Guard called out, and martial law. And that's what you wanted." Kennedy asked if King and the people in the church were safe, but the governor refused to answer. RFK lost his temper; he told Patterson to stop his exercise in rhetoric and get Adjutant General Henry Graham, the officer in command, on the phone. "You're destroying us politically," Patterson protested. But the attorney general now had other priorities. "John, it's more important that these people in the church survive physically than for us to survive politically," he answered.[53]

When the Freedom Riders decided to resume their protest and drive on to Mississippi, the Kennedys braced themselves for more mayhem. Alabama had been bad; Mississippi might get worse. John Patterson had been a loyal friend of John Kennedy up until the Freedom Rides. In the beginning of May, shortly before the first riders got on the bus in Washington, the president and the governor actually had lunched together in the nation's capital. But Ross Barnett never had such ties with JFK, as leader of the unpledged elector movement in his state. James Coleman cautioned Burke Marshall that Barnett was a political agitator of the worst kind who could not be trusted. In the end, the president and his brother turned to Jim Eastland to keep things under control in the Magnolia State. Eastland's attitude toward civil rights activism was of course well known, but at least he had actively supported the ticket in 1960 and possessed a wide network of political friends in Mississippi. The senator liked John and Robert Kennedy, and these feelings were mutual. In an interview with *New York Times* columnist Anthony Lewis, RFK said that during his confirmation hearings he received the strongest support from southern senators such as James Eastland, John McClellan of Arkansas, Sam Ervin of North Carolina, and Olin Johnston of South Carolina. As attorney general,

Robert Kennedy often relied on Eastland's counsel in matters concerning Mississippi and the South.[54]

With the assistance of Eastland, the White House managed to control the Freedom Riders' journey through Mississippi. In contrast with Alabama, no major protests erupted along the route. The president and his brother had been apprehensive about what would happen in Mississippi, because state authorities seemed to be in a rebellious mood. Governor Barnett, always ready to take a defiant stand for the Southland, sent a telegram to Robert Kennedy proclaiming he should keep the "agitators" out of the state. The attorney general of Mississippi, Joe Patterson, accused the Freedom Riders of "Communist conduct." James Coleman told Marshall he doubted the civil rights activists would make it to Jackson alive. When the Trailways bus left Montgomery and set course for Mississippi on May 24, Robert Kennedy was constantly in touch with Eastland. The U.S. attorney general sometimes talked to him twelve times a day. Eastland promised there would not be any rioting. The Freedom Riders would go straight to jail once they reached Jackson, however. Barnett, Eastland, and Robert Kennedy—the state and national Democratic establishment—all benefitted from this deal: the administration did not have to worry about embarrassing outbursts of violence and the dispatch of federal troops, and Mississippi leaders were given the opportunity to lock up a group of civil rights workers without much trouble, thus demonstrating the primacy of states' rights in this kind of matter. Moreover, the state leadership could prove that they were able to maintain order without bloodshed. The Mississippi National Guard escorted the travelers from the Alabama border to Jackson, where they were whisked away to the city jail. During the spring and summer of 1961, more than three hundred Freedom Riders descended on the capital of Mississippi. With the detention centers in town quickly filling up, the police started sending activists to Parchman penitentiary, a notorious prison farm in the middle of the Delta. Although the continued attention of the press probably prevented extreme forms of brutality toward the riders, the time they spent in jail was grueling, particularly in the stifling summer heat.[55]

The Freedom Rider episode solidified the bonds between James Eastland and the Kennedy administration. Three years after the rides, Robert Kennedy still had a great degree of respect for Mississippi's senior senator. According to RFK, Eastland was straightforward, kept his word, and was always available. Whenever the administration had to deal with developments in Mississippi, government officials turned to Eastland. He informed them who could be trusted in the state, and whether he was in a position to help. Robert Kennedy recalled that Eastland's advice "was very, very helpful" and that he "found it much more pleasant to deal with him than with many of the so-called liberals on the House Judiciary Committee, or in other parts of Congress or the Senate."[56]

Both Eastland and the Kennedys had an interest in minimizing forceful civil rights activity in the South. For Eastland, the stakes were clear: any challenge to the perpetuation of Jim Crow was dangerous and needed to be suppressed. For the president, international politics had a higher priority than desegregation. The Freedom Riders started their crusade at a critical point in foreign policy, between the failed Bay of Pigs invasion of April 1961 and a summit meeting with Nikita Khrushchev in Vienna in June. The attempt to topple Fidel Castro had gone horribly wrong, and JFK needed no more embarrassing situations right before a conference with the leader of the Soviet Union. The United States preferred to showcase itself as a beacon of freedom and democracy in the worldwide fight against communism. Southern racists beating up peaceful travelers did not fit into this image.[57] Within the framework of the Cold War, Eastland and the Kennedy brothers teamed up to counter their own versions of the Red Menace. Eastland wanted to keep the "communist agitators" coming into the South at bay, while John Kennedy desired to win the hearts and minds of the nonaligned countries in the conflict with the Soviet Union. The Cold War brought Eastland and Kennedy closer together.

James Eastland saw a clear connection between the domestic and international fight against communism. He outlined the global dimension of the Freedom Rider movement in a speech before the Georgia States' Rights Council in Atlanta on July 24, 1961. The address brought together many of the points Eastland had made during his career. The planter-politician did not doubt whites everywhere shared the racist beliefs of southern segregationists. "It is my fixed and sincere opinion that white people, not only in the South, but in the United States generally and throughout the world, are not yet willing to forfeit their birthright on the altar of integration and miscegenation." This premise formed the basis for Eastland's confidence that the tide could be turned against forced desegregation.[58]

Another central element of the senator's worldview was the idea that the American civil rights movement was part of a global communist conspiracy and that the South formed the front line in the battle to preserve western civilization. "The Masters of the Communist Conspiracy sit at the console of a giant organ," Eastland ominously explained. These masters, by simply pressing the keys, had the power to set off an international chain reaction that fanned the flames of racial strife and class warfare. They did not wage war with conventional weapons, but employed insidious methods that ate away the core of American society. From Eastland's point of view, the organizers of the Freedom Rides were dangerous communist agents, and their followers mere puppets who danced to the wishes of their Marxist overlords.[59]

The liberal verdicts of the Supreme Court exacerbated the threat of communist infiltration, Eastland argued. After the Brown ruling of 1954, the Court became the most prominent nemesis in Eastland's rhetoric. He reviled how the institution acted "as a super legislature, misinterpreting and perverting the Constitution through judicial fiat, and usurping power and authority not delegated to it by the Constitution, which is responsible for the plight in which the States of this Union find themselves today." His research staff had started gathering data about the decisions rendered by the judges and compiling charts that demonstrated their Marxist leanings. On July 10, 1958, Eastland introduced the first findings of this research on the floor of the U.S. Senate. In 1961, he presented an update to the Georgia States' Rights Council. Eastland placed himself in a long American tradition of opposition to the Supreme Court. "Thomas Jefferson was the first to characterize the United States Supreme Court as the potential Achilles Heel in the fabric of our Republican form of government," the senator stated. Eastland accused the judges of rewriting the Constitution on the basis of subversive doctrines, completely disregarding the original intent of the founding fathers. The Court passed the Brown v. Board of Education and the Boynton v. Virginia decisions, Eastland reasoned, so the judges were responsible for the closing down of public schools in Prince Edward County in Virginia and the unrest caused by the Freedom Rides.[60]

After depicting the Supreme Court as a leftist stronghold that posed a danger to the American system of government, Eastland placed the Freedom Riders in the same category. The Congress of Racial Equality (CORE) had been a major force behind the Freedom Rides. At least twelve members of the CORE advisory committee were members of communist or communist-front organizations, according to reports written by the Senate Internal

Security Subcommittee and the House Un-American Activities Committee. CORE employed strategies that were used by communists all over the world, Eastland claimed; the Freedom Riders tried to destroy state sovereignty with their protests. Through the creation of conflict, the riders wanted to generate a federal response to end the violence. Such a transfer of police power from the states to the central government would result in a national police state, Eastland argued, which was exactly what the communists were after. They recognized that states' rights constituted the most important bulwark against political centralization. The destruction of states' rights would inevitably lead to the overthrow of the Constitution and the political system of the United States. On these ruins, the communists could then build their despotic super state.

Because the Freedom Riders subscribed to this agenda, Eastland considered them traitors. He singled out CORE leader James Peck as the ultimate symbol of treachery. Peck participated in the first Freedom Ride and received a severe beating in Birmingham. This man was not only a coward who dodged military service as a conscientious objector during World War II, Eastland snarled, but also a terrorist who attempted to break into nuclear testing facilities multiple times. The senator called him "a Communist agitator and organizer of the most dangerous kind," and repeated a description of the Freedom Riders he had previously delivered in the Senate: "the core of the 'Peace Riders' was not student trainees, but agent provocateurs with the longest possible record of experience in activities inimical to the security and welfare of the United States." Their travels through the South were nothing more than a diversionary tactic, Eastland cautioned. The real goal of the activists was "a complete integration of the white and colored races," starting with children in public schools.[61]

The senator told his audience the white South needed to regroup, reorganize, and then go on the offensive to protect the southern way of life and reestablish constitutional government. Northern whites should be enlisted in this cause. Eastland saw fertile ground for southern ideas in the North. Forced racial integration, rising crime rates, property devaluation, and the breakdown of the public school system brought the white population in eastern and western cities close to revolt, he observed. Southern whites should come to the aid of their countrymen in other parts of the nation. Eastland also talked about change: the change of public opinion outside the South. "We must accelerate this change—continue lawful and effective resistance to integration in every area of the South and spread the gospel throughout the land."[62]

James Eastland used the framework of the Cold War to castigate the enemies of the southern way of life as part of a global communist conspiracy. Supreme Court justices and civil rights activists thus became ultimate symbols of un-Americanism, and segregation was turned into a long-standing American tradition. "Mississippi is proud to be known as the hard core of resistance against any integration of the white and Negro races," Eastland declared. The massive invasion of Freedom Riders only testified to the state's reputation. Their efforts to desegregate bus terminals was the first time Mississippians experienced an "open manifestation of the Communist Conspiracy in its attempt to achieve the next best thing to proletarian revolution."[63]

Although the president and the attorney general shared Eastland's anticommunism, they were not opposed to the extension of civil rights. They preferred to do so through more conventional political procedures, however. The direct action strategy employed by civil rights activists did not fit in the gradualist approach the Kennedys advocated. The Supreme Court had declared segregation in public schools and in interstate terminals unconstitutional, but instead of supporting civil rights workers in their attempts to carry out these decrees, the Kennedy administration turned to southern politicians like James Eastland to minimize the impact of direct action. From a foreign policy perspective, such a course of action might make sense, despite the fact that the Freedom Riders were merely exercising their constitutional rights as interstate passengers. Robert Kennedy acknowledged that the federal government was obliged to protect these travelers when local authorities were incapable or unwilling to do so. But he also thought the riders and the white rioters had a patriotic duty to prevent unrest. "I think we should all bear in mind that the President is about to embark on a mission of great importance," the attorney general said on the day the Freedom Riders entered Mississippi. "Whatever we do in the United States at this time, which brings or causes discredit on our country, can be harmful to his mission."[64] The anticommunism of the Kennedy administration on the international scene dovetailed nicely with Eastland's fight against communist infiltration on the domestic scene.

According to the Kennedys, the ballot box was the surest road to black advancement in the South. Shortly after his brother's inauguration, Robert Kennedy told Martin Luther King that segregationists like James Eastland "would not be so fresh" if the reverend could "get enough of them [African Americans] on the voting rolls in Mississippi."[65] RFK said the federal government had a clear mandate in protecting the right to vote. Nobody—not even southern segregationists—could legitimately oppose voting rights, and suffrage provided blacks the opportunity to change the electoral landscape in the South. The Kennedy administration also hoped the increase in black voters would enhance prospects for the president's reelection, ensure the passage of more liberal measures through the election of progressive southerners to Congress, and eventually transform the southern Democratic Party into a more moderate organization. Once black southerners started voting, Robert Kennedy argued, other rights would automatically follow.

In order to realize these goals, the White House initiated the Voter Education Project (VEP) during the summer of 1961. The government brought together the NAACP, King's Southern Christian Leadership Conference (SCLC), SNCC, CORE, and the Urban League to organize voter registration activities. Funding for the operation was arranged through progressive philanthropic associations. The Justice Department pledged to provide aid, although officials did not give details on the nature of this assistance. When the activists fanned out across the South to start their registration drives, they soon discovered the limits of federal protection.[66]

Many of the civil rights workers who participated in the meeting were suspicious of the true intentions of the administration. Particularly the young and militant activists of SNCC mistrusted the liberal establishment and the more conservative civil rights groups. They suspected that the government was trying to steer the movement into a less radical course by giving money to voter registration, but not to direct action protests. SNCC and the other organizations nonetheless agreed to participate in the VEP, because they needed financial resources and because they expected that the administration would protect them against harassments from southern racists.[67]

The Justice Department had a different definition of protection, however. During the Freedom Rides, the president and the attorney general had already been reluctant to send federal troops to uphold the law. This attitude did not change when the VEP started. The government again relied on local law enforcement to keep the peace. CORE and SNCC, the two organizations that were active in the segregationist heartland of the South, thus depended on the white power structure for their safety. FBI agents only observed what was going on, but did not offer viable security. In its quest for justice, the White House depended on southern federal courts. But with judges like Eastland appointee William Harold Cox on the bench, civil rights workers did not expect fair trials. They logically became frustrated with liberal institutions and with the inability of the federal government to enforce the Constitution in the South. When a civil rights worker asked Mayor Charles Dorrough of Ruleville, a town a few miles north of Eastland's plantation, about his opinion of the U.S. Constitution, he answered: "That law hasn't come here yet."[68]

The introduction of government-backed civil rights programs such as the VEP did not prevent more direct action demonstrations. During the fall of 1962, federal and state authorities clashed over integration at the University of Mississippi, the state's flagship school and a bastion of the Old South. In September of that year, after a protracted legal battle, a black Mississippian named James Meredith aspired to register at Ole Miss. Meredith was not the first African American to undertake such a courageous attempt. In 1958, Clennon King had traveled to Oxford to sign up as a student at the university. Governor Coleman eventually ordered a lunacy hearing for King. He ended up in the state mental hospital for twelve days. Coleman followed the politics of practical segregation and strived to keep integration activities out of the spotlight. Ross Barnett, Coleman's eccentric successor, was considerably less pragmatic. And in contrast with King, James Meredith had a Supreme Court decree that explicitly ordered his admission to the university.

The Kennedy administration had little choice but to fulfill its executive duty and implement the decision of the Court. The president preferred to do so with as little federal force as possible, however, and through negotiations with Barnett. The Mississippi police force had dealt effectively with the Freedom Riders, and the White House hoped a similar agreement could be reached on Meredith's enrollment at Ole Miss. The university could not refuse Meredith, but Kennedy did not want a spectacle around his registration. The midterm elections were coming up, and a violent altercation between the federal government and the Mississippi governor might endanger the reelection of southern moderates. Moreover, the president did not want to upset the members of the powerful Southern Caucus.[69]

But Ross Barnett had no eye for Kennedy's considerations. He had been elected governor of the sovereign state of Mississippi and he intended to defend its rights. Barnett was a demagogue who reveled in the adulation of the crowds and took his political advice from the Citizens' Councils. On September 13, Barnett delivered a defiant speech, broadcast across the state on television and radio. He invoked the Tenth Amendment of the U.S. Constitution, pledged an absolute defense of segregation, and accused "a motley array of un-American pressure groups" of causing the integration crisis. "The Kennedy administration is lending the power of the Federal Government to the ruthless demands of these agitators," Barnett charged.[70]

Two days after the speech, Robert Kennedy contacted Barnett to discuss Meredith's registration at Ole Miss. Although the phone conversation was cordial, the governor initially clung to his right of interposition. The Mississippi press had reported favorably on his strong stand and Barnett enjoyed his newfound hero status in the state. The governor of course remembered the Freedom Rider episode, when the White House practically gave him carte blanche to deal with the riders, instead of offering them federal protection to exercise their constitutional rights. Barnett thought that as long as he could maintain law and order, the president would not enforce desegregation.[71]

Barnett's assumptions about Kennedy's resolve proved to be wrong, however, and his ability to keep the peace proved to be overrated. In fact, Barnett's behavior exacerbated the entire situation. He continued to talk to the president and the attorney general about finding a solution. Facing contempt of court charges, the governor seemed to realize that Meredith's admission had become inevitable. In the negotiations with the federal government, he came up with all sorts of Wild West scenarios that involved increasing numbers of federal marshals drawing guns on him before his surrender. After repeatedly telling the people of Mississippi he would protect the southern way of life at all costs, Barnett needed such a show of force to save face. But when Kennedy and Barnett were finally close to a deal, the governor appeared at a night game of the Ole Miss Rebels against the University of Kentucky in Jackson's Memorial Stadium. A crowd of forty-one thousand whites waved Confederate flags and cheered loudly as the governor again promised to uphold Mississippi's traditions. Buoyed by the exuberant reception in the stadium, Barnett called Kennedy after the football game to tell him he refused to yield. The administration subsequently started final preparations to federalize the Mississippi National Guard and, if necessary, deploy the army.[72]

When Meredith flew to Oxford on September 30, tensions in the state had reached fever pitch, not in a small degree due to Barnett's inflaming speeches.

On the night of Meredith's arrival, the governor again hit the airwaves. He announced that Meredith was on campus but asked Mississippians to stay calm. He reiterated his dedication to states' rights and southern principles, and he vilified the Kennedy brothers for trampling on the sovereignty of Mississippi. By nightfall, an angry mob had gathered in front of the Lyceum, the administrative heart of the university. A contingent of U.S. marshals protected the building, but they had trouble controlling the horde, especially after state authorities ordered the highway patrol to pull out. Among the rioters was former major general Edwin A. Walker, who commanded the 101st Airborne Division during the Little Rock crisis in 1957. Four years later he had resigned because he was convinced the Kennedy administration colluded "with the international Communist conspiracy."[73]

On the night of the riot, Walker spurred on the protesters to force the marshals from their positions. In the meantime, John Kennedy addressed the nation about Meredith's imminent admission. The president, unaware of the escalation of violence at Ole Miss, praised Barnett, the university, and local authorities for their compliance with the Supreme Court order. The marshals desperately tried to hold back the mob with tear gas, and the White House eventually ordered the army to reinforce the troops on campus. Shortly after midnight, twenty-five thousand soldiers arrived on the scene and restored order. The next day, on the morning of October 1, James Meredith became the first known black student at the University of Mississippi. Two people died in the riot preceding his registration, and more than two hundred marshals and soldiers were injured.[74]

On September 26, Eastland denounced the maneuverings of the Justice Department as "judicial tyranny."[75] But this statement did not satisfy Barnett's supporters. As the crisis in Oxford unfolded, Mississippians started petitioning their congressional representatives to take a more forceful stand for the maintenance of segregation at Ole Miss. A huge number of telegrams flooded Eastland's office. "Do Ross and John Bell have to stand alone for Mississippi," one telegram asked. Another one expressed concern about "the silence of our representatives in Washington in this time of crisis. . . . Why haven't southern representatives taken the position that if the administration is to be the enemy of the South that none of its programs will be supported by them?"[76]

These appeals could not be ignored. On September 28, the Mississippi members of the House and Senate sent a declaration to the White House, imploring the president not to enforce Meredith's registration with military power. They put the responsibility for possible bloodshed and the escalation of racial conflict in Kennedy's hands. "We respectfully appeal to and urge you to stop this demonstration of federal might which has moved the people of our state and is now moving those of other states to the highest degree of heat and tension," the delegation wrote. "A holocaust is in the making."[77]

Shortly after the riot, Eastland and Stennis sent staff members of the Judiciary Committee and the Armed Services Committee to investigate the confrontation between U.S. marshals and the protesters. According to their reports, the marshals had instigated the violence by recklessly shooting tear gas canisters into the crowd, which also forced the highway patrol to retreat.[78] "I think it will undoubtedly be shown by evidence that the Marshals, almost unprovoked, started the rioting on the campus and, of course, everyone knows that this whole affair is permeated with political considerations to secure the Negro vote in the key, big States of the country which have so much weight in the electoral college," Eastland wrote to an admirer from Kansas.[79] Although Eastland dispatched researchers to the scene and asked for a congressional inquiry into the conduct of federal troops at Ole Miss, a Senate investigation apparently never materialized.[80]

In contrast with the arrest of the Freedom Riders in Mississippi a year earlier, Eastland's involvement in the Ole Miss crisis was rather ambiguous. He defended his initial detachment from developments surrounding Meredith's registration as a states' rights issue. "I thought it would be extremely inappropriate for me to have interceded other than I did when the matter was being handled by Governor Barnett and the action was taking place in Jackson," Eastland explained to a friend from Columbus, Mississippi. "As soon, however, as the matter moved to a Federal level and it became appropriate for me to have my say, I believed it satisfied nearly everybody."[81]

Another reason for Eastland's tardy response to the situation at the University of Mississippi might be his strained relationship with the governor. Since Barnett's election in 1959, the alliance between the two politicians had slowly deteriorated. Barnett had deceived not only Robert Kennedy but also Eastland about the events preceding the integration of Ole Miss. The senator had little patience with people who tried to double-cross him.[82] Eastland discussed Barnett's unreliability with Deputy Attorney General Nicholas Katzenbach, who was in Oxford at the end of September. When the violence had subsided and Meredith had registered, Katzenbach received a phone call from James Eastland. Eastland's daughter studied at the University of Mississippi, and the senator wanted to know if the campus was safe. On Eastland's invitation, Katzenbach drove to the plantation in a border patrol car to give an update. When he arrived at the farm in Doddsville, the first thing he noticed was a broken television set. "What happened to your TV?" Katzenbach asked. "Well," Eastland said, "I had some guests Sunday night and we turned on the set to hear President Kennedy's address. One of them got so mad he threw a chair through the screen." Katzenbach's account of General Edwin Walker's role in the riot particularly amused Eastland. Because the senator knew how untrustworthy Barnett was, he thought Robert Kennedy should not have tried to negotiate with the governor. In comparison with other southern politicians, James Eastland was mild in his criticism of how the Kennedys handled Meredith's admission to Ole Miss. He later confided to RFK that Barnett's erratic behavior during the crisis had been unacceptable.[83]

Robert Kennedy and Ross Barnett obviously had different ideas about the implementation of James Meredith's enrollment. The journey of the Freedom Riders through Mississippi formed an important frame of reference for both men. The attorney general thought the Mississippi governor would eventually cooperate with Meredith's registration and provide law and order, while Barnett remembered the administration's reluctance to use the power of the national government to enforce desegregation. Without Eastland as mediator, the conflict between federal and state authorities reached a bloody climax. "As far as Eastland is concerned, he never made any effort to stop us from doing anything in the state of Mississippi," said Robert Kennedy.[84] But Kennedy clearly overestimated his own ability to negotiate effectively with the upper echelons of the massive resistance movement in the state.

In the direct aftermath of the riot, white southerners criticized the president and his brother for their disregard of states' rights, prompting the administration to go into damage control mode. Robert Kennedy tried to pacify southern lawmakers. He explained to Senator Stennis's wife that the administration's involvement in the registration of James Meredith had nothing to do with integration or segregation, but with the enforcement of federal law. President Kennedy's approval ratings in the South dropped fourteen points during the weeks following Meredith's admission, but quickly recovered. By November 1962, the ratings had rebounded to 65 percent, the level before the riot.[85]

The immediate political fallout in the South was limited for President Kennedy, and his image improved among black voters and in foreign politics.[86] But Ross Barnett and the massive resisters did not reap many benefits from their strategy to keep Ole Miss segregated. A report on the economic impact of racial unrest outlined the negative consequences of massive resistance in the Magnolia State. William B. Selah Jr., director of the Southwest Mississippi Area Development Commission, expressed the feelings of many entrepreneurs in the state when he declared that violence hurt business. Northern industrialists reconsidered their intentions to open new plants in Mississippi after the riots at Ole Miss. "It looks like you people are being led by the wrong element," a manufacturer from the Midwest told his colleagues in Mississippi. The Southern Association of Colleges and Schools put the University of Mississippi on "extraordinary status" because of the campus riots and the school's submission to political interference by the governor. By the spring of 1963, an increased number of professors had announced their resignation from Ole Miss, and the Association of American Law Schools notified the law school at the university that it would lose its membership in the association if "a suitable educational atmosphere is not quickly created."[87] White Mississippians needed to decide whether massive resistance to desegregation trumped economic and educational concerns.

While businessmen reconsidered investments in Mississippi, Barnett's opponents called for economic sanctions against the state. Former governor James Coleman advised President Kennedy to threaten Barnett with the suspension of federal aid to Mississippi.[88] On September 21, 1962, John Morsell of the NAACP followed suit. Morsell, acting on behalf of Roy Wilkins, asked President Kennedy to use the full force of the national government to break Barnett's defiance. "We believe that this can best be done by withdrawal of all Federal services and payments from the State of Mississippi for as long as necessary to induce compliance with and respect for the U.S. Constitution and the laws enacted thereunder," wrote the NAACP official. Almost a month later, the White House finally responded to Morsell's suggestions. "Although this particular approach to enforcing the laws of the United States and the orders of the Federal Judicial system is worthy of consideration, it does raise some serious questions," Lee White equivocated. White actually thought that the deployment of the army in Oxford was "in some ways more desirable" than the implementation of economic measures.[89]

Lee White's answer did not silence the call for financial penalties against the state of Mississippi, however. After a meeting in Indianapolis on March 30, 1963, the Civil Rights Commission (CRC) voiced a message that was strikingly similar to Morsell's request. The commission reported about the "open and flagrant violation of the Constitution" in Mississippi since the Ole Miss crisis. "Even children, at the brink of starvation, have been deprived of assistance by the callous and discriminatory acts of Mississippi officials administering Federal funds." Chairman John Hannah of the CRC therefore appealed to the president to stop the violence and lawlessness under the Barnett regime and provide federal protection for Mississippians who tried to exercise their constitutional rights. Hannah specifically asked Kennedy to consider withholding federal funds from Mississippi until the state complied "with the Constitution and laws of the United States."[90]

Upon receiving Hannah's report, Lee White immediately got in touch with the Department of Defense to check the numbers on defense expenditures in Mississippi provided by the CRC. In a memorandum drafted for the president, White refuted most of the charges made in the report and he called the proposed cuts in federal spending in Mississippi a great abuse of executive authority. Moreover, "in many of these programs . . . Negroes would be hurt as much or more than Whites by any withholding," White asserted. He thought the radical proposals of the commission did more harm than good to the reputation of the CRC and to the enactment of the administration's civil rights agenda. In addition, financial sanctions against Mississippi might increase the hostility of southern segregationists. The president, not an admirer of the CRC, told Hannah in April 1963 that the proposals of the commission would be "properly and carefully reviewed within the Executive Branch."[91] Kennedy had no desire to stop the flow of federal dollars to Mississippi, however, or to antagonize powerful southerners such as James Eastland.[92]

After the 1960 presidential race, Senator Eastland became less visible in the politics of the national Democratic Party. By disassociating himself from the liberal tendencies of the national Democrats, Eastland retained his credibility in Mississippi as a defender of white southern interests. As a Senate Democrat, he had the power to thwart the points in his party's platform that were obnoxious to him and his supporters. And behind the scenes, he kept his influence on the Kennedy administration, whose officials regularly turned to Mississippi's senior senator for help and advice. The Freedom Rides confirmed

Eastland's effectiveness as a power broker. During the Rides, the president and the attorney general negotiated with Ross Barnett and the massive resistance establishment in the state through Eastland, which prevented the eruption of open violence that had happened in Alabama. But when the White House tried to cut a direct deal with Barnett during the integration crisis at Ole Miss, events spun completely out of control. Without Eastland as intermediary, the governor's volatile behavior proved to be impossible to restrain. Barnett's theatrics eventually led to federal intervention and deployment of the U.S. Army in Mississippi, and thus demonstrated the impracticability of massive resistance when it was carried to its extreme. In the end, the crises surrounding the Freedom Riders and James Meredith established Eastland as the more reliable alternative to negotiate with, instead of administrators in the state.

CHAPTER 7

SOUTHERN REPUBLICANS AND FREEDOM DEMOCRATS

ASTLAND KNEW HOW to manipulate the Kennedy brothers and exploit the deference they had for him. When the Freedom Riders entered Mississippi, the attorney general turned to Eastland for advice. "Eastland was always a man of his word," Robert Kennedy's deputy Nicholas Katzenbach said.[1] The senator personally liked Robert Kennedy and his younger brother Edward, who won election to John Kennedy's old Senate seat in 1962. In his memoirs, Ted Kennedy vividly described how he got his three subcommittee assignments—and how things worked in the backrooms of the U.S. Senate. The young senator-elect from Massachusetts soon realized he needed to talk to Eastland to get the positions he wanted. "Power flowed through him and a handful of other senators, mostly southern, such as Richard Russell of Georgia, Strom Thurmond of South Carolina, and Eastland's fellow Mississippian John Stennis," Kennedy wrote. Eastland's authority did not manifest itself on the Senate floor, but behind the scenes. Kennedy observed that the Mississippi senator was "rather detached from the full life of the Senate." During daytime, oilmen from Mississippi and other areas on the Gulf Coast were often in Eastland's office, and oil maps covered his desk. They spent most of the week discussing oil deals. Committee work happened after 5 p.m., when Eastland invited the senior members of Judiciary for a drink. These men were the Old Bulls, conservative Democrats and Republicans, who ran the committee. At the get-togethers in Eastland's office, the senators decided on eligible candidates for federal judgeships. "They controlled Judiciary as a sort of fiefdom," Kennedy recounted.[2]

When Edward Kennedy met with Eastland to discuss his committee assignments, he learned that the chairman had developed a keen eye for the priorities of the Kennedys. He also learned that a well-developed taste for scotch was useful in negotiations with Eastland. Each time Eastland would appoint Kennedy to a Judiciary subcommittee, he ordered the freshman senator to finish a big glass of whiskey first. "You Kennedys always care about the Negras," Eastland said in his Mississippi Delta drawl. "Always hear you caring about those. You finish that off, and you're on the civil rights subcommittee." When Eastland was not watching, Kennedy poured some of the whiskey into a potted plant near the senator's desk—otherwise he would have been drunk before the meeting was over. Less than two hours later, Ted Kennedy was again outside Eastland's office, inebriated, but with the committee assignments he wanted—constitutional rights, civil rights, and immigration. He had not expected such a level of accommodation from the conservative Mississippian.[3]

The anecdote about Kennedy's committee assignments reveals the workings of power in the inner sanctum of the U.S. Senate. Edward Kennedy's meeting with Eastland resembled a rite of passage, during which the senior senator from Mississippi clearly established his authority. Kennedy would get the committee seats he preferred, but only after he downed a glass of whiskey after each assignment. Chairman Eastland was magnanimous toward Kennedy, and thus created a reciprocal relationship with the young senator. This system of reciprocity also governed Eastland's negotiations with Robert Kennedy about the Freedom Riders. Eastland guaranteed safety for the travelers, but they would end up in jail. The deal benefitted the Kennedy administration and the segregationist regime in Mississippi, but not the riders.

The system of white supremacy that the civil rights movement tried to break extended from the small towns in the Mississippi Delta all the way up to the corridors of Congress, where an informal but influential network of high-ranking senators decided on all sorts of judicial matters after business hours. Through their settlement with Eastland, the president and the attorney general participated in and sustained this system. Despite pledges by the Kennedy White House to protect the voting rights of southern blacks, civil rights workers became frustrated by the lack of commitment from the federal government to the establishment of racial equality in the South. They began to realize that only revolutionary measures could break the segregationist status quo.

The Battle of Ole Miss constituted a watershed in the Kennedy approach to desegregation, and it had fundamental repercussions for the political structure of the South. "Within the larger black freedom struggle, events in Oxford established that the Kennedy administration would use federal power to enforce the law," historian Charles Eagles wrote. James Meredith's registration at the University of Mississippi provided inspiration for the civil rights movement to intensify its direct action protests. A few weeks after Meredith's enrollment, African American students in Jackson started a boycott against white businesses that discriminated against blacks.[4] Less than a year later, direct action and brutal segregationist opposition in Alabama led to the introduction of concrete civil rights legislation by the president. This active involvement of the federal government kindled partisan realignment in the South. The civil rights movement entered a more radical phase during a Democratic administration, and southern segregationists therefore held Democrats culpable for the breakdown of Jim Crow.

In the Deep South, moderate Democrats experienced difficult reelection bids in 1962. Mississippi congressman Frank Smith, a faithful ally of John Kennedy, lost against his segregationist colleague Jamie Whitten after the merging of their districts. Eastland tried to dispel any rumors that he had negotiated with Smith and the Kennedys about Meredith's admission to the University of Mississippi.[5] Besides these rumors that Eastland had negotiated with the president and Mississippi moderates about Meredith's admission, the senator also received flak for his intention to come to Alabama and campaign for Senator Lister Hill, who faced a tough campaign against states' rights Republican James D. Martin. Hill had been in the Senate since 1938 and was an avid supporter of the New Deal. By the 1950s, he had established a reputation as an economic liberal and a moderate on the race question, at least by Deep South standards. Martin, a business leader and a former conservative Democrat, called for "a return to the Spirit of '61—1861, when our fathers formed a new nation." With these words, Martin restructured the image of the southern Republican. He was no longer a scalawag, but an heir to the founding fathers of the Confederate States of America. "Make no mistake my friends, this will be a fight," Martin shouted. "The bugle call is loud and clear! The South has risen!"[6]

Martin based his campaign strategy on mobilizing anti-Kennedy sentiment in the state and linking his opponent with the administration. He called Hill a "Kennedycrat," whose liberal economic views were in line with the program of the national Democratic Party. Martin stressed that economic conservatism was essential for the protection of individual and local freedoms. He presented himself as the defender of personal liberty and local control against outside interference and redirected discussions about segregation from traditional race baiting to states' rights rhetoric. Conservative Republicans across the South employed similar strategies, political scientist Walter Dean Burnham noted. "Not only does it dispense with the cruder forms of demagogy, but it presents a goal of political action which—if achieved—would effectively protect the local power structure," described Burnham. "This approach also has the virtue of being as satisfactory in dealing with economic as with racial issues, and it serves to establish voter perception of a link between congruent attitudes regarding these broad fields of public policy." To counter these charges, Hill pointed at the economic accomplishments of the New Deal in Alabama— projects such as the Tennessee Valley Authority—and conjured up images of Reconstruction and Herbert Hoover's "Republican Depression." He also declared that his seniority enabled him to do useful work for constituents.[7]

Yet the issue that swamped all other campaign themes was the race question. Martin put Hill on the defensive on this front, in particular after President Kennedy's deployment of troops in Oxford. At a rally in Mobile on October 2, Hill told his audience that he "strongly deplored" the actions of the federal government in Mississippi and stated that he stood by Governor Barnett "in defense of our rights and the sovereignty of our states."[8] Despite such statements, Hill's record on segregation needed a boost, preferably from a renowned defender of Jim Crow like James Eastland.

But Alabama conservatives were not looking forward to Eastland's visit. They asked him to stay out of the politics of another state. "Senator Hill does not, and has not represented the conservative white people of his state in many years," wrote Luther Ingalls, a member of the Citizens' Council who had escorted Eastland when he spoke at a Council gathering in Montgomery.[9] A resident from Dothan, Alabama, told Eastland that Martin "would serve Alabama better and would be more cooperative with you and the other Southern Conservative Senators."[10] W. B. Hand, chairman of the Mobile County Rebels for Martin, acknowledged Eastland's "stature in the field of conservative and constitutional government, as opposed to socialistic trends." According to Hand, Eastland's support of Hill was inconsistent with his voting behavior. He also criticized the assumed close association of the Alabama senator with the national Democratic Party.[11] Eastland's office received a great amount of similar letters and telegrams from Alabama after voters there learned the Mississippi senator would come to Alabama and campaign for his longtime colleague.

Lister Hill managed to defeat his Republican opponent, but barely. Hill received 201,937 votes and Martin 195,134, which means Hill won by only 6,803 votes. He received 50.8 percent of the votes cast. Martin's racial and economic conservatism appealed to a majority of white voters, while rural whites in northern Alabama and the few registered black voters in the state supported Hill. Northern Alabama had benefitted enormously from the TVA, which explains Hill's popularity there. Martin's base of support was primarily located in the Black Belt counties and in the cities.[12] Many Alabama Democrats voted for the Republican candidate in 1962. "The organization I speak for in this letter is statewide and impressive in its numerical membership," claimed Hand. "It is composed, in a majority, of Democrats."[13]

By 1962, the Great Melding of economic and racial conservatism and the concomitant migration of southern whites from the Democratic Party to the GOP began to form a problem for southern Democrats such as Lister Hill, a U.S. senator with twenty-four years of seniority. Eastland's voting record was more conservative than Hill's and his chance of political survival was therefore bigger in the Deep South. The Mississippi Democrat nonetheless had to take stock of the fact that in the old Confederacy, the Party of Lincoln had started to gain on the Democratic Party.

The first real sign of Republican resurgence in Mississippi came in 1963, when Rubel Lex Phillips participated in the gubernatorial election on the GOP ticket. "The year 1963 marked a sharp turning point in Mississippi politics," Eastland confidante Erle Johnston indicated. "For the first time since Reconstruction, the Republican Party fielded a formidable candidate for governor."[14] Phillips was the son of a cotton planter and had served as chairman of the Public Service Commission before he switched from the Democrats to the Republicans. As the Democratic chair of the commission, Phillips was already close to people connected with Wirt Yerger, the leader of the state Republican Party. Although he supported Stevenson in 1956, Phillips's sympathy for the GOP increased after he participated in a debate at Ole Miss that year with states' rights partisan McGowan and Yerger. His conversion to the Republican Party was completed in 1960 when he witnessed the calculated tactics of the Kennedy forces to win the nomination at the national convention in Los Angeles. Two years later, he met with U.S. senator Barry Goldwater of Arizona, who visited Mississippi to attend a fund-raising dinner for the state Republican Party. Mississippi Republicans appreciated Goldwater's conservatism, particularly his forceful opposition to communism and Big Government. At the meeting, Goldwater asked Phillips to run for governor in 1963.

Behind the scenes, Democrats also tried to arrange a Phillips bid under the GOP label. Lieutenant Governor Paul B. Johnson Jr. intended to run for the governorship in 1963, but he feared Phillips's popularity among Democratic voters, especially in the northeastern corner of the state. Johnson's brother, Pat, set up a meeting in Memphis with a group of affluent businessmen, who agreed to offer financial support to Phillips if he ran as a Republican. A few days later, Rubel Phillips took the bait and announced as Republican candidate for governor. Although the Johnson family thus secured campaign funds for their opponent, they no longer had to worry about a strong challenge from him in the Democratic primaries. History taught that Republicans did not stand a chance in the subsequent general election.[15]

John Kennedy's policies would dominate the 1963 campaign for governor, including the primaries of the state Democrats. Two old rivals met in the contest for the Democratic nomination. Paul B. Johnson Jr. decided to run a fourth time, while James Coleman also entered the race. As lieutenant governor, Johnson presided over the State Senate. Coleman was a member of the Mississippi House of Representatives. Although the two men worked in different chambers of the legislature, observers noticed how a rivalry quickly developed between them. Moderates and business representatives foresaw another Barnett-style explosion of segregationist fervor if Johnson won the governorship, and they therefore urged Coleman to participate in the primary. The former governor agreed to oppose Johnson, but he did so reluctantly. Coleman realized he had a major political handicap: his association with John Kennedy. He had actively campaigned for JFK in 1960 and never made a secret of his sympathy for the president. After the crisis at Ole Miss, such connections were a serious liability for candidates running for public office in Mississippi.[16]

Paul Johnson's plan of action in the primary consisted of depicting his opponent as a Kennedy henchman and therefore an enemy of segregation. Johnson also reminded voters of his own role during the Battle of Ole Miss, when he worked with Barnett to protect the university against the federal enforcement of racial integration. A picture of the lieutenant governor refusing James Meredith and federal marshals access to the campus played a prominent role in his campaign. Johnson presented himself as the man "standing tall for

Mississippi." Coleman, on the other hand, was accused of actively supporting Kennedy in 1960. Mississippi Democrats had responded enthusiastically when JFK came to the state in 1957, yet six years later newspaper ads adopted a more negative attitude to Kennedy's visit and blamed Coleman for letting him sleep in the governor's mansion. Johnson promised to continue Barnett's economic agenda of industrial development, but the Ole Miss crisis, antipathy to the Kennedys, and states' rights were the real issues that characterized his campaign.

It was a remarkable metamorphosis: in previous elections, Johnson had run as a racial moderate and a Loyalist Democrat. By 1963, however, he denounced the national party and its leaders and took an aggressive stand on segregation and state sovereignty. This agenda delivered him the support of groups in the state that had previously opposed him. Powerful legislators from the Delta and old money entrepreneurs in Mississippi (particularly the oil industry) now considered Johnson the most qualified politician to protect them against federal encroachment. Their support transformed Johnson from the perennial neopopulist underdog to the candidate who represented the segregationist establishment and business elite in the state. And thanks to their financial backing, Johnson's money problems also belonged to the past.[17]

James Eastland again provided Paul Johnson assistance in the primaries and the general election. Johnson faced Charles Sullivan and James Coleman in the first primary and then proceeded to the runoff against Coleman. In June 1963, Johnson asked for Courtney Pace's help. Coleman was trying to play down his relation with the Kennedys by pointing at Eastland's own work for the Democratic ticket in 1960. "Mr. Coleman has been hiding behind the Senator's shirttail on this Kennedy support matter," Johnson informed Pace. "Of course this, in some ways, is not helping Jim." Johnson also wanted to know more about Coleman's role in the disbursement of federal patronage in Mississippi, particularly information about people who unsuccessfully applied for positions with the post office. "Those who did not receive these appointments, I am sure are sore and I need to put blame quietly with all applicants who did not receive appointments," Johnson wrote.[18]

When states' righter Charles Sullivan endorsed Coleman in the runoff primary, Eastland attempted to get businessmen supporting the former governor into the Johnson camp. Staff assistant L.P.B. Lipscomb asked Tom Hederman of the *Clarion-Ledger* if he could form a nonpartisan committee of entrepreneurs to convince the business community in the state that a vote for Johnson would be good for economic development. Eastland's office had drafted a letter this so-called Mississippi Anti-Kennedy Committee could use to accomplish its goals. "The salvation of Mississippi and the business interests generally throughout the South lies with the removal of the Kennedy Administration," it read. The president received blame for all sorts of bureaucratic measures that prohibited economic growth in the southern states. "If sacrifices are necessary for our survival, then Coleman himself should be more than willing to suffer an overwhelming defeat if the result could be to help lift the incubus of Federal dictatorship from the shoulders of the people of Mississippi and the South."[19]

Eastland's staff had already noticed that protests against "the Kennedy dictatorship" were on the rise across the nation. "We know you do not want to be an instrument in reversing a trend that can easily result in the defeat of the Administration in 1964," the letter concluded. "A vote for Paul Johnson will be another nail in the Kennedy political coffin."[20] In 1960, Eastland had joined James Coleman on the Mississippi campaign trail for Kennedy. Three years later, the senator's assistants helped Johnson discredit the president. They fused economic interests with segregation and local control to lure the state's businessmen away from Coleman.

From the start of the campaign, James Coleman recognized that he needed to disassociate himself from the Kennedy administration. Part of his strategy was to remind voters that Eastland and Stennis had also endorsed JFK in the presidential election, and that 108,000 Mississippians had voted for the Democratic ticket that year. "We thought it was the best thing to do at the time. We saved Senator Eastland's Judicial Committee chairmanship, and we're glad of that."[21] Coleman declared the president had no chance to win Mississippi in 1964 and spoke out in favor of a "southern remedy" to assert regional political power at the national level. "Do not let any demagogue tell you that a vote for Coleman is a vote for Kennedy," he warned. "The truth is exactly the other way. If you are really and truly AGAINST Kennedy and the Kennedy policies, you will vote for the one and only man in this race who has had the training, the experience, and the determination to successfully win our battles with the Kennedys."[22]

Coleman ended second in the first primary, with a difference of 5.6 percent between him and Johnson. The lieutenant governor apparently convinced more voters that he was the man to protect Mississippi's "segregated way of life" and that he would be a capable leader in the fight against the Kennedy White House. "The Kennedys are out to put you flat on your back with the Negro's heel on your throat," Johnson shouted at a rally in Scott County, where both he and James Eastland grew up. "The focal point of this campaign is whether the Kennedys will break the back of Mississippi and Southern resistance to federal encroachment."[23] Coleman was unable to find an efficient answer to this virulent style. He tried to convince the electorate he was the statesman who guaranteed a "safe, tranquil, peaceable four years ahead."[24] But Coleman's appeals to reason fell on deaf ears in Mississippi just one year after the integration of Ole Miss. Paul Johnson easily defeated Coleman in the second primary with a margin of more than 14 percent.

The *Memphis Commercial Appeal* considered Johnson's victory a clear indication that the white voters of Mississippi wanted an all-out defense of segregation and a strong stand against the Kennedy administration. The newspaper wondered how Johnson was going to deal with Rubel Phillips in the general election, because the Republican candidate could not be linked to JFK, the Ole Miss crisis, or integration. The race against Phillips was not only important for Johnson's political career, but also for Eastland's position in Mississippi. "Should Mr. Johnson win in November, Senator James O. [Eastland] could be regarded as undisputed political leader in the state," the paper reported. "Senator Eastland quietly but effectively was instrumental in helping Mr. Johnson gain the nomination, and the two have been longtime personal and political friends."[25]

The electoral map of Mississippi shows how Eastland's influence helped Johnson defeat Coleman in the runoff primary. Despite the traditional enmity of the Delta toward the Johnson family, Coleman won only four counties in this part of the state, including Charles Sullivan's home county of Coahoma and Washington County, home base of Hodding Carter's *Delta Democrat-Times*.[26] Eastland knew Johnson could win the Delta with racist appeals, and the lieutenant governor acted on this advice. At a rally in Jackson, for instance, Johnson asked his audience if they knew what "NAACP" stood for. When the crowd shouted "No," Johnson answered: "Niggers, Apes, Alligators, Coons, and Possums."[27] Coleman's predicament grew even worse when the *New York Times* called him the best qualified candidate in the contest for governor. "One thing for sure is that the South-hating, race-baiting ultra-liberal *New York Times* will not be allowed to tell the people of the State of Mississippi how to vote," the *Clarion-Ledger* bristled.[28]

In the face of these odds, Coleman had to go to extremes if he wanted to defeat Johnson. He came up with a plan to organize a separate conference of southern states before the conventions of the national parties in 1964 and said it would be futile to send a state delegation to the Democratic National Convention.[29] Only seven years earlier, Coleman had completely opposed such separatist activities. Political commentator William S. White equated the downfall of Coleman with the destruction of moderation in Mississippi, and he saw Kennedy's use of the military to enforce integration as the main cause for this development. "The fruit will be bitter, and not only for that Administration whose actions have just helped the probable defeat of one of the President's strongest former supporters in all of the Deep South," White wrote after the first primary.[30] According to White, the president's increased attention for the civil rights struggle in the South stimulated the growth of racist extremism among southern whites.

Southern Republicans like Rubel Phillips politically exploited the escalation of civil rights activity in the region and the concomitant response of the federal government. "Up until last fall, Phillips was a good Democrat," columnists Rowland Evans and Robert Novak wrote. "Now, he is a Republican in a state whose Republican Party, up until 1960, had an influence roughly equal to the influence of a Hottentot in a convention of Baptists." But the president's growing attention to civil rights had dramatically changed the outlook of the GOP in Mississippi. "The Hottentots may still have a long way to go before they take over the Baptist convention, but their banging at the door is getting louder every minute, mostly because of the Kennedy administration's declaration of war on the race issue."[31]

Phillips was an articulate, youthful lawyer who was widely respected. He was representative of the bloc of young conservative legal professionals and businessmen that took control of the Mississippi Republican Party in 1956. The group's ascendance was partly the result of increased urbanization, but their appeal among the largely rural population in Mississippi was based on resentment against Kennedy's civil rights agenda. The *New York Times* welcomed the development of a two-party system in the South, yet deplored the strategy of the Republican Party to pick up the white southern vote by fielding segregationist candidates. "If the Republican Party is going to have its banner in the South carried by the opponents of constitutional rights for Negroes, it can kiss goodbye to some millions of votes in the West and North."[32] The national Republican Party now faced the same dilemma the national Democrats had grappled with since the New Deal. The electoral strength of the South represented a coveted political asset, but a commitment to Dixie meant diminished support by African American voters in the North. In 1963, southern blacks did not yet possess enough strength at the ballot box to make Republicans reconsider their right-wing campaign strategy in the Deep South.

Civil rights activists were setting up different projects to improve the political situation of black southerners. By the summer of 1963, the NAACP, SNCC, CORE, and the SCLC had united in the Council of Federated Organizations (COFO) to coordinate civil rights activities in Mississippi. Despite their differences, the organizations realized that cooperation was necessary to confront the segregationist power structure in the Magnolia State. Aaron Henry, a black pharmacist from Clarksdale and state chairman of the NAACP, became president of COFO, and Bob Moses of SNCC served as its program director. Moses was one of the main catalysts behind the Freedom Vote campaign of 1963, an attempt to counter Senator Eastland's charges that the "small Negro vote is merely a result of lack of interest."[33] The Freedom Vote was a mock election for governor, organized parallel to the contest between Johnson and Phillips. Because state authorities went to extremes to bar blacks from voting in the official race, COFO decided to hold alternative elections instead, primarily to show "Mississippi, Washington, and the rest of the nation that the Negro people of Mississippi would vote if they were allowed to register free from intimidation and discrimination."[34]

COFO also wanted to use the project to expand its sphere of influence to other parts of the state. Until the 1963 gubernatorial election, civil rights activities had mostly been limited to the Delta and central Mississippi. A statewide race offered the opportunity to reach out beyond these areas. Another reason to initiate the Freedom Vote was educational. The campaign could teach local blacks how the process of voting worked and might inspire them to set up their own independent political organization. Activists hoped the drive would attract national media coverage as well and thus elicit a response from the Kennedy administration to voter discrimination in Mississippi.[35]

The idea to set up a mock election originally came from Allard Lowenstein, a liberal Democrat from New York, who had witnessed a similar project in

South Africa. After discussing the initiative with Moses, Lowenstein got permission to recruit students from Stanford and Yale to assist with the organization of the campaign. Not all members of the Mississippi movement agreed with the plan to invite whites from elite schools to promote the Freedom Vote. They feared that the presence of these students would intensify the reaction of local whites and increase the danger for all participants. Yet COFO needed extra manpower to cover the entire state. Eventually, more than seventy students came to Mississippi to help get out the vote for Aaron Henry, who ran for governor, and Ed King, a white chaplain at Tougaloo College who ran for lieutenant governor.[36]

On October 6, COFO organized a convention at the Masonic Temple in Jackson to officially launch the campaign. The conference adopted a platform calling for racial justice, the desegregation of schools, and the right to vote. The economic paragraph of the platform focused on improving conditions for poor farm workers and small landowners and on protecting the rights of unions to organize laborers. During the following month, the COFO candidates stumped Mississippi while civil rights activists fanned out across the state to set up polling places and reach out to voters. At rallies, Henry emphasized the main thrust of the Freedom Vote drive: education, voting rights, and racial justice. King underscored the symbolic value of the race, reminding audiences it was the first time since Reconstruction that a black and a white had run on the same ticket.[37]

The organizers hoped to convince at least two hundred thousand people to cast their ballots, which amounted to about 40 percent of blacks eligible to vote. Preparation time had been short, however, and the activists encountered intense harassment by whites and the police. In the end, more than eighty-three thousand African Americans voted for Henry and King, which was still considered an impressive result in the closed society of Mississippi. The Freedom Vote demonstrated that blacks would not refrain from exercising their constitutional rights if they were given the chance, but the project revealed new problems as well. Almost 40 percent of the votes came from the area around Clarksdale. White resistance had prevented successful voter mobilization in other regions of the state. "This election also makes it clear that the Negroes of Mississippi will not get the vote unless the equivalent of an army is sent here," Moses concluded after the ballots had been counted. In addition, media treatment of the campaign had been rather superficial. If journalists covered the events surrounding the Freedom Vote at all, they concentrated on the white students. This focus caused resentment among black activists, but it also showed that bringing in young people from the North increased attention from the national media.[38]

Despite these setbacks, the Freedom Vote was important in many ways. "We conclude that Negroes would vote if they were able to register, and that they would vote for candidates who would stand for freedom," COFO organizers wrote James Eastland in a telegram. "We believe that you have had continuing influence in preventing Negroes in Mississippi from registering to vote."[39] Segregationists not only worried about the biracial character of the Henry-King ticket, but also about the progressive political philosophy the two men espoused. The "platform of the Freedom Party raised issues at the heart of the depressing problems in Mississippi, a state that seems to rank fiftieth in almost every field," a commentator for *The Nation* observed.[40] Norman Thomas, presidential candidate for the Socialist Party, even compared Mississippi's devotion to segregation with communist totalitarianism. After speaking at a rally of the Freedom Party in Greenwood, he gave John Kennedy his impression of the state's obsession with the maintenance of the color line: "It is a religion which, like communism to its believers, cleanses and sanctifies lies, perjury, perversion of law, perhaps even murder to maintain itself." He then told the president that this "situation is America's business. I do not write as a sensationalist, but as a veteran campaigner who has frequently covered the United States without finding a parallel or precedent for what I found in Mississippi."[41] In order to expose this reality to a nationwide audience, many COFO members understood that they had to build on the Freedom Vote project and expand its scope. During the months following the election, civil rights activists in Mississippi discussed the future direction of the movement.[42]

While the mock election organized by COFO challenged the dominance of the Regular Democratic Party from the left, Rubel Phillips and the Mississippi Republicans formed a threat on the right. In the race for governor, Phillips attempted to turn the tables on Johnson and connect his opponent with the Kennedys and the national Democratic Party. The Republican told voters he was the only candidate who had "no ties or obligations to the Kennedys or any part of the New Frontier." He also called himself a "staunch segregationist" and declared "Negroes are all Democrats."[43]

The race took an unexpected turn for Johnson when *Newsweek* published a piece in October about the negotiations between the Kennedys, Barnett, and Johnson during the Meredith crisis at Ole Miss. The magazine stated the transcript was official, a claim the Johnson camp desperately tried to refute. Journalist Curtis Wilkie later revealed that Kennedy had leaked the transcript to his political ally James Coleman for use in the primary against Johnson. Coleman considered the material too explosive, however, and passed it on to Mississippi reporter Bill Minor, who worked for *Newsweek*. Phillips of course did not hesitate to use Minor's revelations against his opponent. The Republicans reprinted the entire dialogue in an advertisement and called Johnson the Kennedy candidate, an integrationist, and a double-crosser. Johnson denied he ever negotiated with the Kennedy administration about the integration of Ole Miss and branded publication of the transcript as "merely another effort on the part of Jack and Robert Kennedy to defeat Paul Johnson's candidacy for governor of Mississippi."[44]

The Democrats countered by declaring that a two-party system in the state formed the real threat to the survival of Jim Crow. Johnson and his allies warned that a disruption of Democratic unity would put the balance of power in the hands of blacks. They assured that Mississippi Democrats were completely independent from both national parties.[45] James Eastland insisted the one-party system had been instrumental in defeating "the carpetbaggers and scalawags one hundred years ago. It is still serving its purpose perfectly." Walter Sillers concurred with Eastland and also put the threat of Republicanism within the framework of the Civil War and Reconstruction: "It was a Republican president and party that occupied Mississippi, placing us under the heel of federal Negro troops and scalawags and carpetbag rule, the overthrow of which finally came in 1875 and 1876."[46]

Phillips was smart enough not to deny the perceived horrors of Reconstruction, but he also pointed out that these problems were the result of one-party rule. The Republican candidate declared he had not left the Democratic Party, but that the Democratic Party had left him. "Over the years, the principles of the Democratic Party have fallen apart," he stated. "Its basic precepts have decayed, and its platform now is composed of foreign matter, foreign ideas, and socialism." According to Phillips, competition between two parties would more clearly reveal ideological differences, strengthen the political structure, and improve the image of Mississippi in the rest of America.[47]

The growing interest for the Republican Party in Mississippi was an unintended consequence of past third-party experiments by the state Democrats, their unrelenting harangues against the national Democratic Party, and peculiar political constructs such as the Democrats for Eisenhower groups. This course had its impact on Mississippi's conservative electorate. Once the state Republican Party began to move out of the margins, it became an attractive alternative for those who had become disillusioned with the Democratic Party, notwithstanding the arguments voiced by Eastland and others about the distinct differences between Mississippi Democrats and national Democrats. Although Johnson and Phillips had a similar pro-business, segregationist message, white-collar workers and businessmen preferred the polished and restrained style of the Republican candidate to Johnson's demagoguery. They also identified with the laissez-faire economic agenda of the national Republican Party.[48]

But Phillips tried to appeal to working-class whites as well. He called himself a redneck and used country music at rallies. His campaign jingle had the following lyrics: "Rubel, Rubel / We're all rebels / Fighting for our native land / Against the Kennedy carpetbaggers / Bobby, Jack and all the clan."[49] The song had obvious Civil War overtones, with Republican rebels fighting to save their country from the Democratic carpetbag regime of John and Robert Kennedy. Cullen Curlee attended Phillips's opening rally in Corinth, on a cold, damp night at the end of September. About five thousand people showed up to see Roy Acuff and the Smokey Mountain Boys perform before Phillips appeared on stage. "Rubel criticized Governor Barnett, Paul Johnson and talked about the 'Great Deal' with the Kennedy Boys," Curlee reported to Eastland. "He also criticized the Hederman Brothers stating that they had a heavy investment in Paul in the past five campaigns and he would not believe anything the *Jackson Daily News* would publish about the campaign." Eastland's assistant thought the audience was disappointed in Phillips's speech, because the Republican attacked "too many of our friends and own people." The Republicans were spending a significant amount of money in Alcorn County, but Curlee doubted Phillips would be able to carry it. He counted on the partisan loyalty of the people from the countryside, who traditionally voted for the Democratic nominee.[50]

Phillips's bid for the governorship nonetheless worried the state Democratic Party. In previous elections, the Republicans had hardly put up any opposition, but Phillips changed that tradition of apathy. Large, full-color billboards appeared across the state, promoting the Republican candidate. The GOP invested heavily in television commercials, while Phillips barnstormed Mississippi, enthusiastically shaking hands with people who had always learned to despise Republicans. The Democrats did not know how to formulate an effective response to this kind of post-primary activity. Paul Johnson went on statewide television, but interest for his speech was minimal. The Democratic Party even organized a large dinner gathering in Jackson, where people could listen to Senator Eastland and other members of the state's political establishment for $25 per plate. Johnson railed against the "Republican carpetbaggers" who tried to split the white vote, while Ross Barnett told the audience he was "fed up with these fence-riding, pussyfooting, snow-digging Yankee Republicans."[51]

State Representative Jack Turner from the Delta town of Tunica appreciated Eastland's contribution to the Democratic rally. "You can help here and throughout the rest of the Delta where it appears to me the Republican propaganda has gained some foothold," Turner told Eastland.[52] But Edley Jones, an insurance agent from Vicksburg, had a different opinion about Eastland's performance in Jackson. "If my memory serves me correctly, you have been successful in obtaining much Republican support in Congress," he wrote the senator. "The ill-chosen and highly inaccurate term of 'scalawag' will not set well with your Republican constituents when you solicit their aid in the forthcoming civil rights fight."[53]

After almost a century of Democratic hegemony, Paul Johnson had significant trouble rallying voters in the general election. "No one doubts that Mississippi has enough Democrats to defeat Republican Phillips," *Time* reported in October 1963. "But those Democrats have become so accustomed to perfunctory, no-contest general elections that they might not take the trouble to vote." The organizers of the Jackson meeting expected a crowd of seventy-five hundred, but eventually only thirty-five hundred people showed up, leaving the hall half empty.[54] On Election Day, November 5, Rubel Phillips managed to garner almost 40 percent of the vote, which came as a shock to many Mississippians.[55] The Republican carried seven counties, including three in the Delta and James Coleman's home county of Choctaw. He almost won the Delta counties of Leflore, Panola, and Tunica, and did well in the state capital of Jackson and on the Gulf Coast.[56] Phillips thus combined the suburban vote with parts of the Black Belt.

Banker M. W. Swartz from Indianola expressed his thoughts on the contest between Johnson and Phillips shortly before the election. "Mr. Phillips has got the Democrats scared," Swartz boasted to Eastland. "Of course, we want a two party system in Mississippi. I do not know of anything better to happen for Phillips to carry the state." He also encouraged the senator to come out "against this mischief making man JFK." Eastland replied after the general election. "You certainly did have us scared," he conceded, "but I believe the best man won!" Eastland promised to visit Swartz in the fall for "a long talk."[57] Political developments in the state and the country probably warranted such a conversation.

Democrats and Republicans interpreted the outcome of the 1963 gubernatorial election in Mississippi differently. The *Jackson Clarion-Ledger* concluded "the Magnolia State wants nothing to do with the two-party system," while Democratic chairman Bidwell Adam telegraphed Phillips to ask when he would "deliver the funeral oration" for the GOP. The *Delta Democrat-Times* saw Phillips's impressive result as a clear and long-awaited breakthrough in the one-party tradition of Mississippi, however. The paper predicted that "within the next decade, the Republicans . . . will be on par with the Democrats. When that day arrives, the GOP will look back on this election as the real starting point."[58]

Rubel Phillips could not agree more with the *Democrat-Times*. He believed his showing against Johnson signified the establishment of a new political structure in Mississippi, based on the competition between two parties. He also described the Republican Party as the choice that stood for tradition and free enterprise. "In my opinion, the Mississippi Republican Party will be successful in the future of our state only to the extent that it offers the people of Mississippi a clear-cut and definite program of conservatism and fiscal concern," Phillips stated. "Unless it offers this choice, the Republican Party in Mississippi will not be successful, and it should not be successful."[59]

Paul Johnson tried to prevent any future form of Republican success as soon as he became governor. After his inauguration he submitted twenty-two bills to "end this Republican upstart movement once and for all." The legislation would seriously obstruct Mississippi Republicans from participating in the state's political process, including elections. But Wirt Yerger successfully mobilized local Republicans against Johnson's initiatives, and also drew the attention of national journalists, who strongly rebuked the governor for his attempts to maintain Democratic hegemony. The Mississippi legislature, disturbed by the commotion caused by the introduction of the anti-GOP bills, eventually decided to reject Johnson's proposals. Yerger later called this triumph his greatest accomplishment as party chairman.[60] The Republican vote in the 1963 gubernatorial election clearly showed the discontent of Mississippi's conservative electorate with the national Democratic Party and especially with John Kennedy.

Phillips's campaign slogan—K.O. the Kennedys—acquired a bitter connotation when the president was assassinated in Dallas on November 22, 1963. Eastland was en route to Mississippi when he found out about the shooting. Driving through Virginia with his wife, they noticed that flags were flying at half-staff. Eastland turned on the radio and heard that JFK was dead. "Good God, Lyndon's President," the senator muttered to his wife. "He's gonna pass a lot of this damn fool stuff."[61] Eastland did not mistake Johnson's resolve to put Kennedy's growing dedication to civil rights into legislation. Five days after the assassination, the new president addressed Congress. "No memorial oration or eulogy could more eloquently honor President Kennedy's memory than the earliest possible passage of the civil rights bill for which he fought," LBJ declared. "We have talked long enough in this country about civil rights. We have talked for one hundred years or more. It is now time to write the next chapter—and to write it in the books of law."[62] In response to the violent suppression of peaceful civil rights protests in Birmingham, Alabama, in the spring of 1963, Kennedy had finally announced a comprehensive civil rights law. It was a turning point in JFK's presidency. Johnson was determined to build on this legacy.[63]

LBJ had various motives to take a strong stand on civil rights. First of all, simply because he came from below the Mason-Dixon Line, Johnson felt pressured to debunk stereotypes about the racist attitudes of white southerners. Lofty words had initially been enough for Kennedy. But if Johnson failed to deliver on desegregation, Americans would undoubtedly hold it against the Texan. LBJ also thought the dismantlement of Jim Crow was necessary for the liberation of southern blacks *and* whites. By removing white supremacy, the South could finally focus on the economic and social problems that had plagued the region for such a long time. Only through desegregation could the South truly reunite with the rest of the nation, Johnson believed. At the same time, he also saw the political benefits of advocating civil rights. By the election year of 1964, the number of Americans supporting more vigorous federal action against southern apartheid had increased significantly. LBJ took advantage of this development and pushed JFK's civil rights bill through Congress.[64]

He warned his old mentor Richard Russell in advance that he was not going to be stopped. "Dick, you've got to get out of my way," Johnson instructed Russell. "I'm going to run over you. I don't intend to cavil or compromise." The leader of the Southern Caucus replied: "You may do that . . . But by God, it's going to cost you the South and cost you the election."[65] Russell and his southern colleagues knew they were defeated. They had been able to control the young and inexperienced Kennedy, but Johnson was a Senate veteran and he had momentum on his side. Abandoned by their Republican allies, the southern senators were unable to filibuster the bill into oblivion. "We had Kennedy stopped," Eastland lamented, "But I'm afraid we can't stop Johnson."[66]

Lyndon Johnson's dedication to the structural reorganization of southern race relations had its limits, however. In July, COFO set up the Mississippi Freedom Democratic Party (MFDP) to challenge the state's Regular Democratic Party, the party of James Eastland and Paul Johnson. The MFDP was one of many initiatives developed by COFO to follow up on the Freedom Vote project, culminating in Freedom Summer of 1964. In August, the Freedom Democrats traveled to the Democratic National Convention in Atlantic City to dispute the credentials of the Regulars, whose racism and disloyalty to the national party was notorious. The president was not happy with this move. He considered the convention his own coronation as the undisputed leader of a united Democratic Party and he did want any divisions in the ranks or dramatic walkouts by southern delegations.[67]

Behind the scenes, LBJ frantically tried to force a compromise on the MFDP and the Regulars. Johnson picked Aaron Henry and Ed King as delegates at large, while the other Freedom Democrats could stay at the convention as nonvoting guests. The Regular Democrats were supposed to pledge their support to the ticket and bar discriminatory practices in future selections of delegates to the national convention. The president called James Eastland several times during the days leading up to the gathering in Atlantic City, asking him to use his influence and make Governor Johnson accept the compromise. Eastland was in Kentucky at the time of the convention. He probably expected the MFDP challenge to cause uproar and decided to keep a low profile. Instead of heading the state delegation, Paul Johnson stayed in

Jackson. In the phone conversations with Eastland, LBJ praised the Mississippi governor for his cooperation with the administration during Freedom Summer. But despite the president's flattery and Eastland's arbitration, Paul Johnson did not budge. When his delegates were forced to sign a loyalty oath, he instructed them to come home. Only three members of the Regular delegation eventually chose to stay in Atlantic City until the end of the convention.[68]

The fate of the Freedom Democrats resembled a tragedy. They went to the convention in the hope that the president and the Democratic Party would stand up for them. Fannie Lou Hamer, a sharecropper from Ruleville, not far from Eastland's farm, delivered a forceful plea why the credentials committee should acknowledge the MFDP as the official Democratic Party of Mississippi. In a dramatic speech broadcast on national television, she recounted the violence and suffering she had to endure just to exercise her right to vote. Yet Lyndon Johnson was unwilling to favor the MFDP over the Regular Democrats. He knew Mississippi and Alabama were lost for the Democratic ticket, but he anticipated a white backlash across the entire South if the convention recognized the Freedom Democrats. One by one, supporters of the MFDP challenge withdrew as political pressure from the White House increased. Civil rights veteran Bayard Rustin thought it necessary to explain the difference between protest and politics to the Mississippi activists. "The former is based on morality and the latter is based on compromise," Rustin lectured. "You must accept the compromise. If you don't, then you are still protesting."[69]

But the MFDP delegates refused to compromise, after everything they had been through. Coming from a state where Democrats and Republicans espoused the same segregationist message, where the political establishment and the police worked hand in hand to protect racism, the Freedom Democrats expected that the national Democratic Party would be on their side. Those expectations proved to be false. "Atlantic City was a watershed in the movement because up until then the idea had been that you were working more or less within the Democratic Party," Bob Moses concluded. "We were working with them on voting, other things like that. With Atlantic City, a lot of movement people became disillusioned. . . . You turned around and your support was puddle-deep."[70] At the convention in Atlantic City, the party leadership desperately tried to minimize the impact of the MFDP through compromise. President Johnson used his old Senate colleagues as middlemen to reach such an agreement. James Eastland received instructions to strike a deal with Paul Johnson, while Hubert Humphrey, the civil rights hero of the 1948 convention, had to convince the MFDP to trade idealism for pragmatism. The Freedom Democrats were the victims of these attempts to maintain the status quo and placate the southern wing of the party.

In a speech in Cleveland, Ohio, in April 1964, Malcolm X had already scorned the close cooperation between the Democratic leadership and southern racists, which impeded true racial change. "The titular head of the Democrats is also the head of the Dixiecrats, because the Dixiecrats are a part of the Democratic Party," he said of Lyndon Johnson. "They have got a con game going on, a political con game, and you and I are in the middle. It's time for you and me to wake up and start looking at it like it is, and trying to understand it like it is; and then we can deal with it like it is." Malcolm X gave his own description of the catch-22 the Democratic Party found itself in. Because of the system of segregation, reactionary Democrats like James Eastland won election to Congress. And because the national Democrats were unable to dismantle Jim Crow with racist southerners in their ranks, these Dixiecrats built up seniority and occupied the positions of power on Capitol Hill:

> The Dixiecrats in Washington, D.C., control the key committees that run the government. The only reason the Dixiecrats control these committees is because they have seniority. The only reason they have seniority is because they come from states where Negroes can't vote. This is not even a government that's based on democracy. It is not a government that is made up of representatives of the people. Half of the people in the South can't even vote. Eastland is not even supposed to be in Washington. Half of the senators and congressmen who occupy these key positions in Washington, D.C., are there illegally, are there unconstitutionally.[71]

Malcolm X castigated the Democrats for harboring Dixiecrats, but southern blacks had equally little to expect from the Republican Party in the region. In 1964, the Party of Lincoln decided to go hunting where the ducks were: disgruntled white southern Democrats. During the presidential election of 1964, states' rights Republican Barry Goldwater followed this strategy and carried five states in the Deep South, plus his home state of Arizona. Although

Goldwater lost to Johnson in a landslide, his victory in the old heartland of the Democratic Party signified a dramatic political transformation. He received 87 percent of the vote in Mississippi. Voters in the state's fourth district elected Prentiss Walker to the House, the first Republican to represent the Magnolia State in Congress since the end of Reconstruction. Walker, a strong segregationist, managed to defeat veteran Democrat Arthur Winstead on Goldwater's coattails.

Democratic senator Strom Thurmond of South Carolina, the former standard-bearer of the Dixiecrats, joined the GOP that year. When Thurmond announced his party switch, letters from across the country arrived at Eastland's office asking the senator to follow his colleague's lead and join Goldwater to reverse "the march toward Socialism." Horace Harned, a member of the Mississippi House of Representatives, the Citizens' Council, and the Sovereignty Commission, wrote to Eastland that it was "apparent that Mr. Reuther and organized labor, Dr. King and organized Negroes have succeeded in capturing our old party." He urged the senator to "begin the serious consideration of a party change-over."[72] A group of women from Vicksburg praised Strom Thurmond, thanking "God for *one* man of integrity and honor, possessed with the courage to stand for his principles, come what may." They had less appreciation for Eastland's continuing membership in the Democratic Party and were "deeply ashamed of and angry with you, our elected official, for not speaking out publicly against this rotten administration."[73] All these constituents no longer considered the Democratic Party their political home. Barry Goldwater, Strom Thurmond, and the Republicans became the new saviors of the white southern way of life.

Yet Eastland was unmoved by the pleas from Mississippi voters to secede from the Democratic Party. Although he did not campaign for LBJ in 1964, he courteously welcomed Lady Bird Johnson when her campaign train made a stop in Mississippi. Senator Stennis and Governor Johnson also came to Biloxi, the latter handing the First Lady a bouquet of yellow roses, the state flower of Texas. Johnson said he was delighted about the visit, "regardless of political differences that may transcend." Eastland refrained from making any political statements. "We are certainly glad to welcome Mrs. Johnson to this great state and its great people," the senator declared, and that was it.[74]

By the mid-1960s, James Eastland had more than twenty years of seniority and occupied the chairs of two influential Senate committees, the Judiciary

Committee and the Internal Security Subcommittee. When Strom Thurmond switched parties, he did not hold any major chairmanships and the Republicans gave him the same rank he had when he was still a Democrat.[75] Eastland's affiliation with the national Democratic Party thus helped him to counter the rise of southern Republicans. He had very little to gain from a defection to the GOP. Because of Eastland's seniority and conservative record, Republican challengers were unable to remove him from power.

Not all of Eastland's constituents were content with their senator's performance, however. Charles Clark from Clarksdale, Mississippi, told Thurmond he was "much heartened by your recent action in leaving the Democratic Party" and welcomed him "to the club." Clark had done "the same thing immediately after 'our' unsuccessful campaign in 1948." He was "still trying to figure what good Mr. Eastland's judicial committee chairmanship has done us." After all, Eastland had been unable to prevent the nomination of liberals such as Earl Warren, John Minor Wisdom, and Thurgood Marshall to the federal bench, and he had not obstructed the appointment of Robert Kennedy as attorney general.[76] Renegade Democrats such as Clark formed the vanguard of Republicanism in the Magnolia State. After the Dixiecrat campaign, he had urged Eastland to abandon partisan loyalty and cooperate with the GOP—perhaps even form a third party together with conservative Republicans. Eastland and other southern Democrats had to make sure not too many of their constituents followed Clark's example and started voting for Republican candidates in congressional elections.

Southern Democratic representatives who promoted the conservative course of the Republican Party faced the risk of losing their influence on Capitol Hill. In January 1965, with the inauguration of the new Congress, Representative John Bell Williams of Mississippi was stripped of his seniority for openly supporting Goldwater in the presidential race. Congressman Albert Watson of South Carolina, another Goldwater Democrat, met a similar fate. Williams in particular paid a heavy price for his defection. Watson lost only two years of seniority, but Williams had been in the House since 1947 and was the second-ranking Democrat on the Interstate and Foreign Commerce Committee, right after Chairman Oren Harris. The two rebels held a press conference, where Williams called the punishment by the Democratic caucus "repugnant," an "assault upon the time-honored seniority system." The congressmen declared that their votes were "not for sale for patronage or party position" and refused to apologize for their stand in the 1964 presidential contest. They also recalled that "a Harlem Congressman was rewarded with a committee chairmanship" for supporting the candidate of another party. This congressman was Adam Clayton Powell, a black Democrat who had endorsed Eisenhower in 1956. Watson resigned from Congress and was reelected as a Republican the same year, to fill the vacancy caused by his own resignation. The Democrats had relegated "white Southerners . . . to the kitchen where we get the crumbs, while others are rewarded in the banquet hall," Watson stated shortly after losing his seniority.[77] Williams stayed in Congress until 1967, when he won the race for governor of his state after conducting a strong segregationist campaign as a "Mississippi Democrat."[78]

Besides the sanctioning of Williams, other partisan problems loomed for the Mississippi Regulars at the start of the new Congress. The Freedom Democrats, thwarted in their attempt to gain access to the convention in Atlantic City, made another effort to achieve recognition from the national party in January 1965. This time, they challenged the credentials of the entire Mississippi delegation in the U.S. House. In December 1964, attorneys for the MFDP officially contested the seating of the five House members from the state, because African Americans had been "systematically and deliberately excluded from the electoral process."[79] Victoria Gray, Annie Devine, and Fannie Lou Hamer had won the Freedom Vote ballot after they were barred from the regular election. The FDP lawyers argued that Gray, Devine, and Hamer should therefore be recognized as the legitimate U.S. representatives of their districts. Because the legal grounds for the latter element of the MFDP challenge were tenuous, the Freedom Democrats decided to focus on their first goal: the removal of the Regulars and Republican Prentiss Walker from the House and the organization of new elections.

Prospects for the challenge seemed promising at first. Although the five Mississippi congressmen were allowed to take the oath of office, 149 representatives (more than one-third of the House membership) voted against their seating. The House also authorized the contestants to continue their case against the Regulars and Walker. "We are not dismayed at the action of the House on January 4th, 1965," the MFDP declared in response to the admittance of Walker and the Regular Democrats. "We know that after we present the evidence of officially sanctioned and initiated violence, intimidation, bombings and other forms of terrorism used to keep Negroes in Mississippi from voting, the nation and the Congress will have no alternative but to unseat the undemocratically selected Mississippians."[80]

During the following months, both the Freedom Democrats and the contested congressmen organized to defend their positions. The MFDP returned to Mississippi, where they received help from more than 150 attorneys to gather evidence about voter discrimination in the state.[81] On the other side of the spectrum, a remarkable show of unity occurred. The Mississippi Republicans and the different factions of the Regular Democratic Party temporarily buried the hatchet and banded together to protect white privilege. Democrats Jamie Whitten, John Bell Williams, William Colmer, and Thomas Abernethy joined with Republican Prentiss Walker "in a full-scale battle to retain their seats." Although James Coleman had not been particularly close with any of the congressmen (especially not with Williams), he served as counselor for the Regulars, while B. B. McLendon assisted Walker. Democrat Joe Patterson represented all members as state attorney general. "Those eight men have varying political beliefs—some in agreement, others not," the *Jackson Daily News* observed. "But they are in accord on one topic: Mississippi's representation in Congress must be retained."[82]

In December 1964, Coleman was already setting up the defense for the congressmen, including Walker. He instructed them to "use all our research facilities in Washington to dig up all precedents" on election contests, and do "all the personal work possible with the Leadership to see to it that the oath is administered pending the disposition of the contest."[83] Despite considerable opposition from their colleagues in the House, the Mississippi delegation managed to accomplish the latter objective when the new Congress started. This recognition gave them a solid base from which they could counter the attacks mounted by the MFDP.

In the seating contest, the Freedom Democrats once again could not count on the backing of the White House. Despite their support for the Johnson-Humphrey ticket in the 1964 race, LBJ chose to pacify the white southerners in Congress. In his 1965 State of the Union address, Johnson announced his Great Society program, a massive initiative by the federal government to end poverty and social injustice in the United States. The president feared that southern opposition to his progressive plans would become insurmountable if the House members from Mississippi were forced to give up their seats. Such a revolt had to be prevented at all costs, Johnson believed. Just a few months before, the Freedom Democrats had derailed his convention and now they put the realization of his legislative agenda at risk. LBJ had little sympathy for the tactics employed by the MFDP to break the traditional power structure in Mississippi and in Congress.[84]

Opponents of the MFDP argued that the congressional challenge was a communist plot. On February 3, James Eastland delivered a speech in the Senate about the Marxist leanings of the Freedom Democrats and their supporters. "The State of Mississippi has been subjected to an invasion which the Communists regard as only the opening maneuver in the coming Negro revolution," said the senator.[85] Thomas Abernethy regarded the efforts by the MFDP as extremely threatening. "I have just returned after three weeks in Mississippi, fighting a bunch of well heeled political bandits who are challenging the right of our State to have representation in the U.S. House of Representatives," he wrote to one of his constituents. "This is a genuine challenge, made in all seriousness, well financed and aggressively pressed." Abernethy recounted that a great army of "smart attorneys" had descended upon Mississippi, and that they had plenty of staff and high-tech equipment to do their research on behalf of the Freedom Democrats. The congressman did not doubt that these legal advisers received help from the Department of Justice.[86]

The Mississippi delegation set up headquarters in the King Edward Hotel in Jackson, where they spent "money like water trying to keep up with these invaders." The phone bill ran up to $250 a day and the representatives had to fly all over the state to brief lawyers on defensive tactics. "Incidentally, many of their group are well known Commies and others are affiliated with communist front organizations," Abernethy declared. "But this does not keep them from being smart nor does it keep them out of the offices of the Department of Justice where many are welcome, and where they also took some depositions against us and our State."[87]

During the spring of 1965, civil rights groups employed different strategies to gain access to the political process. The Freedom Democrats followed the legal route with their seating challenge, while Martin Luther King, the SCLC, and local activists in Selma, Alabama, chose to confront racial oppression through direct action. On Sunday, March 7, a group of more than six hundred African Americans and a few whites began a march from Selma to the state capital of Montgomery, where they intended to hold a voting rights demonstration. The protesters did not get far; at the Edmund Pettus Bridge, a posse of state troopers and vigilantes under the command of Colonel Al Lingo and Sheriff James Clark stood ready to stop them. When the marchers started crossing the bridge, the white troops attacked. Using tear gas and nightsticks, the patrolmen, some of them on horseback, charged into the group of unarmed protesters. Journalists were on the scene to report the brutal violence used by Alabama law enforcement. The nation reacted with disgust when they saw the images on television and in the newspapers.[88]

The protest also had an effect on the White House. President Johnson first called on Governor George Wallace of Alabama to come to Washington to discuss the civil rights situation in his state. Wallace tried to convince LBJ that the troops had only tried to preserve law and order and keep outside agitators under control, but Johnson had little patience with such arguments. During the remainder of the conversation, he mercilessly grilled the governor about black voting rights in Alabama. "Hell," Wallace later confessed, "if I'd stayed in there much longer, he'd have me coming out for civil rights."[89]

Two nights after the meeting with Wallace, on March 15, Johnson proposed a voting rights bill to a joint session of Congress. "There is no Negro problem," the president said, explaining the voting rights issue in his speech. "There is no Southern problem. There is no Northern problem. There is only an American problem."[90] Johnson had already instructed his attorney general to write "the goddamndest, toughest voting rights act that you can devise" before Selma, but the clash at the Edmund Pettus Bridge expedited the process. Like the Kennedys, LBJ believed that a true change in southern politics and race relations could come if blacks got the right to vote.[91]

Reverend Frank Dunn of the First Christian Church in Savannah, Georgia, was less optimistic, however. He believed that the direct action demonstrations organized by "a handful of . . . Negro leaders and white agitators" had in fact obstructed black advancement across the United States. "You know and I know that the people of the north are no more for integration than the southern people are," Dunn wrote Eastland on the day the president introduced the Voting Rights Act to Congress. The senator agreed with Dunn, but he saw little hope for the white southern cause, because of the national outcry against the events in Selma. "Clergymen and politicians, negro leaders and communist leaders fed by television, are all contributing to the emotionalism of the hour," Eastland grumbled. "Even in Congress, people are just not stopping to reason or to think and I shudder at the prospect of what can happen before sanity returns."[92] Both the White House and southern segregationists argued that the race issue was not regional, but national in scope.

Like in the debate on the 1964 Civil Rights Act, the southern bloc in Congress was unable to muster enough support to stop the Voting Rights Act of 1965. After Selma, the call for such a measure was strong nationwide. "There is a lot of hysteria in the country relative to the Civil Rights question," Eastland explained to one of his constituents, who wanted an investigation of Martin Luther King's "Communist affiliations."[93] Eastland had little hope the senators from the South could prevent enactment of Johnson's voting bill. On May 17, exactly eleven years after *Brown*, the Citizens' Council of Jackson held its tenth anniversary. The organizers invited James Eastland, George Wallace, and John Bell Williams. But Eastland was not sure he could come to Jackson. "I will attend the meeting if it is possible for me to leave Washington," he replied to Bill Simmons. "The Voting Rights Bill is up, and, of course, it will pass, but we have got to do everything we can against it."[94]

At the beginning of August, Congress indeed passed the Voting Rights Act with overpowering bipartisan endorsement—in the Senate, Strom Thurmond was the only Republican who voted against the legislation. On August 6, an elated President Johnson signed the bill into law. "Today, the Negro story and the American story fuse and blend," he stated. "And I pledge you that we will not delay or we will not hesitate or we will not turn aside, until Americans of every race and color and origin in this country have the same right as all others to share in the process of democracy." Five days later, race riots set Chicago and the Los Angeles district of Watts on fire.[95]

The enactment of the Voting Rights Act once again proved the effectiveness of direct action protests to initiate a federal response against discrimination. The legal route followed by the MFDP to unseat the Mississippi congressmen bore less fruit, although the Regulars initially expressed genuine fear about losing their positions in Congress. "We are doing our best to meet these liberals but our resources as compared to theirs leaves us at a terrible disadvantage," Abernethy confessed. He considered the seating challenge not just an attack on the congressional delegation, but a condemnation of the entire state of Mississippi and its way of life. "It is actually a fight against our State, a gargantuan effort put forth by nationwide liberal organizations to deny our State representation in the House of Representatives."[96]

The Committee on House Administration finally decided the case in favor of Prentiss Walker and the Regular Democrats on September 15, 1965. Five members of the committee voted against dismissal of the congressmen, citing that the "record in this case clearly indicates disfranchisement of voters in the State of Mississippi, due to inadequate official protection of their rights, as well as of their lives and limbs." They were hopeful that the new Voting Rights Act would protect the franchise of southern blacks in the future, however.[97] Abernethy was relieved, describing the entire episode as "the meanest, most nauseating thing I have ever been forced to endure. . . . This is an organized conspiratorial political push."[98] In his correspondence, Abernethy frequently projected the traditional image of the South as an embattled and victimized region, the last vestige of American conservatism under siege by the entire nation.

The decision of the Committee on House Administration meant that Mississippi retained its segregationist representation in Congress. All of its Democratic members had been elected during the 1930s and 1940s. They were therefore well entrenched in national politics when Lyndon Johnson signed the Voting Rights Act. The only exception was John Bell Williams, elected in 1947, who lost his seniority and afterward became governor of Mississippi, thanks to his stand for Goldwater and against the national Democratic Party. James Coleman charged almost $16,000 for his work as legal counsel for the congressmen.[99] The U.S. government paid each member of the contested Mississippi delegation $2,000 for their expenses in the seating challenge.[100]

In the spring of 1965, President Johnson nominated Coleman to the Fifth Circuit Court of Appeals. LBJ had several reasons to appoint a practical segregationist like Coleman to a southern circuit court known for its pro–civil rights stand and for its liberal members, judges such as John Minor Wisdom and Elbert Tuttle. First of all, he expected that the appointment of another progressive judge might endanger a possible reelection bid in 1968. Second, Coleman had openly endorsed the Kennedy-Johnson ticket in 1960. Because of his long-standing friendship with the Kennedys, even Robert Kennedy supported the nomination. Third, both John Stennis and James Eastland had promoted Coleman for the judgeship and Johnson was afraid that these two powerful politicians would cause even more obstruction to his Great Society plans if he ignored their wishes. Despite strong protest from Martin Luther King, SNCC, and other civil rights activists, Johnson did not renounce the nomination and Coleman became the new judge on the Fifth Circuit.[101] The president thus engendered goodwill with the Mississippi segregationists on Capitol Hill. Once again, the Regulars benefitted from their affiliation with the national Democratic Party. As long as they could keep the Freedom Democrats outside the party and the Goldwater Democrats in their ranks, their positions of power in national politics were secure.

CONCLUSION

ASTLAND SPENT HIS last years on the family plantation in the Delta. In the fall of 1985, journalist Joe Atkins drove to Doddsville to interview the senator. The "Godfather" of Mississippi politics struck a powerless pose, almost seven years after he had made his final speech on the Senate floor. His wife, Elizabeth, told Atkins about the ailments that plagued her husband and about the lonely life in the Delta. Many relatives and old friends had died or moved away. An elderly man who helped manage the plantation said the senator would "sometimes go down to the graveyard and just look at it." James Eastland did not talk much with Atkins, peering instead "across his bed and out the window toward the cotton, soybean, and rice fields that stretch over 5,800 acres of family-owned land."[1] Four months later he was dead.

Eastland's rural background and segregationist worldview defined his politics, not only on civil rights, but also toward organized labor and federal farm policies. He placed the challenge to the South's social and economic structure within the context of the Cold War, depicting it as part of a global communist conspiracy. James Eastland never disconnected the entitlements of race from the entitlements of class. What started out as a fight for the interests of white middle-class southerners eventually turned into a fight for the interests of white middle-class America. From the senator's standpoint, the battle for the southern way of life was not just an attempt to preserve segregation, but a much larger crusade to defend the American system of government and individual liberty against supposed alien forces that wanted to replace federalism with a despotic super state based on a Soviet model. Eastland was shrewd enough to eventually couch his segregationist beliefs in patriotic language and to connect the racist underpinnings of his states' rights ideology with anticommunism, personal freedom, and free enterprise. After the Voting Rights Act, ideas about small government and local control gained national traction. Between 1941 and 1965, Eastland's rhetoric changed from outright racist to a more constitutionalist style, but the underlying motives remained the same: to retain the status quo.

While working in Mississippi during Freedom Summer, SNCC activist Jane Stembridge discovered that the federal government was part of this status quo. "America is controlled by men who simply do not want justice: but who want power and—most of all—things to remain precisely as they are," she concluded.[2] The radicalization of parts of the civil rights movement and the emergence of Black Power were some of the more visible results of the difficulties of articulating an effective, widely shared answer to the systemic nature of race and class inequality in the United States. Eastland actually welcomed the change in tactics and in the regional orientation of civil rights activists, because he believed it would open the eyes of northern whites. By 1966, he perceived a marked shift in public opinion about civil rights legislation. "Northern people are beginning now to see where it is taking them and I think we are on the verge of seeing a radical change in the public sentiment of this country," he told one of his constituents.[3] Eastland even attributed the failure of the 1966 Civil Rights Act to the racial unrest that gripped the nation. He wrote the following to a Republican friend in Clarksdale, Charles Clark: "There is one thing about this rioting, pillaging and looting in the North, and that is it has given the American people a grandstand view of this civil rights movement. It is helping us in the South and I think it is responsible for our being able to stop the Civil Rights Bill in the Senate two weeks ago. You can feel the change in the Senate itself and, of course, you can observe it in the nation's press. We still have a long way to go, but these excesses are certainly working in our favor."[4]

During his career, Eastland contributed to various segregationist organizations, such as the States' Rights Democrats, the Citizens' Councils, and the Federation for Constitutional Government. These groups not only sought to sustain established racial structures, but also the economic status of middle-class whites. The FCG was an organization that combined its opposition to integration with a strong stance against socialized medicine and organized labor. For white middle-class Americans, a Black Power revolution inspired by communist doctrine obviously formed an explicit threat.

After World War II, the preservation of segregation had become "the cause of middle-class and elite whites," historian Pete Daniel wrote. "Southern whites who had recently entered the middle class, in particular, feared that integration would threaten their status, privilege, and upward mobility."[5] Eastland expressed and played upon these fears by linking integration with Big Government and communism. During the 1950s, upwardly mobile whites in the South did not want desegregation, but neither did they want to donate their newly acquired wealth to Washington. The economic ideology of free enterprise and laissez-faire government that was central to Eastland's worldview resonated with them. He presented racial separation and free-market capitalism as the American way, while forced integration and communism formed its antithesis.

Southern Republicans began to appropriate this neobourbon agenda of local control, in both racial and financial matters. Their most important political achievement was the reversal of the arguments made by segregationist Democrats. Eastland put the defense of segregation in the first place, followed by economic motives. He claimed that the survival of the American Republic depended on the survival of Jim Crow. Southern Republicans turned this line of reasoning around: their opposition to government interference rested on fiscal concerns and anticommunism, while more white supremacist notions eventually disappeared behind the coded veil of colorblind racism. By the time the Republican Party began to form a serious threat to southern Democrats, whites in the South understood the link between race and class privilege and they therefore understood the racial prejudice implicit in the Republican message. For many years, segregationist leaders like James Eastland had conditioned them to automatically make this connection.

After his participation in the Dixiecrat Revolt, James Eastland faced increased scrutiny by his constituents, who rapidly lost faith in the national Democratic Party. Forced to rejoin the political camp he had so strongly denounced during the 1948 campaign, the senator had to find ways to stay effective within the national party while the home front simultaneously impelled him to live up to his status as a defender of southern traditions. Ironically, the Supreme Court decision in Brown v. Board of Education played a critical role in boosting Eastland's political career. The verdict by the Warren Court enabled him to redirect his accusations of conspiratorial activities from his own party to the judicial branch. Moreover, during the 1950s both the Democrats and the Republicans committed themselves to civil rights in vaguely worded platforms. By the time the Eisenhower administration became involved in the integration crisis in Little Rock, Eastland's reasoning that the difference between the Democratic Party and the GOP was negligible started to sound more plausible to his constituents. The entire American political system appeared to be taken over by alien doctrines; all that seemed to matter now was not party affiliation, but the ability to prevent this infiltration from spreading to the southern states.

When Eastland obtained the chairmanship of the Senate Judiciary Committee in 1956, he could argue that his new position of power was enough reason for Mississippians to keep him in Washington. For years, James Eastland effectively downplayed his membership in the national Democratic Party and stressed the importance of his committee assignments in the fight against external intrusion. By placing himself outside the American factional division between national Democrats and national Republicans, and by emphasizing the significance of his power in the Senate, Eastland himself in fact became a political institution, the embodiment of conservative ideology and the defender of the southern way of life.

The Mississippi GOP tried to dispel this image during the 1960s and 1970s. Prentiss Walker, Eastland's Republican challenger in the 1966 Senate race, questioned his opponent's political sincerity. He tried to convince voters that the senator was spreading his conservative message in Mississippi one day and making deals with the Democratic establishment in Washington the next. In a letter announcing his candidacy for the Senate, Walker stated that the 1966 election would be "the first time in many years that we have had a choice in Mississippi between a Conservative Republican and a Double-Standard Democrat." Walker believed Eastland had never been a true representative for the average Mississippian. "Senator Jim Eastland, an elderly and wealthy plantation owner, has, in my opinion, become very unconcerned about Mississippi and her problems," he wrote. "Why would he promote Bobby Kennedy for Attorney General . . . ? How could he promote Lyndon Johnson for President and then ask the good people of Mississippi to support him for the U.S. Senate?" According to the Republican candidate, a vote for the Democratic Party would be a vote for "the politicians, money men, and the so-called Great Society promoting Senator Eastland."[6] But Walker's attempts to link Eastland with Lyndon Johnson's Great Society did not work. Only 27 percent of Mississippi voters eventually went Republican in the Senate contest.

The reason why the conservative electorate in Mississippi did not support a states' rights Republican like Walker is clear: the average white voter in the state was content with Eastland's political record. By 1966, the senator's Democratic Party unity score hovered around 20 percent.[7] Clarke Reed, who became chairman of the Mississippi Republican Party in 1966, thought Eastland was in fact much closer to the ideology of the GOP than the Democratic Party, based on his voting behavior. The most important rationale for the Democrats to keep such a right-wing politician in their ranks was his contribution to achieving congressional majorities.[8]

At the same time, Eastland managed to create enough goodwill among the more liberal members of his party. In September 1965, *Los Angeles Times* reporter John Averill wrote a piece about this apparent contradiction, titled "Sen. Eastland Is Top Paradox in the Senate." The article discussed the ambivalent image of Eastland and revealed that the standard, one-dimensional depiction of Eastland as the ignorant and paranoid racist villain did not quite match with the opinion most of his Senate colleagues had of him. "Even those liberals who disagree most violently with Eastland paradoxically regard him with great respect and perhaps even a degree of affection," Averill wrote.[9]

In a way, Averill's observations confirmed Walker's portrayal of James Eastland as a double-standard Democrat. This was not a sign of ideological weakness, however. Eastland's ability to work with professed liberals (and to keep this cooperation quiet) was instead the surest way to sustain the southern way of life, and his own career. At the same time, he managed to stay on the good side of racist America. Eastland did not become a member of the Citizens' Council because he thought it would be politically inexpedient, but he frequently attended meetings of the organization. Journalist Jerry Mitchell claimed the senator also had close ties with the Ku Klux Klan, including Klan leader Edgar Ray Killen, who was convicted in 2005 for his involvement in the murder of three civil rights workers in Neshoba County, Mississippi, in the summer of 1964. Killen called Eastland his "No. 1 hero" and "a second father," and stated he worked for the senator to "stop the communist Jews or their soldiers." Despite FBI records that confirm a relationship between Eastland and the Klan, people who knew the powerful Mississippi politician strongly deny such a connection existed.[10] Whether or not Killen's story is true, one of Eastland's most important political skills was his ability to make sure such rumors did not negatively affect his work in Washington or his standing with liberal Democrats like Ted Kennedy or John Pastore.

Eastland decided to retire in 1978. After thirty-four years in Washington, he was not up for another Senate race. The times had changed for politicians like him. His political party had become the defender of liberalism and minority rights, and a new style of campaigning had emerged in the South. "I can see from the beginning of the [1970s] when I started to the end of the decade that the regional differences [in campaigning]—which are still there to some extent—have narrowed," pollster Patrick Caddell observed. "The country has become more homogenous."[11] The daylong political rallies with barbecues and fried catfish had become a thing of the past. PR consultants now ran campaigns. They relied heavily on mass media to send their nicely wrapped messages to the voters. Some veteran politicians from the South were able to adjust themselves to the television era, but Eastland was not. "Perhaps he instinctively realized campaigns had changed and knew he wanted no part of the television-driven, candidate-packaged approach to winning elections," two students of Mississippi politics wrote. "Eastland was a master of a political world that is unrecognizable today. Personal relationships formed the basis for political success when Eastland started his political career. . . . Reaching large numbers of voters through press conferences, television, direct mail, and phone banks were techniques foreign to Eastland."[12]

By distancing himself from the liberal ideology of Lyndon Johnson and George McGovern (the Democratic presidential candidate in 1972), Eastland initially managed to hold on to his conservative voter base. After his last Senate campaign, in 1972, that strategy would become increasingly more difficult to pursue, however. From the mid-1970s onward, many southern Democrats had to be able to build biracial coalitions in order to defeat their Republican opponents, who relied heavily on the white vote.[13] Forming such a biracial coalition was problematic for a politician like James Eastland. His reputation as an ultraconservative segregationist probably would not attract a large part of the African American electorate, whose influence increased as the years (and voter registration) continued. Like his colleague Strom Thurmond in 1964, Eastland could have switched parties in 1972. Although there were rumors shortly after the Senate race that the Mississippi senator was thinking about such a move, Eastland himself vehemently denied these reports. "Why do these people keep writing something they know nothing about," he said. "I am not going to turn Republican. . . . There's nothing to it."[14]

In spite of his affiliation with the Democratic Party, Eastland received the tacit backing of the Nixon administration in 1972. His powerful position in

Congress, his statewide network, and his conservative ideology made him the candidate the White House preferred for reelection. Simultaneously, Eastland's seniority and his position on a number of key Senate committees were essential in attracting voters during the 1966 and 1972 campaigns. Although the senator faced Republican opposition for the first time in these years, he could always fall back on his reputation in the state. "'Personalism' remains a dominant characteristic of the southerner," Jack Bass and Walter De Vries wrote. "Politically, personalism appears in the barber shop discussions in which any politician who has truly arrived is referred to by his first name—'Big Jim' for Senator Eastland in Mississippi, 'Ol' Strom' or 'Fritz' for Senators Thurmond and Hollings in South Carolina, or 'Young Harry' for Senator Harry Byrd, Jr. in Virginia."[15] A trusted cadre of straight-party voters had always supported the Mississippi senator through the decades, but their numbers were dwindling at the beginning of the 1970s.

With the leftward turn of the national Democrats, the GOP became a viable alternative for voters in Mississippi and across the South. The southern strategy of Barry Goldwater (and later Richard Nixon) was clearly aimed at winning the white voters in the South for the Republican Party. Eastland's Republican opponents used his membership in the national Democratic Party as a weapon against the senator in their campaigns. At the same time, they revived an old dichotomy in Mississippi politics: the division between the Delta and the Hills. "I'll have to give you my opinion on Jim Eastland. I think Jim absolutely was what I call a paternalistic politician," Gil Carmichael said of his opponent in the 1972 election. "My redneck east Mississippi background family was being taken care of, in fact. A lot of my white Carmichaels in east Mississippi probably got disenfranchised in 1890 or somewhere along there, too, because they couldn't pay the poll tax. So, he came out of that mentality, they sacrificed a lot of poor."[16] By representing themselves as working-class Republicans and by depicting Eastland as a neobourbon elitist, both Walker and Carmichael were able to gain a foothold in the eastern parts of the state and along the southern edge of the Mississippi River. But they never came close to defeating Big Jim Eastland.

Eastland's career spanned a period of protracted political change in the South. His death signified the symbolic end of massive resistance in the region. In 1956, *Time* magazine still described him as "the authentic voice of most of the South's 30 million whites, including the respectable and the educated."[17] But twenty-two years later, when Eastland was thinking about running for a seventh full term in the U.S. Congress, he had to pay the price for his ultraconservative politics. The growth of the African American electorate troubled the senator. He probably knew that a Democratic candidate needed at least some support from black voters, and he also realized that his record as a staunch defender of white supremacy, a record that had delivered him so many victories in previous campaigns, would not be a great asset in 1978. Shortly before Eastland announced his retirement, he met with Aaron Henry and asked if black Mississippians would vote for him in the upcoming Senate elections. Henry, who was the head of the state's NAACP at that time, frankly answered: "Your chances of getting support in the black community are poor at best. You have a master-servant philosophy with regard to blacks."[18]

The Mississippi GOP profited from the senator's retirement. Republican Thad Cochran won the race for Eastland's seat against Democrat Maurice Dantin and independent Charles Evers, the brother of the slain civil rights leader Medgar Evers. With the election of Cochran, a century of Democratic dominance in Senate elections came to an end in Mississippi. As southern Democrats like James Eastland disappeared from the political scene, the Republican Party continued to carry their torch.

NOTES

1. "Ringmaster of Power Lunches, Duke Zeibert, Is Dead at 86," *New York Times,* August 16, 1997.

2. William A. Rusher, *Special Counsel: An Inside Report on the Senate Investigations into Communism* (New Rochelle: Arlington House, 1968), 22.

3. "Eastland Pledges Impartial Rule as Judiciary Head," *Jackson Daily News,* March 3, 1956.

4. "Sen. Eastland Is Top Paradox in the Senate," *Los Angeles Times,* September 15, 1965.

5. Bobby Baker, *Wheeling and Dealing: Confessions of a Capitol Hill Operator* (New York: Norton, 1978), 100.

6. "Senator 'Got Things Done': Associates Recall Power of the 'Machine,'" *Jackson Clarion-Ledger,* October 27, 1985.

7. "Dixie Demagogue: The Story of Sen. Eastland," *New York Post,* February 13, 1956.

8. See for example Byron E. Shafer and Richard Johnston, *The End of Southern Exceptionalism: Class, Race, and Partisan Change in the Postwar South* (Cambridge: Harvard Univ. Press, 2006), Matthew D. Lassiter, *The Silent Majority: Suburban Politics in the Sunbelt South* (Princeton: Princeton Univ. Press, 2006), and Matthew D. Lassiter and Joseph Crespino, ed., *The Myth of Southern Exceptionalism* (New York: Oxford Univ. Press, 2010).

9. Chris Danielson, "'Lily White and Hard Right': The Mississippi Republican Party and Black Voting, 1965–1980," *Journal of Southern History* 75, no. 1 (February 2009): 87–88.

10. Dan T. Carter, "More than Race: Conservatism in the White South since V. O. Key Jr.," in *Unlocking V. O. Key Jr.: Southern Politics for the Twenty-First Century,* ed. Angie Maxwell and Todd G. Shields (Fayetteville: Univ. of Arkansas Press, 2011), 149.

11. Glenn Feldman, review of *The Myth of Southern Exceptionalism,* ed. Matthew D. Lassiter and Joseph Crespino, *Journal of Southern History* 77, no. 3 (August 2011): 785. "The South's *partisan* allegiances are transitory," Feldman stated on the same page, "its fundamental *political* allegiance is unchanging." See also "Introduction: Has the South Become Republican?" in *Painting Dixie Red: When, Where, Why, and How the South Became Republican,* ed. Glen Feldman (Gainesville: Univ. Press of Florida, 2011), 3.

CHAPTER 1. A PRODUCT OF TWO CULTURES

1. Chris Myers Asch, "No Compromise: The Freedom Struggles of James O. Eastland and Fannie Lou Hamer" (Ph.D. diss., University of North Carolina at Chapel Hill, 2005), 19; Chris

Myers Asch, *The Senator and the Sharecropper: The Freedom Struggles of James O. Eastland and Fannie Lou Hamer* (New York: New Press, 2008), 38.

2. Woods C. Eastland to the Honorable Oscar F. Bledsoe, May 6, 1942, in File Series 1, Subseries 2, Folder 1-12, in James O. Eastland Collection, 1930–1978, Archives and Special Collections, J. D. Williams Library, University of Mississippi (hereafter referred to as JOE Collection).

3. V. O. Key Jr., *Southern Politics in State and Nation* (New York: Knopf, 1949), 231.

4. William Alexander Percy, *Lanterns on the Levee: Recollections of a Planter's Son*, 1st ed. (1941; reprint, Baton Rouge: Louisiana State Univ. Press, 2006), 149.

5. Key, *Southern Politics in State and Nation*, 230–246.

6. Dan W. Smith Jr., "James O. Eastland: Early Life and Career" (Master's thesis, Mississippi College, 1978), 5.

7. Stephen Cresswell, *Rednecks, Redeemers, and Race: Mississippi After Reconstruction, 1877–1917* (Jackson: Univ. Press of Mississippi, 2006), 197–200, 225.

8. Albert D. Kirwan, *Revolt of the Rednecks: Mississippi Politics, 1876–1925* (New York: Harper and Row, 1951), 313.

9. Cresswell, *Rednecks, Redeemers, and Race*, 209.

10. Smith, "James O. Eastland," 8–9.

11. Ibid., 11.

12. Curtis Wilkie, *Dixie: A Personal Odyssey Through Events That Shaped the Modern South* (New York: Scribner, 2001), 82; Charles W. Eagles, *The Price of Defiance: James Meredith and the Integration of Ole Miss* (Chapel Hill: Univ. of North Carolina Press, 2009), 14.

13. Smith, "James O. Eastland," 10–14; Asch, *The Senator and the Sharecropper*, 38–40.

14. James O. Eastland to Joe Howorth, February 27, 1927, in Folder 1: 1927 Correspondence, in Joseph M. Howorth Collection, Archives and Special Collections, J. D. Williams Library, University of Mississippi.

15. Smith, "James O. Eastland," 15–17.

16. Ibid., 18–25; Cresswell, *Rednecks, Redeemers, and Race*, 212–213; Key, *Southern Politics in State and Nation*, 241–242; Kirwan, *Revolt of the Rednecks*, 313–314; Chester M. Morgan, *Redneck Liberal: Theodore G. Bilbo and the New Deal* (Baton Rouge: Louisiana State Univ. Press, 1985), 42–44.

17. Morgan, *Redneck Liberal*, 46.

18. Asch, "No Compromise," 22–24; Asch, *The Senator and the Sharecropper*, 41–43; Smith, "James O. Eastland," 26–36.

19. Kari Frederickson, *The Dixiecrat Revolt and the End of the Solid South, 1932–1968* (Chapel Hill: Univ. of North Carolina Press, 2001), 15–17.

20. William E. Leuchtenburg, *The White House Looks South: Franklin D. Roosevelt, Harry S. Truman, Lyndon B. Johnson* (Baton Rouge: Louisiana State Univ. Press, 2005), 80.

21. Ibid., 79.

22. Ibid., 75–80; John Egerton, *Speak Now Against the Day: The Generation Before the Civil Rights Movement in the South* (New York: Knopf, 1994), 110.

23. Egerton, *Speak Now Against the Day*, 110; Leuchtenburg, *The White House Looks South*, 78.

24. Egerton, *Speak Now Against the Day*, 110–115.

25. George B. Tindall, *The Emergence of the New South, 1913–1945*, 2nd ed. (Baton Rouge: Louisiana State Univ. Press, 1983), 553.

26. Frank Freidel, *F.D.R. and the South* (Baton Rouge: Louisiana State Univ. Press, 1965), 96–97.

27. Tindall, *The Emergence of the New South*, 553, 630; Martha H. Swain, *Pat Harrison: The New Deal Years* (Jackson: Univ. Press of Mississippi, 1978); Frederickson, *The Dixiecrat Revolt*, 23–27.

28. Chester M. Morgan, "Senator Theodore G. Bilbo, the New Deal, and Mississippi Politics (1934–1940)," *Journal of Mississippi History* 47, no. 3 (August 1985): 157.

29. Ibid., 150–151.

30. W. C. Eastland to Paul B. Johnson, August 3, 1937, in File Series 1, Subseries 2, Folder 1-7, in JOE Collection.

31. W. C. Eastland to Paul B. Johnson, October 29, 1937, in File Series 1, Subseries 2, Folder 1-7, in JOE Collection.

32. Morgan, "Senator Theodore G. Bilbo," 161–162; Erle Johnston, *Politics: Mississippi Style* (Forest, Miss.: Lake Harbor Publishers, 1993), 51–55. The 1939 governor's election in Mississippi made strange bedfellows: in 1918, Paul Johnson opposed Bilbo in the race for U.S. Congress; in the 1935 gubernatorial campaign, Bilbo backed Hugh White, who ran against Paul Johnson. In that election, Johnson received the support of Mike Conner. In the 1936 Senate race, Bilbo switched his support to Conner, who opposed incumbent Pat Harrison. Three years later, Bilbo campaigned for Johnson, while Pat Harrison and Hugh White backed Conner.

33. Smith, "James O. Eastland," 8, 34–36. Chester Eastland was a cousin of James Eastland.

34. Swain, *Pat Harrison*, 36–39; Asch, *The Senator and the Sharecropper*, 89–90; Smith, "James O. Eastland," 38.

35. *Congressional Record* 87 (July 24, 1941): 6292.

36. Woods C. Eastland to James O. Eastland, August 11, 1941, in File Series 1, Subseries 2, Folder 1-12, in JOE Collection.

37. Asch, "No Compromise," 73–75; James O. Eastland, "Brazilian Cotton, Henderson, and Cottonseed Oil" (Washington, D.C.: United States Government Printing Office, 1941), 2, 7.

38. Asch, "No Compromise," 75–76; James O. Eastland, "World Cotton: The Farmer's Gateway Through the Tariff Wall—Bankhead-Eastland Cotton Bill" (Washington, D.C.: United States Government Printing Office, 1941), 2, 5.

39. Asch, "No Compromise," 69, 77.

40. Ibid., 79; "Jim Eastland, Champion of the Farmer and the South," campaign brochure, in File Series 1, Subseries 19, Folder 8-20, in JOE Collection.

41. "Positions and Policy Statements," in File Series 1, Subseries 19, Folder 9-3, in JOE Collection.

42. *Farm Bureau Co-Op News*, in File Series 1, Subseries 19, Folder 8-1, in JOE Collection.

43. Marcus Kaufman to James O. Eastland, August 12, 1941, in File Series 1, Subseries 20, Folder 1-2, in JOE Collection.

44. James O. Eastland to Marcus Kaufman, August 15, 1941, in File Series 1, Subseries 20, Folder 1-2, in JOE Collection.

45. Woods C. Eastland to Harry K. Murray, June 17, 1942, in File Series 1, Subseries 2, Folder 1-12, in JOE Collection.

46. M. G. Vaiden to James O. Eastland, August 27, 1942, in File Series 1, Subseries 19, Folder 7-22, in JOE Collection.

47. Woods C. Eastland to M. G. Vaiden, September 1, 1942, in File Series 1, Subseries 19, Folder 7-22, in JOE Collection.

48. Wall Doxey in *McComb-Enterprise Journal,* in File Series 1, Subseries 19, Folder 8-20, in JOE Collection.

49. Theodore G. Bilbo to James O. Eastland, February 18, 1942, in File Series 1, Subseries 19, Folder 7-9, in JOE Collection.

50. James O. Eastland to Theodore G. Bilbo, February 27, 1942, in File Series 1, Subseries 19, Folder 7-9, in JOE Collection.

51. Key, *Southern Politics in State and Nation,* 246.

52. Asch, "No Compromise," 79; *Tupelo Daily News,* September 15, 1941, in File Series 1, Subseries 19, Folder 8-20, in JOE Collection.

53. FDR quoted in Robert Sherrill, *Gothic Politics in the Deep South: Stars of the New Confederacy* (New York: Grossman Publishers, 1968), 186.

54. Asch, "No Compromise," 83–84.

55. Ibid., 84–85; Robert Ormond to James O. Eastland, June 20, 1947, in File Series 1, Subseries 3, Folder 1-78, in JOE Collection.

56. W. J. Godbold to James O. Eastland, April 7, 1945, in File Series 1, Subseries 3, Folder 1-51, in JOE Collection.

57. Asch, "No Compromise," 87–95.

58. Chris Myers Asch, "Revisiting Reconstruction: James O. Eastland, the FEPC, and the Struggle to Rebuild Germany, 1945–1946," *Journal of Mississippi History* 67, no. 1 (2005): 7–8.

59. Ibid., 9–12.

60. James A. Dombrowski to Dear Editor, July 18, 1945, in File Series 3, Subseries 1, Folder: Civil Rights—1945 (1 of 3), in JOE Collection. Newspaper quotes from "Southern Editors Defend Negro GI's," attached to Dombrowski letter.

61. Clark Foreman to James O. Eastland, July 19, 1945, in File Series 3, Subseries 1, Folder: Civil Rights—1945 (1 of 3), in JOE Collection.

62. Frank B. Sharbrough to James O. Eastland, July 24, 1945, in File Series 3, Subseries 1, Folder: Civil Rights—1945 (1 of 3), in JOE Collection.

63. James O. Eastland to Frank B. Sharbrough, July 27, 1945, in File Series 3, Subseries 1, Folder: Civil Rights—1945 (1 of 3), in JOE Collection.

64. James O. Eastland to M. G. Mann, July 27, 1945, in File Series 3, Subseries 1, Folder: Civil Rights—1945 (1 of 3), in JOE Collection.

65. Walter Sillers to James O. Eastland, July 23, 1945, in File Series 3, Subseries 1, Folder: Civil Rights—1945 (3 of 3), in JOE Collection.

66. Ibid.

67. Asch, "Revisiting Reconstruction," 21–27.

68. Asch, *The Senator and the Sharecropper,* 116.

69. See Jack Bass and Walter De Vries, *The Transformation of Southern Politics: Social Change and Political Consequence Since 1945* (Athens: Univ. of Georgia Press, 1995), 193. They wrote: "There was

no basic difference between the Delta planter and Bilbo on the place of the Negro. The difference was one of style, an unspoken understanding by one and vulgar demagoguery by the other."

70. Steven F. Lawson, *Black Ballots: Voting Rights in the South, 1944–1969* (New York: Columbia Univ. Press, 1976), 133–134.

71. Walter Sillers to James O. Eastland, June 14, 1944, in Box 24, Folder 19, in Walter Sillers Jr. Papers, Charles W. Capps Jr. Archives, Delta State University (hereafter referred to as WS Papers).

72. John W. Partin, "Roosevelt, Byrnes, and the 1944 Vice-Presidential Nomination," *Historian* 42, no. 1 (November 1979): 87. See also Robert H. Ferrell, *Choosing Truman: The Democratic Convention of 1944* (Columbia: Univ. of Missouri Press, 1994), for a detailed account of Truman's selection for the vice presidency. Partin wrote the following about Truman's qualities: "Truman 'just dropped into the slot'; he had compiled an admirable record as chairman of the Senate Committee to Investigate the National Defense Program, had supported labor legislation, was sympathetic to veteran problems, added geographic diversity, and understood the workings of big-city Democratic organizations." Partin, "Roosevelt, Byrnes, and the 1944 Vice-Presidential Nomination," 92.

73. Leuchtenburg, *The White House Looks South*, 158.

74. "Senator James O. Eastland and Speaker Walter Sillers are credited with leading the movement which resulted in Mississippi switching from Senator Bankhead to Senator Truman for vice-president at the Chicago convention which started off the fire-works that resulted in President Truman's nomination," in Box 24, Folder 19, in WS Collection.

75. Ibid.; Ferrell, *Choosing Truman*, 86–88.

76. "Southern Revolt on Race Issue Blasted," *Jackson Clarion-Ledger*, July 21, 1944.

77. "South's Revolt Leads to Third Party Talk," *Jackson Clarion-Ledger*, July 22, 1944.

78. "Eastland Promises Support to Party Nominees; Conner Feels South Must Organize Strength," *Jackson Clarion-Ledger*, July 23, 1944.

79. James O. Eastland to the Honorable Tom M. McDonald, August 15, 1944, in File Series 1, Subseries 20, Folder 1-5, in JOE Collection; Leuchtenburg, *The White House Looks South*, 158–162

80. Sillers quoted in Leuchtenburg, *The White House Looks South*, 162.

81. James O. Eastland to Billy Snider, September 16, 1946, in File Series 1, Subseries 20, Folder 1-7, in JOE Collection.

82. Patricia Sullivan, *Days of Hope: Race and Democracy in the New Deal Era* (Chapel Hill: Univ. of North Carolina Press, 1996), 7–8.

CHAPTER 2. JAMES EASTLAND'S RADICALISM

1. Leuchtenburg, *The White House Looks South*, 165–178; Joseph Pierro, "'Everything in My Power': Harry S. Truman and the Fight Against Racial Discrimination" (Master's thesis, Virginia Polytechnic Institute, 2004), 34–38.

2. Michael R. Gardner, *Harry Truman and Civil Rights: Moral Courage and Political Risks* (Carbondale: Southern Illinois Univ. Press, 2002), 80.

3. Leuchtenburg, *The White House Looks South*, 178–181.

4. Key, *Southern Politics in State and Nation*, 229.

5. James Eastland, "Joint Assembly of the Mississippi Legislature in Jackson, Mississippi," in File Series 2, Subseries 6, Box 1, Folder: 29 January 1948, in JOE Collection.

6. Ibid.

7. Frederickson, *The Dixiecrat Revolt*, 78–79.

8. "Senator Urges People to Act," *New Orleans Times-Picayune*, February 10, 1948.

9. *Congressional Record* 94 (February 9, 1948): 1193.

10. Ibid., 1194.

11. Ibid.

12. Ibid., 1194–1198.

13. Walter Sillers to James O. Eastland, February 14, 1948, in File Series 1, Subseries 20, Folder 1-9, in JOE Collection.

14. Charles G. Hamilton to the editor of the *Post-Dispatch*, February 19, 1948, in File Series 2, Subseries 4, Folder: February 1948—Dixiecrats, in JOE Collection. See also Frederickson, *The Dixiecrat Revolt*, 83.

15. Leuchtenburg, *The White House Looks South*, 182–185; Frederickson, *The Dixiecrat Revolt*, 78–80.

16. "Gauging the South's Revolt," *U.S. News and World Report*, March 26, 1948, 22. See also Leuchtenburg, *The White House Looks South*, 185–189.

17. Frederickson, *The Dixiecrat Revolt*, 85.

18. Harold W. Gautier to W. W. Wright et al., April 1, 1948, in File Series 1, Subseries 20, Box 1, Folder 1-9, in JOE Collection.

19. Ibid.

20. Ibid.

21. Frederickson, *The Dixiecrat Revolt*, 104–107.

22. Ibid.

23. James O. Eastland to the Honorable Fielding L. Wright, May 10, 1948, in File Series 1, Subseries 20, Folder 1-9, in JOE Collection.

24. George W. Armstrong to James O. Eastland, January 30, 1948, in File Series 1, Subseries 19, Folder 10-17, in JOE Collection. W. Lee O'Daniel was a senator from Texas. John Rankin represented Mississippi's first district in the U.S. House. Both men were strong anticommunists.

25. James O. Eastland to the Honorable Leon S. White, March 3, 1948, in File Series 1, Subseries 19, Folder 10-17, in JOE Collection.

26. Gary A. Donaldson, *Truman Defeats Dewey* (Lexington: Univ. Press of Kentucky, 1999), 136–144; Harold I. Gullan, *The Upset That Wasn't: Harry S Truman and the Crucial Election of 1948* (Chicago: Ivan R. Dee, 1998), 79–84; Robert H. Ferrell, *Harry S. Truman: A Life* (Columbia: Univ. of Missouri Press, 1994), 268; Frederickson, *The Dixiecrat Revolt*, 120–121; Alonzo L. Hamby, *Man of the People: A Life of Harry S. Truman* (New York: Oxford Univ. Press, 1995), 435–436, 446–447.

27. Frederickson, *The Dixiecrat Revolt*, 107; "Mississippi Walkout Is Slated If Truman Receives Nomination," *Memphis Commercial Appeal*, June 23, 1948. For the resolutions adopted at the Mississippi Democratic Convention, see File Series 1, Subseries 20, Folder 1-9, in JOE Collection.

28. James Eastland, "Keynote Speech at the Mississippi Democratic Convention in Jackson, Mississippi," in File Series 2, Subseries 6, Box 1, Folder: 22 June 1948, in JOE Collection.

29. Ibid.

30. Walter Sillers to Judge Horace Wilkinson, June 24, 1948, Mississippi Digital Library, accessed May 19, 2014, http://collections.msdiglib.org/cdm/ref/collection/dsu/id/306.

31. "Dixie Information Bureau Objective," *Meridian Star,* June 28, 1948.

32. Walter Sillers to John U. Barr, June 29, 1948, Mississippi Digital Library, accessed May 19, 2014, http://collections.msdiglib.org/cdm/ref/collection/dsu/id/81.

33. "Mississippi Walkout Is Slated If Truman Receives Nomination," *Memphis Commercial Appeal,* June 23, 1948.

34. James O. Eastland to H. L. Hunt, August 7, 1948, in File Series 1, Subseries 20, Box 1, Folder 1-9, in JOE Collection.

35. Donaldson, *Truman Defeats Dewey,* 160–162; Hubert H. Humphrey, *The Education of a Public Man: My Life and Politics,* ed. Norman Sherman (Garden City: Doubleday, 1976), 110–112.

36. Humphrey, *The Education of a Public Man,* 111.

37. Ibid., 112–113.

38. Frederickson, *The Dixiecrat Revolt,* 129.

39. Carl Solberg, *Hubert Humphrey: A Biography* (New York: Norton, 1984), 17–19.

40. Ibid., 16–17; Donaldson, *Truman Defeats Dewey,* 163–164; Frederickson, *The Dixiecrat Revolt,* 129–130; Humphrey, *The Education of a Public Man,* 114–115.

41. Frederickson, *The Dixiecrat Revolt,* 130.

42. Dan T. Carter, *The Politics of Rage: George Wallace, the Origins of the New Conservatism, and the Transformation of American Politics,* 2nd ed. (Baton Rouge: Louisiana State Univ. Press, 2000), 88. Carter wrote: "He [Wallace] attached himself to the head of the loyalists, Senator Lister Hill, who, like most mainline white southern politicians, elected to swallow the platform as meaningless blather. After all, Dixie's senators still had the filibuster to block Truman's civil rights legislation. And they had no intention of jeopardizing their links to the national party by joining the unruly mob of third-party Dixiecrats."

43. Robert A. Garson, *The Democratic Party and the Politics of Sectionalism, 1941–1948* (Baton Rouge: Louisiana State Univ. Press, 1974), 280, 304–305; Hamby, *Man of the People,* 450–451; Zachary Karabell, *The Last Campaign: How Harry Truman Won the 1948 Election* (New York: Vintage Books, 2001), 158–160. Half a vote went to former Indiana governor Paul McNutt (see Karabell, 159). Of all the southern states, only a part of the North Carolina delegation voted for Truman, see Garson, 280.

44. Harry S. Truman, "Acceptance Speech," in *History of U.S. Political Parties,* vol. 4, *1945–1972, The Politics of Change,* ed. Arthur M. Schlesinger Jr. (New York: Chelsea House Publishers, 1973), 2724.

45. "Dixiecrats Open Meeting Today, Plan Opposition Slates; Congress May Quit on Truman," *Memphis Commercial Appeal,* July 17, 1948.

46. Virginia M. Simmerman to Cullen B. Curlee, July 6, 1948, in File Series 1, Subseries 21, Folder 1-6, in JOE Collection.

47. "The Authentic Voice," *Time,* March 26, 1956.

48. Asch, *The Senator and the Sharecropper,* 116. According to Asch, the Supreme Court's 1954 decision in *Brown v. Board of Education* was the real catalyst for Eastland's political career,

"transforming him from a little-known senator . . . into the South's most visible segregationist politician, a nationally recognized symbol of racism and resistance." See ibid., 133.

49. "States' Rights Movement Is Born, Cradled and Raised by Sympathetic Mississippians," *Jackson Clarion-Ledger,* July 25, 1948. See also Frederickson, *The Dixiecrat Revolt,* 70, and Asch, *The Senator and the Sharecropper,* 123.

50. "Eastland Backs Wright's Stand," *New Orleans Times-Picayune,* January 21, 1948.

51. Frederickson, *The Dixiecrat Revolt,* 70.

52. "Govs. Thurmond, Wright, to Head Southern Ticket," *New Orleans Times-Picayune,* July 18, 1948.

53. Ibid.; Frederickson, *The Dixiecrat Revolt,* 136; J. Barton Starr, "Birmingham and the 'Dixiecrat' Convention of 1948," *Alabama Historical Quarterly* 32 (spring/summer 1970), 37.

54. Starr, "Birmingham and the 'Dixiecrat' Convention of 1948," 39–40.

55. Ibid.; Nadine Cohodas, *Strom Thurmond and the Politics of Southern Change* (Macon: Mercer Univ. Press, 1994), 175.

56. Courtney C. Pace to Melvin Howard, August 23, 1957, in File Series 3, Subseries 1, Folder: Civil Rights—1957 (3 of 5), in JOE Collection.

57. Cohodas, *Strom Thurmond,* 175–176; Frederickson, *The Dixiecrat Revolt,* 137–138.

58. "Govs. Thurmond, Wright, to Head Southern Ticket," *New Orleans Times-Picayune,* July 18, 1948; Courtney C. Pace to Melvin Howard, August 23, 1957, in File Series 3, Subseries 1, Folder: Civil Rights—1957 (3 of 5), in JOE Collection; Starr, "Birmingham and the 'Dixiecrat' Convention of 1948," 41. See also "Thurmond, Candidate of Rebels, Decries 'White Supremacy' Idea," *New York Times,* July 20, 1948.

59. Cohodas, *Strom Thurmond,* 177; Frederickson, *The Dixiecrat Revolt,* 139–140; "Govs. Thurmond, Wright, to Head Southern Ticket," *New Orleans Times-Picayune,* July 18, 1948; "Thurmond, Candidate of Rebels, Decries 'White Supremacy' Idea," *New York Times,* July 18, 1948; Starr, "Birmingham and the 'Dixiecrat' Convention of 1948," 42–43.

60. "Mississippi to Ballot on Vote," *New Orleans Times-Picayune,* July 25, 1948.

61. "Dixiecrats Call for Stand by Officials, Candidates," August 8, 1948. See also Frederickson, *The Dixiecrat Revolt,* 144–145.

62. "Nominee of Dixiecrats Welcomed at Houston," *New Orleans Times-Picayune,* August 11, 1948.

63. James O. Eastland to E. J. Bailey, August 5, 1948, in File Series 3, Subseries 1, Folder: Civil Rights—1948 (2 of 3), in JOE Collection.

64. M. Scott Sosebee, "The Split in the Texas Democratic Party, 1936–1956" (Master's thesis, Texas Tech University, 2000), 79–81.

65. "Thurmond Begins Nation-Wide Fight," *Dallas Morning News,* August 12, 1948.

66. H. L. Bramlett to James O. Eastland, August 12, 1948, in File Series 1, Subseries 20, Box 1, Folder 1-9, in JOE Collection.

67. James O. Eastland to H. L. Bramlett, September 6, 1948, in File Series 1, Subseries 20, Box 1, Folder 1-9, in JOE Collection.

68. "Capital Brevities," *New Orleans Times-Picayune,* August 15, 1948.

69. "It's Dewey vs. Thurmond, Says Eastland at Rally," *Memphis Press-Scimitar,* September 11, 1948.

70. Ibid.

71. Ibid.

72. Ibid.

73. "Truman Forces Name Mississippi Electors," *Memphis Commercial Appeal*, September 20, 1948.

74. Ibid.; "Sister State's Vote Tuesday Is Expected to Top 200,000," *New Orleans Times-Picayune*, October 31, 1948. In 1944, the independent Republicans received 7,859 votes, while Howard received 3,700.

75. "Dixiecrats to Open Campaign in Texas," *Dallas Morning News*, October 7, 1948.

76. "Eastland to Lead 'Operation Texas,'" *Jackson Clarion-Ledger*, October 17, 1948.

77. "States' Righters Start Texas Blitz," *Dallas Morning News*, October 19, 1948.

78. "Capital Brevities," *New Orleans Times-Picayune*, October 31, 1948.

79. P. E Whittington to James O. Eastland, November 6, 1948, in File Series 1, Subseries 20, Folder 1-9, in JOE Collection.

80. James O. Eastland to P. E. Whittington, in File Series 1, Subseries 20, Folder 1-9, in JOE Collection.

81. Leuchtenburg, *The White House Looks South*, 213.

82. Charles W. Clark to James O. Eastland, November 8, 1948, in File Series 1, Subseries 20, Folder 1-9, in JOE Collection.

CHAPTER 3. TAKING CONTROL

1. "Eastland Thinks He's No. 1 on HT's Unpopular List," *Memphis Press-Scimitar*, April 30, 1949.

2. "McGrath Will Bar South's Dissidents as Party Leaders," *New York Times*, November 9, 1948.

3. Frederickson, *The Dixiecrat Revolt*, 189; Sean J. Savage, "To Purge or Not to Purge: Hamlet Harry and the Dixiecrats, 1948–1952," *Presidential Studies Quarterly* 27, no. 4 (fall 1997), 781.

4. "Ask Barring of Four Senators," *New York Times*, December 13, 1948.

5. Savage, "To Purge or Not to Purge," 782.

6. "McGrath Will Bar South's Dissidents as Party Leaders," *New York Times*, November 9, 1948.

7. "'Bolters' Face Cut in Job Patronage," *New York Times*, December 30, 1948.

8. "Set Mississippi Patronage Plan," *New Orleans Times-Picayune*, January 16, 1949.

9. Courtney C. Pace to Cullen B. Curlee, January 24, 1949, and C. B. Curlee to Courtney C. Pace, January 27 and February 9, 1949, in File Series 1, Subseries 21, Box 1, Folder 1-7 (1949), in JOE Collection.

10. "Bolters Are Likely to Keep Patronage," *New York Times*, January 7, 1949.

11. "Truman on Horns of Patronage Dilemma: Loyal Democrat Versus Southern Senator," *New York Times*, April 30, 1949.

12. "Eastland Thinks He's No. 1 on HT's Unpopular List," *Memphis Press-Scimitar*, April 30, 1949.

13. "Mississippi Officials Defy Truman Patronage Action," *Meridian Star*, April 29, 1949.

14. "Truman Men Plan Mississippi Slate," *New York Times*, May 24, 1949.

15. "Urges New Democratic Party for Mississippi," *Meridian Star*, May 26, 1949.

16. Ibid.

17. C. B. Curlee to James O. Eastland, May 9, 1949, in File Series 1, Subseries 21, Box 1, Folder 1-7 (1949), in JOE Collection.

18. "States' Rights Group Maps Fight on Rival," *Memphis Commercial Appeal*, June 24, 1949.

19. Kenneth Toler, "Democratic Friction Flares in Mississippi," in File Series 1, Subseries 20, Box 1, Folder 1-10 (1949), in JOE Collection.

20. "collect night press—clarion ledger—jackson miss.," in File Series 1, Subseries 20, Folder 1-10 (1949), in JOE Collection.

21. C. B. Curlee to James O. Eastland, July 15, 1949, in File Series 1, Subseries 21, Box 1, Folder 1-7 (1949), in JOE Collection.

22. "Mississippians Rebel," *New York Times,* July 16, 1949.

23. "What Are They After? . . . ," *Neshoba Democrat,* July 22, 1949.

24. C. B. Curlee to James O. Eastland, July 15, 1949, in File Series 1, Subseries 21, Box 1, Folder 1-7 (1949), in JOE Collection.

25. "Resolutions of Attala County Executive Committee, July 19, 1949," in File Series 1, Subseries 20, Box 1, Folder 1-10 (1949), in JOE Collection.

26. "Southern Problems," *Washington Evening Star,* August 9, 1949.

27. "Democrats Battle on State Righters," *New York Times,* August 24, 1949; "Party Purges Five: Truman Approves," *New York Times,* August 25, 1949.

28. "Remarks at Dinner Honoring William Boyle, New Chairman of the Democratic National Committee," *Public Papers of the Presidents of the United States: Harry S. Truman, 1949* (Washington: U.S. Government Printing Office, 1964), 439.

29. James O. Eastland to J. M. Talbot, September 5, 1949, in File Series 1, Subseries 20, Box 1, Folder 1-10 (1949), in JOE Collection.

30. C. B. Curlee to James O. Eastland, July 28, 1949, in File Series 1, Subseries 21, Box 1, Folder 1-7 (1949), in JOE Collection.

31. J. M. Talbot to James O. Eastland, August 19, 1949, in File Series 1, Subseries 20, Box 1, Folder 1-10 (1949), in JOE Collection.

32. James O. Eastland to J. M. Talbot, September 5, 1949, in File Series 1, Subseries 20, Box 1, Folder 1-10 (1949), in JOE Collection.

33. "Radicals Back Truman Group, States' Righter Eastland Says," *Memphis Commercial Appeal,* September 16, 1949.

34. "Eastland Says Move to Oust Fly Has Undisclosed 'Angle,'" *Jackson Clarion-Ledger,* September 16, 1949.

35. *Jackson Daily News,* September 18, 1949.

36. Kirman quoted in Jerome E. Edwards, *Pat McCarran: Political Boss of Nevada* (Reno: Univ. of Nevada Press, 1982), 67.

37. Michael J. Ybarra, *Washington Gone Crazy: Senator Pat McCarran and the Great Communist Hunt* (Hanover: Steerforth Press, 2004), 5.

38. Ibid., 141–143.

39. Newspaper clippings attached to letter from C. B. Curlee to James O. Eastland, October 3, 1949, in File Series 1, Subseries 21, Folder 1-7 (1949), in JOE Collection.

40. William C. Berman, *The Politics of Civil Rights in the Truman Administration* (Columbus: Ohio State Univ. Press, 1970), 161–162.

41. Ybarra, *Washington Gone Crazy,* 459–462.

42. Ibid., 463–467.

43. *Congressional Record* 95 (October 15, 1949): 14698.

44. Ibid., 14700; *Time*, October 24, 1949; Ybarra, *Washington Gone Crazy*, 470–471. The other Democratic senators who voted for the Cain-Eastland motion were Robert Kerr and Elmer Thomas of Oklahoma, Virgil Chapman of Kentucky, Carl Hayden and Ernest McFarland of Arizona, Sheridan Downey of California, and Edwin Johnson of Colorado.

45. Leonard Dinnerstein, *America and the Survivors of the Holocaust* (New York: Columbia Univ. Press, 1982), 185, 242–243. The *Volksdeutsche* were ethnic Germans born and living outside Germany, particularly in Eastern Europe.

46. *Congressional Record* 95 (October 15, 1949): 14698.

47. *Congressional Record* 96 (March 3, 1950): 2736–2737.

48. Lehman quoted in Dinnerstein, *America and the Survivors of the Holocaust*, 243.

49. Ibid., 183–184; Ybarra, *Washington Gone Crazy*, 469.

50. *Congressional Record* 96 (March 2, 1950): 2634.

51. Ybarra, *Washington Gone Crazy*, 482–483; Dinnerstein, *America and the Survivors of the Holocaust*, 247–253; *Time*, April 17, 1950. In 1952 Congress passed the McCarran-Walter Act over Truman's veto. The act put severe restrictions on immigration and authorized the deportation of immigrants who had been identified as communists.

52. *Congressional Record* 95 (October 15, 1949): 14698.

53. Ybarra, *Washington Gone Crazy*, 485–487.

54. Ibid., 509–534.

55. *Congressional Record* 96 (November 30, 1950): 15965–15966.

56. Richard M. Fried, *Nightmare in Red: The McCarthy Era in Perspective* (New York: Oxford Univ. Press, 1990), 145.

57. J. Strom Thurmond to James O. Eastland, December 7, 1948, in File Series 1, Subseries 18, Folder 10-10, in JOE Collection.

58. James O. Eastland to J. Strom Thurmond, December 11, 1948, in File Series 1, Subseries 18, Folder 10-10, in JOE Collection.

59. Frederickson, *The Dixiecrat Revolt*, 187–188.

60. Editorial attached to letter from Dalton B. Brady to James O. Eastland, December 1948, in File Series 1, Subseries 20, Folder 1-9 (1948), in JOE Collection.

61. "Hill Disproves His Own Propaganda By Citing States' Rights Influence," in File Series 2, Subseries 4, Box 4, Folder: "April 1950—Politics—Lister Hill," in JOE Collection. See also Frederickson, *The Dixiecrat Revolt*, 200–201.

62. Ibid.

63. Earl Black and Merle Black, *The Rise of Southern Republicans* (Cambridge: Harvard Univ. Press, 2002), 42–59.

64. Neil R. McMillen, "Perry Howard, Boss of Black-and-Tan Republicanism in Mississippi, 1942–1960," *Journal of Southern History* 48, no. 2 (1982): 205; Jere Nash and Andy Taggart, *Mississippi Politics: The Struggle for Power, 1976–2006* (Jackson: Univ. Press of Mississippi, 2006), 35–36.

65. Fred Virkus to the members of the National Republican Roundup Committee, no date, 1950, in File Series 1, Subseries 20, Folder 1-11 (1950), in JOE Collection.

66. Ibid.

67. Fred Virkus to John U. Barr, November 17, 1950, in File Series 1, Subseries 20, Folder 1-11 (1950), in JOE Collection.

68. Fred Virkus invitation to Jackson meeting, November 10, 1950, in File Series 1, Subseries 20, Folder 1-11 (1950), in JOE Collection. Emphases in original.

69. John U. Barr to Fred A. Virkus, November 20, 1950, in File Series 1, Subseries 20, Folder 1-11 (1950), in JOE Collection.

70. C. B. Curlee to James O. Eastland, December 2, 1950, in File Series 1, Subseries 21, Folder 1-8 (1950), in JOE Collection.

71. Frederickson, *The Dixiecrat Revolt,* 199.

72. Glen Feldman, "Southern Disillusionment with the Democratic Party: Cultural Conformity and the 'Great Melding' of Racial and Economic Conservatism in Alabama During World War II," *Journal of American Studies* 43, no. 2 (2009): 199–230.

73. Robert J. Donovan, *Tumultuous Years: The Presidency of Harry S. Truman, 1949–1953* (New York: Norton, 1982), 114–118, 332–339.

74. *Congressional Record* 97 (February 21, 1951): 1447–1448.

75. Ibid.

76. Frank Mize and Clarence Hood to Harry S. Truman, February 23, 1951, in *Documentary History of the Truman Presidency,* ed. Dennis Merrill, vol. 28 (Bethesda: Univ. Publications of America, 2000), 112–113. Mize and Hood sent a similar telegram to William Boyle. See Frank Mize and Clarence Hood to William M. Boyle, February 23, 1951, in File Series 1, Subseries 20, Folder 1-12 (1951), in JOE Collection.

77. Cross Reference Sheet, February 23, 1951, White House Central Files, Official File 1644, Truman Papers, Harry S. Truman Presidential Library (hereafter referred to as HSTL).

78. "Democratic Leader in Mississippi Ousted," *New York Times,* February 27, 1951. For the text of the resolution (S. Res. 87) introduced by Stennis, see *Congressional Record* 97 (February 27, 1951): 1561.

79. U.S. Senate, *Activities of the Mississippi Democratic Committee: Hearings Before the Investigations Subcommittee of the Committee on Expenditures in the Executive Departments,* 82nd Cong. (Washington, D.C.: United State Government Printing Office, 1951), 3–5 (statement of Hon. John Stennis, a senator from the State of Mississippi). The hearings eventually were conducted under the broader S. Res. 51, instead of S. Res. 87. Eastland, as coauthor of the resolution, also planned to be present in the U.S. Courthouse in Jackson, but he could not attend because his wife had to undergo surgery.

80. C. B. Curlee to James O. Eastland, April 14, 1951, in File Series 1, Subseries 21, Folder 1-9 (1951), in JOE Collection.

81. "Ousted Democrat Tells of 'Contacts,'" *New York Times,* April 12, 1951.

82. U.S. Senate, *Activities of the Mississippi Democratic Committee,* 33 (testimony of Frank F. Mize).

83. *Congressional Record* 97 (June 20, 1951): 6781.

84. "Twelve Are Indicted in Mississippi in Federal Job Sales Conspiracy," *New York Times,* July 21, 1951; "10 Truman Men Free in Mississippi 'Plot,'" *New York Times,* February 2, 1952.

85. U.S. Senate, *Activities of the Mississippi Democratic Committee,* 391, 398 (testimony of Curtis Rogers, Sylverana, Miss.).

86. James O. Eastland to C. B. Curlee, January 4, 1947, in File Series 1, Subseries 21, Folder 1-5 (1947), in JOE Collection. At the time of his appointment in 1947, Curlee received a gross salary from the federal government of $7,075 a year, including extras.

87. U.S. Senate, *Activities of the Mississippi Democratic Committee,* 448–449 (testimony of Joseph J. Lawler, Assistant Postmaster General in charge of Bureau of Post Office Operations), 526 (testimony of Postmaster General Jesse M. Donaldson).

88. *Congressional Record* 97 (April 17, 1951): A2127.

89. Frank D. Barber interview, May 30, 1990, University of Southern Mississippi Oral History Program, McCain Library and Archives.

90. C. B. Curlee to James O. Eastland, February 20, 1951, in File Series 1, Subseries 21, Folder 1-9 (1951), in JOE Collection. Barber was a campaign worker for Johnson in his failed bid for governor in 1947 and he later worked for Eastland as legislative assistant and field man.

91. Clipping attached to letter from C. B. Curlee to James O. Eastland, February 4, 1951, in File Series 1, Subseries 21, Folder 1-9 (1951), in JOE Collection.

92. Jesse Lamar White Jr., "Mississippi Electoral Politics, 1903–1976: The Emerging Modernization Consensus" (Ph.D. diss., Massachusetts Institute of Technology, 1979), 371–373.

93. Ibid., 375; Barber interview.

94. White, "Mississippi Electoral Politics," 368–369, 373–374.

95. "Senator Eastland Should Resign," *Brandon News,* June 14, 1951, in File Series 4, Subseries 2, Box 4, Folder: August 1951—Politics, in JOE Collection.

96. "I have noticed . . . ," in File Series 1, Subseries 20, Folder 1-12 (1951), in JOE Collection.

97. Newspaper article attached to letter from S. T. Pilkington to James O. Eastland, August 15, 1951, in File Series 1, Subseries 20, Folder 1-12 (1951), in JOE Collection.

98. "White Predicts Big Majority; Johnson Praised by Eastland," *Memphis Commercial Appeal,* August 24, 1951.

99. "Yes, the South is confronted . . . ," in File Series 1, Subseries 20, Folder 1-12 (1951), in JOE Collection.

100. Jos. F. Ellis to James O. Eastland, August 10, 1951, in File Series 1, Subseries 20, Folder 1-12 (1951), in JOE Collection.

101. Paul Clark to James O. Eastland, September 1, 1951, in File Series 1, Subseries 20, Folder 1-12 (1951), in JOE Collection.

102. James O. Eastland to S. T. Pilkington, September 1, 1951, in File Series 1, Subseries 20, Folder 1-12 (1951), in JOE Collection.

103. James O. Eastland to Paul Clark, September 28, 1951, in File Series 1, Subseries 20, Folder 1-12 (1951), in JOE Collection.

104. Clipping attached to letter from C. B. Curlee to James O. Eastland, June 15, 1951, in File Series 1, Subseries 21, Folder 1-9 (1951), in JOE Collection.

105. White, "Mississippi Electoral Politics," 375.

106. C. B. Curlee to James O. Eastland, August 31, 1951, in File Series 1, Subseries 21, Folder 1-9 (1951), in JOE Collection. Frank Barber concurred with Curlee. He said: "He [Johnson] took the Truman side and he paid for it. He probably would have been governor in the election of '51 but for that issue." See Barber interview.

107. Eastland also supported Johnson financially. See Hugo Newcomb to John C. Stennis, January 22, 1954, in Series 50, Box 5, Folder 1, in John C. Stennis Collection, Congressional and Political Research Center, Mississippi State University (hereafter referred to as JCS Collection). Newcomb wrote: "The money that was put into Paul's campaign in 1951 on account of Senator Eastland's appealing to his friends was a considerable amount and could well be a decisive factor for Paul next time."

108. Clark Clifford, "Memorandum for the President," November 19, 1947, pages 1, 3, 8–9, 11, in Political File, Box 22, Folder: Confidential Memo to the President [2 of 2], in Clark M. Clifford Papers, HSTL.

109. Clifford, "Memorandum for the President." See also Frederickson, *The Dixiecrat Revolt*, 68–69.

110. Clifford, "Memorandum for the President."

111. Frederickson, *The Dixiecrat Revolt*, 220.

CHAPTER 4. DEMOCRATIC UNITY AFTER THE DIXIECRAT REVOLT

1. William F. Winter to John C. Stennis, May 27, 1952; William F. Winter to John C. Stennis, May 31, 1952, both in Series 50, Box 8, Folder 32, in JCS Collection.

2. John C. Stennis to William F. Winter, June 9, 1952, in Series 50, Box 8, Folder 32, in JCS Collection.

3. "Address of the Honorable Hugh White, Governor of Mississippi, at the States Right Convention, June 26, 1952," in President Harry S Truman's Office Files, 1945–1953, reel 4, microfilm edition, Roosevelt Study Center, Middelburg, the Netherlands (hereafter referred to as RSC).

4. "Dem. Convention, Miss. 1952," in File Series 1, Subseries 20, Folder 2-1 (1952), in JOE Collection.

5. "Third-Party Bolt Mississippi Threat," *New York Times*, June 27, 1952.

6. "Ex-SR Dem Chieftain Thinks Clark Faction Will Win in Chicago," *Jackson Clarion Ledger*, July 6, 1952.

7. "White Denies Plan to Bolt Dem Convention," *Jackson Clarion Ledger*, June 28, 1952.

8. J. P. Coleman to John C. Stennis, July 2, 1952, in Series 50, Box 10, Folder 18, in JCS Collection.

9. James O. Eastland to C. B. Curlee, June 30, 1952, in File Series 1, Subseries 21, Folder 1-10 (1952), in JOE Collection.

10. "Brief of the Facts and the Law (With the Supporting Affidavits) Filed With the Subcommittee on Credentials of the Democratic National Committee on Behalf of the Delegates of the Regular Democratic Party in the State of Mississippi," in File Series 1, Subseries 20, Folder 2-1 (1952), in JOE Collection.

11. "Mississippi Still on Inside Looking Out but Situation Is Not Yet Fully Clarified," *Jackson Daily News*, July 23, 1952.

12. John Robert Greene, *The Crusade: The Presidential Election of 1952* (Lanham: Univ. Press of America, 1985), 156–162. See also James R. Sweeney, "Revolt in Virginia: Harry Byrd and the 1952 Presidential Election," *Virginia Magazine of History and Biography* 86, no. 2 (April 1978): 184–188.

13. Greene, *The Crusade*, 145–147; Berman, *The Politics of Civil Rights in the Truman Administration*, 211–215.

14. Robert A. Caro, *The Years of Lyndon Johnson: Master of the Senate* (New York: Vintage Books, 2002), 467–471; John A. Goldsmith, *Colleagues: Richard B. Russell and His Apprentice Lyndon B. Johnson* (Macon: Mercer Univ. Press, 1998), 27–29; Greene, *The Crusade*, 162–169.

15. H. Rey Bonney to James O. Eastland, July 28, 1952, in File Series 1, Subseries 20, Folder 2-1 (1952), in JOE Collection.

16. James O. Eastland to the Honorable H. Rey Bonney, in File Series 1, Subseries 20, Folder 2-1 (1952), in JOE Collection.

17. "White, Wright, See Stevenson," *Jackson Clarion Ledger,* August 6, 1952.

18. "Research Memorandum on Developments in Eight States Involved in 'Loyalty Oath' Controversies at Democratic National Conventions in 1944, 1948, and 1952," in Library Clippings Files, Box 157, Folder: Disposition of Party Loyalty Oath (Chicago Meeting), November 1955, in Records of the Democratic National Committee, HSTL.

19. "Eastland Says Pinks of Party Thwarted," *Jackson Clarion Ledger,* August 21, 1952; "Stevenson is more conservative than Roosevelt or Truman . . ." in File Series 1, Subseries 20, Folder 2-1 (1952), in JOE Collection.

20. Ibid.

21. Mrs. R. J. Burt to James O. Eastland, October 4, 1952, in File Series 1, Subseries 20, Folder 2-1 (1952), in JOE Collection

22. "Radio Address by E. O. Spencer," October 20, 1952, in File Series 1, Subseries 20, Folder 2-1 (1952), in JOE Collection.

23. M. W. Swartz to James O. Eastland, September 22, 1952, in File Series 1, Subseries 20, Folder 2-1 (1952), in JOE Collection. Swartz also happened to be the chairman of the Democrats for Eisenhower chapter in Sunflower County, where Eastland's plantation was located.

24. Thomas J. Tubb to Stephen Mitchell, September 20, 1952, in Sam Wilhite Papers, Box 1, Folder: Correspondence September 19–30, 1952, in Special Collections, Mississippi State University (hereafter referred to as SW Papers).

25. William M. Whittington to L. Hamer McKenzie, September 23, 1952, in Box 1, Folder: Correspondence September 19–30, 1952, in SW Papers.

26. "Southern Senators Refuse to Be Tied by Party Platform," in File Series 2, Subseries 4, Box 4, Folder: 1952—Politics, in JOE Collection.

27. "Senator Eastland Asks South to Be on Guard in Coming Election," in File Series 2, Subseries 4, Box 4, Folder: 1952—Politics, in JOE Collection.

28. "Says Nothing Indecisive in His Position," *Jackson Clarion Ledger,* October 1, 1952.

29. "Address by Governor Adlai E. Stevenson at Nashville, Tennessee, Saturday Evening, October 12, 1952," in File Series 1, Subseries 20, Folder 2-1 (1952), in JOE Collection.

30. Ibid.

31. "Stevenson Holds Mississippi Edge," *New York Times,* November 2, 1952.

32. Numan V. Bartley, *The Rise of Massive Resistance: Race and Politics in the South During the 1950s* (Baton Rouge: Louisiana State Univ. Press, 1969), 49–50.

33. William F. Winter, "New Directions in Politics, 1948–1956," in *A History of Mississippi,* vol. 2, ed. Richard Aubrey McLemore (Jackson: Univ. and College Press of Mississippi, 1973), 149.

34. Thomas J. Tubb to James O. Eastland, November 12, 1952, in File Series 1, Subseries 20, Folder 2-1 (1952), in JOE Collection.

35. James O. Eastland to Thomas J. Tubb, November 20, 1952, in File Series 1, Subseries 20, Folder 2-1 (1952), in JOE Collection.

36. Nash and Taggart, *Mississippi Politics,* 36; White, "Mississippi Electoral Politics," 377, n. 73; Winter, "New Directions in Politics," 149.

37. E. O. Spencer to James O. Eastland, January 10, 1953, in File Series 1, Subseries 20, Folder 2-2 (1953), in JOE Collection.

38. White, "Mississippi Electoral Politics," 377, n. 73.

39. Asch, *The Senator and the Sharecropper,* 148–149.

40. *Jackson Daily News,* February 25, 1953, in File Series 1, Subseries 19, Folder 20-22, in JOE Collection.

41. C. B. Curlee to James O. Eastland, February 3, 1953, in File Series 1, Subseries 21, Folder 1-11 (1953), in JOE Collection.

42. "Eastland's Statement Seen as Announcement to Offer Again for His Senate Post," *Jackson Daily News,* August 7, 1953.

43. "Aspirants for Governorship Want Eastland's Assurance He Will Keep 'Hands Off,'" *Memphis Commercial Appeal,* August 30, 1953.

44. Ibid.

45. James O. Eastland to C. B Curlee, February 4, 1953, in File Series 1, Subseries 21, Folder 1-11 (1953), in JOE Collection.

46. Ibid.

47. Dorothy M. Zellner, "Red Roadshow: Eastland in New Orleans, 1954," *Louisiana History* 33, no. 1 (1992): 34.

48. Ibid., 50; Asch, *The Senator and the Sharecropper,* 144–145.

49. Transcript, Clifford and Virginia Durr oral history interview by Michael L. Gillette, March 1, 1975, tape 1, pages 41–45, Lyndon Baines Johnson Presidential Library (hereafter referred to as LBJL).

50. Ibid.; Zellner, "Red Roadshow," 35–36, 58–59.

51. Asch, *The Senator and the Sharecropper,* 145.

52. Ibid., 145–149.

53. *Congressional Record* 100 (May 27, 1954): 7251–7257.

54. Ibid.

55. Johnston, *Politics: Mississippi Style,* 111.

56. Ibid., 112.

57. C. Arthur Sullivan to Louis E. Gardner, June 23, 1954, in File Series 1, Subseries 19, Folder 21-21, in JOE Collection.

58. Barber interview.

59. "Thousands to Converge on Laurel for Gartin Rally," *Laurel Leader-Call,* June 15, 1954.

60. W. F. Minor, "Gartin Scores Eastland Record," in File Series 1, Subseries 19, Folder 20-23, in JOE Collection.

61. Ibid.

62. "Opening Speech Scott County, June 26, 1954," in File Series 1, Subseries 19, Folder 20-5, in JOE Collection.

63. Ibid.

64. Ibid.

65. Ibid.

66. "Eastland Opens Reelection Bid," *New Orleans Times-Picayune,* June 27, 1954.

67. Map of Field Men, in File Series 1, Subseries 19, Folder 20-5, in JOE Collection.

68. Newspaper clipping, July 22, 1954; Kenneth Toler, "Eastland's Foe Will Pitch His Campaign on Farm Issue," June 12, 1954, in File Series 1, Subseries 19, Folder 20-23, in JOE Collection.

69. Hugh Allen Boren to Phillip Sheffield, August 9, 1954, in Box 3, Folder 3-1, in Carroll Gartin Collection, Archives and Special Collections, J. D. Williams Library, University of Mississippi (hereafter referred to as CG Collection).

70. H. A. Womack to James O. Eastland, June 3, 1954, in File Series 1 Subseries 19, Folder 21-21, in JOE Collection.

71. James O. Eastland to H. A. Womack, June 5, 1954, in File Series 1 Subseries 19, Folder 21-21, in JOE Collection.

72. Televised speech by Wilma Sledge, Station WLBT, Jackson, Mississippi, Tuesday Night, Aug. 17, 1954—9:05 to 9:20, transcript, in File Series 1, Subseries 19, Folder 21-7, in JOE Collection.

73. Hodding Carter III, *The South Strikes Back* (Garden City: Doubleday, 1959), 44–45.

74. Ibid., 45.

75. A. F. McDaniel to All Representatives of Miss. Leg. Board, July 3, 1954, in Box 3, Folder 3-4, in CG Collection.

76. Televised speech by Wilma Sledge. According to Sledge, Starnes said the following in April 1954: ". . . we will be in the middle of the Senatorial Race, and I agree with you that it is a bit early to do anything in this matter. I was in Jackson a short while ago and some of the people I talked with indicated that Gartin has an uphill fight ahead of him."

77. "Why the *Daily News* Supports Eastland," *Jackson Daily News,* June 29, 1954.

78. "How We'll Vote," *Greenville Delta Democrat-Times,* August 5, 1954.

79. James O. Eastland to E. O. Spencer, September 17, 1954, in File Series 1, Subseries 19, Folder 21-21, in JOE Collection.

CHAPTER 5. THE POLITICS OF COMPROMISE

1. Walter Sillers to James O. Eastland, August 26, 1954, in Box 105, Folder 13, in WS Papers.

2. Bartley, *Rise of Massive Resistance,* 17–19. U.S. Senator Harry Flood Byrd of Virginia coined the term "massive resistance." See ibid., 117. For a discussion of Byrd's initial discussion of massive resistance, see George Lewis, *Massive Resistance: The White Response to the Civil Rights Movement* (London: Hodder Arnold, 2006), 1–5.

3. See for example Lewis, *Massive Resistance,* 5–12, 19, 24; Clive Webb, introduction to *Massive Resistance: Southern Opposition to the Second Reconstruction,* ed. Clive Webb (Oxford: Oxford Univ. Press, 2005), 8–9, 13–15.

4. Joseph Crespino, *In Search of Another Country: Mississippi and the Conservative Counterrevolution* (Princeton: Princeton Univ. Press, 2007), 19.

5. Carter, *The South Strikes Back,* 104.

6. Bartley, *The Rise of Massive Resistance*, 118.

7. Crespino, *In Search of Another Country*, 18–19.

8. Neil R. McMillen, *The Citizens' Council: Organized Resistance to the Second Reconstruction, 1954–1964* (Urbana: Univ. of Illinois Press, 1994), 16–18. Brady's book was titled *Black Monday*.

9. Pete Daniel, *Lost Revolutions: The South in the 1950s* (Chapel Hill: Univ. of North Carolina Press, 2000), 196.

10. Tom Brady to Walter Sillers, May 17, 1954, in Box 66, Folder 5, in WS Papers.

11. John Dittmer, *Local People: The Struggle for Civil Rights in Mississippi* (Urbana: Univ. of Illinois Press, 1995), 45–46.

12. Carter, *The South Strikes Back*, 49.

13. "Address Before the Mississippi Association of Citizens' Councils, August 16, 1955," in File Series 2, Subseries 9, Folder 1-92, in JOE Collection.

14. Barber interview.

15. White, "Mississippi Electoral Politics," 385–396.

16. For the text of the interposition resolution, see "Joint Statement of United States Senator James O. Eastland, Judge Tom P. Brady, and Congressman John Bell Williams," in File Series 2, Subseries 9, Folder 1-95, in JOE Collection. See also "Historic Fight on Desegregation Ruling Planned by Sen. Eastland, Rep. Williams and Judge Brady" and "State Leaders Map Segregation Fight," in File Series 2, Subseries 4, Folder: December 1955—Civil Rights, in JOE Collection. Numan Bartley described the concept of interposition as follows: "Despite ambiguities, legal gymnastics, and fantasies, interposition did rest upon a basic foundation: a commitment to use state power to oppose the *Brown* decision." See Bartley, *The Rise of Massive Resistance*, 127.

17. "Bias Against the South," press release, October 29, 1955, in File Series 2, Subseries 9, Folder 1-93, in JOE Collection.

18. Bartley, *The Rise of Massive Resistance*, 121.

19. "The Charter of Incorporation of [the] Federation for Constitutional Government," in File Series 4, Subseries: Subject Files, Folder: Federation for Constitutional Government—John U. Barr—1949–1960, in JOE Collection.

20. Bartley, *The Rise of Massive Resistance*, 123.

21. "New Group Formed to Balk Integration," *Memphis Commercial Appeal*, December 29, 1955.

22. "Excerpts From Speech Made by Senator James O. Eastland" and "The Purpose of the Federation for Constitutional Government," both in File Series 4, Subseries: Subject Files, Folder: Federation for Constitutional Government—John U. Barr—1949–1960, in JOE Collection.

23. T. R. Waring to James O. Eastland, October 31, 1955, and W. Lee Guice to James O. Eastland, October 31, 1955, both in File Series 3, Subseries 1, Folder: Civil Rights—1955 (1 of 2), in JOE Collection.

24. C. E. Browning to James O. Eastland, January 5, 1956; R. K. Daniel to James O. Eastland, January 6, 1956; James O. Eastland to R. K. Daniel, January 10, 1956, all in File Series 3, Subseries 1, Folder: Civil Rights—1956 (2 of 3), in JOE Collection.

25. Daniel, *Lost Revolutions*, 197. See also Joseph B. Atkins, *Covering for the Bosses: Labor and the Southern Press* (Jackson: Univ. Press of Mississippi, 2008), 67–70.

26. McMillen, *The Citizens' Council*, 116.

27. Bartley, *The Rise of Massive Resistance*, 124.

28. Ibid., 122–123.

29. Carter, *The South Strikes Back*, 67.

30. "Coleman Rejects Nullification Idea," *Jackson Daily News*, December 14, 1955.

31. Yasuhiro Katagiri, *The Mississippi State Sovereignty Commission: Civil Rights and States' Rights* (Jackson: Univ. Press of Mississippi, 2001), 3–5.

32. Ibid., 11–12; Carter, *The South Strikes Back*, 62–63.

33. Clarence Pierce interview conducted by Maarten Zwiers, May 22, 2011, Vaiden, Mississippi, digital recording in Maarten Zwiers's possession.

34. Edwards, *Pat McCarran*, 197–199.

35. Rusher, *Special Counsel*, 20–21.

36. Ibid.

37. "Jim Eastland Tells Why He Opposes Harlan," *Jackson Clarion-Ledger* and *Jackson Daily News*, March 13, 1955.

38. Ibid.

39. Robert Franklin Maddox, *The Senatorial Career of Harley Martin Kilgore* (East Rockaway: Cummings and Hathaway Publishers, 1997), 322–328.

40. Meeting of the Democratic Steering Committee, March 2, 1956, in Box 9, Folder 9-11, in Felton M. Johnston Collection, Archives and Special Collections, J. D. Williams Library, University of Mississippi (hereafter referred to as FMJ Collection).

41. Transcript, James O. Eastland oral history interview I by Joe B. Frantz, February 19, 1971, Internet copy, LBJL.

42. Drew Pearson, "Morse Urged Not to Fight Eastland," *Washington Post*, March 8, 1956.

43. "Eastland Pledges Impartial Rule as Judiciary Head," *Jackson Daily News*, March 3, 1956.

44. J. M. Talbot to James O. Eastland, March 14, 1956, and James O. Eastland to J. M. Talbot, March 20, 1956, both in File Series 3, Subseries 1, Folder: Civil Rights—1956 (2 of 3), in JOE Collection.

45. Meeting of the Democratic Steering Committee, March 2, 1956, in Box 9, Folder 9-11, in FMJ Collection.

46. Kefauver quoted in Charles L. Fontenay, *Estes Kefauver: A Biography* (Knoxville: Univ. of Tennessee Press, 1980), 322.

47. Lyndon B. Johnson to Estes Kefauver, January 10, 1957, in Pre-Presidential Papers: Senate Papers, 1949–1961, Box 364, Folder: Committee Assignments, LBJL.

48. Fontenay, *Kefauver*, 122–123, 321–322, 361–362; Pierce interview.

49. Fontenay, *Kefauver*, 11, 321.

50. Caro, *Master of the Senate*, 219–220; Keith M. Finley, *Delaying the Dream: Southern Senators and the Fight Against Civil Rights, 1938–1965* (Baton Rouge: Louisiana State Univ. Press, 2008), 148.

51. John C. Stennis to James O. Eastland, November 8, 1952, and James O. Eastland to John C. Stennis, November 13, 1952, both in File Series 1, Subseries 18, Folder 9-39, in JOE Collection. Other sources also confirm Eastland liked Johnson. See, for example, Barber interview, Eastland interview, in LBJL, and Pierce interview. Senator Eastland's son, Woods, said his father and Johnson were "personal friends." Interview with Woods Eastland conducted by Maarten Zwiers, May 17, 2011, Doddsville, Mississippi, digital recording in Maarten Zwiers's possession.

52. Black and Black, *The Rise of Southern Republicans*, 46, 48–50.

53. Ibid., 51–52; Woods Eastland interview.

54. *Congressional Record* 102 (March 12, 1956): 4460.

55. Bartley, *The Rise of Massive Resistance*, 117.

56. Tony Badger, "Southerners Who Refused to Sign the Southern Manifesto," *Historical Journal* 42, no. 2 (June 1999): 519–520.

57. Mooney quoted in Caro, *Master of the Senate*, 599.

58. James O. Eastland to Messrs. Lyon, Davis & Cook, March 21, 1956, in File Series 3, Subseries 1, Folder: Civil Rights—1956 (2 of 3), in JOE Collection.

59. Coleman quoted in Carter, *The South Strikes Back*, 67.

60. Newspaper clippings, Library Clippings Files, Box 157, Folder: Loyalty Oath Question at New Orleans Meeting, December 1954; Subsequent Action at Chicago, November 1955, and Folder: Disposition of Party Loyalty Oath (Chicago Meeting), November 1955, in Records of the Democratic National Committee, HSTL.

61. Johnston, *Politics: Mississippi Style*, 128–129.

62. Carter, *The South Strikes Back*, 68–69.

63. "Eastland Suggests Caution Toward Demo Convention," *Jackson Clarion-Ledger*, July 12, 1956.

64. "Strengthen Party Unity as Factions Divide Posts," *Jackson Clarion-Ledger*, July 17, 1956.

65. "Coleman No Namby-Pamby; Is Expert of Power Politics," *Jackson Clarion-Ledger*, July 22, 1956.

66. James P. Coleman to Major Frederick Sullens, July 7, 1956, in Box 13, Folder 6, in Z/1877.000: Coleman (J. P.) Papers, Mississippi Department of Archives and History, Jackson, MS (hereafter referred to as JPC Collection).

67. Ibid.

68. "Coleman Still Asks Unity as Adlai Supports Court," *Jackson Clarion-Ledger*, August 8, 1956.

69. Johnston, *Politics: Mississippi Style*, 129.

70. "Eastland Suggests Virginia School Plan," *Jackson Clarion-Ledger*, August 10, 1956; "Eastland Warns That South Has Only Legislative Branch on Which to Lean," *Jackson Clarion-Ledger*, August 12, 1956.

71. Asch, *The Senator and the Sharecropper*, 153.

72. "Eastland Suggests Virginia School Plan," *Jackson Clarion-Ledger*, August 10, 1956.

73. W. C. Neill to James O. Eastland and James P. Coleman, December 20, 1956, in File Series 3, Subseries 1, Folder: Civil Rights—1956 (folder 2 of 3), in JOE Collection.

74. Lyndon Baines Johnson to James O. Eastland, August 8, 1956, and James O. Eastland to Lyndon Baines Johnson, August 11, 1956, both in File Series 1, Subseries 18, Folder 5-44, in JOE Collection.

75. "Acclamation Vote Thwarts JP's Hopes," *Jackson Clarion-Ledger*, August 17, 1956; "Mississippi Vote for Johnson Shut Cleavage in Demos' Ranks," *Jackson Clarion-Ledger*, August 19, 1956.

76. "State Delegates—," *Jackson Clarion-Ledger*, August 17, 1956.

77. Caro, *Master of the Senate*, 827–830; Robert Dallek, *Lone Star Rising: Lyndon Johnson and His Times, 1908–1960* (New York: Oxford Univ. Press, 1991), 502–503.

78. Sean J. Savage, *JFK, LBJ, and the Democratic Party* (Albany: State Univ. of New York Press, 2004), 17.

79. John F. Kennedy to James O. Eastland, September 8, 1956, in File Series 1, Subseries 18, Folder 6-8, in JOE Collection.

80. "State Delegates Miss Pep Talks," *Jackson Clarion-Ledger,* August 18, 1956.

81. "State Delegates—" *Jackson Clarion-Ledger,* August 17, 1956.

82. "Gartin 'Sick' Over Kefauver," in Box 22, Folder 22-24, in CG Collection.

83. A. S. Coody to James O. Eastland, August 29, 1956, in Box 5, Folder 82, in Z/1228.000: Coody (Archibald Stinson) Papers, Mississippi Department of Archives and History, Jackson, Mississippi.

84. Nash and Taggart, *Mississippi Politics,* 38.

85. "Mississippi's Split Vote Is Confusing," *Jackson Clarion-Ledger,* August 20, 1956; "Mississippi's Split G.O.P. Delegation Seated Together," *Jackson Clarion-Ledger,* August 21, 1956.

86. "Spencer Invited to Rejoin Demos," *Jackson Clarion-Ledger,* August 16, 1956.

87. "States' Righters Will Talk Unpledged Electors on Ticket," *Jackson Clarion-Ledger,* August 21, 1956.

88. Johnston, *Politics: Mississippi Style,* 131; "Earl Evans Quits as Demo Elector," *Jackson Clarion-Ledger,* August 30, 1956. DeSapio was a New York politician and Harriman supporter.

89. Johnston, *Politics: Mississippi Style,* 131.

90. "Eastland, Coleman Back Demo Ticket; Invite Adlai Here," *Jackson Clarion-Ledger,* August 22, 1956; "Ladner, Patterson Urge State Go Demo," *Jackson Clarion-Ledger,* August 21, 1956.

91. "Eastland, Coleman Back Demo Ticket; Invite Adlai Here," *Jackson Clarion-Ledger,* August 22, 1956

92. Numan V. Bartley, *The New South, 1945–1980* (Baton Rouge: Louisiana State Univ. Press, 1995), 231; James O. Eastland to Mrs. Pearl Griffin, October 10, 1956, in File Series 1, Subseries 20, Folder 2-5, in JOE Collection.

93. W. M. McLaurin to James O. Eastland, October 22, 1956, in File Series 1, Subseries 20, Folder 2-5, in JOE Collection.

94. Johnston, *Politics: Mississippi Style,* 132.

95. Newspaper clipping, in File Series 2, Subseries 4, Folder: November 1956—Politics, in JOE Collection.

96. Doris Fleeson, "Northern Democrats Look Back," *Washington Evening-Star,* November 9, 1956.

97. "The Congress: The New Chairman," *Time,* March 12, 1956.

98. Mitchell quoted in Jules Witcover, *Party of the People: A History of the Democrats* (New York: Random House, 2003), 463.

99. David A. Nichols, *A Matter of Justice: Eisenhower and the Beginnings of the Civil Rights Revolution* (New York: Simon and Schuster Paperbacks, 2007), 120–123.

100. Steven F. Lawson, *Running for Freedom: Civil Rights and Black Politics in America Since 1941* (New York: McGraw-Hill, 1991), 53–57.

101. Dallek, *Lone Star Rising,* 517–518; Finley, *Delaying the Dream,* 154–156; Nichols, *A Matter of Justice,* 144–145; Howard E. Shuman, "Senate Rules and the Civil Rights Bill: A Case Study," *American Political Science Review* 51, no. 4 (December 1957): 956–957.

102. Dallek, *Lone Star Rising,* 521–522; Finley, *Delaying the Dream,* 165–166; Shuman, "Senate Rules and the Civil Rights Bill," 961–970. On page 969, Shuman wrote: "The other coalition was a revival of cooperation between the Southern and Western Democrats together with the remaining hard core of the Republicans."

103. James O. Eastland to N. E. Dacus, February 4, 1957, in File Series 3, Subseries 1, Folder: Civil Rights—1957 (2 of 5), in JOE Collection.

104. Finley, *Delaying the Dream*, 163–164; Robert Mann, *When Freedom Would Triumph: The Civil Rights Struggle in Congress, 1954–1968* (Baton Rouge: Louisiana State Univ. Press, 2007), 44–48.

105. Dallek, *Lone Star Rising*, 522–527; Finley, *Delaying the Dream*, 166–183; Lawson, *Running for Freedom*, 57–58; Mann, *When Freedom Would Triumph*, 49–59; Nichols, *A Matter of Justice*, 155–168.

106. James O. Eastland to W. E. Morse, February 26, 1957, in File Series 3, Subseries 1, Folder: Civil Rights—1957 (2 of 5), in JOE Collection.

107. Walter Sillers to James O. Eastland, March 6, 1957, in File Series 3, Subseries 1, Folder: Civil Rights—1957 (2 of 5), in JOE Collection

108. James O. Eastland to Walter Sillers, March 15, 1957, in File Series 3, Subseries 1, Folder: Civil Rights—1957 (2 of 5), in JOE Collection; Caro, *Master of the Senate*, 945–946, 951.

109. Walter Sillers to James O. Eastland, June 11, 1957, in File Series 3, Subseries 1, Folder: Civil Rights—1957 (1 of 5), in JOE Collection.

110. James O. Eastland to William F. Appleton, June 24, 1957, in File Series 3, Subseries 1, Folder: Civil Rights—1957 (4 of 5), in JOE Collection.

111. James O. Eastland to W. W. Ramsey, July 5, 1957, in File Series 3, Subseries 1, Folder: Civil Rights—1957 (4 of 5), in JOE Collection.

112. James O. Eastland to Harvey McGehee, August 13, 1957, in File Series 3, Subseries 1, Folder: Civil Rights—1957 (3 of 5), in JOE Collection.

113. James O. Eastland to J. J. Breland, July 16, 1957, in File Series 3, Subseries 1, Folder: Civil Rights—1957 (1 of 5), in JOE Collection.

114. Telegrams from James O. Eastland to Judge Sidney Mize and Judge Allen Cox, July 31, 1957, in File Series 3, Subseries 1, Folder: Civil Rights—1957 (1 of 5), in JOE Collection.

115. James O. Eastland to S. O. Scott, August 12, 1957, in File Series 3, Subseries 1, Folder: Civil Rights—1957 (1 of 5), in JOE Collection.

116. Finley, *Delaying the Dream*, 186.

117. Press release, Senators James O. Eastland and John C. Stennis, August 30, 1957, in File Series 3, Subseries 1, Folder: Civil Rights—1957 (5 of 5), in JOE Collection.

118. James O. Eastland to Jesse Shanks, September 7, 1957, letter #2, in File Series 3, Subseries 1, Folder: Civil Rights—1957 (5 of 5), in JOE Collection.

119. Ibid.

120. James O. Eastland to Mary Margaret Clark, October 17, 1957, in File Series 3, Subseries 1, Folder: Civil Rights—1957 (5 of 5), in JOE collection.

121. Crespino, *In Search of Another Country*, 85.

122. Nash and Taggart, *Mississippi Politics*, 39–40; Christopher Alan Danielson, "The Voting Rights Act and the Creation of Black Politics in Mississippi, 1965–1985" (Ph.D. diss., University of Mississippi, 2006), 7.

123. Carroll Gartin to E. A. Turnage, August 23, 1956, in Box 13, Folder 13-7, in CG Collection.

124. "Meeting of the Democratic Steering Committee," March 2, 1956, in Box 9, Folder 9-11, in FMJ Collection.

125. Woods Eastland interview.

126. Lyndon B. Johnson to James O. Eastland, September 9, 1957, in File Series 1, Subseries 18, Folder 5-44, in JOE Collection.

127. Carroll Gartin told the voters in Mississippi to cast their ballot for the Stevenson-Kefauver

ticket in 1956, because Kefauver's "elevation [to vice president] would remove him from the second seniority spot on the Judiciary Committee headed by Sen. James O. Eastland who has bottled the civil rights program so far in his committee." See *Jackson Clarion-Ledger*, August 23, 1956.

128. James O. Eastland to Jesse Shanks, September 7, 1957, letter #2, in File Series 3, Subseries 1, Folder: Civil Rights—1957 (5 of 5), in JOE Collection.

CHAPTER 6. THE ERA OF POWER POLITICS

1. "Whither Goest Thou, Senator?" *Simpson County News*, September 6, 1956.

2. Mark Stern, *Calculating Visions: Kennedy, Johnson, and Civil Rights* (New Brunswick: Rutgers Univ. Press, 1992), 16–17.

3. Nick Bryant, *The Bystander: John F. Kennedy and the Struggle for Black Equality* (New York: Basic Books, 2006), 192.

4. Theodore C. Sorensen, *Kennedy* (London: Hodder and Stoughton, 1965), 102.

5. Edgar J. Stephens Jr. to John F. Kennedy, October 10, 1957, in Pre-Presidential Papers, Presidential Campaign Files, 1960, Box 950, Folder: Mississippi—Political (N–S), John F. Kennedy Presidential Library (hereafter referred to as JFKL); Caro, *Master of the Senate*, 825–827.

6. Theodore C. Sorensen to Frank E. Smith, October 1, 1957, in Pre-Presidential Papers, Presidential Campaign Files, 1960, Box 950, Folder: Mississippi—Political (N–S), JFKL.

7. Bryant, *The Bystander*, 84.

8. Ibid., 84–85; Sorensen, *Kennedy*, 102–103.

9. "Democrats: Through the Roadblock," *Time*, October 28, 1957.

10. Bryant, *The Bystander*, 86.

11. Theodore C. Sorensen to William F. Minor, November 27, 1957, in Pre-Presidential Papers, Presidential Campaign Files, 1960, Box 950, Folder: Mississippi—Political (H–M), JFKL.

12. Joe T. Patterson to John F. Kennedy, November 1, 1957, in Pre-Presidential Papers, Presidential Campaign Files, 1960, Box 950, Folder: Mississippi—Political (N–S), JFKL.

13. Bartley, *The New South*, 238; Asch, "No Compromise," 187; Chandler to James O. Eastland, July 10, 1959, in File Series 1, Subseries 20, Folder 2-8, in JOE Collection.

14. "General Resume of Southeast Region," May 19, 1958; "Report on the South and Future plans," November 13, 1958, both in Box 3, Folder: Democratic Party: National: Wilhite 1958, in SW Papers.

15. Bryant, *The Bystander*, 132–137. See also W. J. Rorabaugh, *The Real Making of the President: Kennedy, Nixon, and the 1960 Election* (Lawrence: Univ. Press of Kansas, 2009), 68–70.

16. Fred Jones, "TO THE VOTERS OF MISSISSIPPI," in Box 21, Folder 21-23, in CG Collection.

17. Johnston, *Politics: Mississippi Style*, 139–143; White, "Mississippi Electoral Politics," 412–414. Neil McMillen wrote the following about Council influence on the Barnett administration: "The inauguration of Ross Barnett in January, 1960, heralded a new day for the Citizens' Council in Mississippi. Held at arm's length not only by Coleman but also by his predecessor, Governor Hugh L. White, the organization, for all its strength in the state legislature and its more than eighty thousand members, had until that winter day been conspicuously without influence with the state's chief executive. Under the new governor, however, it would enjoy not only official blessings but generous state subsidies." See McMillen, *The Citizens' Council*, 326.

18. Frank D. Barber to Theodore Sorensen, December 4, 1959, in Pre-Presidential Papers, Presidential Campaign Files, 1960, Box 950, Folder: Mississippi—Political (A–C), JFKL; Frank D. Barber to John B. Hynes, September 24, 1959, in Pre-Presidential Papers, Presidential Campaign Files, 1960, Box 950, Folder: Mississippi—Political (A–C), JFKL.

19. Sam Wilhite to John F. Kennedy, August 27, 1959, in Pre-Presidential Papers, Presidential Campaign Files, 1960, Box 950, Folder: Mississippi—Political (T–Z), JFKL.

20. Address by Governor Ross R. Barnett of Mississippi to New Orleans Citizens' Council Rally, March 7, 1960, in Series 50, Box 10, Folder 20, in JCS Collection.

21. Wilburn Buckley to James O. Eastland, February 4, 1960, in File Series 1, Subseries 20, Folder 3-1, in JOE Collection.

22. Frank E. Shanahan Jr. to John B. Hynes, September 21, 1959, in Pre-Presidential Papers, Presidential Campaign Files, 1960, Box 950, Folder: Mississippi—Political (N–S), JFKL.

23. Bartley, *The New South*, 238; "Eloquent Dixie Protests Overridden By Convention," *Jackson Clarion-Ledger*, July 13, 1960.

24. Ross R. Barnett recorded interview by Dennis O'Brien, May 6, 1969, page 8, JFKL Oral History Program.

25. Ibid.; "Reconvened State Convention Coming," *Jackson Clarion-Ledger*, July 14, 1960; "Johnson Is Nominated for No. 2 Demo Post," *Jackson Clarion-Ledger*, July 15, 1960.

26. "Johnson Is Nominated for No. 2 Demo Post," *Jackson Clarion-Ledger*, July 15, 1960.

27. Telegram from Walter Sillers to James O. Eastland, August 16, 1960, in File Series 1, Subseries 20, Folder 3-1, in JOE Collection.

28. Joint statement by Senators James O. Eastland and John C. Stennis, of Mississippi, August 19, 1960, in File Series 1, Subseries 20, Folder 3-1, in JOE Collection.

29. Johnston, *Politics: Mississippi Style*, 145.

30. Clay B. Tucker to James O. Eastland, August 19, 1960, in File Series 1, Subseries 20, Folder 3-1, in JOE Collection.

31. Johnnie R. Copeland to James O. Eastland, August 22, 1960, File Series 1, Subseries 20, Folder 3-1, in JOE Collection. For Johnson's alternating identities as westerner and southerner, see Leuchtenburg, *The White House Looks South*, 267–278.

32. R. K. Daniel to James O. Eastland, October 22, 1960, in File Series 1, Subseries 20, Folder 3-1, in JOE Collection.

33. "Kennedy-Johnson Chances Improve as Democrats Speed Up Campaigning," in Senate Political Files, 1949–1960, Box 198, Folder: Lyndon B. Johnson for Vice President—Mississippi Press, LBJL.

34. Ibid.; "Kennedy-Johnson Ticket Gaining Fast as Loyalists Speed Up Drive in State," in Senate Political Files, 1949–1960, Box 198, Folder: Lyndon B. Johnson for Vice President—Mississippi Press, LBJL.

35. "Jim Raps Platform, Endorses Party," "Laurel Becomes Important Center for Regular Mississippi Democrats," and "Two Mississippi Leaders Indorse Kennedy-Johnson Ticket," in Senate Political Files, 1949–1960, Box 198, Folder: Lyndon B. Johnson for Vice President—Mississippi Press, LBJL.

36. Form letters, in File Series 1, Subseries 20, Folder 3-1, in JOE Collection.

37. White, "Mississippi Electoral Politics," 417.

38. James P. Coleman to John C. Stennis, November 9, 1960, in Series 50, Box 7, Folder 14, in JCS Collection.

39. Frank E. Shanahan Jr. to John F. Kennedy, November 10, 1960, in Pre-Presidential Papers, Transition Files, Box 1068, Folder: Mississippi: Nov. 9, 1960—Nov. 26, 1960, JFKL.

40. "Senator Eastland Merits Support and Confidence of Mississippians," *Jackson Clarion-Ledger*, June 5, 1960.

41. James O. Eastland to Carey N. Gerald, November 22, 1960, in File Series 1, Subseries 20, Folder 3-1, in JOE Collection.

42. Mrs. Joe Crawford Applewhite to James O. Eastland, August 7, 1961, and James O. Eastland to Mrs. Joe Crawford Applewhite, August 22, 1961, in File Series 1, Subseries 20, Folder 3-2, in JOE Collection.

43. "Eastland Keeps Chairmanship of Powerful Judiciary Group," *Jackson Daily News*, January 12, 1961.

44. John C. Stennis to Lawrence F. O'Brien, February 14, 1961, and Lawrence F. O'Brien to John C. Stennis, February 21, 1961, both in White House Central Subject Files, Box 687, Folder: PL/ST24, JFKL.

45. Special Memorandum, March 24, 1961; Senator's comments on various matters, March 28, 1961, both in Series 50, Box 5, Folder 4, in JCS Collection; James O. Eastland and John C. Stennis to Lawrence F. O'Brien, April 5, 1961, in White House Central Name File, Box 766, Folder: Eastland, James O. (Sen), JFKL.

46. Memorandum on conversation with Chairman Bailey and Larry O'Brien, March 1, 1961; memorandum on Senator's conversation with Mr. Abernethy, March 1, 1961, both in Series 50, Box 5, Folder 4, in JCS Collection. See also "Barnett, Winstead Differ on Electors," in File Series 2, Subseries 4, Folder: August 1960—Politics, in JOE Collection.

47. James O. Eastland to E. J. Hines Jr., February 27, 1961, in File Series 1, Subseries 20, Folder 3-2, in JOE Collection.

48. Memorandum from Lee White to Larry O'Brien, March 16, 1961, in President's Office Files, Reference Box 49, Folder: Legislative Files: 3/1–17/61, JFKL; Sorensen, *Kennedy,* 345. Sorensen wrote: "Kennedy, particularly in his first year—despite the advantages of being the first President in a hundred years to have served in both houses—felt uncomfortable and perhaps too deferential with these men who the previous year had outranked him."

49. Bryant, *The Bystander,* 286; "William Harold Cox, Outspoken U.S. Judge," *New York Times,* February 27, 1988.

50. Nicholas deB. Katzenbach, *Some of It Was Fun: Working with RFK and LBJ* (New York: Norton, 2008), 56; Stern, *Calculating Visions,* 50; William Harold Cox to John F. Kennedy, May 16, 1959, in Pre-Presidential Papers, Presidential Campaign Files, 1960, Box 950, Folder: Mississippi—Political (A–C), JFKL.

51. Raymond Arsenault, *Freedom Riders: 1961 and the Struggle for Racial Justice* (New York: Oxford Univ. Press, 2006), 189–190, Bryant, *The Bystander,* 266.

52. Arsenault, *Freedom Riders,* 193, 204–205; Bryant, *The Bystander,* 267–268; Dittmer, *Local People,* 92; David Niven, *The Politics of Injustice: The Kennedys, the Freedom Rides, and the Electoral Consequences of a Moral Compromise* (Knoxville: Univ. of Tennessee Press, 2003), 70–73.

53. Bryant, *The Bystander,* 268–273.

54. Arsenault, *Freedom Riders,* 256; Niven, *The Politics of Injustice,* 101; Robert F. Kennedy interview by Anthony Lewis, Part 1, December 4, 1964 (hereafter referred to as RFK interview), in American Political Archive, C-SPAN Radio, broadcast November 17, 2004.

55. Arsenault, *Freedom Riders,* 256–257; Dittmer, *Local People,* 93–97; Niven, *The Politics of Injustice,* 102–105; RFK interview, Part 2, in American Political Archive, C-SPAN Radio, broadcast November 23, 2004.

56. RFK interview, Part 1.

57. Jonathan Rosenberg and Zachary Karabell, *Kennedy, Johnson, and the Quest for Justice: The Civil Rights Tapes* (New York: Norton, 2003), 31.

58. Speech before the Georgia States' Rights Council, July 24, 1961, in File Series 2, Subseries 6, Folder: 25 July 1961—Georgia States' Rights Council, Atlanta, Georgia, in JOE Collection.

59. Ibid.

60. Ibid.

61. Ibid.

62. Ibid.

63. Ibid.

64. Bryant, *The Bystander,* 276.

65. Niven, *The Politics of Injustice,* 33.

66. Ibid., 32–26; Lawson, *Running for Freedom,* 81–83.

67. Lawson, *Running for Freedom,* 82–83.

68. Dittmer, *Local People,* 128; Lawson, *Running for Freedom,* 84–86; J. Todd Moye, *Let the People Decide: Black Freedom and White Resistance Movements in Sunflower County, Mississippi, 1945–1986* (Chapel Hill: Univ. of North Carolina Press, 2004), 94.

69. Bryant, *The Bystander,* 331–332.

70. A Statewide Address on Television and Radio to the People of Mississippi by Governor Ross R. Barnett, 7:30 PM—September 13, 1962, in File Series 3, Subseries 1, Folder: Civil Rights—1962 (1 of 6), in JOE Collection.

71. Bryant, *The Bystander,* 333.

72. Ibid., 335–343; Eagles, *The Price of Defiance,* 336–339.

73. Bryant, *The Bystander,* 340; Eagles, *The Price of Defiance,* 355–356.

74. Bryant, *The Bystander,* 345–350; Eagles, *The Price of Defiance,* 356–370, 428–429, 433–434.

75. Bryant, *The Bystander,* 339.

76. A collection of these telegrams can be found in File Series 3, Subseries 1, Folder: Civil Rights—1962 (5 of 6), in JOE Collection.

77. "The highest state of heat and tension prevails in Mississippi . . . ," in File Series 1, Subseries 16, Folder 1-13, in JOE Collection.

78. James O. Eastland to A. G. Paxton, October 9, 1962; statement by L.P.B. Lipscomb, October 3, 1962, both in File Series 3, Subseries 1, Folder: Civil Rights—1962 (1 of 6), in JOE Collection.

79. James O. Eastland to Verne F. Ryland, October 9, 1962, in File Series 3, Subseries 1, Folder: Civil Rights—1962 (1 of 6), in JOE Collection.

80. Eagles, *The Price of Defiance,* 428.

81. James O. Eastland to Louis Wise, October 9, 1962, in File Series 3, Subseries 1, Folder: Civil Rights—1962 (1 of 6), in JOE Collection.

82. Pierce interview.

83. Katzenbach, *Some of It Was Fun*, 81; Bryant, *The Bystander*, 352.

84. RFK interview, Part 1.

85. Bryant, *The Bystander*, 352–355.

86. Eagles, *The Price of Defiance*, 426.

87. "The Economic Impact of Racial Unrest," in Civil Rights During the Kennedy Administration, 1961–1963, Part 1, White House Central Files, Staff Files, and POF, reel 9, microfilm edition, RSC.

88. Bryant, *The Bystander*, 339.

89. John A. Morsell to John F. Kennedy, September 21, 1962, and Lee C. White to John A. Morsell, October 17, 1962, both in Civil Rights During the Kennedy Administration, 1961–1963, Part 1, White House Central Files, Staff Files, and POF, reel 5, microfilm edition, RSC.

90. "Resolution of the United States Commission on Civil Rights," in Civil Rights During the Kennedy Administration, 1961–1963, Part 1, White House Central Files, Staff Files, and POF, reel 19, microfilm edition, RSC.

91. Robert F. Steadman to Lee C. White, April 9, 1963, "Memorandum for the President, April 10, 1963," and "Text of letter from the president to the chairman, United States Commission on Civil Rights, Dr. John A. Hannah, April 19, 1963," all in Civil Rights During the Kennedy Administration, 1961–1963, Part 1, White House Central Files, Staff Files, and POF, reel 14, microfilm edition, RSC. See also Bryant, *The Bystander*, 376–379.

92. Dittmer, *Local People*, 197.

CHAPTER 7. SOUTHERN REPUBLICANS AND FREEDOM DEMOCRATS

1. Katzenbach, *Some of It Was Fun*, 46.

2. Edward M. Kennedy, *True Compass: A Memoir* (London: Little, Brown, 2009), 191–192.

3. Ibid., 193–194.

4. Eagles, *The Price of Defiance*, 431.

5. Press release, in File Series 2, Subseries 9, Folder 2-27, in JOE Collection. "Some of my friends have reported over the telephone that there is a rumor in the State that I attended a meeting on the Meredith case with Attorney General Kennedy, former Governor Coleman, Senator Stennis, and Congressman Frank Smith," Eastland declared in the press release. "I cannot imagine how such a report could originate since there is not a fringe of substance to it."

6. Walter Dean Burnham, "The Alabama Senatorial Election of 1962: Return of Inter-Party Competition," *Journal of Politics* 26, no. 4 (November 1964): 810.

7. Ibid., 811.

8. Ibid., 812.

9. Luther Ingalls to James O. Eastland, October 22, 1962, in File Series 1, Subseries 18, Folder 5-18, in JOE Collection.

10. E. E. Dorroh to James O. Eastland, October 23, 1962, in File Series 1, Subseries 18, Folder 5-18, in JOE Collection.

11. Telegram from W. B. Hand to James O. Eastland, October 17, 1962, in File Series 1, Subseries 18, Folder 5-18, in JOE Collection.

12. Black and Black, *The Rise of Southern Republicans*, 126–127; Burnham, "The Alabama Senatorial Election of 1962," 812, 815.

13. Telegram from W. B. Hand to James O. Eastland, October 17, 1962, in File Series 1, Subseries 18, Folder 5-18, in JOE Collection.

14. Johnston, *Politics: Mississippi Style*, 150.

15. Ibid., 151–153.

16. White, "Mississippi Electoral Politics," 418–419.

17. Ibid., 421–425.

18. Paul B. Johnson to Courtney Pace, May 23, 1963, in File Series 1, Subseries 20, Folder 3-4 (1963), in JOE Collection.

19. L.P.B. Lipscomb to Tom Hederman, August 14, 1963, in File Series 1, Subseries 20, Folder 3-4 (1963), in JOE Collection.

20. Ibid.

21. Johnston, *Politics: Mississippi Style*, 155.

22. Ibid., 154; White, "Mississippi Electoral Politics," 426–427.

23. Johnston, *Politics: Mississippi Style*, 154.

24. "Where Does Coleman Stand On the Kennedys?" in File Series 2, Subseries 4, Folder: 1963—Politics, in JOE Collection.

25. "Choice of Johnson Reveals Sharp Image of Voters Mind," *Memphis Commercial Appeal*, August 28, 1963.

26. "How Johnson Won—By Counties," *Memphis Commercial Appeal*, August 28, 1963.

27. White, "Mississippi Electoral Politics," 427–428.

28. "Liberal, Race-Baiting, Northern Paper Chooses State Candidate," *Jackson Clarion-Ledger*, August 12, 1963.

29. "Where Does Coleman Stand on the Kennedys?" in File Series 2, Subseries 4, Folder: 1963—Politics, in JOE Collection.

30. "JFK Extremism Casts Long Shadow Over J.P.," *Jackson Daily News*, August 13, 1963.

31. "The New South," *Washington Post*, August 20, 1963.

32. Billy Burton Hathorn, "Challenging the Status Quo: Rubel Lex Phillips and the Mississippi Republican Party (1963–1967)," *Journal of Mississippi History* 47, no. 4 (November 1985): 243.

33. Leslie Burl McLemore, "The Mississippi Freedom Democratic Party: A Case Study of Grass-roots Politics" (Ph.D. diss., University of Massachusetts, 1971), 101. McLemore wrote that the "idea of a 'Freedom Vote' was conceived largely by one man, Robert Moses."

34. Dittmer, *Local People*, 200.

35. Ibid., 200–201.

36. Moye, *Let the People Decide*, 114–115; Charles Payne, *I've Got the Light of Freedom: The Organizing Tradition and the Mississippi Freedom Struggle* (Berkeley: Univ. of California Press, 1996), 294–295.

37. Dittmer, *Local People*, 201–205.

38. Ibid., 205–207 (Moses quoted on page 206); Moye, *Let the People Decide*, 115; Payne, *I've Got the Light of Freedom*, 295–298.

39. Moye, *Let the People Decide*, 116.

40. McLemore, "The Mississippi Freedom Democratic Party," 103.

41. Ibid., 105.

42. Ibid., 105–106; Dittmer, *Local People*, 207; Moye, *Let the People Decide*, 116–118.

43. White, "Mississippi Electoral Politics," 430.

44. Johnston, *Politics: Mississippi Style*, 160–164. See also Crespino, *In Search of Another Country*, 90–91.

45. White, "Mississippi Electoral Politics," 431–432.

46. Johnston, *Politics: Mississippi Style*, 164–165.

47. Ibid.

48. White, "Mississippi Electoral Politics," 432.

49. Hathorn, "Challenging the Status Quo," 250.

50. C. B. Curlee to James O. Eastland, September 30, 1963, in File Series 1, Subseries 20, Folder 3-4 (1963), in JOE Collection.

51. "Mississippi: The Upset of Upsets?" *Time*, October 25, 1963.

52. Jack N. Turner to James O. Eastland, October 16, 1963, in File Series 1, Subseries 20, Folder 3-4 (1963), in JOE Collection.

53. Edley H. Jones Jr. to James O. Eastland, October 19, 1963, in File Series 1, Subseries 20, Folder 3-4 (1963), in JOE Collection.

54. "Mississippi: The Upset of Upsets?" *Time*, October 25, 1963.

55. White, "Mississippi Electoral Politics," 432.

56. Hathorn, "Challenging the Status Quo," 256; "Official Vote," *Jackson Clarion-Ledger*, November 22, 1963. Phillips carried Washington County (61 percent), Coahoma County (57.3 percent), Choctaw County (56.1 percent), Lowndes County (53.2 percent), Harrison County (53 percent), Warren County (51 percent), and Jones County (50.6 percent).

57. M. W. Swartz to James O. Eastland, October 15, 1963; James O. Eastland to M. W. Swartz, November 12, 1963, both in File Series 1, Subseries 20, Folder 3-4 (1963), in JOE Collection.

58. Hathorn, "Challenging the Status Quo," 256–257.

59. Johnston, *Politics: Mississippi Style*, 165.

60. Nash and Taggart, *Mississippi Politics*, 44.

61. Leuchtenburg, *The White House Looks South*, 302.

62. Lawson, *Black Ballots*, 298.

63. Robert Dallek, *Flawed Giant: Lyndon Johnson and His Times, 1961–1973* (New York: Oxford Univ. Press, 1998), 32.

64. Ibid., 111–114; Lawson, *Black Ballots*, 298; Leuchtenburg, *The White House Looks South*, 300–302.

65. Dallek, *Flawed Giant*, 112.

66. Leuchtenburg, *The White House Looks South*, 308.

67. Dallek, *Flawed Giant*, 162–164.

68. "Mississippi Regulars Bolt Convention," *Philadelphia Bulletin*, August 26, 1964; David Johnson, *All the Way with LBJ: The 1964 Presidential Election* (Cambridge: Cambridge Univ. Press, 2009), 161–167; President Johnson and James Eastland, 12:13 P.M., August 17, 1964, Tape WH6408.26, Citation # 4992, LBJ Presidential Recordings, Miller Center, accessed January 7, 2012, http://millercenter.org/scripps/archive/presidentialrecordings/johnson/1964/08_1964.

69. Dittmer, *Local People*, 285–300.

70. Ibid., 300–302.

71. Malcolm X, "The Ballot or the Bullet," April 3, 1964, Cleveland, Ohio, SoJust: Speeches on Social Justice, accessed April 11, 2012, http://www.sojust.net/speeches/malcolm_x_ballot.html.

72. Horace Harned to James O. Eastland, September 1, 1964, in File Series 3, Subseries 1, Folder: Elections—Presidential 1964, in JOE Collection.

73. R. L. Hallberg to James O. Eastland, September 18, 1964, in File Series 3, Subseries 1, Folder: Elections—Party Switching 1964, in JOE Collection.

74. "Lady Bird Courteously Received by Officials," *Jackson Clarion-Ledger,* October 10, 1964.

75. Cohodas, *Strom Thurmond,* 360–361.

76. Charles W. Clark to Strom Thurmond, September 22, 1964, in Subject Correspondence Series, Box 24 (1964), Folder 8-2, in Strom Thurmond Collection, Special Collections, Clemson University Libraries, Clemson, South Carolina.

77. "Mississippi Solons Face House Seating Duel Today," *Tupelo Daily Journal,* January 4, 1964.

78. Crespino, *In Search of Another Country,* 217. See also Nash and Taggart, *Mississippi Politics,* 28–29, 314. Crespino wrote that "few candidates short of a Klansman could have run to the right of Williams on civil rights" in the 1967 election.

79. Dittmer, *Local People,* 338.

80. McLemore, "The Mississippi Freedom Democratic Party," 189. See also Dittmer, *Local People,* 338–340.

81. Dittmer, *Local People,* 340.

82. "Stand for Congressmen, State Elevates Coleman," *Jackson Daily News,* February 7, 1965.

83. "Memorandum to the Honorable W. M. Colmer, Honorable Jamie L. Whitten, Honorable Thomas G. Abernethy, Honorable John Bell Williams, and Honorable Prentiss Walker," December 16, 1964, in Box 260, Folder: Election Contest January—February 1965, in Thomas G. Abernethy Collection, Archives and Special Collections, J. D. Williams Library, University of Mississippi (hereafter referred to as TGA Collection).

84. Dittmer, *Local People,* 340.

85. *Congressional Record* 111 (February 3, 1965): 1908.

86. Thomas Abernethy to Paul M. Edmondson, February 17, 1965, in Box 260, Folder: Election Contest January—February 1965, in TGA Collection.

87. Ibid.

88. Mann, *When Freedom Would Triumph,* 222–229.

89. Ibid., 229–231.

90. David C. Carter, *The Music Has Gone Out of the Movement: Civil Rights and the Johnson Administration, 1965–1968* (Chapel Hill: Univ. of North Carolina Press, 2009), xi.

91. Mann, *When Freedom Would Triumph,* 221–222.

92. Frank K. Dunn to James O. Eastland, March 15, 1965, and James O. Eastland to Frank K. Dunn, March 18, 1965, both in File Series 3, Subseries 1, Folder: Civil Rights—1965 (1 of 2), in JOE Collection.

93. Mrs. Augustus T. Evans to James O. Eastland, May 6, 1965, and James O. Eastland to Mrs. Augustus T. Evans, June 1, 1965, in File Series 3, Subseries 1, Folder: Civil Rights—1965 (1 of 2), in JOE Collection.

94. James O. Eastland to Bill Simmons, April 30, 1965, in File Series 3, Subseries 1, Folder: Civil Rights—1965 (1 of 2), in JOE Collection

95. Mann, *When Freedom Would Triumph*, 247–251.

96. Thomas G. Abernethy to H. E. Pass, January 29, 1965, in Box 260, Folder: Election Contest January—February 1965, in TGA Collection.

97. "Dismissing the Five Mississippi Election Contests and Declaring the Returned Members Are Duly Entitled to Their Seats in the House of Representatives," Committee Report No. 1008, House of Representatives, 89th Cong., 1st Sess., September 15, 1965.

98. Thomas G. Abernethy to Burris C. Jackson, September 13, 1965, in Box 259, Folder: Election Contest Correspondence August, in TGA Collection.

99. "Fee Statement, J. P. Coleman, Ackerman, Mississippi, for Professional Services to the Following Members of the Mississippi Delegation in Congress, Thomas G. Abernethy, Jamie L. Whitten, John Bell Williams, and William M. Colmer," in Box 260, Folder: Election Contest—Contributions, in TGA Collection.

100. "U.S. Pays Five Miss. Congressmen $2000 Each in Election Challenges," *Washington Post*, March 8, 1966. According to the article, the MFDP was also entitled to a government reimbursement.

101. Anders Walker, *The Ghost of Jim Crow: How Southern Moderates Used* Brown v. Board of Education *to Stall Civil Rights* (Oxford: Oxford Univ. Press, 2009), 141–142.

CONCLUSION

1. "Jim Eastland Winds Down Life of Power," *Jackson Clarion-Ledger*, October 27, 1985.

2. Daniel, *Lost Revolutions*, 302.

3. James O. Eastland to Tom Kemp, August 8, 1966, in File Series 3, Subseries 1, Folder: Civil Rights—1966, in JOE Collection.

4. James O. Eastland to Charles W. Clark, September 26, 1966, in File Series 3, Subseries 1, Folder: Civil Rights—1966, in JOE Collection.

5. Daniel, *Lost Revolutions*, 179.

6. Prentiss Walker, "Dear Fellow Mississippian," in File Series 1, Subseries 19, Folder 31-49, in JOE Collection.

7. Black and Black, *The Rise of Southern Republicans*, 116.

8. Clarke Reed interview conducted by Maarten Zwiers, May 16, 2011, Greenville, Mississippi, digital recording in Maarten Zwiers's possession.

9. "Sen. Eastland Is Top Paradox in the Senate," *Los Angeles Times*, September 15, 1965.

10. "FBI Records: Late Senator Linked to Klan," *Jackson Clarion-Ledger*, October 18, 2009.

11. Joseph B. Parker, "New Style Campaign Politics: Madison Avenue Comes to Dixie," in *Contemporary Southern Politics*, ed. James F. Lea (Baton Rouge: Louisiana State Univ. Press, 1988), 150.

12. Nash and Taggart, *Mississippi Politics*, 75.

13. Black and Black, *The Rise of Southern Republicans*, 172.

14. "Party Changing? Eastland's Reply Emphatic: 'No,'" *Biloxi-Gulfport Daily Herald*, November 13, 1972.

15. Bass and De Vries, *The Transformation of Southern Politics*, 397.

16. Jeff Broadwater, "Interview with Gil Carmichael, 18 July 1991," JCS Collection.

17. *Time*, March 26, 1956.

18. "James O. Eastland Is Dead at 81: Leading Senate Foe of Integration," *New York Times*, February 20, 1986. According to Henry, the "old man just burst into tears" after he told him that blacks would probably not vote for him.

BIBLIOGRAPHY

ARCHIVES
Austin, Texas
UNIVERSITY OF TEXAS, LYNDON BAINES JOHNSON
PRESIDENTIAL LIBRARY
Papers of Lyndon B. Johnson.
   Pre-Presidential Papers.
      Senate Papers, 1949–1961.
      Senate Political Files, 1949–1960.

Boston, Massachusetts
JOHN F. KENNEDY PRESIDENTIAL LIBRARY
Papers of John F. Kennedy.
   Pre-Presidential Papers.
      Presidential Campaign Files, 1960.
      Transition Files.
   Presidential Papers.
      President's Office Files.
      White House Central Name File.
      White House Central Subject Files.

Clemson, South Carolina
CLEMSON UNIVERSITY, CLEMSON UNIVERSITY
LIBRARIES, SPECIAL COLLECTIONS
J. Strom Thurmond Papers.

Cleveland, Mississippi
DELTA STATE UNIVERSITY, CHARLES W. CAPPS JR. ARCHIVES
Walter Sillers Jr. Papers.

Independence, Missouri

HARRY S. TRUMAN PRESIDENTIAL LIBRARY

Clark M. Clifford Papers.

Records of the Democratic National Committee.

Harry S. Truman Papers.

    Presidential Papers.

        White House Central Files.

            Official File, 1945–1953.

Jackson, Mississippi

MISSISSIPPI DEPARTMENT OF ARCHIVES AND HISTORY

James P. Coleman Papers.

Archibald S. Coody Papers.

Middelburg, the Netherlands

ROOSEVELT STUDY CENTER

Civil Rights During the Kennedy Administration, 1961–1963 (microfilm).

President Harry S Truman's Office Files, 1945–1953 (microfilm).

Oxford, Mississippi

UNIVERSITY OF MISSISSIPPI, J. D. WILLIAMS LIBRARY, DEPARTMENT
OF ARCHIVES AND SPECIAL COLLECTIONS

Thomas G. Abernethy Collection.

James O. Eastland Collection.

Carroll Gartin Collection.

Joseph M. Howorth Collection.

Felton M. Johnston Collection.

Starkville, Mississippi

MISSISSIPPI STATE UNIVERSITY, MITCHELL MEMORIAL LIBRARY,
CONGRESSIONAL AND POLITICAL RESEARCH CENTER

John C. Stennis Collection.

MISSISSIPPI STATE UNIVERSITY, MITCHELL MEMORIAL
LIBRARY, SPECIAL COLLECTIONS

Sam Wilhite Papers.

Interviews and Oral Histories

Barber, Frank D. Interview by Reid S. Derr. May 30, 1990. University of Southern Mississippi Oral History Program, McCain Library and Archives.

Barnett, Ross R. Recorded interview by Dennis O'Brien. May 6, 1969. John F. Kennedy Library Oral History Program.

Carmichael, Gil. Interview by Jeff Broadwater. July 18, 1991. John C. Stennis Collection, Congressional and Political Research Center, Mississippi State University.

Durr, Clifford and Virginia. Oral history interview by Michael L. Gillette. March 1, 1975. Lyndon Baines Johnson Library.

Eastland, James O. Oral history interview I by Joe B. Frantz. February 19, 1971. Internet copy. Lyndon Baines Johnson Library.

Eastland, Woods. Interview by Maarten Zwiers. May 17, 2011. Doddsville, Mississippi. Digital recording in Maarten Zwiers's possession.

Kennedy, Robert F. Interview by Anthony Lewis, Parts 1 and 2. December 4, 1964. American Political Archive, C-SPAN Radio, broadcast November 2004.

Pierce, Clarence. Interview by Maarten Zwiers. May 22, 2011. Vaiden, Mississippi. Digital recording in Maarten Zwiers's possession.

Reed, Clarke. Interview by Maarten Zwiers. May 16, 2011. Greenville, Mississippi. Digital recording in Maarten Zwiers's possession.

Periodicals and Newspapers

Biloxi-Gulfport Daily Herald. 1972.
Brandon News. 1951.
Congressional Record. 1941–1965.
Dallas (Tex.) Morning News. 1968.
Farm Bureau Co-Op News. 1942.
Greenville Delta Democrat-Times. 1954.
Jackson Clarion-Ledger. 1944–2009.
Jackson Daily News. 1951–1965.
Laurel Leader-Call. 1954.
Los Angeles Times. 1965.
McComb-Enterprise Journal. 1942.
Memphis (Tenn.) Commercial Appeal. 1948–1963.
Meridian Star. 1948–1949.

Memphis Press-Scimitar. 1948–1949.

Neshoba Democrat. 1949.

New Orleans Times-Picayune. 1948–1954.

New York Post. 1956.

New York Times. 1948–1997.

Philadelphia (Penn.) Bulletin. 1964.

Simpson County News. 1956.

Time. 1949–1957.

Tupelo Daily Journal. 1964.

Tupelo Daily News. 1941.

U.S. News and World Report. 1948.

Washington Evening Star. 1949–1956.

Washington Post. 1956–1966.

Online Databases

Mississippi Digital Library. www.msdiglib.org.

Presidential Recordings Program, Miller Center, University of Virginia. www.miller-center.org/scripps/archive/presidentialrecordings.

SoJust: A Primary Source History of Social Justice. www.sojust.net.

Secondary Sources and Government Publications

Arsenault, Raymond. *Freedom Riders: 1961 and the Struggle for Racial Justice.* New York: Oxford Univ. Press, 2006.

Asch, Chris Myers. "No Compromise: The Freedom Struggles of James O. Eastland and Fannie Lou Hamer." Ph.D. diss., University of North Carolina at Chapel Hill, 2005.

———. "Revisiting Reconstruction: James O. Eastland, the FEPC, and the Struggle to Rebuild Germany, 1945–1946." *Journal of Mississippi History* 67, no. 1 (2005): 1–28.

———. *The Senator and the Sharecropper: The Freedom Struggles of James O. Eastland and Fannie Lou Hamer.* New York: New Press, 2008.

Atkins, Joseph B. *Covering for the Bosses: Labor and the Southern Press.* Jackson: Univ. Press of Mississippi, 2008.

Badger, Tony. "Southerners Who Refused to Sign the Southern Manifesto." *Historical Journal* 42, no. 2 (June 1999): 517–534.

Baker, Bobby. *Wheeling and Dealing: Confessions of a Capitol Hill Operator.* New York: Norton, 1978.

Bartley, Numan V. *The New South, 1945–1980.* Baton Rouge: Louisiana State Univ. Press, 1995.

———. *The Rise of Massive Resistance: Race and Politics in the South During the 1950s.* Baton Rouge: Louisiana State Univ. Press, 1969.

Bass, Jack, and Walter De Vries. *The Transformation of Southern Politics: Social Change and Political Consequence Since 1945.* Athens: Univ. of Georgia Press, 1995.

Berman, William C. *The Politics of Civil Rights in the Truman Administration.* Columbus: Ohio State Univ. Press, 1970.

Black, Earl, and Merle Black. *The Rise of Southern Republicans.* Cambridge: Harvard Univ. Press, 2002.

Bryant, Nick. *The Bystander: John F. Kennedy and the Struggle for Black Equality.* New York: Basic Books, 2006.

Burnham, Walter Dean. "The Alabama Senatorial Election of 1962: Return of Inter-Party Competition." *Journal of Politics* 26, no. 4 (November 1964): 798–829.

Caro, Robert A. *The Years of Lyndon Johnson: Master of the Senate.* New York: Vintage Books, 2002.

Carter, Dan T. "More than Race: Conservatism in the White South since V. O. Key Jr." In *Unlocking V. O. Key Jr.: Southern Politics for the Twenty-First Century,* edited by Angie Maxwell and Todd G. Shields, 129–159. Fayetteville: Univ. of Arkansas Press, 2011.

———. *The Politics of Rage: George Wallace, the Origins of the New Conservatism, and the Transformation of American Politics,* 2nd ed. Baton Rouge: Louisiana State Univ. Press, 2000.

Carter, David C. *The Music Has Gone Out of the Movement: Civil Rights and the Johnson Administration, 1965–1968.* Chapel Hill: Univ. of North Carolina Press, 2009.

Carter, Hodding, III. *The South Strikes Back.* Garden City: Doubleday, 1959.

Cohodas, Nadine. *Strom Thurmond and the Politics of Southern Change.* Macon: Mercer Univ. Press, 1994.

Crespino, Joseph. *In Search of Another Country: Mississippi and the Conservative Counterrevolution.* Princeton: Princeton Univ. Press, 2007.

Cresswell, Stephen. *Rednecks, Redeemers, and Race: Mississippi After Reconstruction, 1877–1917.* Jackson: Univ. Press of Mississippi, 2006.

Dallek, Robert. *Flawed Giant: Lyndon Johnson and His Times, 1961–1973.* New York: Oxford Univ. Press, 1998.

———. *Lone Star Rising: Lyndon Johnson and His Times, 1908–1960.* New York: Oxford Univ. Press, 1991.

Daniel, Pete. *Lost Revolutions: The South in the 1950s.* Chapel Hill: Univ. of North Carolina Press, 2000.

Danielson, Christopher Alan. "'Lily White and Hard Right': The Mississippi Republican Party and Black Voting, 1965–1980." *Journal of Southern History* 75, no. 1 (February 2009): 83–118.

———. "The Voting Rights Act and the Creation of Black Politics in Mississippi, 1965–1985." Ph.D. diss., University of Mississippi, 2006.

Dinnerstein, Leonard. *America and the Survivors of the Holocaust*. New York: Columbia Univ. Press, 1982.

Dittmer, John. *Local People: The Struggle for Civil Rights in Mississippi*. Urbana: Univ. of Illinois Press, 1995.

Donaldson, Gary A. *Truman Defeats Dewey*. Lexington: Univ. Press of Kentucky, 1999.

Donovan, Robert J. *Tumultuous Years: The Presidency of Harry S. Truman, 1949–1953*. New York: Norton, 1982.

Eagles, Charles W. *The Price of Defiance: James Meredith and the Integration of Ole Miss*. Chapel Hill: Univ. of North Carolina Press, 2009.

Eastland, James O. "Brazilian Cotton, Henderson, and Cottonseed Oil." Washington, D.C.: United States Government Printing Office, 1941.

———. "World Cotton: The Farmer's Gateway Through the Tariff Wall—Bankhead-Eastland Cotton Bill." Washington, D.C.: United States Government Printing Office, 1941.

Edwards, Jerome E. *Pat McCarran: Political Boss of Nevada*. Reno: Univ. of Nevada Press, 1982.

Egerton, John. *Speak Now Against the Day: The Generation Before the Civil Rights Movement in the South*. New York: Knopf, 1994.

Feldman, Glen., ed. *Painting Dixie Red: When, Where, Why, and How the South Became Republican*. Gainesville: Univ. Press of Florida, 2011.

———. Review of *The Myth of Southern Exceptionalism*, edited by Matthew D. Lassiter and Joseph Crespino. *Journal of Southern History* 77, no. 3 (August 2011): 783–786.

———. "Southern Disillusionment with the Democratic Party: Cultural Conformity and the 'Great Melding' of Racial and Economic Conservatism in Alabama During World War II." *Journal of American Studies* 43, no. 2 (2009): 199–230.

Ferrell, Robert H. *Choosing Truman: The Democratic Convention of 1944*. Columbia: Univ. of Missouri Press, 1994.

———. *Harry S. Truman: A Life*. Columbia: Univ. of Missouri Press, 1994.

Finley, Keith M. *Delaying the Dream: Southern Senators and the Fight Against Civil Rights, 1938–1965*. Baton Rouge: Louisiana State Univ. Press, 2008.

Fontenay, Charles L. *Estes Kefauver: A Biography*. Knoxville: Univ. of Tennessee Press, 1980.

Frederickson, Kari. *The Dixiecrat Revolt and the End of the Solid South, 1932–1968*. Chapel Hill: Univ. of North Carolina Press, 2001.

Freidel, Frank. *F.D.R. and the South*. Baton Rouge: Louisiana State Univ. Press, 1965.

Fried, Richard M. *Nightmare in Red: The McCarthy Era in Perspective*. New York: Oxford Univ. Press, 1990.

Gardner, Michael R. *Harry Truman and Civil Rights: Moral Courage and Political Risks*. Carbondale: Southern Illinois Univ. Press, 2002.

Garson, Robert A. *The Democratic Party and the Politics of Sectionalism, 1941–1948*. Baton Rouge: Louisiana State Univ. Press, 1974.

Goldsmith, John A. *Colleagues: Richard B. Russell and His Apprentice Lyndon B. Johnson.* Macon: Mercer Univ. Press, 1998.

Greene, John Robert. *The Crusade: The Presidential Election of 1952.* Lanham: Univ. Press of America, 1985.

Gullan, Harold I. *The Upset That Wasn't: Harry S Truman and the Crucial Election of 1948.* Chicago: Ivan R. Dee, 1998.

Hamby, Alonzo L. *Man of the People: A Life of Harry S. Truman.* New York: Oxford Univ. Press, 1995.

Hathorn, Billy Burton. "Challenging the Status Quo: Rubel Lex Phillips and the Mississippi Republican Party (1963–1967)." *Journal of Mississippi History* 47, no. 4 (November 1985): 240–264.

Humphrey, Hubert H. *The Education of a Public Man: My Life and Politics.* Edited by Norman Sherman. Garden City: Doubleday, 1976.

Johnson, Robert David. *All the Way with LBJ: The 1964 Presidential Election.* Cambridge: Cambridge Univ. Press, 2009.

Johnston, Erle. *Politics: Mississippi Style.* Forest, Miss.: Lake Harbor Publishers, 1993.

Karabell, Zachary. *The Last Campaign: How Harry Truman Won the 1948 Election.* New York: Vintage Books, 2001.

Katagiri, Yasuhiro. *The Mississippi State Sovereignty Commission: Civil Rights and States' Rights.* Jackson: Univ. Press of Mississippi, 2001.

Katzenbach, Nicholas deB. *Some of It Was Fun: Working with RFK and LBJ.* New York: Norton, 2008.

Kennedy, Edward M. *True Compass: A Memoir.* London: Little, Brown, 2009.

Key, V. O., Jr. *Southern Politics in State and Nation.* New York: Knopf, 1949.

Kirwan, Albert D. *Revolt of the Rednecks: Mississippi Politics, 1876–1925.* New York: Harper and Row, 1951.

Lassiter, Matthew D. *The Silent Majority: Suburban Politics in the Sunbelt South.* Princeton: Princeton Univ. Press, 2006.

Lassiter, Matthew D., and Joseph Crespino, ed. *The Myth of Southern Exceptionalism.* New York: Oxford Univ. Press, 2010.

Lawson, Steven F. *Black Ballots: Voting Rights in the South, 1944–1969.* New York: Columbia Univ. Press, 1976.

———. *Running for Freedom: Civil Rights and Black Politics in America Since 1941.* New York: McGraw-Hill, 1991.

Leuchtenburg, William E. *The White House Looks South: Franklin D. Roosevelt, Harry S. Truman, Lyndon B. Johnson.* Baton Rouge: Louisiana State Univ. Press, 2005.

Lewis, George. *Massive Resistance: The White Response to the Civil Rights Movement.* London: Hodder Arnold, 2006.

Maddox, Robert Franklin. *The Senatorial Career of Harley Martin Kilgore.* East Rockaway: Cummings and Hathaway Publishers, 1997.

Mann, Robert. *When Freedom Would Triumph: The Civil Rights Struggle in Congress, 1954–1968*. Baton Rouge: Louisiana State Univ. Press, 2007.

McLemore, Leslie Burl. "The Mississippi Freedom Democratic Party: A Case Study of Grass-roots Politics." Ph.D. diss., University of Massachusetts, 1971.

Merrill, Dennis, ed. *Documentary History of the Truman Presidency*. Bethesda: Univ. Publications of America, 2000.

McMillen, Neil R. *The Citizens' Council: Organized Resistance to the Second Reconstruction, 1954–64*. Urbana: Univ. of Illinois Press, 1994.

———. "Perry Howard, Boss of Black-and-Tan Republicanism in Mississippi, 1942–1960." *Journal of Southern History* 48, no. 2 (1982): 205–224.

Morgan, Chester M. *Redneck Liberal: Theodore G. Bilbo and the New Deal*. Baton Rouge: Louisiana State Univ. Press, 1985.

———. "Senator Theodore G. Bilbo, the New Deal, and Mississippi Politics (1934–1940)." *Journal of Mississippi History* 47, no. 3 (August 1985): 147–164.

Moye, J. Todd. *Let the People Decide: Black Freedom and White Resistance Movements in Sunflower County, Mississippi, 1945–1986*. Chapel Hill: Univ. of North Carolina Press, 2004.

Nash, Jere, and Andy Taggart. *Mississippi Politics: The Struggle for Power, 1976–2006*. Jackson: Univ. Press of Mississippi, 2006.

Nichols, David A. *A Matter of Justice: Eisenhower and the Beginnings of the Civil Rights Revolution*. New York: Simon and Schuster Paperbacks, 2007.

Niven, David. *The Politics of Injustice: The Kennedys, the Freedom Rides, and the Electoral Consequences of a Moral Compromise*. Knoxville: Univ. of Tennessee Press, 2003.

Parker, Joseph B. "New Style Campaign Politics: Madison Avenue Comes to Dixie." In *Contemporary Southern Politics*, edited by James F. Lea, 148–175. Baton Rouge: Louisiana State Univ. Press, 1988.

Partin, John W. "Roosevelt, Byrnes, and the 1944 Vice-Presidential Nomination." *Historian* 42, no. 1 (November 1979): 85–100.

Payne, Charles. *I've Got the Light of Freedom: The Organizing Tradition and the Mississippi Freedom Struggle*. Berkeley: Univ. of California Press, 1996.

Percy, William Alexander. *Lanterns on the Levee: Recollections of a Planter's Son*, 1st ed. 1941. Reprint, Baton Rouge: Louisiana State Univ. Press, 2006.

Pierro, Joseph. "'Everything in My Power': Harry S. Truman and the Fight Against Racial Discrimination." Master's thesis, Virginia Polytechnic Institute, 2004.

Reid, Warren R., ed. *Public Papers of the Presidents of the United States: Harry S. Truman, 1949*. Washington: U.S. Government Printing Office, 1964.

Rorabaugh, W. J. *The Real Making of the President: Kennedy, Nixon, and the 1960 Election*. Lawrence: Univ. Press of Kansas, 2009.

Rosenberg, Jonathan, and Zachary Karabell. *Kennedy, Johnson, and the Quest for Justice: The Civil Rights Tapes*. New York: Norton, 2003.

Rusher, William A. *Special Counsel: An Inside Report on the Senate Investigations into Communism*. New Rochelle: Arlington House, 1968.

Savage, Sean J. *JFK, LBJ, and the Democratic Party*. Albany: State Univ. of New York Press, 2004.

———. "To Purge or Not to Purge: Hamlet Harry and the Dixiecrats, 1948–1952." *Presidential Studies Quarterly* 27, no. 4 (fall 1997): 773–790.

Schlesinger, Arthur M., Jr., ed. *History of U.S. Political Parties*, vol. 4, *1945–1972, The Politics of Change*. New York: Chelsea House Publishers, 1973.

Schultz, Nancy Lusignan. Preface to *Fear Itself: Enemies Real and Imagined in American Culture*, edited by Nancy Lusignan Schultz, i–xvii. West Lafayette: Purdue Univ. Press, 1999.

Shafer, Byron E., and Richard Johnston. *The End of Southern Exceptionalism: Class, Race, and Partisan Change in the Postwar South*. Cambridge: Harvard Univ. Press, 2006.

Sherrill, Robert. *Gothic Politics in the Deep South: Stars of the New Confederacy*. New York: Grossman Publishers, 1968.

Shuman, Howard E. "Senate Rules and the Civil Rights Bill: A Case Study." *American Political Science Review* 51, no. 4 (December 1957): 955–975.

Smith, Dan W., Jr. "James O. Eastland: Early Life and Career." Master's thesis, Mississippi College, 1978.

Solberg, Carl. *Hubert Humphrey: A Biography*. New York: Norton, 1984.

Sorensen, Theodore C. *Kennedy*. London: Hodder and Stoughton, 1965.

Sosebee, M. Scott. "The Split in the Texas Democratic Party, 1936–1956." Master's thesis, Texas Tech University, 2000.

Starr, J. Barton. "Birmingham and the 'Dixiecrat' Convention of 1948." *Alabama Historical Quarterly* 32 (spring/summer 1970): 23–50.

Stern, Mark. *Calculating Visions: Kennedy, Johnson, and Civil Rights*. New Brunswick: Rutgers Univ. Press, 1992.

Sullivan, Patricia. *Days of Hope: Race and Democracy in the New Deal Era*. Chapel Hill: Univ. of North Carolina Press, 1996.

Swain, Martha H. *Pat Harrison: The New Deal Years*. Jackson: Univ. Press of Mississippi, 1978.

Sweeney, James R. "Revolt in Virginia: Harry Byrd and the 1952 Presidential Election." *Virginia Magazine of History and Biography* 86, no. 2 (April 1978): 180–195.

Tindall, George B. *The Emergence of the New South, 1913–1945*, 2nd ed. Baton Rouge: Louisiana State Univ. Press, 1983.

U.S. Senate. *Activities of the Mississippi Democratic Committee: Hearings Before the Investigations Subcommittee of the Committee on Expenditures in the Executive Departments*. 82nd Cong. Washington, D.C.: United States Government Printing Office, 1951.

Walker, Anders. *The Ghost of Jim Crow: How Southern Moderates Used* Brown v. Board of Education *to Stall Civil Rights*. Oxford: Oxford Univ. Press, 2009.

Webb, Clive. Introduction to *Massive Resistance: Southern Opposition to the Second Reconstruction,* edited by Clive Webb, 3–17. Oxford: Oxford Univ. Press, 2005.

Wilkie, Curtis. *Dixie: A Personal Odyssey Through Events That Shaped the Modern South.* New York: Scribner, 2001.

White, Jesse Lamar, Jr. "Mississippi Electoral Politics, 1903–1976: The Emerging Modernization Consensus." Ph.D. diss., Massachusetts Institute of Technology, 1979.

Winter, William F. "New Directions in Politics, 1948–1956." In *A History of Mississippi,* vol. 2, edited by Richard Aubrey McLemore, 140–153. Jackson: Univ. and College Press of Mississippi, 1973.

Witcover, Jules. *Party of the People: A History of the Democrats.* New York: Random House, 2003.

Ybarra, Michael J. *Washington Gone Crazy: Senator Pat McCarran and the Great Communist Hunt.* Hanover: Steerforth Press, 2004.

Zellner, Dorothy M. "Red Roadshow: Eastland in New Orleans, 1954." *Louisiana History* 33, no. 1 (1992): 31–60.

INDEX